CHRISTIAN FAITH AND
THE PROBLEM OF EVIL

CHRISTIAN FAITH AND THE PROBLEM OF EVIL

Edited by

Peter van Inwagen

William B. Eerdmans Publishing Company
Grand Rapids, Michigan / Cambridge, U.K.

Wm. B. Eerdmans Publishing Co.
255 Jefferson Ave. S.E., Grand Rapids, Michigan 49503 /
P.O. Box 163, Cambridge CB3 9PU U.K.

Printed in the United States of America

09 08 07 06 05 04   7 6 5 4 3 2 1

ISBN 0-8028-2697-0

www.eerdmans.com

Contents

CONTENTS

Introduction

Theists often ask why a loving and all-powerful God allows terrible things to happen. Atheists have a simple answer: if there were a loving and all-powerful God, he *wouldn't* allow terrible things to happen, and, since terrible things *do* happen, it follows that a loving and all-powerful God does not exist. This argument for the non-existence of God is sometimes called the argument from evil — "evil" being just another way of saying "terrible things."

In June and July of 1999, I directed a six-week seminar devoted to the argument from evil. The seminar was one of a series of "Summer Seminars in Christian Scholarship" sponsored by Calvin College and funded by a grant from the Pew Charitable Trusts. Participation in the seminar was limited to Christian scholars teaching at North American colleges and universities. The thirteen members of the seminar were chosen from thirty-six very able applicants. It was expected that in the year following the seminar, each member of the seminar would write an essay, an original piece of scholarly research, on the topic to which the seminar was devoted.

The essays that the members of the seminar wrote were presented at a conference at Calvin the following spring. In addition to the members of the seminar, three distinguished philosophers who had not participated in the seminar — Paul Draper, Alvin Plantinga, and Richard Otte — were invited to present papers at the conference. The papers presented at that conference are collected in this volume. (But three participants in the seminar and the conference asked permission to publish their papers elsewhere, and I reluctantly granted it. It should also be mentioned that the papers by Professors Draper and Otte in this volume are not the papers presented at the conference, although there is considerable overlap between the papers they have contributed to this book and their conference papers. In addition to the papers presented at the conference, I have included in the volume a paper of my own, which was read to a general audience at Calvin during the time at which the seminar was going on.)

The members of the seminar were mostly philosophers (of the analytical school), but not all: Barbara Omolade is a sociologist, John Schneider is a theologian, Robert Stanley is a specialist in French literature, and Carol Winkelmann is a linguist who teaches in a department of English literature.

Although the topic of the original seminar was the argument from evil, the essays in this volume are not confined to that narrow topic. That is, many of them cannot be described as attempts to consider the strengths and weaknesses of a certain argument for the non-existence of God. The topic of this book can only be described as "the problem of evil," even though it is very hard to say *what* problem the problem of evil is. (Philosophers will see in the question implied by this statement an echo of many similar questions: What problem, exactly, is the problem of free will? What problem is the problem of knowledge? The problem of perception? The mind-body problem?) The phrase "the problem of evil" seems to me to be a shorthand way of referring to a complex of many philosophical and theological problems about God and evil — a complex unified by the undeniable fact that there is a fundamental opposition between the existence of a loving and all-powerful God and the existence of evil in the world this God has made. (The phrase "a fundamental opposition" is as vague as any meaningful phrase could be; I have chosen it for its very vagueness.) One of the problems that belongs to the complex of problems loosely called "the" problem of evil is this: How shall the theist reply to the argument from evil? But this problem is almost certainly not the problem — to choose one example from an array of many possible examples — that faces the pastor who must offer spiritual counsel to a mother whose child is dying of leukemia. It would be that problem if the mother had said to the pastor, "I no longer believe that there is a God, for a loving and all-powerful God would not have allowed this to happen." But, almost certainly, the mother will not have said this or anything like it. She will have said, "Why has God done this?" or "How can I love and trust a God who would let this happen?" or "I love God and I trust him and I know that he loves me and my child and I don't need to know the reason for anything he does, but what can I say to my husband? His faith isn't like mine" . . . or any of a thousand things. The problem that faces the pastor is much closer to what most people mean by "the problem of evil" than is the philosopher's problem, the problem of how to reply to the argument from evil. This problem, the philosopher's problem, is only one of many problems that belong to the complex called the problem of evil.

Many of the essays contained in this volume are about the problem of evil in the narrow sense, the philosopher's problem. And some of these are very much like what other philosophers have written about the philosopher's problem. (I mean that they are essays of the same sort as many other essays; I don't mean to imply that they are unoriginal in content.) Even when it is understood in the light of the parenthetical qualification that follows it, that sentence sounds condescending, and I have considered (and rejected) several alternatives to it. But it says what I want to say. Perhaps it will help to show that I do not mean to condescend to anyone if I say that my own contribution to the volume is one of the essays that are very much like what other philosophers have written about the philosopher's problem. The essays in this group are very like most of the classic essays on the philosopher's problem that are found in anthologies like Robert and Marilyn Adams's *The Problem of Evil* and Michael L. Peterson's *The Problem of Evil: Selected Readings* and Daniel Howard-Snyder's *The Evidential Argument from Evil*.[1] (These collections, together with a large number of photocopies of essays very similar to the essays they contain, were the texts that formed the basis for the discussions in the seminar meetings.) Besides my own essay, the essays of Paul Draper, Stephen Griffith, Del Kiernan-Lewis, Richard Otte, and Keith Wyma fall into this category.

In a much-read and frequently cited essay now about fifteen years old,[2] Paul Draper had defended the following conclusion: given the distribution of pain and pleasure in the human and animal worlds since the beginning of life on the earth, a certain form of naturalism is more probable than theism. And this conclusion, Draper maintained, entails that it is irrational to accept theism. In Richard Otte's essay, Otte criticizes the ar-

---

1. Marilyn McCord Adams and Robert Merrihew Adams, eds., *The Problem of Evil* (Oxford: Oxford University Press, 1990); Michael L. Peterson, ed., *The Problem of Evil: Selected Readings* (Notre Dame, Ind.: University of Notre Dame Press, 1992); Daniel Howard-Snyder, ed., *The Evidential Argument from Evil* (Bloomington: Indiana University Press, 1996).

2. Paul Draper, "Pain and Pleasure: An Evidential Problem for Theists," *Noûs* 23 (1989): 331-50.

gument of Draper's essay. In his contribution to the present volume, Draper replies to Otte's criticism of his earlier argument. Stephen Griffith, in his contribution to the volume, contends that a problem about God and non-optimality that is in its logical structure exactly parallel to the "logical" problem of evil could be raised in any non-optimal world, even if that world contained no evil at all. It is, Griffith maintains, obvious what the theist should say in response to the non-optimality problem; and, owing to the shared logical structure of the two problems, reflection on the non-optimality problem suggests strategies that the theist can employ in response to the logical problem of evil (and to the "evidential" problem of evil as well). Del Kiernan-Lewis's essay concerns the argument from evil. The conclusion of the argument from evil is that there exists no being who is omniscient, omnipotent, and morally perfect. Kiernan-Lewis attempts to show that the argument from evil must employ premises whose truth is not entailed by the existence of an omnipotent, omniscient, perfectly good being, and that, therefore, the argument from evil can be rejected by any theist who is willing to reject these additional premises.

Keith Wyma's essay is a defense of the Calvinist (and, many would say, the Pauline) doctrine that God's foreordaining all the acts of human beings, including their sinful acts, implies neither that human beings are not responsible for their own sinful acts nor that God cannot justly punish them for having performed these acts.

Three of the essays — those of Eduardo Echeverria, Laura Waddell Ekstrom, and Alvin Plantinga — are about the philosopher's problem, but they approach it in ways that are quite different from the ways in which philosophers have typically approached it. Echeverria's essay is an attempt to present the thoughts of John Paul II on the meaning of suffering and the sense in which our suffering when united with the sufferings of Christ may partake in the historical working out of God's plan of salvation. Ekstrom's essay explores the idea that suffering may be a path to the experience of God. (Other philosophers have had similar thoughts, but only very recently. The interested reader is directed to recent work by Marilyn McCord Adams and Eleonore Stump.[3] It is an interesting speculation that the idea of suffering as a path to experiential knowledge of God may be due to an insight into the nature of God that occurs more

3. Marilyn McCord Adams, *Horrendous Evils and the Goodness of God* (Ithaca, N.Y.: Cornell University Press, 1999); Eleonore Stump, *Faith and the Problem of Evil: The Stob Lectures, 1998-99* (Grand Rapids: The Stob Lectures Endowment, 1999).

readily in women than in men. To make a typically left-brained, male calculation: if one assumes that one-third of the analytical philosophers
writing on the problem of evil are women — an estimate that is probably
on the high side — and if one assumes that none of the three women I
have mentioned was influenced in her choice to explore the idea that suffering is a path to the knowledge of God by the fact that earlier work on
this topic was done by a woman, the antecedent probability of the three
philosophers who have explored this topic all being women is less than
four percent.) Plantinga's essay is a defense of the medieval speculation
that the fall of humanity and the consequent entry into the world of the
two things that were never made, sin and death, was a *felix culpa*, ordained by God in order that the unfathomably great good of the Incarnation might occur.

The remaining essays are on topics wholly different from those that
have been addressed by philosophers who have written on the problem
of evil.

Richard McClelland, the only philosopher to write an essay belonging to this group, addresses the question of the hidden motives of philosophers and theologians who engage in what he calls "theodictic projects"
(which may be very roughly identified with the sort of thing that is done
in the essays that I have already discussed — with, of course, the exception of Professor Draper's essay: Draper is engaged in an "anti-
theodictic" project). Drawing on recent Freudian theory, McClelland
maintains that narcissism is not only, as in classical Freudianism, a pathology. He maintains that there is a "normal" narcissism, a component
of the normal, non-pathological maintenance of psychological equilibrium, and (he disclaims any "reductivist" or "deconstructionist" intent)
that considerations related to normal narcissism afford insights into the
unconscious motives that underlie theodictic projects.

Robert Stanley presents the account of the meaning of evil, a deeply
Christ-centered account, that is to be found in the writings of the French
thinker Simone Weil. (It is very hard to find a category that fits this highly
idiosyncratic writer. The only classification that comes to mind that is
more informative than "writer" or "thinker" is the vulgar and overused
"intellectual.") Weil was strongly drawn to the Catholic Church (as was
the case with most of her compatriots, no other church or denomination
had any reality for her), although she could never bring herself actually
to enter the Catholic Church. For that reason, it is interesting to compare
the points of contact in her thinking about Christ and evil (as Stanley
presents them) with John Paul's thoughts on the same topic (outlined in

Echeverria's essay). It is also interesting to compare her treatment of Christ and evil with the treatment of evil in the incarnational narrative in Mark's Gospel (as it is represented in John Schneider's essay).

Schneider — drawing on, but revising, the work of Eleonore Stump on the book of Job[4] — maintains that Job does receive an answer to his question, and that one part of this answer is that God is the absolute master of everything evil in the world (represented allegorically by Leviathan): that evil is not the work of a primal chaos that exists independently of God and outside his control (on the point, Job stands in stark contrast to the myths of Israel's Semitic neighbors and conquerors, in which Leviathan — the dragon of chaos — was a primordial enemy of the gods). Schneider goes on to contend that this same theme, the theme of God's mastery of all evil things, is present in Mark's Gospel. In Mark, however, it is the incarnate God who is represented as the master of evil things. The incarnate God's absolute authority over evil things is represented in Mark by the placement of the story of the stilling of the storm, which represents the primordial chaos ("What manner of man is this, that even the wind and the sea obey him?"), between stories whose message is that evil spirits have no choice but to obey the commands of Jesus.

The remaining two papers in the volume represent an even more radical departure than do McClelland's, Stanley's, and Schneider's from the sort of paper one might expect to find in a volume edited by a philosopher and entitled *Christian Faith and the Problem of Evil*. Evil makes its presence felt in the writings of philosophers — and even in the writings of John Paul II and Simone Weil — as an abstract category, something as removed from the particularity of any concrete experience, any single episode in the life of any one human being, as any of Kant's or Aristotle's categories. If a book club composed of Martians, Martians wholly ignorant of life on our planet, read the essays in this book — other than the two essays I am about to discuss — they would learn that the earth was a vale of tears, but they would learn very little about what it was like to be one of the inhabitants of the earth, one of the real human beings who shed real tears over particular things. (Angels may weep because the world is filled with suffering. A human being weeps because his daughter, she and not another, has died of leukemia this very night, or because her village, the only world she knows, is burning and the mutilated bodies of her husband and her son lie at her feet.) The essays of Barbara Omolade and Carol Winkelmann are about the real world, the actual

4. In *Faith and the Problem of Evil*.

earth we walk on, the planet that has had one particular sorry history and no other. They present no solution to the problem of evil, and in them there is no discussion of the difficulties that face someone else's solution to the problem of evil. They rather record the ways in which certain Christians (not the church, not theologians, not a synod of respected elders), certain individuals, certain marginalized human persons, have found the resources to confront and deal with actual, particular evils. These two essays provide a perspective on the question of God and evil of an entirely different kind from the perspective provided by the writings of philosophers and theologians. It is good for philosophers to realize that evil can confront Christians in ways that have only the most remote and tenuous connection (if even that) with the problems of philosophical theology. It is good for philosophers to realize that there are Christians for whom the existence of a loving and all-powerful God is no more in question than is the existence of the wind and the rain — and who yet daily face oppression and suffering that can have no more than an intellectual reality for affluent academics putting words together in their studies.

I think, I hope, that the seminar convinced Omolade and Winkelmann that what philosophers have to say about the problem of evil has its own sort of value. (I think they will forgive me if I reveal that they needed at least a little convincing on this point.) I also hope that Omolade and Winkelmann have convinced some philosophers (and will, by the publication of their essays, convince more of them) of the value of studies of the concrete reality of evil in human lives.

The seminar was a wonderful intellectual experience for me. I am very glad I was able to have the opportunity to discuss the problem of evil with the fine scholars who were members of the seminar. If I may switch just for a moment to the second person, thank you all. Thank you very much indeed.

I wish to express my gratitude (I know that the members of the seminar and the participants in the conference will join me in this) to the Pew Charitable Trusts for their generous financial support of the seminar and the conference. I wish also to express our gratitude to Calvin College for the splendid facilities and institutional support it provided for the seminar and conference, and to Anna Mae Bush, the Coordinator of the Calvin Summer Seminars, for the tireless work she and her staff did in support of every aspect of the seminar and the conference and in ensuring the comfort and happiness of the participants and their families. I wish finally to thank Professor Susan Felch of the Calvin College English Department, the Director of the Calvin College Summer Seminars, for the very existence of the seminar and the conference. We hope (I speak for all the participants in the seminar and the conference) that the essays collected in this volume will demonstrate to her that her labors have borne fruit in which she can take pride. We are very grateful to her for all that she has done for us.

PETER VAN INWAGEN
Notre Dame, Indiana
December 1st, 2003

Supralapsarianism, or 'O Felix Culpa'

Alvin Plantinga

Among the tenets of a certain sort of Calvinism is supralapsarianism, a claim about the order of the decrees of God. God has decreed to permit humanity to fall into sin; he has also decreed to save at least some of the fallen.[1] Does the former decree precede or succeed the latter? According to supralapsarianism the decree to save some of the fallen precedes the decree to permit sin; according to infralapsarianism, it's the other way around. The debate between Supra and Infra has sometimes been held up as an example of Protestant scholasticism run amok. That is because, in part, it is extremely hard to see just what the debate is. The main problem here is the 'precede' and 'succeed'. As the disputants saw, the question isn't about temporal precedence (it isn't that God promulgated part of his decree at one time and part at a later); they therefore suggested that the precedence in question is logical. As Carl Henry says, "The terms supra and infra stipulate whether the divine decree to elect some to salvation comes logically before or after the decrees to create and to permit the fall."[2] But what would that mean? Would the idea be that one of the decrees entailed but was not entailed by the other? But then, apparently, the Infras would have to think the decree to permit the fall entails but is not entailed by the decree to save some of the fallen. The Infras may have been misguided, but they weren't as obtuse as all that; surely they saw

---

1. Many Supras also held that God's first decree included that some should be damned as well as that some should be saved; perhaps this accounts for the association of supralapsarianism with the sterner sort of Calvinism.

2. *God Who Stands and Stays*, vol. VI of *God, Revelation, and Authority* (Waco, Tex.: Word, 1983), p. 88.

that the proposition *God decrees to save some of the fallen* entails but is not entailed by the proposition *God decrees to permit some to fall;* but then presumably that's compatible with their infralapsarianism. So what does this dispute amount to?

One understandable reaction is that it doesn't much matter what the dispute amounts to; the question concerns wholly arcane matters where Scripture is for the most part silent; why waste time on something like that? Isn't this something like arguing about how many angels can dance on the head, or maybe even the point, of a pin? I have some sympathy for this reaction. Nevertheless, I think we can see which of these is right and what kind of priority is relevant. And we can see which is right by thinking about the problem of evil.

Suffering and Evil

The late and unlamented twentieth century displayed an absolutely appalling amount and variety both of suffering and of evil; no previous century rivals it. As I'm thinking of the matter, suffering encompasses any kind of pain or discomfort: pain or discomfort that results from disease, injury, oppression, overwork, old age, sorrow for one's sins, disappointment with one's self or with one's lot in life (or that of persons close to one), the pain of loneliness, isolation, betrayal, unrequited love, and awareness of the suffering of others. I'm thinking of evil, on the other hand, as, fundamentally, a matter of free creatures' doing what is wrong and/or displaying vicious character traits. Often pain and suffering is a result of evil, as in some of the events for which our century will be remembered — the horrifying seventy-year-long Marxist experiments in eastern Europe and China with their many millions of victims, the Holocaust, genocide in late twentieth-century Europe and Africa, and the like. Of course much suffering and evil is banal, prosaic, commonplace, and is none the better for that.

It isn't only the twentieth century that has featured suffering and evil. Christians and other believers in God have long been baffled and perplexed by its presence, or by the amount of it, or by certain especially heinous displays of it, some of which are so horrifying that it seems callous and unfeeling to bring them up in the context of a scholarly discussion. Why does God permit evil, or why does he permit so much of it, or why does he permit those horrifying varieties of it? This bafflement and perplexity is widely represented in the Bible: perhaps especially in the

Psalms and the book of Job, but elsewhere as well. And the perplexity is by no means merely theoretical: faced with an especially abhorrent example of suffering or evil in her own life, or the life of someone she loves, a believer can find herself tempted to take towards God an attitude she herself hates — an attitude of mistrust, or suspicion, or bitterness, or rebellion. A person in this condition may not be much tempted to doubt the existence or even the goodness of God; nevertheless she may resent God, fail to trust him, be wary of him, be unable to think of him as a loving father, think of him as distant and indifferent.

Now many have urged that knowledge of the extent, variety, duration and distribution of suffering and evil ("the facts of evil," for short) confronts the believer with a problem of quite another sort.[3] The facts of evil, they argue, can serve as the premise of a powerful argument against the very existence of God — against the existence, that is, of an all-powerful, all-knowing, and wholly good person who has created the world and loves the creatures he has created. Call such an argument 'atheological'; atheological arguments go all the way back to the ancient world — at least to Epicurus, whose argument is repeated in the eighteenth century by Hume: Epicurus' old questions are yet unanswered.

> Is he willing to prevent evil, but not able? then he is impotent. Is he able, but not willing? then he is malevolent. Is he both able and willing? whence then is evil?[4]

And the claim is that the facts of evil constitute a defeater for theistic belief for those theists who are fully aware of them — and if for theistic belief, then also for Christian belief. Christians may find this argument less than compelling;[5] nevertheless they may also find the facts of evil disturbing, both from a practical and from a theoretical point of view; un-

---

3. It is worth noting that there are many *different* problems, questions, and topics that fall under the rubric of the problem of evil. There are, for example, the problems of *preventing* suffering and evil, that of *alleviating* it (knowing how to comfort and help those that suffer from it), that of maintaining the right attitude towards those who suffer, the pastoral or spiritual problem I mentioned above, and more; and of course a proper response to one of these problems might be totally inappropriate as a response to another.

4. *Dialogues concerning Natural Religion*, ed. Richard Popkin (Indianapolis: Hackett Publishing, 1980), p. 63. Hume puts the argument in the mouth of Philo, widely thought to represent Hume's own views.

5. See, e.g., Chapter 14 of my book *Warranted Christian Belief* (New York: Oxford University Press, 2000).

derstanding of evil and its place in God's world is an important goal for Christians, one where philosophers can perhaps be of some help.

Christian philosophers have for the most part concentrated on the apologetic effort of rebutting the various versions of the argument from evil. These rebuttals have taken several forms. One sort of response specifies some particular kind of good, and suggests that God could not have created a world displaying that kind of good without permitting evil. Thus perhaps the world is a vale of soul-making, with evil and suffering permitting human beings to achieve certain desirable spiritual states they couldn't otherwise attain. Alternatively, evil arises from creaturely free will: God wanted a world in which there are free creatures who freely obey his commands and enter into personal relationship with him; but of course whether a creature freely obeys God's commands is not up to God: it is up to the creature in question; and the counterfactuals of freedom are such that God couldn't actualize a really good world with free creatures without permitting evil. There is also the 'no-see-um re-sponse':[6] God has his reasons for permitting evil, but the epistemic distance between him and us is such that we can't really hope to know what those reasons are, or why they require him to permit the evil we see.[7] Still another response: Donald Turner suggests that (to put it roughly and inaccurately) perhaps God creates concrete worlds or cosmoi corresponding to all of the possible worlds that are on balance good.[8] Some of these worlds, of course, will contain a great deal of evil (and even more good); our world is one of those worlds.

These responses are useful and important. But in addition to rebut-

6. A no-see-um is a very small midge with a bite out of all proportion to its size. The reference is to the fact that your failing to see a no-see-um in your tent is no evidence that there aren't any there; similarly, failing to see what God's reason is for a given evil is no reason to think he doesn't or couldn't have a reason.

7. See, e.g., Steve Wykstra, "Difficulties in Rowe's Argument for Atheism, and in One of Plantinga's Fustigations against It," read on the *Queen Mary* at the Pacific Division Meeting of the American Philosophical Association, 1983, and "The Humian Obstacle to Evidential Arguments from Suffering: On Avoiding the Evils of 'Appearance,'" *International Journal for Philosophy of Religion* 16 (1984): 73-94.

8. See Donald Turner's 1994 Ph.D. dissertation *God and the Best of All Possible Worlds* (University of Pittsburgh). Here we must be careful: there is a good world W where you wear your blue shirt today, and another that differs from W only (substantially) in that you wear your yellow shirt today; a good world W where you have a Coke with lunch and another just like it except that you have coffee. God does not, of course, create cosmoi corresponding to all of these. That is because you yourself could not be in more than one cosmos; so while he creates cosmoi corresponding to each of the good possible worlds, the appropriate function is many-one. For details see Turner's dissertation.

ting these arguments, Christian philosophers should also turn to a different task: that of understanding the evil our world displays from a Christian perspective. Granted, the atheological arguments are unsuccessful; but how should Christians think about evil?[9] I therefore want to suggest still another response, or rather I want to reinvent the wheel and propose for further consideration a response that has been with us for a long time. I don't claim that this response answers all our questions or relieves all of our perplexity. It does make a contribution along these lines, however, and in what follows I want to explore it, to see what it has to offer us.

Suppose initially we think about the matter as follows. God intends to create a world; to do so, he must weakly actualize a possible world.[10] He considers all the uncountably many possible worlds, each with its own degree of excellence or value. How shall we think of the value or goodness of a possible world? Well, what sorts of things are good or valuable or excellent, on the one hand, or bad or unhappy or deplorable on the other? The answer is easy; states of affairs (perhaps among other things) are good or bad.[11] John's being in pain is a bad state of affairs, and John's suffering pain magnificently, a good one; there being many people who treat each other in accord with the law of love is a good state of affairs; there being people who hate God and each other is a bad. Since possible worlds are states of affairs, they are precisely the sorts of things that are good or bad, valuable or disvaluable. Perhaps there is no best possible world (there is a tie, or for each world, no matter how good, there is another better yet) but in any event what God intended, in creating, was to actualize (weakly actualize) a really good possible world.

---

9. Here Marilyn Adams and Eleonore Stump have led the way: see, for example, Stump's "Aquinas on the Sufferings of Job" in *The Evidential Argument from Evil*, ed. Daniel Howard-Snyder (Bloomington, Ind.: Indiana University Press, 1996) and "Second Person Accounts and the Problem of Evil," in *Faith and the Problem of Evil*, Stob Lectures at Calvin College, January 1999 (Grand Rapids: Calvin College, 1999), and Adams' "Horrendous Evils and the Goodness of God" in *The Problem of Evil*, ed. Marilyn McCord Adams and Robert Merrihew Adams (New York: Oxford University Press, 1990).

10. For the notion of possible worlds in play here, see my *The Nature of Necessity* (Oxford: Clarendon Press, 1974), Chapter 4, and "Actualism and Possible Worlds," *Theoria* 1976: 139ff., reprinted in Michael Loux, *The Actual and the Possible* (Ithaca, N.Y.: Cornell University Press, 1979). For the notions of strong and weak actualization, see the Profiles volume *Alvin Plantinga*, ed. James Tomberlin and Peter van Inwagen (Dordrecht: D. Reidel Publishing Co., 1985) (hereafter Profiles), pp. 49ff.

11. I don't mean to address here the question whether it is states of affairs or objects or events that are the primary locus of value; in either case states of affairs will be good or bad.

Now many of these possible worlds, I take it, are such that it is not within God's power to weakly actualize them. I've argued for this elsewhere;[12] here I'll just sketch the argument. For a given possible world W, let T(W) be the largest state of affairs God strongly actualizes in W.[13] Assuming that there are nontrivial true counterfactuals of freedom,[14] God would be able to weakly actualize a given possible world W only if the counterfactual

(1) If God were to strongly actualize T(W), then W would be actual

were true. Now there are possible worlds W and W* such that God strongly actualizes the same states of affairs in W as in W*; that is, there are many possible worlds W and W* such that T(W) = T(W*). Where T(W) = T(W*), it is of course impossible that both (1) and

(2) If God were to strongly actualize T(W*), then W* would be actual

be true; that is because it is not possible that both W and W* be actual. Accordingly, either W or W* is a world God could not have actualized. Following Thomas Flint, we could say that the worlds God could have weakly actualized are the feasible worlds. God's aim in creating, then, is to create an extremely good feasible world.

So far so good; but what are good-making qualities among worlds — what sort of features will make one world better than another? Here one thinks, for example, of the amount of creaturely happiness; a world with a great deal of creaturely happiness (i.e., a world such that if it were actual, there would be a great deal of creaturely happiness) is so far forth a better world than one in which there is little such happiness. Other characteristics on which the goodness of a world depends would be the

12. *The Nature of Necessity*, pp. 180ff., and Profiles, pp. 50ff.

13. God strongly actualizes a given state of affairs S just if he causes S to be actual.

14. I don't have the space here to respond to objections to this assumption. Perhaps the most important of these objections is the so-called 'grounding' objection offered by Robert Adams in "Middle Knowledge and the Problem of Evil," *American Philosophical Quarterly*, 1977, and William Hasker in "A Refutation of Middle Knowledge," *Noûs*, December 1986. This objection goes all the way back to the Jesuit/Dominican controversy in the sixteenth century, a dispute whose increasing rancor finally induced the Pope to forbid the disputants to vilify one another in public (although he apparently didn't object to vilification among consenting adults in the privacy of their own quarters). The grounding and founding objection has been dealt with in magisterial fashion in my colleague Thomas Flint's book *Divine Providence: The Molinist Account* (Ithaca, N.Y.: Cornell University Press, 1998).

amount of beauty, justice, creaturely goodness, performance of duty, and the like. The existence of creatures who conform to the divine law to love God above all and their neighbor as themselves (which presumably holds not just for humans but for other rational creatures — angels, other rational species in our universe, if there are any others) would also be an important determinant of a world's goodness or excellence. And of course there are also badmaking characteristics of a world: containing much suffering, pain, creaturely rejection of God, hatred, sin, and the like. Fundamentally, a world W is a better world than a world W* just if God would prefer the actuality of W to the actuality of W*.

The above list of good-making characteristics, however, omits the two most important. First, any world in which God exists is enormously more valuable than any world in which he does not exist. According to the traditional doctrine of God's necessary existence, of course, God is both concrete and necessarily existent, and the only being who displays both those characteristics. If this doctrine is correct, then there aren't any worlds in which God does not exist. Still further, regardless of whether there are any such worlds, God will be able to choose only among those in which he exists; hence this great-making characteristic, trivially, will be present in any world he chooses for weak actualization.

Given the truth of Christian belief, however, there is also a contingent good-making characteristic of our world — one that isn't present in all worlds — that towers enormously above all the rest of the contingent states of affairs included in our world: the unthinkably great good of divine incarnation and atonement. Jesus Christ, the second person of the divine Trinity, incomparably good, holy, and sinless, was willing to empty himself, to take on our flesh and become incarnate, and to suffer and die so that we human beings can have life and be reconciled to the Father. In order to accomplish this, he was willing to undergo suffering of a depth and intensity we cannot so much as imagine, including even the shattering climax of being abandoned by God the Father himself: "My God, my God, why have you forsaken me?" God the Father, the first being of the whole universe, perfectly good and holy, all-powerful and all-knowing, was willing to permit his Son to undergo this suffering, and to undergo enormous suffering himself, in order to make it possible for us human beings to be reconciled to him. And this in face of the fact that we have turned our back upon God, have rejected him, are sunk in sin, indeed, are inclined to resent God and our neighbor. Could there be a display of love to rival this? More to the present purpose, could there be a good-making feature of a world to rival this?

Suppose we think about these points a bit further. We are considering just the worlds in which God exists; for present purposes, let's assume that traditional theism is true, and that these are all the worlds there are. The first thing to note, I think, is that all of these worlds — all possible worlds, then — are very good. For God is unlimited in goodness and holiness, as well as in power and knowledge; these properties, furthermore, are essential to him; and this means, I believe, that God not only has created a world that is very good, but that there aren't any conditions under which he would have created a world that is less than very good. It isn't possible that he create such a world; every possible world in which God creates is very good. For every possible world containing creatures is a world such that it is possible, in the broadly logical sense, that God weakly actualize it;[15] none is such that God's goodness or love or mercy would make it impossible for him to actualize it. There is therefore no level of value among possible worlds such that God couldn't actualize possible worlds whose value falls below that level (and such that some possible worlds fall below that level). The class of possible worlds God's love and goodness prevents him from actualizing is empty. All possible worlds, we might say, are eligible worlds: worlds that God's goodness, mercy, and love would permit him to actualize.

Now I don't mean to suggest that every imaginable or in some sense conceivable world is a very good world. Perhaps we can imagine or in some sense conceive of worlds in which the only things that exist are persons always in excruciating pain. No such world is in fact possible, however, if God, as we are assuming, is a necessary being who has essentially such properties as unlimited goodness, love, knowledge, and power. For first, of course, every world includes the existence of God. But neither would any world contain just God and creatures always in excruciating pain: God wouldn't create such worlds. So perhaps there are imaginable or even conceivable worlds that are not very good; the fact is, however, no such world is possible. All possible worlds are very good.

Of course it is also possible that God refrain from creating altogether. If he had done so, however, the world still would have been very good; for his own existence, of course, would have been actual. Indeed, any world in which God exists is in a good sense infinitely valuable. I don't mean to suggest that we can apply Cantorian infinitary mathematics to these topics. I don't mean to suggest that there are proper units of

15. This is trivial; every possible world W containing creatures is such that there is some possible world in which God actualizes W: W itself.

goodness — felicifics, for example — such that any world containing God displays infinitely many of those units of goodness. Still, God himself, who is unlimited in goodness, love, knowledge, power, and the like, exists in any such world; it follows, I suggest, that the value of any state of affairs in which God alone exists is itself unlimited.

But what is the force of 'unlimited' here? I take it to mean that there are no nonlogical limits to God's display of these great-making properties: no nonlogical limit to his goodness, love, knowledge, and power. From this it follows, I believe, that any state of affairs containing God alone — any state of affairs that would have been actual had God not created anything at all — is also in a sensible sense infinite in value. It is not that any such world W is of maximal value, so that there are no possible worlds better than W. On the contrary: a world that also contains very good creatures — free creatures, perhaps, who always do what is right — would be a better world than W. No: it's something else. To see what, consider a possible world W and then consider the state of affairs W- consisting just in the existence and properties of the free creatures W contains. Let us also suppose that we have a coherent sense of entailment in which W- does not entail the existence of God, even though the latter is a necessary state of affairs. (I believe there are such senses, but don't have the space to pursue the matter here.) Now the way in which such a world W is unlimited in value is that W-, no matter how good, and no matter how many wonderful creatures with splendid properties it displays, is not as good as the state of affairs consisting in the existence of God. We might say that in this way the good of God's existence is incommensurable with creaturely goods. But it is also incommensurable with creaturely evils. No matter how much sin and suffering and evil W- contains, it is vastly outweighed by the goodness of God, so that W is a good world, and indeed a very good world. It follows, once more, that every possible world is a very good world.

But that doesn't mean that none are more valuable than others. The fact is: some possible worlds are much better than others. For there is a second and enormously impressive good-making feature of our world, a feature to be found only in some and not in all possible worlds. This is the towering and magnificent good of divine incarnation and atonement. According to the traditional Christian way of looking at the matter, God was ~~way~~ obliged to provide a way of salvation for his erring creatures. It ~~been~~ consistent with his love, goodness, and mercy not to in~~~~elous plan by which we sinful creatures can have life and ~~~~God. Hence there are possible worlds in which there are free creatures who go wrong, and in which there is no atonement; in these worlds all these free creatures suffer the consequences of their sin and are ultimately cut off from God. Such a world, I say, is not as good — perhaps not nearly as good — as a world in which sinful creatures are offered redemption and salvation from their sins.

In fact I believe we can go further. I believe that any world with incarnation and atonement is a better world than any without it — or at any rate better than any world in which God does nothing comparable to incarnation and atonement. It is hard to imagine what God could do that is in fact comparable to incarnation and atonement; but perhaps this is just a limitation of our imagination. But since this is so hard to imagine, I propose that we ignore those possible worlds, if there are any, in which God does not arrange for incarnation and atonement, but does something else of comparable excellence. So consider the splendid and gracious marvel of incarnation and atonement. I believe that the great goodness of this state of affairs, like that of the divine existence itself, makes its value incommensurable with the value of states of affairs involving creaturely good and bad. Thus the value of incarnation and atonement cannot be matched by any aggregate of creaturely goods. No matter how many excellent creatures there are in a world, no matter how rich and beautiful and sinless their lives, the aggregated value of their lives would not match that of incarnation and atonement; any world with incarnation and atonement would be better yet. And no matter how much evil, how much sin and suffering a world contains, the aggregated badness would be outweighed by the goodness of incarnation and atonement, outweighed in such a way that the world in question is very good. In this sense, therefore, any world with incarnation and atonement is of infinite value by virtue of containing two goods of infinite value: the existence of God, and incarnation and atonement. Under this assumption, there will be a certain level L of excellence or goodness, among possible worlds, such that all the worlds at that level or above contain incarnation and atonement. Call this 'the strong value assumption', and say that any world whose value equals or exceeds it, is a highly eligible world.

I am inclined to accept the strong value assumption, but I don't need anything quite as powerful as all that for my argument. I can hold something weaker. Contrast two kinds of possible worlds. In the first kind, there are free creatures who always do only what is right, who live in love and harmony with God and each other, and do so, let's add, through all eternity. Now for each of these worlds W of this kind, there is a world W* of the second kind. In W* God creates the very same creature as in W; but in W* these free creatures rebel against him, fall into sin and wickedness, turn their backs upon God. In W*, however, God graciously provides a means of salvation by way of incarnation and atonement. My claim is that for any such worlds W and W*, W* is a better world than W. Unlike the strong value assumption, this claim does not entail that every world with incarnation and atonement is better than any world without them, and it does not entail that there is a level of value such that every world at or above that level contains incarnation and atonement. What it does imply, however, is that there is no level of value such that none of the worlds at or above that level contain incarnation and atonement. Call this the moderate value assumption.

But my argument doesn't require even the moderate value assumption.[16] All it really requires is that among the worlds of great value, there be some that include incarnation and atonement. Indeed, we can go further: given that all of the possible worlds including creatures are worlds sufficiently good for God to actualize them, all that is really required, for my argument, is that incarnation and atonement be possible, i.e., that there be possible worlds that include them. Since, according to Christian thought, this state of affairs is actual, it is a fortiori possible.

I shall conduct the argument under the strong value assumption, merely reminding the reader that the argument can also be conducted under the moderate or weak assumptions. Under the strong assumption, the value of any world which displays incarnation and atonement will exceed that of any world without those features. Perhaps, even, the value of incarnation and atonement, (i.e., the complex event involving the actions of God the Father and God the Son) is so great that any world in which it occurs is as valuable as any other world, so that the value of all the worlds in which atonement occurs is equal. We needn't go as far as all that, however; more modestly, we can say that the value of the worlds with atonement exceeds that of worlds without atonement, and the value of the former are clumped together in such a way that while some may be more valuable than others, none is very much more valuable than any other. More modestly still, we can say simply that all the worlds in which incarnation and atonement are present are worlds of very great goodness, achieving that level L of goodness such that no world without incarnation and atonement achieves that level.

Accordingly, if God proposes to actualize a really good possible

---

16. As was pointed out to me by Tom Flint, for whose penetrating comments on this and other topics of this paper I am extremely grateful.

world, one whose value exceeds L, he will create a world containing incarnation and atonement. But of course all the worlds with incarnation and atonement contain evil. For atonement is among other things a matter of creatures' being saved from the consequences of their sin; therefore if there were no evil, there would be no sin, no consequences of sin to be saved from, and hence no atonement. Therefore a necessary condition of atonement is sin and evil. But all the highly eligible worlds contain atonement; hence all the highly eligible worlds contain sin and evil, and the suffering consequent upon them. You can't have a world whose value exceeds L without sin and evil; sin and evil is a necessary condition of the value of every really good possible world. O Felix Culpa indeed![17] But then this gives us a very straightforward and simple response to the question "Why is there evil in the world?" The response is that God wanted to create a highly eligible world, wanted to actualize one of the best of all the possible worlds; all those worlds contain atonement, hence they all contain sin and evil. I've claimed elsewhere that theodicies are unsuccessful: "And here I must say that most attempts to explain why God permits evil — theodicies, as we may call them — strike me as tepid, shallow, and ultimately frivolous."[18] But doesn't the above furnish us with an answer to the question "Why does God permit evil?" The answer is: because he wanted to actualize a possible world whose value was greater than L; but all those possible worlds contain incarnation and atonement; hence all those worlds contain evil. So if a theodicy is an attempt to explain why God permits evil, what we have here is a theodicy — and, if I'm right, a successful theodicy.

And as a bonus, we get a clear resolution of the Supra/Infra debate: the Supras are right. God's fundamental and first intention is to actualize an extremely good possible world, one whose value exceeds L; but all those worlds contain incarnation and atonement and hence also sin and evil; so the decree to provide incarnation and atonement and hence salvation is prior to the decree to permit fall into sin. The priority in question isn't temporal, and isn't exactly logical either; it is a matter, rather, of ultimate aim as opposed to proximate aim. God's ultimate aim, here, is to create a world of a certain level of value. That aim requires that he aim to create a world in which there is incarnation and atonement — which, in turn, requires that there be sin and evil. So there is a clear sense in which

17. The Roman Catholic Easter Vigil liturgy contains the words, "O felix culpa, quae talem ac tantum meruit habere Redemptorem."

18. Profiles, p. 35.

the decree to provide salvation precedes the decree to permit sin; but there is no comparable sense in which the decree to permit sin precedes the decree to permit evil.

One final point before we turn to objections. In "Salvifici Doloris," a recent apostolic letter from Pope John Paul II on the Christian meaning of suffering, we read that

> Each one is also called to share in that suffering through which the Redemption was accomplished. He is called to share in that suffering through which all human suffering has also been redeemed. . . . Thus each man, in his suffering, can also become a sharer in the redemptive suffering of Christ. (p. 31)

Here the suggestion seems to be that we human beings, by virtue of suffering, can participate and take part in, can contribute to the divine suffering by which humankind is redeemed. Now this seems to suggest that Christ's suffering and sacrifice was somehow incomplete: if my contribution is genuinely useful, must there not be something in some sense lacking in what Christ himself did in the Atonement? From a Christian perspective, this seems a bit suspect. But the same suggestion is made by the apostle Paul, whose credentials here are certainly beyond question: "Now I rejoice in what was suffered for you, and I fill up in my flesh what is still lacking in regard to Christ's afflictions, for the sake of his body which is the church" (Colossians 1:24).[19] "What is still lacking in regard to Christ's affliction"? What could still be lacking? What could this lack be?

From the present perspective there is an answer: highly eligible possible worlds, those whose value exceeds level L, also contain creaturely suffering, suffering on the part of victims and perpetrators of sin. This suffering is a necessary condition of the goodness of the world in question. In suffering, then, we creatures can be like Christ. We get to take part and participate in his redemptive activity. So, for a highly eligible world to be actualized, more is needed than just the suffering of Christ. All of these worlds contain atonement; so they all contain divine suffering; but they also all contain creaturely suffering. Creatures, therefore, can fill up what is lacking in regard to Christ's suffering in the following way: there is a necessary condition of the goodness of truly good (highly eligible) possible worlds that is not and cannot be satisfied by Christ's suffering; it

---

19. The same idea is to be found elsewhere in Paul's writings: see, e.g., Romans 1:17.

requires creaturely suffering as well. It is in this sense that Paul as well as the rest of us can fill up what is still lacking in regard to Christ's suffering.

Objections

Accordingly, the Felix Culpa approach can perhaps provide us with a theodicy. But of course it does so properly only if it isn't itself subject to fatal flaws. Is it? What might be objections to it? There are at least three principal objections to this line of thought, or perhaps three kinds of difficult questions to answer. First, why does God permit suffering as well as sin and evil? Second, why does God permit so much suffering and evil? And third, if God permitted human suffering and evil in order to achieve a world in which there is incarnation and atonement, wouldn't he be manipulative, calculating, treating his creatures like means instead of ends? There is a sort of psychological disorder called 'Munchausen syndrome by proxy'[20] in which parents harm their children and then rush them to the hospital in order to look heroic and get attention; wouldn't this be a bit like that? In the interests of decency and good order I will take these up one at a time and in order.

Why Suffering?

I said above that the Felix Culpa line of thought offers a theodicy: an answer to the question "Why does God permit evil?" But perhaps a serious theodicy would have to answer other questions as well: for example, why does God permit so much evil, and why does God permit suffering? Concede that you can't have atonement without evil; why do you also need suffering? Incarnation and atonement requires sin and evil: why think it also requires suffering? Wouldn't the cosmos have been better if God had permitted sin and evil, so that there was occasion for incarnation and atonement, but no suffering? Maybe the Felix Culpa line of thought explains the existence of sin and evil; how does it help with respect to suffering?

The answer is twofold: (a) significantly free creatures are free to do evil, and some of them in fact do evil, causing suffering; (b) suffering itself is instrumentally valuable. So first, one goodmaking feature of a

20. Here I am indebted for a correction to Tom Flint.

world is the existence, in it, of free and rational creatures. But free creatures come in a variety of versions, and not all free creatures are equal with respect to value, i.e., to the value of the worlds in which they exist. In general, the more free creatures resemble God, the more valuable they are and the more valuable are the worlds in which they exist. In particular, creatures that have a great deal of power, including power to do both good and evil, are more valuable than creatures who are free, but whose power is limited or meager. God therefore created a world in which there are creatures with at least two features: (a) a great deal of power, including the power to work against God, and (b) the freedom to turn their backs upon God, to rebel against him, fight against what he values. Thus Milton's Satan declares "Evil, be Thou my Good!"; in so doing he announces his intention to take up arms against God, to resist him, to try to destroy what God values, to do his best to wreck God's world, to promote what God hates. Suffering is intrinsically a bad thing; accordingly God hates it; Satan therefore aims to promote suffering, to cause as much of it as he can. Much of the suffering in the world results in this way from the free actions of creatures who actively oppose God and what he values. But free creatures also cause suffering, sometimes, not because they intend in this way actively to oppose God, but just because they don't have any objection to inflicting suffering on others in order to achieve their own selfish or foolish ends. Here one thinks of the enormous suffering inflicted, in the twentieth century, on the population of the former Soviet Union in order to attain that Marxist paradise; Stalin and his henchmen recklessly ran roughshod over the rights and goods of others in order to achieve something they saw as valuable. At least some of the suffering the world displays results from the free actions of significantly free creatures.

But what about so-called natural evil, evil that cannot be attributed to the free actions of human beings? What about the suffering due to disease, earthquake, flood, famine, pestilence, and the like? What about animal suffering and the savagery displayed in the natural world? What about the Ichneumonid wasp Darwin found so upsetting, a wasp that lays its eggs in a live caterpillar, so that when the eggs hatch, the pupae eat the caterpillar alive from the inside? Well, perhaps, as Peter van Inwagen suggests, this is the price God had to pay for a regular world. But there is another and more traditional suggestion here. Perhaps the term 'natural evil' is something of a misnomer, or perhaps, at any rate, the contrast between natural evil and moral evil is misleading in that the former is really an instance of the latter. It is plausible to think that there are deeper layers to the sin and evil the world displays, than that exhibited by human beings and embodied in their actions. According to the apostle Paul, the whole creation is groaning, and groaning because of sin.[21] Here a traditional suggestion is that suffering and evil of this sort is to be attributed to the actions of Satan and his cohorts; Satan is a mighty non-human free creature who rebelled against the Lord long before human beings were on the scene; and much of the natural evil the world displays is due to the actions of Satan and his cohorts.[22]

This suggestion is not at present widely popular in Western academia, and not widely endorsed by the contemporary intellectual elite. But it is less than clear that Western academia has much to say by way of evidence against the idea. That beings of these sorts should be involved in the history of our world seems to me (as to, e.g., C. S. Lewis and many others) not at all unlikely, in particular not unlikely with respect to Christian theism. The thought that much evil is due to Satan and his cohorts is of course entirely consistent with God's being omnipotent, omniscient, and perfectly good; furthermore it isn't nearly as improbable with respect to "what we now know" as most philosophers seem to assume. Objections to it consist much more in amused contempt or instinctive revulsion

21. "For the creation was subjected to frustration, not by its own choice, but by the will of the one who subjected it, in hope that the creation itself will be liberated from its bondage to decay and brought into the glorious freedom of the children of God. We know that the whole creation has been groaning as in the pains of childbirth right up to the present time" (Romans 1:18-22).

22. Thus, for example, Dom Bruno Well:

> So the fallen angels which have power over the universe and over this planet in particular, being motivated by an intense angelic hatred of God and of all creatures, have acted upon the forces of matter, actuating them in false proportions so far as lay in their power, and this from the very outset of evolution, thus producing a deep-set disorder in the very heart of the universe which manifests itself today in the various physical evils which we find in nature, and among them the violence, the savagery, and the suffering of animal life. This does not mean that, for instance, an earthquake or a thunderstorm is due directly to satanic action. It is due to purely natural causes, but these causes are what they now are owing to the deep-set disorder in the heart of nature resulting from this action of fallen spirits, most subtly mingled with the action of good spirits, throughout the long ages of the world's formation — 'an enemy came and sowed tares also amid the wheat'.

Why Does God Permit Evil? (London: Burns, Oates & Washbourne Ltd., 1941), pp. 49-50. Aquinas approvingly quotes Damascene to the same effect: "The devil was one of the angelic powers who presided over the terrestrial order" (ST I, Q. 110, a. 1, ad 3).

16

than in reasoned refutation. They are like those incredulous stares David Lewis complains of — not much by way of considered thought. But how much evidential value should be attached to a thing like that?

So suffering results, at least in part, from the actions of free creatures; and perhaps it wasn't within the power of God to create free creatures who are both capable of causing suffering and turning to evil, but never in fact do cause suffering. But further, perhaps even if God could create such creatures, he wouldn't want to, or wouldn't want to create only them. Perhaps worlds with free powerful creatures who sin but do not cause suffering are not as good as worlds in which they create suffering; for suffering is also itself of instrumental value. First, some suffering has the effect of improving our character and preparing God's people for life in his kingdom;[23] this world is in part a vale of soul-making, as John Hick and many others (including the apostle Paul) before him have suggested. Some suffering may also be the price of a regular world, as Peter van Inwagen suggests.[24] But according to the apostle Paul, there are other subtle ways in which suffering is of instrumental value. He suggests, for example, that our present suffering is a means to the eternal weight of glory prepared for those who follow him:

> We always carry around in our body the death of Jesus, so that the life of Jesus may also be revealed in our body. For we who are alive are always being given over to death so that his life may be revealed in our mortal body. (2 Corinthians 4:10-11, 14)

> We are . . . fellow heirs with Christ, provided we suffer with him in order that we may also be glorified with him. I consider that the sufferings of this present time are not worthy to be compared. . . . (Romans 8)

> For our light and momentary troubles are achieving for us an eternal glory that far outweighs them all. (2 Corinthians 4:17)

Our suffering can enable us to be glorified, and achieve for us an eternal glory; but we aren't told how this works: how is it that our suffering is a means to this eternal glory? Elsewhere there are tantalizing suggestions:

---

23. "God disciplines us for our good, that we may share in his holiness. No discipline seems pleasant at the time, but painful. Later on, however, it produces a harvest of righteousness and peace for those who have been trained by it" (Hebrews 12:10-11).

24. See, e.g., "The Magnitude, Duration, and Distribution of Evil" in *God, Knowledge, and Mystery* (Ithaca, N.Y.: Cornell University Press, 1995), p. 118.

> I want to know Christ and the power of his resurrection, and the fellowship of sharing in his sufferings, becoming like him in his death, and so, somehow, to attain to the resurrection from the dead. (Philippians 3:10-11)

I believe three things are suggested. First, there is the suggestion that sharing in the suffering of Christ is a means to attain "the resurrection from the dead," i.e., salvation. Second, it is a good thing that the followers of Christ share in his sufferings because this is a means of fellowship with him at a very profound level and a way in which they achieve a certain kind of solidarity with him; and third, in thus sharing his suffering, his followers come to resemble Christ in an important respect, thus displaying more fully the image of God.[25] Although these are deep waters, I'd like to say just a bit about the second and third suggestions. Consider the idea of fellowship with Christ in his suffering, then: what is valuable about fellowship in sharing in the sufferings of Christ? The suggestion, I think, is just that our suffering with Christ, thus joining him in the most profound expression of his love and enjoying solidarity with him in his central mission, is a good state of affairs; it is good that creatures, whose sins require this activity on his part, join him in it. Secondly, those who suffer resemble Christ in an important respect, thus displaying more fully the image of God, i.e., displaying that image more fully than they could have without the suffering. An absolutely central part of Christ's mission is his suffering; it is through this suffering that he atones for human sin and enables human beings to achieve union with God. But then if it is a good thing that creatures resemble Christ, it is a good thing that they resemble him in this respect as well. According to Jonathan Edwards, by virtue of our fall and subsequent redemption, we can achieve a level of intimacy with God that can't be achieved in any other way; by virtue of suffering we are invited to join the charmed circle of the Trinity itself. And according to Abraham Kuyper, the angels see this and are envious.[26] Perhaps another part of what is required for membership in this circle is solidarity with Christ and resemblance to him with respect to suffering. The really mature Christian, furthermore, one like St. Paul, will

---

25. Simone Weil: ". . . the distress of the abandoned Christ is a good. There cannot be a greater good for us on earth than to share in it." "The Love of God and Affliction" in *On Science, Necessity and the Love of God* (London: Oxford University Press, 1968), p. 177.

26. *To Be Near unto God*, trans. John Hendrik de Vries (Grand Rapids: Wm. B. Eerdmans, 1918,) p. 307.

welcome this opportunity. Furthermore, perhaps all of us who suffer will welcome the opportunity in retrospect. Julian of Norwich suggests that those who suffer will receive God's gratitude[27] and will of course much rather have had the suffering and received the divine gratitude than to have had neither. That too is a good state of affairs.

I say that our fellowship and solidarity in Christ's suffering and our resembling him in suffering are good states of affairs; I do not say that we can clearly see that they are indeed good states of affairs. My reason for saying that they are in fact good is not that it is simply obvious and apparent to us that they are good states of affairs, in the way in which it is simply apparent that severe suffering is intrinsically a bad thing. Perhaps this is indeed apparent to some especially mature or especially favored human beings, but it isn't to the rest of us. So I don't say this because it is evident to us, but rather because we learn from Scripture that these are good states of affairs — or, more modestly, we learn this from what seems to me to be the best understanding of the scriptural passages in question. Someone might object that in a theodicy, one cannot appeal to goods we can't ourselves recognize to be goods; but why think a thing like that? A theodicy will of course make reference to states of affairs that are known to be good, or reasonably thought to be good. How this information is acquired is neither here nor there.

So why is suffering present in the really good possible worlds; why is it that they contain not just sin, evil, and rebellion, but also suffering? Because, first, some of the free creatures God has created have turned their backs on God and behaved in such a way as to cause suffering; and second, because suffering is itself of instrumental value, and thus will be found in really good worlds. Suffering is of instrumental value, furthermore, in several different ways. In addition to the ways suggested by Hick, Swinburne, and van Inwagen, there is also the fact that the suffering of God's children enables them to be in fellowship and solidarity with the Lord Jesus Christ; it also enhances the image of God in them.

Why So Much Sin and Suffering?

But why is there so much sin and suffering? Concede that every really good world contains both evil and suffering; but why does there have to be as much of these dubious quantities as our world in fact manifests?

27. *Revelation of Divine Love,* Chapter 14.

Wouldn't a world with much less sin and suffering than ours be a better world, even if it contains both incarnation and atonement and also some sin and suffering? Here there are two considerations. First, perhaps the counterfactuals of freedom come out in such a way that a world as good as ours will contain as much sin and suffering as ours. But secondly, there is the question how much sin and suffering a highly eligible world contains. This is not an easy question. As I've argued, the best worlds contain incarnation and atonement. But for all we know, there isn't any maximal amount of sin and suffering contained in such worlds; that is, there isn't an amount a of sin and suffering such that some world in this class contains a units (turps, perhaps) of sin and suffering and no world in this class contains more. Perhaps for every degree of sin and suffering contained in some highly eligible world, there is another highly eligible world with more. In the same way, for all we know there is no minimum degree of suffering among these highly eligible worlds. Perhaps for every degree of sin and suffering contained in some highly eligible world, there is another highly eligible world with less.

This is compatible with the degree of sin and suffering, in such worlds, being bounded both above and below: perhaps there is a degree of suffering and evil a such that every highly eligible world contains at least that much suffering and evil, and a degree a^* such that no highly eligible world contains more than that amount of suffering and evil. Then it could also be that for any given evil, God could have actualized a highly eligible world without permitting that evil; it doesn't follow that he would be unjustified in permitting it. It could also be that God could have actualized a world that is better than alpha, the actual world; it doesn't follow that he ought to have done so, since perhaps for every possible world there is a better he could have actualized.

A second complication: how much sin is required to warrant incarnation and atonement? Suppose the extent of sin were one small misstep on the part of an otherwise admirably disposed angel: would that be sufficient to warrant such drastic and dramatic action on the part of God? Wouldn't such a response on the part of God be somehow inappropriate, something like overkill, perhaps? Probably, although one hardly knows what to say. It might be objected that God, given the unlimited extent of his love, would be willing to undergo the suffering involved in incarnation and atonement, even to save just one sinner. Perhaps so; but that is compatible with its being more appropriate that God's magnificent action here save many, perhaps indefinitely many. Christian doctrine includes, of course, the teaching that human beings are immortal, and can spend eternity with God; the more creatures who attain that state, presumably, the better. Jonathan Edwards and Abraham Kuyper believe, as we saw above, that fallen creatures who are redeemed can be admitted to a greater degree of intimacy with God (can join that charmed circle) than creatures who have not fallen. If so, the highly eligible worlds would no doubt contain a good deal of sin and evil — and, also, consequently, a good deal of suffering. How much sin and evil, then, will a highly eligible world contain? That is hard to say; and again, of course, there may be no answer.

Considering all of these then — our lack of knowledge of the relevant counterfactuals of freedom, the fact that suffering is of instrumental value in a variety of ways — it seems to me that we have no way at all of estimating how much suffering the best worlds will contain, or where the amount of suffering and evil contained in alpha stands in comparison with those worlds. This objection, therefore, is inconclusive.

Munchausen Syndrome by Proxy?

Finally, an objection that has no doubt been clamoring for attention; this objection is powerful, but a little hard to state. The basic idea, however, goes something like this: wouldn't God, in the scenario we're thinking about, be using his creatures, treating them like means, not ends?[28] God has this magnificent end of actualizing a highly eligible possible world (one in which he incidentally plays the stellar role); this requires suffering and evil on the part of his creatures, and apparently requires a good deal of innocent suffering and evil: is that fair, or right? More crucially, would this be consistent with God's loving these creatures,[29] as according to Christian belief he certainly does? If he loved them, would he compel them to suffer in this way so that he can achieve these fine ends? Or perhaps we could put it like this: isn't there something unduly calculating about this procedure? Isn't this a scenario for a sort of cosmic Munchausen syndrome by proxy?[30] Isn't it too much like a father who

28. This way of putting the objection was suggested to me by Michael Schrynamacher.

29. See Marilyn Adams, "Horrendous Evils and the Goodness of God" in *The Problem of Evil*, ed. Marilyn McCord Adams and Robert Merrihew Adams (New York: Oxford University Press, 1990).

30. "[Child abuse] includes not only children who have suffered physical abuse with fractures and bruises ('the battered child') but also those who have experienced

throws his children into the river so that he can then heroically rescue them, or a doctor who first spreads a horrifying disease so that he can then display enormous virtue in fighting it in heroic disregard of his own safety and fatigue? Could we really think God would behave in this way? How could it be in character for God to riffle through the whole range of possible creatures he could create and the circumstances in which he could create them, to find some who would freely sin, and then create them, so that he could display his great love by saving them? How could God be so manipulative?

According to my dictionary, manipulation, in the currently relevant sense, is "management with the use of unfair, scheming, or underhanded methods, especially for one's own advantage"; and calculating behavior is "marked by coldhearted calculation as to what will most promote self-interest." Manipulation thus involves seeking one's own advantage by unfair means; and the problem with calculating behavior is that it is "coldhearted." The idea, then, is that if God acted according to the Felix Culpa line of thought, he would be unfair to his creatures and would be acting in a coldhearted, i.e., unloving way. This coldheartedness part of the present strand of the objection, therefore, reduces to the charge of un-lovingness, the other strand in the objection. This leaves the charge of un-fairness. But why would it be unfair of God to behave in this way toward his creatures? For two reasons, perhaps: (a) this way of behaving on God's part requires suffering on the part of his creatures; and it is unfair of God to act in such a way as to require suffering on the part of his creatures in order to attain or achieve his own ends as opposed to what is good for them; and (b) involving his creatures in this way is unfair be-cause it fails to respect their autonomy. And both of these could be thought of as treating his creatures as means, not ends.

Of course it isn't always wrong for you to treat me as a means rather than an end. You hire me to weed your garden or repair your car or in-struct your children: are you not then treating me as a means rather than an end? You are not thinking first, or perhaps at all, of my needs and in-terests, but of your own; and you get me to do something that serves your ends. Of course I am perhaps also treating you as means under those con-ditions: I take the job so that I can earn some money, enabling me to ac-complish some of my own ends. So exactly why would it be out of char-

---

emotional abuse, sexual abuse, deliberate poisoning, and the infliction of fictitious ill-ness on them by their parents (Munchausen syndrome . . .)" *Encyclopedia Britannica,* 11th ed., s.v. "child abuse."

acter for God to treat his creatures as a means? Perhaps the problem is along the following lines: you offer to hire me to weed your garden, and of course I can refuse; similarly, I don't force you to hire me. But with God, of course, it is quite different. He doesn't ask our permission before creating us, before actualizing this world in which we are called upon to suffer. We don't accept the suffering voluntarily; we don't get a choice; God doesn't consult us before actualizing this world, this world that requires our suffering. Obviously he couldn't have consulted us about whether we wish to be created in a world such as this, but still he doesn't; and isn't that somehow unfair? So with respect to this strand of the objection, the charge is twofold: (a) God requires his creatures to suffer, not for their own good, but in order to advance some aims or ends of his own; and (b) God does this without asking their permission.

The second strand of the objection — the strand according to which if God loved his creatures, he would not act in accord with the Felix Culpa scenario — reduces to the same charge: God's love for his creatures is incompatible with his requiring them to suffer in order to advance divine aims or ends that do not advance the creatures' good or welfare. The claim is that if God loves creatures the way he is said to, he would not treat them in that fashion. Marilyn Adams and Eleonore Stump, both extraordinarily thoughtful writers on evil and suffering, have both proposed what Adams calls "agent centered restrictions" on the way in which a holy, just and loving God would treat us. Asking how Christian philosophers can now best contribute to the solution of the problem of evil, she replies that they "should focus on God's agent centered goodness: the very dimension rendered so baffling in the face of horrific individual sufferings." And Stump says . . . The thought is that Christian philosophers should recognize that God is wholly good, but also perfectly loving, loves each of his creatures with a perfect love. If so, could it be that he would permit a person S to suffer for the good of someone else, (or, more abstractly, permit S to suffer because S's suffering is an element in the best world God can actualize)? If God perfectly loves his creatures, he would not require one of them to suffer in order to advance an end or aim that wasn't directly connected with that agent's own welfare. God wouldn't require me to suffer in order to benefit someone else; he wouldn't even require me to suffer in order to actualize an extremely good world; he wouldn't require me to suffer, unless that suffering was necessary for some good for me myself.

Now as we have seen, some suffering is directly connected with the agent's good. But it doesn't appear that all suffering is. So suppose some suffering is not. How shall we think about this? Here we must make some distinctions. First, of course, God might, in perfect consonance with his love, permit me to suffer in order to benefit someone else or to achieve a highly eligible good world if I freely consent to it and (like Christ) voluntarily accept the suffering. But suppose I don't voluntarily accept it: perhaps I am unable, for one reason or another, to make the decision whether or not to accept the suffering in question. (Perhaps the suffering is childhood suffering.) Well, of course we sometimes quite properly make important decisions for someone (in a coma, say) who can't make the decision for herself; we try to determine what the person in question would decide if she could make the decision herself. So suppose further that God knew that if I were able to make that decision, I would freely accept the suffering: then too, so far as I can see, his being perfectly loving wouldn't at all preclude his permitting me to suffer for the benefit of others, or to enable him to achieve his end of actualizing a highly eligible good world. But suppose still further, that I am able to make the decision and in fact would not accept the suffering; but suppose God knows that this unwillingness on my part would be due only to ignorance: if I knew the relevant facts, then I would accept the suffering. In that case too, God's perfect love, as far as I can see, would not preclude his permitting me to suffer. Finally, suppose further yet that God knows that I would not accept the suffering in question, but only because of disordered affections; if I had the right affections (and also knew enough), then I would accept the suffering: in this case too, as far as I can see, his being perfectly loving would not preclude his allowing me to suffer. In this case God would be like a mother who, say, insists that her eight-year-old child take piano lessons or go to church or school.

There is another distinction that must be made. Perhaps God's reason for permitting me to suffer is not that by undergoing this suffering I can thus achieve a greater good (the good of enjoying his gratitude, for example: see footnote 27) but because he can thus achieve a better world overall. Nevertheless, perhaps it is also true that he would not permit me to suffer for that end, an end outside my own good, unless he could also bring good for me out of the evil. Then his reason for permitting me to suffer would not be that this suffering contributes to my own improvement; nevertheless he would not permit me to suffer unless the suffering could somehow be turned to my own good.[31] A constraint on God's reasons (induced, perhaps, by his being perfectly loving) is one thing; a con-

31. See, e.g., Romans 8:28.

straint on the conditions under which he would permit involuntary and innocent suffering is another. To return to an earlier example (above, p. 7), perhaps God sees that the best worlds he can actualize are ones that include the unthinkably great good of divine incarnation and atonement. Suppose he therefore actualizes a highly eligible world that includes incarnation and atonement, and in which human beings fall into sin, evil, and consequent suffering. Suppose also that the final condition of human beings, in this world, is better than it is in the worlds in which there is no fall into sin but also no incarnation and redemption; they receive God's thanks, enjoy a greater intimacy with him, are invited to join that charmed circle. Then God's actualizing the world in question involves suffering for many human beings; his reason for permitting that suffering is not that thereby the suffering individuals will be benefited (his reason is that he wishes to actualize a highly eligible world, one with the great goods of incarnation, atonement, and redemption). Nevertheless his perfect love perhaps mandates that he actualize a world in which those who suffer are benefited in such a way that their condition is better than it is in those worlds in which they do not suffer.

By way of conclusion: the Felix Culpa approach does not dispel all the perplexity surrounding human suffering and evil; I suppose nothing can do that. But perhaps it reduces the perplexity, and perhaps it provides the means for a deeper grasp of the salvific meaning of suffering and evil.

Probability and Draper's Evidential Argument from Evil

Richard Otte

Introduction

The problem of evil has taken many forms, but much of the recent discussion has focused on what is known as the probabilistic or evidential argument from evil. According to these arguments the evil in our world lowers the probability of God existing or is evidence against the existence of God, even though evil is logically consistent with God's existing. Based on this it may be claimed it is irrational to believe one of the traditional theistic religions, unless there is overwhelming positive evidence to counter this negative evidence, or one may simply say that this presents an epistemic problem for believers. One of the most important versions of this argument comes from Paul Draper. Although quite sophisticated, this argument is unsuccessful; it makes fundamental errors that are fatal to the argument. But the failures are instructive and relevant to any probabilistic argument from evil. I will begin by discussing Draper's claims and will then briefly look at a reply that could be made to my argument. Looking at this objection will allow us to discuss the epistemic framework he assumes in more detail. After discussing Draper's argument, I will then briefly discuss the prospects for developing a successful probabilistic argument from evil.

Draper's Argument[1]

Draper's argument is intended to show that the pain and pleasure that we are aware of in the world gives us a prima facie reason to reject theism. By theism, Draper means there "exists an omnipotent, omniscient, and morally perfect person who created the universe."[2] Whereas ordinary probabilistic arguments from evil look only at how likely it is that God exists given the evil in the world, Draper approaches the problem differently. Draper claims that previous discussions of the evidential argument from evil are deficient because they fail to take into account alternative explanations of the pain and pleasure in the world. The strategy of looking at alternative explanations is familiar to philosophers of science who look at how evidence confirms or disconfirms a theory, and as Draper notes, it was employed by Hume in his attack on religious belief. Draper's unusual strategy is to compare theism with an alternative, the hypothesis of indifference, and to see which best explains the evil in the world. According to the hypothesis of indifference, "neither the nature nor the condition of sentient beings on earth is the result of benevolent or malevolent actions performed by nonhuman persons."[3] It is clear that theism and the hypothesis of indifference are inconsistent with each other. Draper compares theism (T) and the hypothesis of indifference (HI) by looking at how well they explain the observed human and animal pain and pleasure in our world (O), which he interprets as how likely O is on T and on HI. He argues that O is a problem for theism by arguing for principle C:

> C: Independent of the observations and testimony O reports, O is much more probable on the assumption that HI is true than on the assumption that theism is true.[4]

Draper then introduces some nonstandard probability notation: $P(x/y)$ will be the probability of x, "independent of the observations and testi-

1. Most of this section is taken from my "Evidential Arguments from Evil," *International Journal for Philosophy of Religion* 48, no. 1 (2000): 1-10. Reprinted with kind permission of Kluwer Academic Publishers.

2. Paul Draper, "Pain and Pleasure: An Evidential Problem for Theists," *Noûs* 23 (1989): 333. The essay is reprinted in *The Evidential Argument from Evil*, ed. Daniel Howard-Snyder (Bloomington, Ind.: Indiana University Press, 1996), pp. 12-29.

3. Draper, "Pain and Pleasure," p. 332.

4. Draper, "Pain and Pleasure," p. 333.

mony O reports," given y.[5] Given this notation, Draper rewrites C as follows:

C: $P(O/HI)$ is much greater than $P(O/T)$.

Draper claims that C is a prima facie reason to reject theism. He then gives several arguments for the truth of C.

Although I reject the epistemological framework Draper assumes in this argument, I will begin by granting that framework for the purposes of discussion and will focus on his argument within that framework. The main problem with Draper's argument is that even if principle C were true, it would have no consequences for the rationality of most theists' religious beliefs. Most theists are not mere theists, but instead are Christians, Muslims, or Jews. So unless principle C gives one a reason to not be a Christian, a Muslim, or a Jew, it will not be a successful argument. Since it is clear that Draper does not intend his argument to be restricted to mere theists, we must investigate whether his argument applies to Christians, Muslims, and Jews, as well as to mere theists. I will concentrate on the applicability of his argument to Christianity, but similar responses could be given for Islam and Judaism.

To support Draper's position one might appeal to what looks like an obvious argument. Christians, Muslims, and Jews are all theists, simply because they believe that an omnipotent, omniscient, and morally perfect being created the universe; Christianity, Islam, and Judaism logically imply theism. Thus one might argue that if we have a reason to not be a theist, we also have a reason to not be a Christian, Muslim, or Jew. However this argument is not persuasive. It might be persuasive if the reason to not be a theist was because theism was logically inconsistent. If so, then Christianity, Islam, and Judaism would be committed to the same logical inconsistency, which would provide an argument that they are irrational. But the problem Draper finds in theism is not that it is logically inconsistent. Rather, he finds theism problematic because there is a better alternative, the hypothesis of indifference. Draper's reason to reject theism is not because of anything internal to theism, but is because of something external to theism: there is a better alternative that is inconsistent with theism. To conclude from this that we have a reason to reject Christianity, Draper would need to rely on some general principle such as the following:

5. Draper, "Pain and Pleasure," p. 333.

If hypothesis H implies hypothesis K, and we have a reason to reject K because there is a better alternative hypothesis AH that is inconsistent with K, then we have a reason to reject H because of this alternative hypothesis that is inconsistent with H.

If we let H be Christianity, K be theism, and AH be the hypothesis of indifference, then this principle would claim that we have a reason to reject Christianity because the hypothesis of indifference is a better alternative to theism. We can explicitly state this as follows:

If Christianity implies mere theism and we have a reason to reject mere theism because the hypothesis of indifference explains some phenomenon better than mere theism and is inconsistent with mere theism, then we also have a reason to reject Christianity because of the hypothesis of indifference (which is inconsistent with Christianity).

When stated like this the problems with this principle are evident. Just because the hypothesis of indifference is a better alternative to mere theism does not mean that the hypothesis of indifference is a better alternative to Christianity, Islam, or Judaism. On the contrary, we can easily argue that Christianity, Islam, or Judaism is a better alternative to the hypothesis of indifference. It is possible that the hypothesis of indifference can explain evil much better than mere theism, but Christianity (for example) can explain evil better than the hypothesis of indifference.

Draper used principle C to compare theism and the hypothesis of indifference by looking at the probability of the observed evil in our world conditional on each of them. We can follow his reasoning and compare the hypothesis of indifference and Christianity (CH) by looking at the probability of evil conditional on HI and on Christianity. I propose principle C* to be true:

C*: Independent of the observations and testimony O reports, O is much more probable on the assumption that Christianity is true than on the assumption that HI is true.

Using Draper's notation, we can rewrite this as follows:

C*: $P(O/CH)$ is much greater than $P(O/HI)$.

Since we are working within Draper's framework, we could reason similarly to Draper and conclude that the truth of C* gives us a prima facie reason to reject the hypothesis of indifference. Thus Christians, and perhaps even naturalists, have a reason to reject HI.

Draper has given several arguments for the truth of principle C, but since principles C and C* are logically consistent with each other, we do not need to refute his arguments and argue that C is false in order to argue that C* is true. Fortunately, our argument for the truth of C* can be quite brief. I'm not sure what Draper intends O to include, but it is important to realize that Christianity, Islam, and Judaism logically imply that there is evil in this world, and even imply much about the specific evils that occur. Of course mere theism itself does not imply this, which is one reason principle C may appear plausible, but Christianity, Islam, and Judaism make many claims about evil, pain, and pleasure in the world. Some of these are general claims about the types of evil we find in the world, and others are claims about specific evils. If Draper's O is simply a broad description of the types of pain and pleasure we observe, then Christianity logically implies O. In that case, $P(O/CH) = 1$, which is much greater than $P(O/HI)$. Under this interpretation of O, CH is obviously preferable to HI. If instead we take O to include the specific instances of pain and pleasure that we've actually observed, then of course Christianity does not imply O. But since Christianity implies the type of pain and suffering that occur in the world, O will still be much more probable on Christianity than on the hypothesis of indifference. Under this interpretation of O, CH is also preferable to HI. Under both of these construals of O we find that O is more probable on CH than on HI, and following Draper's reasoning we conclude that CH is preferable to HI. The Christian has no reason to prefer HI to CH.

We now have two principles, C and C*. For the purposes of argument we will grant that both are true. We can do this because it is logically consistent that CH logically implies T, $P(O/T)$ is low, and that $P(O/CH) = 1$. We can summarize these two principles by: $P(O/CH) > P(O/HI) > P(O/T)$. We also have two arguments: one uses principle C to argue against theism, and the other uses principle C* to argue against the hypothesis of indifference. The question that arises is which one is to be accepted by a theist. If the person is only a theist and is not a Christian, Muslim, or Jew, then principle C would be applicable to his or her beliefs. Draper's argument would then be relevant and worthy of consideration. But consider a theist who is not a mere theist, but instead is a Christian, Muslim, or Jew. Such a person will know that when the hypothesis of indifference is compared with a small part of his or her religious beliefs (simple theism), that the hypothesis of indifference is the better alternative. But when the hypothesis of indifference is compared with his or her complete religious beliefs, the complete religious beliefs are the better alternative. It is clear in this case that the agent has no reason to give up the religious beliefs. Simply because there is a better alternative to part of what one believes does not give one a reason to give up one's beliefs; one's total beliefs may be better than the alternative.

If it were legitimate to argue against a Christian, Muslim, or Jew by taking a subset of that person's beliefs (theism) and showing that the evil in our world is less likely on that subset than on some other hypothesis, a mere theist should be able to reason similarly against someone who accepts the hypothesis of indifference. Someone who believes the hypothesis of indifference believes many other things, and undoubtedly there is a subset of those beliefs that is such that the probability of the evil in our world conditional on it is not as high as it is conditional on mere theism. The pattern of reasoning Draper uses can be used to support any position; it is completely unconvincing.

So we see that Draper's argument fails because it looks only at a narrow subset of a religious person's beliefs. By focusing on mere theism instead of Christianity, Islam, or Judaism, Draper's argument loses all relevance. Even if Draper is correct and principle C is true, this has no implications for the rationality of being a Christian, Muslim, or Jew. They can easily admit that O is unlikely on T, that their religious beliefs logically imply T, and yet they can also consistently hold that O is very likely, even certain, on their religious beliefs. Furthermore, Christians, Muslims, and Jews can appeal to principle C* to support their religious beliefs and to claim that we have a prima facie reason to reject the hypothesis of indifference.

It is well known that when Pascal died they found in the lining of his coat a piece of paper on which was written: "The God of Abraham, Isaac, and Jacob, not the God of the philosophers." The rationality of believing in the god of the philosophers may have very little to do with the rationality of believing in the God of Abraham, Isaac, and Jacob. Since we are interested in the rationality of believing in Christianity, we should look directly at that and not at the rationality of mere theism.

Draper's Response

Let us now look at a response that could be made to my reasoning. This response is worth considering in detail, because it points to further and deeper problems with Draper's argument. I will begin with Draper's account of alternative hypotheses, and then briefly look at the probabilities he makes use of in his argument.

In response to my argument Draper has objected that he is not claiming that there is a problem for some hypothesis H1 simply because some truth is antecedently less probable on H1 than on some alternative H2.[6] He says this is of little significance, because there will always be alternatives to H1 on which that truth is certain. What gives the fact importance or significance is that Draper wants to add the requirement that the alternative hypothesis be what he calls a serious alternative. Although I do not find this requirement in his main paper, "Pain and Pleasure: An Evidential Problem for Theists," in a later article Draper explains this concept as follows: "Specifically, one hypothesis is a 'serious' alternative to another only if (i) it is not ad hoc — the facts to be explained are not arbitrarily built into it — and (ii) it is at least as plausible initially as the other hypothesis."[7] Let us grant Draper the requirement that the alternative hypothesis be a serious alternative. Draper then claims that CH is not a serious alternative to HI, because it fails both of the tests: "it is both ad hoc with respect to O and intrinsically much less probable than HI."[8] It appears Draper is claiming that HI creates a problem for T because HI is a serious alternative to T, but CH does not create a problem for HI because CH is not a serious alternative to HI. Thus one cannot follow Draper's style of reasoning and use C* to support the claim that CH presents a problem for HI. On this objection Draper is not claiming principle C* is false (although he may believe that), but rather that it is irrelevant to what it is rational to believe. He could admit C* is true, but claim that since CH is not a serious alternative to HI, principle C* does not give him a reason to reject HI. Of course, this objection does not affect the main point of my argument (that principle C is irrelevant to Christian belief), because even if HI is a serious alternative to CH, it is not the case that O is more likely on HI than on CH. Thus this objection does not give a reason to reject my main claim that Draper's reasoning fails to show that HI presents a problem for CH. However this objection does raise very interesting philosophical problems.

The problem that immediately arises is that Christians and natural-

6. Paul Draper, personal correspondence with the author, 27 June 1999.
7. Paul Draper, "Probabilistic Arguments from Evil," *Religious Studies* 28 (1993): 316.
8. Draper, "Probabilistic Arguments," p. 316.

ists will most likely disagree on what the serious alternatives are. For example, Draper thinks CH is not a serious alternative to HI. As a result, principle C* does not give Draper a reason to reject HI. And since he considers HI to be a serious alternative to CH (it is at least as probable as CH) he thinks principle C gives him a reason to reject CH. However, I disagree with Draper and think CH is a serious alternative to HI. Because of this, principle C* gives me a reason to reject HI. Since people disagree on the initial probabilities of CH, T, and HI, they will disagree on what the serious alternatives to CH and HI are; as a result they will disagree on the relevance of principles C and C* to what it is rational to believe. Since so much turns on this requirement of being a serious alternative, we need to investigate this in more detail.

One reason Draper thinks CH is not a serious alternative to HI is that CH is "intrinsically much less probable than HI" (1999). One problem with this is that it is not at all clear what it means for something to be intrinsically less probable or initially less plausible than something else. Ignoring the possibility that there may not even be such a thing as intrinsic or initial epistemic probabilities, I see no reason for Christians to think CH is intrinsically less probable than HI, or that HI is even close to being as intrinsically probable as CH. It is difficult to think of any plausible reason that might be given for this. Neither Draper nor anyone else that I know of has given a convincing reason to think that CH is intrinsically less probable than HI in any interesting or relevant sense of probability.

In presenting an argument against CH and in favor of HI, one cannot begin by making the very controversial assumption that HI is much more intrinsically probable than CH. If Draper wants to convince Christians by his argument, and does not want it to be accepted by only those who already agree with his conclusion, he cannot use assumptions that Christians reject.

It appears Draper believes Christians should think that HI is initially more probable than CH, but due to natural theology, religious experience, or some other argument, Christians come to believe that CH is more probable than HI when all the evidence is considered. This is connected with Draper's view that a Christian should begin with mere theism (T), compare that with the alternatives, and then later bring in specific Christian doctrines. In his article Draper considers the effect of theodicies on $P(O/T)$, and this is where he thinks specific religious doctrines should enter the discussion. But why should a Christian think this is the way to proceed? In effect, Draper is claiming that a Christian should compare only part of his or her beliefs with something that

Draper claims is a serious alternative to it, and then later bring in his or her other beliefs to see if they can salvage religious belief. Draper has given us no reason to think this is the proper way to proceed, and many Christians will likely reject this whole way of approaching their beliefs.

Let us now turn to Draper's other reason for thinking CH is not a serious alternative to HI, which is that CH is ad hoc with respect to O. In claiming that CH is ad hoc with respect to O Draper presumably means that the facts to be explained, O, are arbitrarily built into CH. It is not easy to see what is wrong with ad hoc hypotheses, if this is what they are, because most successful scientific theories build in the facts to be explained. In science we often know what the observations are (what the theory must predict in order to be empirically adequate) and so we built these into the theory to get the right predictions. As Kuhn, Putnam, van Fraassen, and others have noted, this is considered perfectly acceptable in science. For example, we may have a theory in which a constant plays a certain role, but the theory does not tell us the value of the constant. Through experimentation we may discover that the value of this constant must be r in order to get the right predictions. In this situation scientists often simply build into the theory that the value of the constant is r. One might claim this is ad hoc, because the constant r is included in the theory for the sole reason of getting the right predictions, which were already known. We knew the constant had to have the value r in order for the theory to be empirically adequate, and actual scientific practice considers it perfectly acceptable to construct theories in this way.

Perhaps what is important about ad hoc hypotheses is that they involve arbitrariness in some way, and for the sake of argument let us grant that we don't want the facts to be explained to be arbitrarily built into a hypothesis. But O is not arbitrarily built into CH. CH is a historical religion and makes many historical claims, many of which involve pain and pleasure. It also includes many stories that describe aspects of our lives that are connected with pain and pleasure. Assuming that the facts to be explained (O) are contained in or implied by the historical stories of CH (I agree with that part of this objection), it is difficult to argue that they are arbitrarily built into CH. For example, consider the story of the Israelites suffering in Egypt. This story describes pain and suffering, and so it would be included in O. But there is no reason to think this story was arbitrarily put into CH in order to explain O. The stories related to O that are part of CH are not included arbitrarily in any interesting sense of arbitrariness.

The idea of some known predictions being arbitrarily added to a hypothesis fits well with the picture of a hypothesis being invented or constructed in order to explain certain phenomenon. In such situations one might object to simply putting the observations to be explained into the model we're constructing. This is connected with the view that religious beliefs are hypotheses constructed in order to explain or bring order to our experience. According to this view it might be natural to start with a minimal religious hypothesis T, and then see if we can modify it to explain O. But very few Christians would consider their religion to be a theory that was constructed in order to account for our experience, which includes O. In fact, some of them might feel that several of their religious doctrines present difficulties, and they would have done things very differently if they were simply constructing a religion to explain various things. So we see the ad hoc charge is not very convincing. There is no reason to think a Christian will consider CH to be ad hoc with respect to O.

We have seen that Draper has given no reason for a Christian to believe that CH is not a serious alternative to HI, or even think that HI is a serious alternative to CH. Perhaps Draper himself believes that CH is not a serious alternative to HI, and thus principle C* does not give him a reason to reject HI. But since most theists will reject these claims, they will not find Draper's argument convincing.

Draper's Antecedent Probabilities

We saw that Draper claims that O is antecedently much more probable given the hypothesis of indifference than it is given theism. We now need to look at Draper's antecedent probabilities, and see whether they are appropriate for his argument. This is very important, because evidence is only evidence relative to a set of beliefs (and maybe a set of experiences). Thus in order to determine any antecedent probabilities and whether O is evidence against T and CH, we need to be very clear about what background information is conditionalized on.

Let us first think about what the goal of the argument is. I take it to be that *individual* theists or Christians have an epistemic problem because of evil. We are not interested in social rationality (if there is any such thing), but in whether individual believers are rational. We need to look at Draper's proposals and decide whether they help us attain this goal. If we follow his suggestion about what to conditionalize on, will the resultant probabilities be relevant to whether an individual believer is rational?

Draper's argument makes use of P(O/HI) and P(O/T). Recall Draper's account of what background information we should conditionalize on:

> For the sake of brevity, I will use P(x/y) to represent the probability of the statement x, *independent of the observations and testimony O reports*, on the assumption that the statement y is true.[9]

I believe Draper's intuition behind this proposal is that we need to eliminate any reports or observations of O from what is conditionalized on; otherwise theism, CH, and HI would be irrelevant to the probability of O. On the other hand, we are interested in what it is rational for an individual to believe, and this is dependent upon all of the experiences and beliefs the individual has; thus we will want to conditionalize on as many of the individual's beliefs as possible. One proposal, which may be what Draper intended in the above account, is to take the individual's complete set of beliefs, and simply subtract the observations and testimony for O. This has the advantage of eliminating only what is obviously necessary to eliminate, while keeping as much as possible of the evidence we'd like to retain.

Although the above proposal has some advantages, it turns out to be very problematic and numerous difficulties arise. In addition to O, beliefs in T, CH, and HI will also have to be eliminated. Otherwise the probabilities we're interested in might not even be defined.[10] As Plantinga noted in a different context, we also need to eliminate any beliefs that logically imply O, because this would also result in T and HI being irrelevant to the likelihood of O.[11] Another problem arises because we might have some beliefs that when combined with T or HI, imply O.[12] Certainly Draper would not want us to conditionalize on beliefs like this; thus we need to subtract any of our beliefs, that in conjunction with T or HI, imply O, or not O. But, of course, it doesn't matter if these beliefs actually imply O; it is enough if they affect the probability of O. As a result we also have to exclude beliefs X that in conjunction with T or HI affect the probability

9. Draper, "Pain and Pleasure," p. 333.

10. For example, if a theist were certain of theism and assigned P(HI) = 0, then P(O/HI) would be undefined.

11. Alvin Plantinga, "On Being Evidentially Challenged," in *The Evidential Argument from Evil*, ed. Daniel Howard-Snyder (Bloomington, Ind.: Indiana University Press, 1996), pp. 244-61.

12. For example, beliefs such as 'T materially implies O' and 'not-HI or O'.

of O: *if (T and X) then O is very likely,* or *it is not likely that both (HI and X) and O, etc.*[13] Since we need to exclude any beliefs, that in conjunction with HI or T, are relevant to the probability of O, nothing will be left to conditionalize on that affects the probability of O.

The result is that we are left with simply looking at the a priori probability of O on HI and on T. Since we've excluded any information that in conjunction with HI or T is relevant to the probability of O, all we are left with is irrelevant information; but this is equivalent to looking at the a priori probability of O on T, and O on HI. Returning to the question of what it is rational for an individual to believe, it is difficult to see why the a priori probability of O on T, or HI, is relevant to what it is rational for a specific individual to believe. The individual has learned many things that may be relevant to T, O, and HI, and this evidence should not be ignored.

Another problem arises because if we don't exclude enough, neither HI nor T will be able to affect the probability of O. To see this, consider any specific situation where someone is in significant physical pain. For example, suppose I were to observe Paul putting his hand in a very hot flame. I observe him yanking his hand out of the flame, his rolling around on the floor while screaming, his being rushed to a hospital in an ambulance, his being treated in the emergency room, his being kept for a few days in a hospital room, his receiving lots of 'get well' cards and visits from friends, his rehabilitation, and so on. According to Draper's proposal, in this situation we do not conditionalize on any claim of Paul's to be in pain. Perhaps we wouldn't even conditionalize on the observations of his pain behavior. But we would conditionalize on all of the other things that are closely connected with the pain behavior. These observations may not imply Paul was in pain, but they make it very likely. The more details of the situation we fill in, the more likely it becomes that Paul is feeling pain instead of pleasure. It is difficult to be aware of all of the details, except Paul's being in pain and perhaps his pain behavior, and to claim that he is not in pain. And if we start with a complete description of our experience, and only subtract the observation or testimony that Paul is in pain and leave everything else in, then it becomes overwhelmingly likely that Paul is in pain, regardless of whether theism is true or the hypothesis of indifference is true. This has the result that the probability of O will not change when we add T or HI to what is

---

13. We also need to exclude beliefs such as: the objective probability of O given T is high.

conditionalized on. Given enough details, O becomes very likely and neither T nor HI will change that. Thus conditionalizing on this background information will not allow Draper to distinguish between HI and T. The lesson to be learned from these problems is that there is no hope for this epistemic framework; the whole approach is bankrupt. The epistemic framework that Draper's argument assumes is very problematic.

What Is the Benefit of Using Probability in These Arguments?

We have seen that a major probabilistic argument from evil is deficient. We now need to think more generally about formulating arguments from evil in some sort of probabilistic framework. I want to briefly discuss whether using probability in the discussion of evil is likely to be fruitful, and what are the prospects for developing a successful probabilistic argument from evil.

Probability can be a very useful tool in philosophy and in managing our beliefs. It helps us avoid incoherence and helps us pursue having consistent beliefs. Like deductive logic, probability places various formal restrictions on what we can consistently believe.

The deductive argument from evil was powerful and appeared convincing to so many because it started with assumptions that theists accept, and proceeded to show an apparent logical inconsistency within them. This was a problem for theists no matter what their epistemic framework. The argument did not obviously depend on any controversial views about the use of deductive logic or on any other suspicious assumptions. The argument received its strength because it did *not* assume anything that theists rejected. Thus theists found themselves in the position of apparently being committed to a logical inconsistency, which was very problematic.

But the probabilistic argument from evil is not at all like this. First of all, it does not start with the theist's or Christian's beliefs and show an internal inconsistency or incoherence in them. Second, it does not rely on noncontroversial probabilistic reasoning to derive the conclusions. Let us look at each of these in more detail, beginning with the first. Probabilistic arguments from evil do not rely on assumptions that all theists accept, and instead they tend to rely on assumptions the Christian will specifically reject. For example, we saw that Draper assumed that the Christian would hold that Christianity is not a serious alternative to the hypothesis of indifference, because he assumed the Christian would believe the hypothesis of indifference was at least as intrinsically probable as mere theism and that it is much more probable than Christianity. But few Christians believe that Christianity is not a serious alternative to the hypothesis of indifference. So Draper's argument at most shows something like the following: if Christians thought that Christianity was not a serious alternative to the hypothesis of indifference, then the hypothesis of indifference would give them a reason to reject their religious beliefs. Unlike the deductive argument from evil, Draper's argument depends on assumptions that Christians reject; as a result, Christians will not find that this probabilistic argument provides any reason to modify their beliefs.

One way writers tend to ignore and hide these assumptions is by appealing to epistemic probabilities. But these appeals do not answer any philosophical problems, and instead they push the problem back to the question of deciding what the epistemic probabilities are — what a rational person would believe in the circumstances. The appeal to epistemic probabilities does not reduce the number of philosophical problems or amount of work that needs be done, but often it will hide or disguise an assumption being made. And even bringing in the concept of epistemic probability raises a problem; is there any reason to think these epistemic a priori probabilities even exist or have any relevance to what it is rational for us to believe?

Let us now turn to the second way in which probabilistic arguments from evil differ from the deductive argument from evil; they rely on very controversial reasoning and do not appeal only to patterns of reasoning that Christians will accept. The deductive argument from evil appealed only to standard deductive logic, and argued that the theist was committed to a logical inconsistency, which it was assumed was to be avoided. However, Draper's argument depends on probabilistic reasoning that is suspicious at best, and Christians have no reason to accept this form of reasoning. We saw this reasoning required the Christian to compare a small subset of his or her beliefs with alternative hypotheses, instead of comparing the alternative hypothesis with his or her actual religious beliefs. And even the requirement of having to compare religious beliefs with alternative hypotheses is not obviously correct; certainly it is rejected by many philosophers. Furthermore, Draper assumes we can concentrate on evil, and draw implications about prima facie reasons to reject belief in God; but there is good reason to think a more holistic approach is needed, since evidence (and what is a prima facie reason) is highly dependent upon the other beliefs and experiences a person may have. At best the pattern of reasoning in this probabilistic argument from evil is quite controversial.

We thus see that probabilistic arguments from evil are very different from the deductive argument from evil; they lack the traits that made the deductive argument from evil so powerful. Given this, there is no reason to think a successful or convincing probabilistic argument from evil will be developed.

Conclusion

I've argued that a major probabilistic argument from evil fails. Furthermore, the reason it failed was because of deep structural problems in the argument; it did not fail because of any minor or superficial problem. As a result, no minor modifications of the argument will solve the problems I've raised. Even if we accept the general epistemic framework that Draper is working within, the arguments are problematic at the very core.

Philosophical arguments appealing to probability are most effective when they simply look at consistency among beliefs and rely on few epistemic assumptions about probability and rational belief. But I'm not aware of any probabilistic argument from evil that proceeds in this way. Unless defenders of the probabilistic argument from evil give a reason to accept their epistemic frameworks, their arguments will be dependent upon very suspicious assumptions. Since I believe there are good reasons to reject these epistemic frameworks, I think it is unlikely any probabilistic argument from evil will be successful.

More Pain and Pleasure:
A Reply to Otte

Paul Draper

Introduction

Theists hold that the natural world depends for its existence on a perfect, supernatural, personal entity ("God"). David Hume seems to favor a quite different position, a position I call the "hypothesis of indifference." According to this hypothesis, neither the nature nor the condition of sentient beings on earth results from benevolent or malevolent actions performed by supernatural persons.[1] This hypothesis is very broad. It is compatible both with metaphysical naturalism, which denies the existence of all supernatural entities, and also with a variety of supernaturalist hypotheses, including deism, which affirms a personal supernatural creator, but denies that this creator has any benevolent or malevolent interest in the quality of earthly life. Hume prefers the hypothesis of indifference to theism and to all other alternatives as well, because he believes

1. I assume that the character Philo comes very close to speaking for Hume, at least in Part XI of Hume's *Dialogues Concerning Natural Religion*. Philo argues for the hypothesis that the first causes of the universe have neither goodness nor malice. I have broadened Philo's hypothesis so that it is true even if there are no causes of the universe (and even if the causes of the universe do have goodness or malice, so long as their actions affecting sentient beings on earth are neither benevolent nor malevolent). I doubt Hume would have objected to making the hypothesis of indifference more flexible in this way. The assumption that the universe is caused does not seem to be essential to Hume's own views, though Philo is committed to it by what he says in Part II of the *Dialogues*. See *Dialogues Concerning Natural Religion,* ed. Norman Kemp Smith (New York: Macmillan Publishing Co., 1947), p. 142.

that it is the only hypothesis that can account for what he calls the "strange mixture" of pain and pleasure in the world. Unfortunately, Hume's argument for this is sketchy at best.

A much more developed argument for a similar position can be found in my 1989 article "Pain and Pleasure: An Evidential Problem for Theists."[2] My argument differs, however, from Hume's in several important ways. First, I make no attempt to argue for the truth or probable truth or even prima facie probable truth of the hypothesis of indifference. Instead, I try to show that we have a good prima facie reason to believe that the hypothesis of indifference is more probable than theism. While this implies that we have a good prima facie reason to believe that theism is probably false (since theism and the hypothesis of indifference are incompatible and so could not both be probable), it does not imply that we have a good prima facie reason to believe that the hypothesis of indifference is true (since theism and the hypothesis of indifference are not jointly exhaustive and so could both be improbable). So my argument is more accurately described as an argument against theism than as an argument for the hypothesis of indifference. Second, my argument appeals not just to the bare fact that the world contains both pain and pleasure, but rather to a statement which I call "O" that reports what one knows about the kinds, amounts, and distribution of pain and pleasure in the world. This knowledge is ultimately grounded upon a variety of experiences, including experiences directly of one's own pain and pleasure, as well as sensory experiences both of other beings experiencing pain and pleasure (when this is known by their behavior) and of testimony concerning pain and pleasure.[3] Third, the premises of my argument make an explicit appeal to probability. While Hume speaks vaguely of the ability or inability of different hypotheses to "account for" the mixture of pain and pleasure in the world, it is my position that the best way to show that the facts O reports provide evidence favoring the hypothesis of indifference over theism, and the only way to accurately assess the strength of that evidence, is to compare the antecedent probability that O is true on the assumption that the hypothesis of indifference is true to the anteced-

---

2. *Noûs* 23 (1989): 331-50.

3. In "Pain and Pleasure," I let "O" stand for a statement directly reporting these experiences rather than for a statement reporting knowledge about pain and pleasure that is grounded on these experiences. There are advantages and disadvantages to both formulations. Cf. Peter van Inwagen, "The Problem of Evil, the Problem of Air, and the Problem of Silence," in *The Evidential Argument from Evil*, ed. Daniel Howard-Snyder (Bloomington, Ind.: Indiana University Press, 1996), note 2, p. 171.

ent probability that O is true on the assumption that theism is true. By the "antecedent" probability of O, I mean its probability *independent of the experiences that ultimately ground one's knowledge of O.*[4]

The central claim of "Pain and Pleasure" is that O is antecedently much more probable given the hypothesis of indifference than it is given theism. I chose to call this claim "C" because it is the conclusion of the main argument in that article. Using "HI" to mean "the hypothesis of indifference," "T" to mean "theism," "Pr" to mean "the antecedent probability of," "/" to mean "given" and ">!" to mean "is much greater than," C can be expressed symbolically as follows:

C: $\Pr(O/HI) >! \Pr(O/T)$.

Although my primary goal in writing "Pain and Pleasure" was to provide an extended argument for the truth of C, that article also contains a second argument, a much less developed argument for the conclusion that the truth of C provides a prima facie good reason to reject theism.

Richard Otte doesn't like this second argument at all. He makes this quite clear in his article "Probability and Draper's Evidential Argument from Evil."[5] Actually, he's not thrilled about the first argument either. He never directly challenges that argument. In fact, he completely ignores both its structure and its premises. If, however, my "epistemic framework" (and in particular my use of "antecedent probabilities" in C) is as problematic as he believes it is, then it would seem that no argument for the truth of C could possibly be convincing. It is my second argument, however, that receives the lion's share of Otte's scorn. He asserts that this argument contains, not just errors, but "fundamental" errors, errors that are "fatal to the argument." What, exactly, are these mortal mistakes? The deadliest one, or at least the one he emphasizes most, is that C compares HI to theism rather than to Muslim theism or to Jewish theism or to his personal favorite, Christian theism. But is this really a mistake? I will show in the next section that it is not. Then, in the last section, I will respond to the Otte's concerns about my notion of "antecedent probabilities."

4. Of course, O is, because of its great specificity, antecedently very improbable on either the hypothesis of indifference or theism. But that's compatible with the claim that O is antecedently much more probable on the hypothesis of indifference than it is on theism. In other words, although $\Pr(O/HI)$ and $\Pr(O/T)$ are each very low in the sense that the *difference* between either of them and O is small, the *ratio* of the first to the second could still be very large.

5. In this book. Citations will be made parenthetically in the text.

Sectarian Theism and the Significance of C

Otte distinguishes between the issue of whether C's truth would present an epistemic problem for mere theists (i.e. theists who do not accept any specific revealed religion) and the issue of whether it would present a problem for Jews, Christians, and Muslims. Concerns about epistemic framework aside, he seems to allow that C could be a problem for mere theists. But this, he believes, is of very limited significance since so few theists are mere theists. I suspect Otte seriously underestimates how many "mere theists" there are. Many people who believe in a personal God do not believe that other more specific sectarian religious claims (e.g. that Jesus rose from the dead and that Noah and his family were the only survivors of a great flood) are literally true. Many of these mere theists nevertheless identify themselves as Muslims or Christians or Jews because they attach great *symbolic* importance to other highly sectarian doctrines, or because they believe that the stories in scripture teach important moral lessons, or because they engage in various distinctively Muslim or Christian or Jewish religious practices. But they are mere theists rather than Muslims, Jews, or Christians by Otte's definition. I won't, however, pursue this point because Otte is wrong about his main point. The truth of C is a threat to all theists, including those who firmly believe all of the many theological and historical claims that Otte implicitly builds into his definition of Christianity.

It is important to recognize that, in claiming that C provides both sectarian and non-sectarian theists with a prima facie good reason to reject theism, I am not thereby committed to the wildly implausible view that, for any statements H1, H2, and E, if E is antecedently much more probable given H1 than it is given H2, then the truth of E provides a prima facie good reason to reject H2. Clearly HI, T, and O have features that not all triads of statements have that contribute to the epistemic significance of C. The fact that O is known to be true is an obvious place to start. A more subtle but equally crucial feature that distinguishes my triad from others is that HI is a *serious* alternative to T. (Otte says he cannot find this requirement in "Pain and Pleasure" [p. 32], but it is stated explicitly at the end of the first section of that paper.) When I say that HI is a serious alternative, I mean that theism is not intrinsically *much* more probable than HI. (I no longer require that an hypothesis not be ad hoc in order to qualify as "serious" and the requirement that HI be at least as probable intrinsically as theism is unnecessarily stringent given that O is antecedently *much* more probable on HI than on theism.)

Returning, then, to the question of how C provides a prima facie good reason to reject theism, the answer is that it serves as the central premise in the following argument, the conclusion of which is clearly a prima facie good reason to reject theism.

A. O is known to be true.
B. T is not much more probable intrinsically than HI.
C. Pr(O/HI) >! Pr(O/T).
So, D. Other evidence held equal, T is probably false.[6]

It is crucial to recognize that the probabilities in this argument are epistemic ones.[7] The epistemic probability of a proposition P for some person S at some time t depends on two things. First, it depends on the evidence (both propositional and non-propositional) for and against P that S has at t (i.e. it depends on various factors in S's epistemic situation that can raise or lower some initial probability of P's being true). Second, it depends on P's intrinsic probability, the probability P has solely by virtue of its content (i.e. P's probability independent of all evidence for and against it). Given this concept of probability, there are three distinct reasons why C does not by itself prove that theism is probably false. First, C can't help to show that theism is improbable if O is not known to be true.

---

6. If the goal is to show that we have a prima facie good reason to believe, not just that theism is probably false, but that it is *very* probably false, then the argument can be formulated as follows:

A. O is known to be true.
B. HI is at least as probable intrinsically as T.
C. Pr(O/HI) >! Pr(O/T).
So, D. Other evidence held equal, T is very probably false.

7. As a first approximation, we may identify the epistemic probability of a proposition relative to some epistemic situation as the degree of confidence a fully rational person in that situation would have in the truth of that proposition. Because epistemic situations vary from one person to another and from one time to another, epistemic probabilities vary from one person to another and from one time to another. Notice also that in many cases, even though we cannot assign a precise numerical value to the epistemic probability of a proposition, we can make comparative judgments about its probability. For example, I can't assign a precise numerical value to the epistemic probability of the proposition that humans are descended from other bipedal primates. But I can correctly claim that this proposition is very probably true, that its probability is much greater than ½ or close to one, and that it is more probable than the proposition that all modern humans are descended from humans living in Africa (though that proposition is also probably true).

This is why premise A is important. Second, even if premises A and C are both true, theism would not be improbable if it were intrinsically *much* more probable than HI. This is why premise B is crucial. Third, not even the truth of all three premises proves that theism is improbable because one might, in addition to the strong evidence favoring HI over theism reported by O, have other evidence favoring theism over HI. This is why D concludes only that T is improbable, *other evidence (besides O) held equal,* and thus the truth of D is a *prima facie* good reason to reject theism. In fairness to Otte, I should mention that this argument was at best hinted at in "Pain and Pleasure." As I said earlier, my main goal in that article was to establish the truth of C. I am grateful to Otte for forcing me to reflect on exactly how an argument for the significance of C should proceed. I am quite sure, however, that Otte would not, upon seeing this argument, feel any inclination to raise a white flag. So let's turn to his main objection.

Otte says that "The main problem with Draper's argument is that even if principle C were true, it would have no consequences for the rationality of most theists' religious beliefs" because "Most theists are not mere theists, but instead are Christians, Muslims or Jews" (Otte, p. 28). But if theism is improbable, then of course so is Christianity or any other broader set of beliefs entailing theism. So what is the significance of Otte's claim that most theists are sectarian theists? Explaining this further, Otte claims that

C*: O is antecedently much more probable given CH (Christianity) than it is given HI.

He doesn't offer much by way of argument for C*, and C* is simply false if, for example, "Christianity" is equated with something like the Nicene Creed. Apparently, however, Otte identifies "Christianity" with something much more specific and much more sectarian than that. For he claims that Christianity entails any broad description of the types of pain and pleasure in the world and also much about the specific evils in the world. It is worth reflecting on how extraordinary this claim is. It is rather obviously false unless Otte means to build into his definition of "Christianity" the various reports of pain and pleasure found in the Bible! Given this ultra-sectarian definition of Christianity, mere theists will no doubt be joined by many (non-literalist) Christians in feeling neglected by Otte's strategy.

Supposing, however, that Otte is right about C* being true, why does he conclude that the truth of C has no implications for the rationality of being a Christian? Otte gives two distinct answers to this question. The first is that "Christians . . . can appeal to principle C* . . . to claim that we have a prima facie reason to reject the hypothesis of indifference" (Otte, p. 31). But Christians can do this only if the following argument is just as strong as A-D.

A*. O is known to be true.
B*. HI is not much more probable intrinsically than CH.
C*. Pr(O/CH) >! Pr(O/HI).
So, D*. Other evidence held equal, HI is probably false.

This argument is not, however, as strong as A-D for the simple reason that, while B is true, B* is false.

B is true primarily because theism is a much more specific hypothesis than the hypothesis of indifference. Theism claims, not just that some sort of supernatural entity exists, but also that this entity is both personal and absolutely perfect. Since it cannot be shown that the existence of such an entity is metaphysically necessary, the claim that such an entity exists starts out with a low probability. In general, the more specific and hence riskier an existential claim like theism is, the *less* probable that claim is intrinsically but the *more* probable its denial is intrinsically. This is why we assume both in science and in everyday reasoning that existential claims, especially specific ones, require stronger evidence to be justified than their denials do. Unlike theism, the hypothesis of indifference has no positive ontological commitments at all. It is entailed by and so is at least as probable as (metaphysical) naturalism, which asserts nothing more than that supernatural entities do not exist and so is compatible with the existence of both natural and non-natural entities. In addition, the hypothesis of indifference is compatible with a wide variety of supernaturalist hypotheses. If any of these hypotheses have a non-zero intrinsic probability, then naturalism is a riskier and hence intrinsically less probable hypothesis than the hypothesis of indifference. When looked at in this light, it should be clear that B is a rather modest claim. For it does not assert that the hypothesis of indifference is more probable intrinsically than theism (although I believe it is). Indeed, it doesn't even deny that theism is more probable intrinsically than the hypothesis of indifference. Rather, it claims only that theism is not *much* more probable intrinsically than the hypothesis of indifference.

Now consider B*. The ultra-sectarian Christian hypothesis appealed to by Otte in B* claims that theism is true and that a whole host of other theological and historical claims are true, including many that are, in the absence of evidence, more or less independent (probabilistically speaking) of theism and of each other. So Christianity as Otte understands it is *obviously* far less probable intrinsically than both theism and the hypothesis of indifference. Moreover, since I did argue in the fourth section of "Pain and Pleasure" that the hypothesis of indifference is more probable intrinsically than theism, and since this entails the denial of B*, Otte's claim that I simply *assume* that Christianity is not a serious alternative to HI is false. I admit that my use of the term "serious" was misleading. The fact that Christianity has a low intrinsic probability does not imply that it is not serious in many ways. Indeed, with enough supporting evidence, it could even be probable all things considered. But as long as the claim that Christianity is not a serious alternative to HI is understood in the technical sense in which I intend it, no theist should deny it. Given how much Otte builds into his definition of Christianity, it would be unreasonable to deny that, prior to considering any evidence at all, the hypothesis of indifference is much more probable than Christianity. Hence, B is true while B* is false, and hence C and C* are not of equal significance.

But Otte is not done yet. For he has, as I said earlier, a second reason for inferring from the truth of C* that the truth of C has no implications for the rationality of Christian theism. He claims that, even if Christianity is not a serious alternative to the hypothesis of indifference, this would "not affect the main point of [his] argument (that principle C is irrelevant to Christian belief), because even if HI is a serious alternative to CH, it is not the case that O is more likely on HI than on CH" (Otte, p. 32). Notice that Otte's first reason for believing that C's truth has no implications for the rationality of Christianity emphasized that O is antecedently more probable given CH than given HI. His second reason emphasizes that O is not antecedently more likely on HI than on CH. This may seem like a tiny difference, but his intent is clear. His first reason involved an attempt to construct an argument from O against HI. His second reason attempts only to undermine any argument from O against CH. The former requires that CH be a serious alternative to HI. The latter, he maintains, does not.

Otte's second reason, however, is no more convincing than his first. He is, in effect, trying to conclude way too much from the fact that the third premise of the following argument is false:

A'. O is known to be true.
B'. CH is not much more probable intrinsically than HI.
C'. Pr(O/HI) is much greater than Pr(O/CH).
So, D'. Other evidence held equal, CH is probably false.

Recall his exact words. He says my point about intrinsic probabilities isn't ultimately crucial to his main point that C is irrelevant to Christianity because "even if HI is a serious alternative to CH" — i.e. even if B' is true — "it is not the case that O is more likely on HI than on CH" — i.e. C' is not true. But while this shows that A'-D' is a bad argument and so fails to establish the truth of D', it does not establish the irrelevance of C to Christianity because it does not show that D' is false! Even if A'-D' is a bad argument, A-D can still be a good argument. And if A-D is a good argument, then that establishes the truth of D and so indirectly establishes the truth of D'. D, recall, is the claim that, other evidence held equal, theism (*not* just "mere theism") is probably false. Since Christianity entails theism and so cannot be more probable than theism, D entails D' — i.e. it entails that, other evidence held equal, Christianity is probably false. Thus, I can happily grant that C' is false and hence that A'-D' fails to show that D' is true and yet continue to maintain that C, together with A and B, provides a prima facie good reason to reject any sort of theism, whether sectarian or non-sectarian. Thus, Otte's belief that intrinsic probabilities are irrelevant to his main objection is false.

It is important to emphasize, however, that I do not deny the potential relevance of other religious beliefs to the issue of whether or not my argument is sound. Indeed, religious or ethical or metaphysical or epistemological beliefs could raise $Pr(O/T)$ (or lower $Pr(O/HI)$) in the way explained in Section III of "Pain and Pleasure." To determine if they do, I recommended applying the following principle, which I called the weighted average principle:

$$Pr(O/T) = Pr(H/T) \times Pr(O/T\&H) + Pr(\sim H/T) \times Pr(O/T\&\sim H).$$

The idea here is that, if H is some Christian doctrine, then $Pr(O/T)$ will be an average of $Pr(O/T\&H)$ and $Pr(O/T\&\sim H)$. What makes it an average is the fact that $Pr(H) + Pr(\sim H) = 1$. But it is not necessarily a straight average because $Pr(H/T)$ and $Pr(\sim H/T)$ may not equal ½. Thus, for example, if $Pr(H/T) = 2/3$ and $Pr(\sim H/T) = 1/3$, then $Pr(O/T\&H)$ is given twice as much weight as $Pr(O/T\&\sim H)$ in calculating the average.

Consider, for example, the doctrine of life after death ("L" for short). I believe that $Pr(L/T)$ is very high. Suppose I am right about this and suppose also that $Pr(O/L\&T)$ is much greater than $Pr(O/HI)$. Then C would be false, because $Pr(O/T) = Pr(L/T) \times Pr(O/L\&T) + Pr(\sim L/T) \times Pr(O/\sim L\&T)$. Of course, I don't believe for a moment that $Pr(O/L\&T)$ is much greater than $Pr(O/HI)$. The hypothesis that we will survive death explains very little of what we know about pain and pleasure. But the point is that I provided a mechanism in "Pain and Pleasure" for evaluating the relevance of other religious and non-religious beliefs to my argument for C. They should be treated and evaluated in the same way as theodicies (or as "defenses," as I explain in "The Skeptical Theist").[8]

Notice also that my procedure treats religious and non-religious beliefs in the same way. Otte, on the other hand, seems to think that religious beliefs form some sort of privileged group that should be evaluated as a whole. This is implicit in his claim that, while C might provide a problem for mere theists, it does not present a problem for Jews, Christians, and Muslims. He also suggests that, if O were much more probable on HI than on CH, then this would present a problem for Christians. But mere theists have other beliefs besides religious ones, as do sectarian theists (not to mention people who believe in the hypothesis of indifference), and Otte provides no reason to believe that all of these are irrelevant. Why, then, Otte's focus on religious beliefs? His criticism of my argument actually commits him to a much more radical view, namely, that in order to show that a fact threatens the rationality of a belief with which that fact is compatible, one would need to show that that fact is evidence against the conjunction of all of a person's beliefs. And since, practically speaking, it is impossible to consider that many beliefs all at once, this in turn commits Otte to the view that evidence could never be used to challenge the rationality of any belief. Of course, this is quite absurd. So Otte's approach is clearly not a viable alternative to my own.

Antecedent Probabilities and the Truth of C

Having refuted Otte's main points, which concern my argument for D, I turn now to Otte's concerns about the "antecedent probabilities" in C. I will show that the proposal about these probabilities that Otte criticizes is a straw man. (Indeed, my formulation of C actually presupposes the falsity of that proposal.) Otte misunderstands my notion of "antecedent probabilities," leading him to conclude that the epistemic framework presupposed by C is bankrupt. Before examining why Otte finds my appeal to antecedent probabilities problematic, it will be useful to explain my reasons for formulating C in terms of such probabilities.

8. In *The Evidential Argument from Evil*, ed. Daniel Howard-Snyder (Bloomington, Ind.: Indiana University Press, 1996), Ch. 9.

Consider the following scenario. A person enters a room in which two large jars filled with jellybeans are seated on a table. In Jar A, almost all of the beans are yellow, but there are also some red beans and some blue ones. A close look reveals that there are about ten times more red ones than blue. Jar B looks just like jar A, except it contains roughly ten times more blue beans than red ones. The lights are then turned off and a bean is randomly drawn from one of the two jars. The lights come on and the person observes that the bean drawn is red. Now consider two hypotheses. Hypothesis A states that the bean was drawn from jar A, and hypothesis B states that the bean was drawn from jar B. Let "R" stand for a statement reporting one's observation that the selected bean is red.

Assuming one knows that the observed bean was randomly drawn from one of the two jars, R obviously reports evidence favoring hypothesis A over hypothesis B. But you cannot detect or measure the degree of R's relevance to A and B if you compare the probability of R given A to the probability of R given B. The problem is that R is certain given either of these two hypotheses, because the observation R reports makes it certain. To put the point simply, you know the bean is red whichever jar it came from because you saw that it is red. Thus, if you want to measure the degree of evidential relevance of R to hypotheses A and B, you must compare, not R's probability but rather its *antecedent* probability on the two different hypotheses. In other words, you must abstract from the effect your observation of the bean's color had on the probability of its being red. Independent of that observation, the probability of R is low both on hypothesis A and hypothesis B. This is because you know the bean was drawn randomly, and you justifiably believe on the basis of your inspection of the two jars that the vast majority of beans in each jar are yellow, not red. Nevertheless, R reports fairly strong evidence favoring hypothesis A over hypothesis B because, antecedently — that is, independent of the observation R reports — R is about ten times more probable on the assumption that A is true than it is on the assumption that B is true. This implies that the observation reported by O has a significant effect on the ratio of the probability of the hypothesis A to the probability of the hypothesis B. It makes it about ten times greater than it would otherwise be. Thus, if A and B started out equally probable, then A will, because of the observation O reports, end up about ten times more likely than B. This explains the need to appeal to antecedent probabilities in the jellybean scenario and ipso facto the need to appeal to antecedent probabilities in C.

So why does Otte find such an appeal so problematic? He emphasizes over and over again that it is crucial to know what one is "conditionalizing on." But the only propositions conditionalized on in C are HI and T. Of course, other things we know affect the probabilities in C, but they aren't conditionalized on. Otte's demand to know what is being conditionalized on mistakenly assumes that epistemic probability is nothing more than a relation between propositions, something like the degree of support that one proposition gives to another. On this sort of view, talk about the epistemic probability of a proposition P (all things considered) is shorthand for talk about a certain conditional probability, either P's probability conditional on some statement reporting everything I know non-inferentially, or less plausibly, everything I know, or, much less plausibly, everything I believe! Even if thinking of epistemic probability in this sort of way can for some purposes be defended as a sort of harmless idealization, it is seriously flawed. Epistemic probabilities are, of course, relative to epistemic situations, and one's epistemic situation includes the fact that one has certain background knowledge. But an "epistemic situation" is much more complicated than this, because it includes everything that affects the degree of confidence that one rationally should have in the truth of a proposition. For example, it may include the fact that one is having certain memory or sense experiences, experiences that may directly confer various degrees of justification on various propositions. Thus, an epistemic situation cannot be represented as a proposition, and even if it could, conditionalizing on it would be appropriate only if that proposition were known to be true with absolute certainty, which is hardly realistic.

Notice also how absurd it is to think that the epistemic probability of a proposition depends on everything else one believes or even on everything else one believes that is evidentially relevant to that proposition. I doubt Otte really believes this, but he certainly suggests this position when he says that "we will want to conditionalize on as many of the individual's beliefs as possible" because "we are interested in what it is rational for an individual to believe, and this is dependent upon all of the . . . beliefs the individual has" (Otte, p. 36). An individual's belief can be evidentially relevant to a proposition without affecting the probability of that proposition for that individual. For example, Bill can believe he'll be lucky at the track this weekend, and that may increase the confidence he has in the truth of the proposition that he will win his bets, but this belief is completely irrational and so has no effect on the epistemic probability of his winning. Epistemic probabilities are relative to epistemic situations, but are not relative to *beliefs* in the simplistic way Otte seems to presuppose.

Now let's focus on Otte's specific criticisms of my use of antecedent probabilities. He begins with a truly absurd proposal about how to understand the antecedent probabilities in C, which he ungenerously says "may be what Draper intended" (Otte, p. 36). According to this proposal, I simply subtract O from my complete set of beliefs and then conditionalize on what's left. That this is not how I intended the antecedent probabilities in C to be understood should be obvious since I do not as a matter of fact conditionalize on *anything* besides HI or T in C. Thus, while I certainly agree with Otte's criticisms of this proposal, I find it most disturbing that he tries to saddle me with it.

So now let's look at my *actual* proposal. What I say in "Pain and Pleasure" is that the antecedent probability of O is its probability "independent of . . . the observations and testimony O reports."[9] In other words, I abstract from certain events (more specifically, observations or experiences), not from any beliefs or propositions, and the events I abstract from are what ultimately grounds my knowledge of O. Similarly, in the jellybean example, my knowledge that the bean is red is ultimately grounded in my observation (visual experience) of the selected bean after the lights in the room are turned on. So to judge the "antecedent" probability of the proposition that the bean is red, I abstract from that observation. If, in addition to making that observation, I had also heard another person in the room say "Look, the bean is red," then I would also have to abstract from (my auditory experience of) that testimony. But I abstract from nothing else. For example, I also know that the bean was drawn randomly, that most of the beans in each jar are yellow, that there are about ten times more red beans than blue beans in jar A, and that there are about ten times more blue beans than red beans in jar B. My knowledge of these facts does not depend on my observation of the red bean and so abstracting from that observation has no effect on this knowledge, which is crucial for my judging that the antecedent probability of R is about ten times more likely on the hypothesis that it came from jar A than on the hypothesis that it came from jar B. By contrast, my knowledge that either the moon is made out of green cheese or the bean is red, which together with my knowledge that the moon is not made out of green cheese entails that the bean is red, does depend on my observation of the bean. Thus, when I abstract from my observation of the bean, I in effect abstract from this knowledge, which prevents the entailment in question from making the antecedent probability of the bean's being red equal on the two hypotheses.

9. Draper, "Pain and Pleasure," p. 333.

The crucial point is that, as long as one makes the correct abstraction, the background knowledge that should affect the crucial probabilities will affect them, and the background knowledge that should not affect them won't. There is no need to list all of our beliefs or all of the propositions we know, subtract some, and then conditionalize on the ones that are left. That would be a truly hopeless procedure (as Otte demonstrates). If, instead, my procedure is followed, then it is clear that the antecedent probability of the bean's being red will be about ten times greater on the assumption that it came from jar A than on the assumption that it came from jar B. This tells us that R reports evidence favoring hypothesis A over hypothesis B, and it also tells us exactly how strong that evidence is — exactly what effect it has on the ratio of the probability of A to the probability of B. I know of no other reasonable approach to assessing the evidential relevance of R to A and B that can match these results!

Granted, the abstraction involved in C is in some sense much "larger" than the abstraction involved in the jellybean example. But I see no reason to believe that size makes a difference in this particular case. I don't, of course, deny that my approach and some of its epistemological assumptions are, despite their advantages, controversial. That's the nature of philosophy. If Otte's worry about probabilistic arguments from evil is that they will turn out to be controversial, then I have no disagreement with him. But the fact that such an argument is controversial implies neither that it is unsound nor that no one can rationally believe that it is sound. More to the point, it does not imply that only non-Christians or non-theists will be or should be convinced by it!

The Argument from Evil

Peter van Inwagen

By the argument from evil, I understand the following argument (or any argument sufficiently similar to it that the two arguments stand or fall together): We find vast amounts of truly horrendous evil in the world; if there were a God, we should not find vast amounts of horrendous evil in the world; there is, therefore, no God.

One might suppose that no argument was exempt from critical examination. But it is often asserted, and with considerable vehemence, that it is extremely wicked to examine the argument from evil with a critical eye. Here, for example, is a famous passage from John Stuart Mill's *Three Essays on Religion:*[1]

> We now pass to the moral attributes of the Deity. . . . This question bears a very different aspect to us from what it bears to those teachers of Natural Theology who are encumbered with the necessity of admitting the omnipotence of the Creator. We have not to attempt the impossible problem of reconciling infinite benevolence and justice with infinite power in the Creator of a world such as this. The attempt to do so not only involves absolute contradiction in an intellectual point of view but exhibits to excess the revolting spectacle of a jesuitical defense of moral enormities. (p. 179)

And here is a second example. The following poem occurs in Kingsley Amis's novel *The Anti-Death League*[2] (it is the work of one of the

1. London: Longmans, Green, 1875.
2. New York: Harcourt, Brace & World, 1966.

characters), and it puts a little flesh on the bones of Mill's abstract Victorian indignation. It contains several specific allusions to just those arguments that Mill describes as jesuitical defenses of moral enormities. Its literary effect depends essentially on putting these arguments, or allusions to them, into the mouth of God.

To a Baby Born without Limbs

This is just to show you who's boss around here.
It'll keep you on your toes, so to speak.
Make you put your best foot forward, so to speak,
And give you something to turn your hand to, so to speak.
You can face up to it like a man,
Or snivel and blubber like a baby.
That's up to you. Nothing to do with Me.
If you take it in the right spirit,
You can have a bloody marvelous life,
With the great rewards courage brings,
And the beauty of accepting your LOT.
And think how much good it'll do your Mum and Dad,
And your Grans and Gramps and the rest of the shower,
To be stopped being complacent.
Make sure they baptize you, though,
In case some murdering bastard
Decides to put you away quick,
Which would send you straight to LIMB-o, ha ha ha.
But just a word in your ear, if you've got one.
Mind you, DO take this in the right spirit,
And keep a civil tongue in your head about Me.
Because if you DON'T,
I've got plenty of other stuff up My sleeve,
Such as leukemia and polio
(Which, incidentally, you're welcome to any time,
Whatever spirit you take this in).
I've given you one love-pat, right?
You don't want another.
So watch it, Jack.[3]

---

3. In the poem as it is printed in the novel there are (for reasons of the plot, as they say) several illiteracies (e.g., 'whose' for 'who's' in l. 1). I have "corrected" them — with apologies to Martin Amis, in whose opinion they are an important part of the intended effect of the poem on the reader (that is, the effect Kingsly Amis intended the

I am not entirely out of sympathy with writers like Mill and the fictional author of the poem in Amis's novel. There *is* one sort of position on God and evil toward which the intellectual scorn of Mill (I'll presently discuss his moral scorn) seems entirely appropriate. I have in mind the idea that — in the most strict and literal sense — evil does not exist. Now it might seem surprising that anyone would say this. Consider the following passage from *The Brothers Karamazov:*

> By the way, a Bulgarian I met lately in Moscow . . . told me about the crimes committed by Turks and Circassians in all parts of Bulgaria through fear of a general rising of the Slavs. They burn villages, murder, outrage women and children, they nail their prisoners by the ears to the fences, leave them so till morning, and in the morning they hang them. . . . These Turks took a pleasure in torturing children, too; cutting the unborn child from the mother's womb, and tossing babies up in the air and catching them on the points of their bayonets before their mothers' eyes. . . .[4]

How can anyone listen to stories like this and say that evil does not exist? Their idea, if I understand it, is something like this. An event like the Turkish massacres in Bulgaria *would* be an evil if it constituted the entire universe. But, of course, no such event does. The universe as a whole contains no spot or stain of evil, but it looks to us human beings as if it did because we view it from a limited perspective. Perhaps an aesthetic analogy will help us to understand this rather obscure idea. (I owe this analogy to Wallace Matson.) Many pieces of music that are of extreme beauty and perfection contain short discordant passages that would sound very ugly if they were played all by themselves, outside the musical context in which the composer intended them to occur. (Bach's *Well-Tempered Clavier* is an example.) But these passages are not ugly in their proper musical context; they are not the kind of passage Rossini was referring to when he said, "Wagner has lovely moments but awful quarters of an hour." Seen, or rather heard, in the context of the whole, they are not only not ugly but are essential elements of the beauty and perfection of that whole. The idea I am deprecating is that the horrors and atrocities

---

poem to have on readers of *The Anti-death League*). For Martin Amis's argument for this conclusion (and the poem without my officious corrections), see his memoir *Experience* (New York: Hyperion, 2000), p. 188.

4. From Chapter 4 ("Rebellion") of Book V. Ivan is speaking. It is very nearly obligatory for writers on the problem of evil to quote something from this chapter.

of our world are analogous to these discordant passages. The *loci classici* of this idea are Leibniz's *Theodicy* and the following well-known lines from Pope's "Essay on Man" (Epistle I, ll. 289 et seq.):

> All nature is but art unknown to thee,
> All chance, direction which thou canst not see;
> All discord, harmony not understood;
> All partial evil, universal good;
> And, spite of pride, in erring reason's spite,
> One truth is clear, Whatever is, is right.

I don't see how anyone could believe this. It seems to me to be a wholly fantastic thesis. Do not misunderstand this statement. I wish to distance myself from the vulgar slander that ascribes moral insensibility (or downright wickedness) to Pope — a slander about which I'll have more to say in a moment. For my part, I accuse him only of intellectual error. But the intellectual error is of enormous magnitude — comparable to the intellectual error of, say, the astronomer Percival Lowell, who believed that Mars was covered with canals or to Descartes's belief that cats and dogs are unconscious automata. If we think of soldiers making mothers watch while they throw their babies in the air and catch them on the points of their bayonets, or of the ancient Mesopotamian practice of Moloch — of throwing living infants into a furnace as a sacrifice to Baal — or of a child born without limbs, we shall, I hope, find it impossible to say that evil is not real. Bad things really do happen, and anyone who, like Pope, says that we call certain things bad only because we don't see them *sub specie aeternitatis* is in grave error. One might as well say that if we could only observe pain from God's point of view, we'd see that it doesn't hurt.

If anyone takes the Leibniz/Pope line on the reality of evil, then, I think, that person deserves some of the scorn that Mill and Amis so eloquently express. I insist, however, that the scorn should be intellectual rather than moral. Given what Pope believed, he is guilty of no moral error; but his intellectual error is profound and not to be imitated.

In any case, the scorn of Mill and the other writers I've alluded to is not directed only at those who deny the reality of evil. This scorn is poured on anyone who is unwilling to admit, without further argument, that the evils of this world entail the non-existence of a good and omnipotent God. And when they imply that all such people, all people who are not immediately converted to atheism by the argument from evil in its simplest form, are morally defective, they go too far — they go *far* too far — and I must accuse them of intellectual dishonesty.

Thinking clearly about God and evil is *hard*. Thinking clearly for an extended period about any topic is hard. It is easier to pour scorn on those who disagree with you than actually to address their arguments. (It was easier for Voltaire to caricature Leibniz's arguments and to mock the caricature than actually to address them. And so he wrote *Candide*. And of all the kinds of scorn that can be poured on someone's views, moral scorn is the safest and most pleasant (most pleasant to the one doing the pouring). It is the safest kind because, if you want to pour moral scorn on someone's views, you can pretty much take it for granted that most people will regard it as unanswerable; you can take it as *certain* that everyone who is predisposed to agree with you will believe that you have made an unanswerable point. You can pretty much take it for granted that your audience will dismiss any attempt your opponent in debate makes at an answer as a "rationalization" — that great contribution of modern depth-psychology to intellectual complacency and laziness. Moral scorn is the most *pleasant* kind of scorn to deploy against those who disagree with you because a display of self-righteousness — moral posturing — is a pleasant action whatever the circumstances, and it is nice to find an excuse for it. No one can tell me that Mill wasn't enjoying himself when he wrote the words, "exhibits to excess the revolting spectacle of a jesuitical defense of moral enormities." (Perhaps he was enjoying himself so much that his attention was diverted from the question, "What would it be to exhibit a revolting spectacle in moderation?")

To people who avoid having to defend the argument from evil by this sort of moral posturing, I can only say, "Come off it." These people are, in point of principle, in exactly the same position as those defenders of law and order who, if you express a suspicion that a man accused of abducting and molesting a child has been framed by the police, tell you with evident disgust that molesting a child is a horrible crime and that you're defending a child molester.

Having defended the moral propriety of critically examining the argument from evil, I will now do just that. The argument presupposes, and rightly, that two features God is supposed to have are "non-negotiable": that he is omnipotent and morally perfect. That he is omnipotent means that he can do anything that doesn't involve an intrinsic impossibility. Thus, God, if he exists, can change water to wine, since there is no intrinsic impossibility in the elementary particles that constitute the water in a cup being rearranged so as to constitute wine. But even God can't draw a round square or cause it both to rain and not to rain at the same place at the same time or change the past because these things are intrinsically impossible. To say that God is morally perfect is to say that he never does anything morally wrong — that he could not possibly do anything morally wrong. If God exists, therefore, and if you think he's done something morally wrong, you must be mistaken: either he didn't do the thing you think he did, or the thing he did that you think is morally wrong isn't. Omnipotence and moral perfection are, as I said, non-negotiable components of the idea of God. If the universe was made by an intelligent being, and if that being is less than omnipotent (and if there's no other being who is omnipotent), then the atheists are right: God does not exist. If the universe was made by an omnipotent being, and if that being has done even one thing that was morally wrong (and if there isn't another omnipotent being, one who never does anything morally wrong), then the atheists are right: God does not exist. If the Creator of the universe lacked either omnipotence or moral perfection, and if he claimed to be God, he would be either an impostor (if he claimed to be omnipotent and morally perfect) or confused (if he conceded that he lacked either omnipotence or moral perfection and claimed to be God anyway).

To these two "non-negotiable" features of the concept of God, we must add one other that doesn't call for much comment: God, if he exists, must know a great deal about the world he has created. Now it is usually said that God is *omniscient* — that he knows *everything*. But the argument from evil doesn't require this strong assumption about God's knowledge — it requires only that God know enough to be aware of a significant amount of the evil that exists in the world. If God knew even the little that you and I know about the amount and extent of evil, that would be sufficient for the argument.

Now consider those evils God knows about. Since he's morally perfect, he must desire that these evils not exist — their non-existence must be what he *wants*. And an omnipotent being can achieve or bring about whatever he wants. So if there were an omnipotent, morally perfect being who knew about these evils — well, they wouldn't have arisen in the first place, for he'd have prevented their occurrence. Or if, for some reason, he didn't do that, he'd certainly remove them the instant they began to exist. But we observe evils, and very long-lasting ones. So we must conclude that God does not exist.

How much force has this argument? Suppose I believe in God and grant that the world contains vast amounts of truly horrible evil. What might I say in reply? I should, and do, think that the place to begin is with an examination of the word 'want'. Granted, in some sense of the word, the non-existence of evil must be what a morally perfect being *wants*. But we often don't bring about states of affairs we can bring about and want. Suppose, for example, that Alice's mother is dying in great pain and that Alice yearns desperately for her mother to die — today, and not next week or next month. And suppose it would be easy for Alice to arrange this — she is perhaps a doctor or a nurse and has easy access to pharmaceutical resources that would enable her to achieve this end. Does it follow that she will act on this ability that she has? It is obvious that it does not, for Alice might have *reasons* for not doing what she can do. Two obvious candidates for such reasons are: she thinks it would be morally wrong; she is afraid that her act would be discovered and that she would be prosecuted for murder. And either of these reasons might be sufficient, in her mind, to outweigh her desire for an immediate end to her mother's sufferings. So it may be that someone has a very strong desire for something and is able to obtain this thing, but does not act on this desire — because he has reasons for not doing so that seem to him to outweigh the desirability of the thing. The conclusion that evil does not exist does not, therefore, follow *logically* from the premises that the non-existence of evil is what God wants and that he is able to bring about the object of his desire — since, for all logic can tell us, God might have reasons for allowing evil to exist that, in his mind, outweigh the desirability of the non-existence of evil. But are such reasons even imaginable? What might they be?

Suppose I believe I know what God's reasons for allowing evil to exist are, and that I tell them to you. Then I have presented you with what is called a *theodicy*. This word comes from two Greek words that mean 'God' and 'justice'. Thus, Milton, in *Paradise Lost,* tells us that the purpose of the poem is to "justify the ways of God to men" — 'justify' meaning 'exhibit as just'. If I could present a theodicy, and if those to whom I presented it found it convincing, I'd have a reply to the argument from evil. But suppose that, although I believe in God, I *don't* claim to know what God's reasons for allowing evil are. Is there any way for someone in my position to reply to the argument from evil? There is. Consider this analogy.

Suppose your friend Clarissa, a single mother, left her two very young children alone in her flat for over an hour very late last night. Your Aunt Harriet, a maiden lady of strong moral principles, learns of this and declares that Clarissa is unfit to raise children. You spring to your friend's defense: "Now, Aunt Harriet, don't go jumping to conclusions. There's probably a perfectly good explanation. Maybe Billy or Annie took ill, and she decided to go over to St. Luke's for help. You know she hasn't got a phone or a car and no one in that neighborhood of hers would come to the door at two o'clock in the morning." If you tell your Aunt Harriet a story like this, you don't claim to know what Clarissa's reasons for leaving her children alone really were. And you're not claiming to have said anything that shows that Clarissa really is a good mother. You're claiming only to show that the fact Aunt Harriet has adduced doesn't prove that she isn't one; what you're trying to establish is that for all you and Aunt Harriet know, she had some good reason for what she did. And you're not trying to establish only that there is some remote possibility that she had a good reason. No lawyer would try to raise doubts in the minds of the members of a jury by pointing out to them that for all they knew his client had an identical twin, of whom all record had been lost, and who was the person who had actually committed the crime his client was charged with. That may be a possibility — I suppose it *is* a possibility — but it is too remote a possibility to raise real doubts in anyone's mind. What you're trying to convince Aunt Harriet of is that there is, as we say, *a very real possibility* that Clarissa had a good reason for leaving her children alone; and your attempt to convince her of this consists in your presenting her with an example of what such a reason *might* be.

Critical responses to the argument from evil — at least responses by philosophers — usually take just this form. A philosopher who responds to the argument from evil typically does so by telling a story, a story in which God allows evil to exist. This story will, of course, represent God as having reasons for allowing the existence of evil, reasons that, if the rest of the story were true, would be good ones. Such a story philosophers call a *defense*. A defense and a theodicy will not necessarily differ in content. A defense may, indeed, be verbally identical with a theodicy. The difference between a theodicy and a defense is simply that a theodicy is put forward as true, while nothing more is claimed for a defense than that it represents a real possibility — or a real possibility given that God exists. If I offer a story about God and evil as a defense, I hope for the following reaction from my audience: "Given that God exists, the rest of the story might well be true. I can't see any reason to rule it out."

A defense cannot simply take the form of a story about how God brings some great good out of the evils of the world, a good that outweighs those evils. At the very least, a defense will have to include the proposition that God was *unable* to bring about the greater good without allowing the evils we observe (or some other evils as bad or worse). And to find a story that can plausibly be said to have this feature is no trivial undertaking. The reason for this lies in God's omnipotence. A human being can often be excused for allowing, or even causing, a certain evil if that evil was a necessary means, or an unavoidable consequence thereof, to some good that outweighed it — or if it was a necessary means to the prevention of some greater evil. The eighteenth-century surgeon who operated without anesthetic caused unimaginable pain to his patients, but we do not condemn him because (at least if he knew what he was doing) the pain was an unavoidable consequence of the means necessary to some good that outweighed it — such as saving the patient's life. But we should not excuse a present-day surgeon who had anesthetics available and who nevertheless operated without using them — not even if his operation saved the patient's life and thus resulted in a good that outweighed the horrible pain the patient suffered.

A great many of the theodicies or defenses that one sees are insufficiently sensitive to this point. Many undergraduates, for example, if they are believers, seem inclined to say something like the following: if there were no evil, no one would appreciate — perhaps no one would even be aware of — the goodness of the things that *are* good. You know the idea: you never really appreciate health till you've been ill, you never really understand how great and beautiful a thing friendship is till you've known adversity and known what it is to have friends who stick by you through thick and thin — and so on. Now the obvious criticism of this defense is so immediately obvious that it tends to mask the point that led me to raise it. The immediately obvious criticism is that this defense may be capable of accounting for a certain amount of, for example, physical pain, but it certainly doesn't account for the degree and the duration of the pain that many people are subject to. But I have brought up the "appreciation" defense — which otherwise would not be worth spending any time on — to make a different point. It is not at all evident that an omnipotent creator would need to allow people really to experience *any* pain or grief or sorrow or adversity or illness to enable them to appreciate the good things in life. An omnipotent being would certainly be able to provide the knowledge of evil that human beings in fact acquire by bitter experience of real events in some other way. An omnipotent being could, for example, so arrange matters that at a certain point in each person's life — for a few years during his adolescence, say — that person have very vivid *nightmares* in which he is a prisoner in a concentration camp or dies of some horrible disease or watches his loved ones being raped and murdered by soldiers bent on ethnic cleansing. It seems evident to me that the supposed good (the capacity for the appreciation of good things) that some say is a consequence of the evils of the world could (if it exists) be equally well achieved by this means. And it is indisputable that a world in which horrible things occurred only in nightmares would be better than a world in which the same horrible things occurred in reality, and that a morally perfect being ought to prefer a world in which horrible things were confined to dreams to a world in which they existed in reality. The general point this example is intended to illustrate is simply that the resources of an omnipotent being are unlimited — or are limited only by what is intrinsically possible — and that a defense must take account of these unlimited resources.

There seems to me to be only one defense that has any hope of succeeding, and that is the so-called free-will defense. In its simplest, most abstract, form, the free-will defense goes as follows:

> God made the world and it was very good. An indispensable part of the goodness he chose was the existence of rational beings: self-aware beings capable of abstract thought and love and having the power of free choice between contemplated alternative courses of action. This last feature of rational beings, free choice or free will, is a good. But even an omnipotent being is unable to control the exercise of the power of free choice, for a choice that was controlled would *ipso facto* not be free. In other words, if I have a free choice between x and y, even God cannot ensure that I choose x. To ask God to give me a free choice between x and y and to see to it that I choose x instead of y is to ask God to bring about the intrinsically impossible; it is like asking him to create a round square, a material body that has no shape, or an invisible object that casts a shadow. Having this power of free choice, some or all human beings misuse it and produce a certain amount of evil. But free will is a sufficiently great good that its existence outweighs the evils that result from its abuse; and God foresaw this.

The free-will defense immediately suggests several objections. The two most pressing of them are these:

> How could anyone possibly believe that the evils of this world are outweighed by the good inherent in our having free will? Perhaps free will is a good and would outweigh a certain amount of evil, but it seems impossible to believe that it can outweigh the amount of physical suffering (to say nothing of other sorts of evil) that actually exists.

> Not all evils are the result of human free will. Consider, for example, the Lisbon earthquake or the almost inconceivable loss of life produced by the hurricane that ravaged Honduras in 1997. Such events are not the result of any act of human will, free or unfree.

In my view, the simple form of the free-will defense I have presented is unable to deal with either of these objections. The simple form of the free-will defense can deal with at best the existence of *some* evil — as opposed to the vast amount of evil we actually observe — and the evil with which it can deal is only that evil that is caused by the acts of human beings. I believe, however, that more sophisticated forms of the free-will defense do have interesting things to say about the vast amount of evil in the world and about those evils that are not caused by human beings. Before I discuss these "more sophisticated" forms of the free-will defense, however, I want to examine an objection that has been raised against the free-will defense that is so fundamental that, if valid, it would refute any elaboration of the defense, however sophisticated. This objection has to do with the nature of free will. There is a school of thought — Hobbes, Hume, and Mill are its most illustrious representatives — whose adherents maintain that free will and determinism are perfectly compatible: that there could be a world in which the past determined a unique future and the inhabitants of which were nonetheless free beings. Now if this school of philosophers is right, the free-will defense fails, for if free will and determinism are compatible, then an omnipotent being can, contrary to the central premise of the free-will defense, create a person who has a free choice between x and y and ensure that that person choose x rather than y. Those philosophers who accept the compatibility of free will and determinism defend their thesis as follows: being free is being free to do what one wants to do; prisoners in a jail, for example, are unfree because they want to leave and can't. The man who desperately wants to stop smoking but can't is unfree for the same reason — even though no barrier as literal as the bars of a cage stands between him and a life without nicotine. The very words 'free will' testify to the rightness of this analysis, for one's will is simply what one wants, and a free will is just exactly an unimpeded will. Given this account of free will, a Creator who wants to give me a free choice between x and y has only to arrange the components of my body and my environment in such a way that the following two 'if' statements are both true: if I were to want x, I'd be able to achieve that desire, and if I were to want y, I'd be able to achieve *that* desire. And a Creator who wants to ensure that I choose x, rather than y, has only to implant in me a fairly robust desire for x and see to it that I have no desire at all for y. And these two things are obviously compatible. Suppose, for example, that there was a Creator who had put a woman in a garden and had commanded her not to eat of the fruit of a certain tree. Could he so arrange matters that she have a free choice between eating of the fruit of that tree and not eating of it — and also *ensure* that she not eat of it? Certainly. To provide her with a free choice between the two alternatives, he need only see to it that two things are true: first, that if she wanted to eat of the fruit of that tree, no barrier (such as an unclimbable fence or paralysis of the limbs) would stand in the way of her acting on that desire, and, secondly, that if she wanted *not* to eat of the fruit, nothing would force her to act contrary to *that* desire. And to ensure that she not eat of the fruit, he need only see to it that not eating of the fruit be what she desires. This latter end could be achieved in a variety of ways; the simplest, I suppose, would be to build into her psychological makeup a very strong desire to do whatever he tells her to and a horror of disobedience — a horror like that experienced by the acrophobe who is forced to approach the edge of a cliff — and then to instruct her not to eat of the fruit. If all this is indeed correct, it would seem that an omnipotent being could both grant its creatures free will and ensure that they never bring any evil into the world by the abuse of it. And, of course, if *that* is true, the free-will defense fails.

But how plausible is this account of free will? Not very, I think. It certainly yields some odd conclusions. Consider the lower social orders in Aldous Huxley's *Brave New World*, the "deltas" and "epsilons." These unfortunate people have their deepest desires chosen for them by others — by the "alphas" who make up the highest social stratum. What the deltas and epsilons primarily desire is to do what the alphas (and the "beta" and "gamma" overseers who are appointed to supervise their labors) tell them. This is their primary desire because it is imposed on them by prenatal and postnatal conditioning. (If Huxley were writing today, he might have added genetic engineering to the alphas' list of resources for determining the desires of their slaves.) It would be hard to think of beings who better fitted the description 'lacks free will' than the deltas and epsilons of *Brave New World*. And yet, if the account of free will that we are considering is right, the deltas and epsilons are exemplars of beings with free will. Each of them is always doing exactly what he wants, after all, and who among us is in that fortunate position? What he wants is to do as he is told by those appointed over him, of course, but the account of free will we are examining says nothing about the *content* of one's desires: it requires only that there be no barrier to acting on them. The deltas and epsilons are not very intelligent, and are therefore incapable of philosophizing about their condition, but the alphas' techniques could as easily be applied to highly intelligent people. It is interesting to ask what conclusions such people would arrive at if they reflected on their condition. If you said to one of these highly intelligent slaves, "Don't you realize that you obey your master only because your desire to obey him was implanted in you by prenatal conditioning and genetic engineering," he would, I expect, reply by saying something like this: "Yes, and a good thing, too, because, you see, they had the foresight to implant in me a desire that my desires be so formed. I'm really very fortunate: I'm not only doing exactly what I want, but I want to want what I want, and I want what I want to be caused by prenatal conditioning and genetic engineering." Despite the fact that (I freely confess) I do not have a philosophically satisfactory account of free will, I can see that this person hasn't got it. Therefore, I contend, the atheist's attempt to show that the story that constitutes the free-will defense is false rests on a false theory about the nature of free will. Now my argument for the falsity of this theory is, I concede, inconclusive. (If it were conclusive, it would convince Hobbes and Hume and Mill and their fellow "compatibilists" that their account of free will was wrong. And experience shows that most compatibilists who hear and understand this argument are unmoved by it.) But let us remember the dialectical situation in which this inconclusive argument occurs. That is, let us remember who is trying to prove what. The atheist has opened the discussion by trying to prove the non-existence of God; the alleged proof of this conclusion is the argument from evil. The theist responds by producing the free-will defense and contends that this defense shows that evil does not prove the non-existence of God. The atheist's rejoinder is that the story called the free-will defense is false and that its falsity can be demonstrated by reflection on the nature of free will. The theist replies that the atheist has got the nature of free will wrong, and he offers a philosophical argument for this conclusion (the "Brave New World" argument), an argument that perhaps falls short of being a proof but has nevertheless seemed fairly plausible to many intelligent people. When we add up all the pluses and minuses of this exchange, it seems that the free-will defense triumphs in its limited sphere of application. When we think about it, we see that, for all the atheist has said, the story called the free-will defense *may well be true* — at least given that there is a God. One cannot show that a story involving creatures with free will is false or probably false by pointing out that the story would be false if a certain theory about free will were true. To show that, one would also have to show that the theory of free will that one has put forward was true or probably true. And the atheist hasn't shown that his theory of free will, the "no barriers" theory, is true or probably true, for the objections to the atheist's theory of free will that I have set out show that this theory faces very serious problems indeed.

The atheist's most promising course of action, I think, is to admit that the free-will defense shows that there might, for all anyone can say, be a certain amount of evil, a certain amount of pain and suffering, in a world created by an all-powerful and morally perfect being, and to stress the amounts and the kinds of evil that we find in the world as it is. The world as it is, I have said, contains vast amounts of truly horrendous evil (that's the point about amounts), and some of the kinds of evil to be found in the world as it is are not caused by human beings — wholly unforeseeable natural disasters, for example (that's the point about kinds). Can any elaboration of our simple version of the free-will defense take account of these two points in any very plausible way?

Let me suggest some elaborations toward this end. The reader must decide whether they are plausible. The free-will defense as I've stated it suggests — though it does not entail — that God created human beings with free will, and then just left them to their own devices. It suggests that the evils of the world are the more or less unrelated consequences of uncounted millions of largely unrelated abuses of free will by human beings. Let me propose a sort of plot to be added to the bare and abstract free-will defense I stated above. Consider the story of creation and rebellion and the expulsion from paradise that is told in the first three chapters of Genesis. Could this story be true — I mean literally true, true in every detail? Well, no. It contradicts what science has discovered about human evolution and the history of the physical universe. And that is hardly surprising, for it long antedates these discoveries. The story is a re-working — with much original material — by Hebrew authors (or, as I believe, a Hebrew author) of elements found in many ancient Middle Eastern mythologies. Like the *Aeneid*, it is a literary refashioning of materials originally supplied by legend and myth, and it retains a strong mythological flavor. It is possible, nevertheless, that the first three chapters of Genesis are a mythico-literary representation of actual events of human pre-history. The following is consistent with what we know of human pre-history. Our current knowledge of human evolution, in fact, presents us with no particular reason to believe that this story is false. (Here and there in the story, the reader will encounter various philosophical *obiter dicta*, asides to the reader thoughtfully provided by the omniscient narrator — myself.)

For millions of years, perhaps for thousands of millions of years, God guided the course of evolution so as eventually to produce certain very clever primates, the immediate predecessors of *Homo sapiens*. At some time in the last few hundred thousand years, the whole population of our pre-human ancestors formed a small breeding community — a few hundred or even a few score. That is to say, there was a time when every ancestor of modern human beings who was then alive was a member of this tiny, geographically tightly knit group of primates. In the fullness of time, God took the members of this breeding group and miraculously raised them to rationality. That is, he gave them the gifts of language, abstract thought, and disinterested love — and, of course, the gift of free will. He gave them the gift of free will because free will is necessary for love. Love, and not only erotic love, implies free will. The essential connection between love and free will is beautifully illustrated in Ruth's declaration to her mother-in-law Naomi:

> And Ruth said, Entreat me not to leave thee, or to return from following after thee: for whither thou goest, I will go; and where thou lodgest, I will lodge: thy people shall be my people and thy God my God: where thou diest, will I die, and there will I be buried; the Lord do so to me, and more also, if aught but death part thee and me. (Ruth 1:16-17)

It is also illustrated by the vow I made when I was married:

> I, Peter, take thee, Elisabeth, to be my wedded wife, to have and to hold from this day forward, for better for worse, for richer for poorer, in sickness and in health, to love and to cherish, till death us do part, according to God's holy ordinance; and thereto I plight thee my troth.

God not only raised these primates to rationality — not only made of them what we call human beings — but also took them into a kind of mystical union with himself, the sort of union that Christians hope for in heaven and call the Beatific Vision. Being in union with God, these new human beings, these primates who had become human beings at a certain point in their lives, lived together in the harmony of perfect love and also possessed what theologians used to call preternatural powers — something like what people who believe in them today call paranormal abilities. Because they lived in the harmony of perfect love, none of them did any harm to the others. Because of their preternatural powers, they were able somehow to protect themselves from wild beasts (which they were able to tame with a word), from disease (which they were able to cure with a touch) and from random, destructive natural events (like earthquakes), which they knew about in advance and were able to avoid. There was thus no evil in their world. And it was God's intention that they should never become decrepit with age or die, as their primate forbears had. But, somehow, in some way that must be mysterious to us, they were not content with this paradisal state. They abused the gift of free will and separated themselves from their union with God.

The result was horrific: not only did they no longer enjoy the Beatific Vision, but they now faced destruction by the random forces of nature, and were subject to old age and natural death. Nevertheless, they were too proud to end their rebellion. As the generations passed, they drifted further and further from God — into the worship of false gods (a worship that sometimes involved human sacrifice), inter-tribal warfare (complete with the gleeful torture of prisoners of war), private murder, slavery, and rape. On one level, they realized, or some of them realized, that something was horribly wrong, but they were unable to do anything about it. After they had separated themselves from God, they were, as an engineer might say, "not operating under design conditions." A certain frame of mind became dominant among them, a frame of mind latent in the genes they had inherited from a million or more generations of ancestors. I mean the frame of mind that places one's own desires and perceived welfare above everything else, and which accords to the welfare of one's immediate relatives a subordinate privileged status, and assigns no status at all to the welfare of anyone else. And this frame of mind was now married to rationality, to the power of abstract thought; the progeny of this marriage were the continuing resentment against those whose actions interfere with the fulfillment of one's desires, hatreds cherished in the heart, and the desire for revenge. The inherited genes that produced these baleful effects had been harmless as long as human beings had still had constantly before their minds a representation of perfect love in the Beatific Vision. In the state of separation from God, and conjoined with rationality, they formed the genetic substrate of what is called original sin or birth-sin: an inborn tendency to do evil against which all human efforts are vain. We, or most of us, have some sort of perception of the distinction between good and evil, but, however we struggle, in the end we give in and do evil. In all cultures there are moral codes (more similar than some would have us believe) and the members of every tribe and nation stand condemned not only by alien moral codes but by their own. The only human beings who consistently do right in their own eyes, whose consciences are always clear, are those who, like the Nazis, have given themselves over entirely to evil, those who say, in some twisted and self-deceptive way, what Milton has his Satan say explicitly and clearly: "Evil, be thou my Good."

When human beings had become like this, God looked out over a ruined world. It would have been just for him to leave human beings in the ruin they had made of themselves and their world. But God is more than a God of justice. He is, indeed, more than a God of mercy — a God who was merely merciful might simply have brought the story of humanity to an end at that point, like someone who shoots a horse with a broken leg. But God is more than a God of mercy: he is a God of love. He therefore neither left humanity to its own devices nor mercifully destroyed it. Rather, he set in motion a rescue operation. He put into operation a plan designed to restore separated humanity to union with himself. This defense will not specify the nature of this plan of atonement. The three Abrahamic religions, Judaism, Christianity, and Islam, tell three different stories about the nature of this plan, and I do not propose to favor one of them over another in telling a story that, after all, I do not maintain is true. This much must be said, however: the plan has the following feature, and any plan with the object of restoring separated humanity to union with God would have to have this feature: its object is to bring it about that human beings once more love God. And, since love essentially involves free will, love is not something that can be imposed from the outside, by an act of sheer power. Human beings must choose freely to be reunited with God and to love him, and this is something they are unable to do of their own efforts. They must therefore cooperate with God. As is the case with many rescue operations, the rescuer and those whom he is rescuing must cooperate. For human beings to cooperate with God in this rescue operation, they must know that they need to be rescued. They must know what it means to be separated from him. And what it means to be separated from God is to live in a world of horrors. If God simply "canceled" all the horrors of this world by an endless series of miracles, he would thereby frustrate his own plan of reconciliation. If he did that, we should be content with our lot and should see no reason to cooperate with him. Here is an analogy. Suppose Dorothy suffers from angina, and that what she needs to do is to stop smoking and lose weight. Suppose her doctor knows of a drug that will stop the pain but will do nothing to cure the condition. Should the doctor prescribe the drug for her, in the full knowledge that if the pain is alleviated, there is no chance that she will stop smoking and lose weight? Well, perhaps the answer is yes. The doctor is Dorothy's fellow adult and fellow citizen, after all. Perhaps it would be insufferably paternalistic to refuse to alleviate Dorothy's pain in order to provide her with a motivation to do what is to her own advantage. If one were of an especially libertarian cast of mind, one might even say that someone who did that was "playing God." It is far from clear, however, whether there is anything wrong with *God's* behaving as if he were God. It is at least very plausible to suppose that it is morally permissible for God to allow human beings to suffer if the result of suppressing the suffering would be to deprive them of a very great good, one that far outweighed the suffering. But God does shield us from *much* evil, from a great proportion of the sufferings that would be a natural consequence of our rebellion. If he did not, all human history would be at least this bad: every human society would be on the moral level of Nazi Germany. But, however much evil God shields us from, he must leave in place a vast amount of evil if he is not to deceive us about what separation from him means. The amount he has left us with is so vast and so horrible that we cannot really comprehend it, especially if we are middle-class Americans or Europeans. Nevertheless, it could have been much worse. The inhabitants of a world in which human beings had separated ourselves from God and he had then simply left them to their own devices would regard our world as a comparative paradise. All this evil, however, will come to an end. At some point, for all eternity, there will be no more unmerited suffering. Every evil done by the wicked to the innocent will have been avenged, and every tear will have been wiped away. If there is still suffering, it will be merited: the suffering of those who refuse to cooperate with God's great rescue operation and are allowed by him to exist forever in a state of elected ruin — those who, in a word, are in hell.

One aspect of this story needs to be brought out more clearly than I have. If the story is true, much of the evil in the world is due to chance. There is generally no explanation of why *this* evil happened to *that* person. What there is is an explanation of why evils happen to people without any reason. And the explanation is: that is part of what being separated from God means: it means being the playthings of chance. It means living in a world in which innocent children die horribly, and it means something worse than that: it means living in a world in which innocent children die horribly *for no reason at all*. It means living in a world in which the wicked, through sheer luck, often prosper. Anyone who does not want to live in such a world, a world in which we are the playthings of chance, had better accept God's offer of a way out of that world.

Here, then, is a defense. Do I believe it? Well, I believe parts of it and I don't disbelieve any of it. (Even those parts I believe do not, for the most part, belong to my faith; they merely comprise some of my religious opinions.) I am not at all sure about "preternatural powers," for example, or about the proposition that God shields us from much evil and that the world would be far worse if he did not. The story I have told is, I remind you, only supposed to be a defense. It is not put forward as a theodicy, as a statement of the real truth of the matter, as I see it, about the co-presence of

God and evil in the world. I contend only that this story is — given that God exists — true for all we know. And I certainly don't see any very compelling reason to reject any of it. In particular, I don't see any reason to reject the thesis that God raised a small population of our ancestors to rationality by a specific action on, say, June 13, 116,027 B.C. — or on some such particular date. It is not a discovery of evolutionary biology that there are no miraculous events in our evolutionary history. It *could* not be, any more than it could be a discovery of meteorology that the weather at Dunkirk on those fateful days in 1940 was not due to a specific and local divine action. Anyone who believes either that the coming-to-be of human rationality or the weather at Dunkirk had purely natural causes must believe this on philosophical, not scientific, grounds. In fact the case for this is rather stronger in the case of the genesis of rationality, for we know a lot about how the weather works, and we know that the rain clouds at Dunkirk are the sort of thing that *could* have had purely natural causes. We most assuredly do not know that rationality could have arisen through natural causes — or, at any rate, we do not know this unless there is some philosophical argument that shows that *everything* has purely natural causes. And this is because everyone who believes that human rationality could have had purely natural causes believes this solely on the basis of the following argument: Everything has purely natural causes; human beings are rational; hence, the rationality of human beings could have had purely natural causes because it in fact did.

Suppose, then, for the sake of argument, that the defense I have presented is a true story. Does it justify the evils of the world? Or put the question this way. Suppose there were an omnipotent and omniscient being and that this being acted just as God has acted in the story I have told. Could any moral case be made against the actions of this being? Is there any barrier to saying that this being is not only omnipotent and omniscient but morally perfect as well? In my view, it is not self-evident that there is no barrier to saying this — but it is not self-evident that there is a barrier, either. The defense I have presented, the story I have told, should be thought of as the beginning of a conversation. If there is anyone who maintains that the story I have told, even if it is true, does not absolve a being who acts as I have supposed God to act from serious moral criticism, let that person explain why he or she thinks this is so. Then I, or some other defender of theism, can attempt to meet this objection, and the objector can reply to the rejoinder and . . . but so philosophy goes: philosophy is argument without end. As J. L. Austin said — also speaking on the topic of excuses — here I leave and commend the subject to you.

The Problem of Evil:
Moral Constraints and
Philosophical Commitments

Del Kiernan-Lewis

In this paper I want to explore an issue that I believe has received insufficient attention in contemporary discussions of the problem of evil, an issue central to the projects of atheologians who construct arguments from evil and to the projects of theists who construct defenses and theodicies. All three — arguments from evil, defenses, theodicies — require a commitment to some background principle of moral justification specifying the conditions that must obtain if a perfect being permits some instance of pain or suffering preventable by that being. My question is this: What are the logical connections between these principles of moral justification and what may be called the "metaphysics of theism"? In other words, to what degree do the justificatory constraints one places on God in the context of addressing the problem of evil depend on (or depend for their plausibility or dialectical usefulness on) nonaxiological philosophical assumptions one brings to the discussion — assumptions, for example about the extent of divine omniscience or about the creatability of various possible worlds?

Suppose it could be shown that there is a strong connection between the principle of moral justification employed by a particular argument from evil and other controversial theological or philosophical claims. In the strongest case, there would be a logical dependence: the moral principle is relevant to God's permission of evil only if some substantive theological or other philosophical claim is true. But it would also be interesting if only a weaker epistemic dependence could be discovered — namely, that no philosopher who did not take herself to reasonably believe the theological/philosophical claim would take herself to reasonably believe that the cited moral principle can be used to impugn or defend God's permission of evil.

In either case, the controversial status of the moral principle would appear to diminish significantly the dialectical force of any argument from evil which presupposes either the philosophical claim's truth or the epistemic preferability of that philosophical claim over its denial. Let me explain. The purported target of arguments from evil is typically what is called *generic theism*. Generic theism is the conjunctive proposition that an omniscient, omnipotent, perfectly good Creator exists. Of course, generic theism is false just in case one of its conjuncts is false. However, since candidates for the kinds of philosophical or theological claims I have in mind are controversial, none of the conjuncts of generic theism will constitute such a claim.

Roughly expressed, possible candidates have the following property: Most theists believe that one can be warranted in believing generic theism even if one is not warranted in believing this philosophical or theological claim. I have in mind such propositions as the following:

- God has middle knowledge.
- God causally determines every human action.
- Human freedom and determinism are logically incompatible.
- God is a necessary being.
- God is timeless.
- God can resurrect the same persons even if a materialist account of mind and personal identity is correct.
- All human beings will in the long run attain salvation from their sins and live in eternal union with God.

These propositions belong to the list of propositions theists of an historically orthodox Christian variety, at any rate, have disputed and disagreed over. Any argument from evil that involves ineliminable commitment to such propositions cannot be an argument against the rationality of generic theism per se.

Boethius famously turned an argument against the compatibility of divine foreknowledge and human freedom into a tool for theological revisionism. He embraced the logic but rejected the theological premise. In the spirit of Boethius, theists committed to the truth of generic theism who already reject some philosophical or theological claim presupposed by an atheologian's argument from evil may consistently endorse the atheologian's logic and thank him for providing them with yet another reason for rejecting that particular claim. Suppose, for example, that an argument from evil presupposes that God has middle knowledge. The theist who rejects middle knowledge may happily embrace this version of the argument from evil insofar as he takes the argument to be a reduction of the claim that God has middle knowledge.

Indeed, I seriously doubt that any remotely plausible theodicy, defense, or argument from evil can be constructed without presupposing, over and above generic theism, the sort of controversial propositions I have in mind. Of course, this may be the case even if such propositions are wholly unrelated to the principles of moral justification used in the argument. But this is to get ahead of the game.

The issue, to repeat, is whether and to what degree the moral constraints one places on God when discussing the problem of evil are related to significant nonethical philosophical claims about God and reality also presupposed in the same context. A recent exchange between William Rowe and Alvin Plantinga provides an ideal place to start our investigation. To adapt a point Plantinga has made about Aquinas and Calvin, few will deny that any claim Rowe and Plantinga agree on is a claim that philosophers of religion should take seriously. Rowe writes:

> What we do know, I believe, are some conditions that must hold between a good g and an evil e if it is to be true both that God exists and that g justifies God in permitting e. And I think Plantinga has elegantly set forth several such conditions. We know, for example, that if God exists and some evil e is actual, then g justifies God in permitting e only if (1) g is actual, (2) g outweighs e, (3) g cannot exist unless e is permitted to exist by a perfect being, and (4) no better world can be brought about if g and e are prevented by a perfect being. Let us, then, following Plantinga, say that if any one of these conditions fails to hold between a good g and an evil e, g fails to stand in J [the required justificatory relation] to e.[1]

Suppose that Rowe has accurately captured Plantinga's position, and that Plantinga and Rowe are correct: (1) through (4) are jointly necessary conditions for God's being justified in permitting whichever evils exist. If these conditions are to function as they do in Rowe's (or any other) argument from evil, then we must add another necessary condition, namely: (5) e exists only if God knows that e stands in J to g. For if God doesn't know that g stands in J to e, his basis for permitting e may be

---

1. William Rowe, "Reply to Plantinga," *Noûs* 32:4 (1998): 54.

undermined. And this implication has no intrinsic connection to constraints on divine action, but would appear to apply in any case where one puts forward necessary conditions which exculpate a moral agent from blame whenever she performs a particular action.

For example, suppose George is sitting in church with a hundred dollar bill in his pocket that he won at a poker game the night before. Moved by the visiting missionary's sermon on the plight of the homeless in Honduras, he wonders whether he should put his gambling winnings into the collection for Honduras hurricane victims. But suppose we place the following moral constraint on his possible donation:

(P1) George is justified in putting a hundred dollar bill in the offering plate only if that bill was never used to purchase illegal drugs.

Suppose George donates the bill and the bill is historically besmirched by a drug deal. Now there is a fact of the matter as to whether or not George is justified when he puts the bill in the collection plate. But, if George simply cannot tell whether the condition in P1 is satisfied, P1 would appear to be irrelevant to passing judgment on George's moral character. Assuming P1, one must say that George's action of donating the hundred dollar bill is unjustified. However, it isn't clear that any negative judgment follows about George himself — that is, about the goodness or badness of George insofar as he is the person who donates this particular hundred dollar bill. A negative judgment about George (that he cannot be perfectly good and have donated the bill) is not warranted unless we believe that George could be expected to know — or is able to know — whether the bill has the morally relevant feature cited in P1. And of course this isn't true of George. In other words, George's ignorance screens off P1 from any judgment about George's character based on our judgment about his action.

Likewise, it makes no sense to ascribe to God a moral defect on the basis of his failure to consider information in principle unavailable to him. Unless God is in a position to know whether conditions (1)-(4) are satisfied in the event that he permits e, then he is not in a position for us to regard conditions (1)-(4) as relevant to our moral judgment of his (real or hypothetical) permission of e. For if God does not know what he must in order to know that conditions (1)-(4) are satisfied, it will only be by chance or luck that God is justified in permitting e. Yet, if God exists and is so justified with respect to e, that g stands in J to e can't be merely fortuitous. This is the reason for making condition (5) explicit.

The significance of condition (5) becomes further apparent as soon as one considers condition (1), which says, "g is actual." What does this mean? (1) is part of what is supposed to follow "if God exists and e is actual." Why doesn't Rowe write "if God exists and e *exists*"? Because he is merely endorsing Plantinga, who proposes that a "good g justifies an evil e if there were a perfect being, and g and e were actual, then b would be justified by g in permitting e." And by the predicate "is actual" Plantinga means "exists in actual world alpha," where alpha is just that determinate possible world which happens to be the actual world. Therefore, g is actual just in case g did, does, or will exist in the history of alpha. And since even God can't know whether actual e stands in J to g unless God knows that g is actual, it follows that God knows that g is actual just in case God knows that g exists before, simultaneous with, or after e. Further suppose, along with Rowe and Plantinga, that goods not yet existing before T or at T, the time when e occurs — that is, goods that come about after T — may, in principle, serve to justify God's permission of e. In that case, given (5), it follows that, insofar as God knowingly permits e at T, he also knows that g will exist after (perhaps even long after) T.

And that, of course, is the rub, metaphysically speaking. It now looks as though condition (1) is relevant to God's permission of e at T only if either God at T foreknows which goods will indeed exist after T or, barring foreknowledge, God timelessly know which goods exist after T. Since it cannot be ruled out *a priori* that some of the goods which would justify God's permission of human suffering at T require the free actions and choices of persons after T, the first view implies divine foreknowledge of free human actions and choices. Notoriously, there is no consensus among contemporary theistic philosophers who endorse generic theism on the plausibility, coherence, or truth of these two views about the nature and extent of divine omniscience. What these two views share is a commitment to the following claim: God knows — either timelessly or beforehand — which possible world is identical to the actual world alpha. This is just a way of saying in possible-worlds jargon that God knows to the smallest detail which events were, are, or will be. This is precisely the sort of claim that is controversial among theistic philosophers.

Condition (2) only magnifies the problem with condition (1). (2) says that g outweighs e. This requires God to know that g is the kind of good whose value, were e to exist and g to stand in the appropriate relation to e, would outweigh the disvalue of e. But even God knows, *pace* Kant, that a possible yet nonexistent g, however much its inherent value relative to e's disvalue, cannot do any justificatory work. And this makes (2) dependent on the satisfaction of (1) if (2) is going to do nonhypothetical justificatory work.

At first glance, it might seem that in (3) we finally get to a condition that has no connection to controversial philosophical claims. But this initial impression won't stand once it is realized what God must know in order to know that, as (3) stipulates, "g cannot exist unless e is permitted to exist by a perfect being." If g exists after e and depends wholly or in part on the free actions or choices of persons in response to e, then the controversial claims generated by (1) arise once again for similar reasons. If, as Marilyn Adams and others have argued, a person's retrospective judgment of the value of some instance of suffering in her life is partly constitutive of the objective value of that suffering, and if that judgment at T2 — long after the suffering ends at T1 — cannot exist but for numerous free actions and choices occurring after T1 and before T2, then only by adopting controversial claims about freedom, foreknowledge or omniscience can we assume that God knows that, were he to permit e, g (which cannot exist unless e exists) will exist.

So much for the general point. But it is worth mentioning a further important difficulty with (3). Metaphysical considerations about omniscience aside, the following question is relevant to God's satisfying condition (3): In cases where the evil permitted is the suffering or pain of person S, must g (in part or entirely) be a good for S? Now eminent philosophical theists disagree on the answer to this question. Eleonore Stump says yes. Peter van Inwagen says no. Note that what we have here is a moral claim that, if it is true at all, is necessarily true. God had better know the answer if he is to act in accordance with (3). And we had better know the answer in order to understand how (3) constrains God's permission of evil. It would seem that any argument from evil which, for example, depends on Stump's answer for its plausibility must be dialectically irrelevant to van Inwagen's variety of theism.

By this point it should be apparent what I am going to say about condition (4), which says that "no better world can be brought about if g and e are prevented by a perfect being." The interpretation of (4) raises questions about which possible worlds God can (knowingly) bring about. These questions cannot be resolved without resolving the disputes over such controversial matters as middle knowledge, timelessness, incompatibilism, and so forth. On some views God can know (in advance or timelessly) which possible world W is alpha, and so that he "brings about" W; on other views not.

It might be objected that my argument so far only shows that Rowe's argument from evil and Plantinga's response thereto involve a commitment to controversial claims in virtue of their shared commitment to the relevant moral constraint they place upon God if he is to act rightly. However, this objection does not weaken the case for my general thesis, because the constraint Rowe and Plantinga apply to God's permission of evil is hardly idiosyncratic. In *God and Inscrutable Evil*, David O'Connor says "it is a virtual orthodoxy among philosophers of religion that the concept of God is incompatible with avoidable evil, divinely avoidable evil in particular. By avoidable or preventable evil I mean evil that could be avoided or prevented without forfeiting any greater or outweighing good."[2] Stephen Wykstra agrees with what he considers a claim essential to Rowe's argument from evil: "God would allow an instance of intense suffering only if doing so serves some outweighing good obtainable only by God's allowing this (or some comparable) evil."[3] Richard Swinburne writes that "if theodicy is to show that God is justified in allowing each of the actual evils of this world e which occur, it needs to show that (1) in allowing e (or an evil equally bad) to occur, God would bring about a logically necessary condition of some good state of affairs g which could not be achieved in any other morally permissible way; (2) if e occurs, g is realised, (3) it is morally permissible that God allow e to occur, (4) the comparative condition is satisfied."[4] It should be obvious that the general argument of this paper extends to these formulations as well.

The upshot of the foregoing discussion is that it is not possible to argue that generic theism is false on the basis of an argument from evil without implicit or explicit commitment to significant, controversial philosophical claims not (noncontroversially) entailed by generic theism — and so possibly false even if generic theism is true. If this is correct, then no argument from evil can succeed as an argument against generic theism. To get an argument against generic theism, the atheologian must supplement the argument from evil with other arguments showing that the extra philosophical claims either really are entailed by generic theism or can be established on independent philosophical grounds.

I do not mean to suggest that the atheologian cannot find what he

2. David O'Connor, *God and Inscrutable Evil: In Defense of Theism and Atheism* (Lanham, Md.: Rowman & Littlefield, 1998), p. 52.

3. Stephen Wykstra, "Rowe's Noseeum Arguments from Evil," in *The Evidential Argument from Evil*, ed. Daniel Howard-Snyder (Bloomington, Ind.: Indiana University Press, 1996), p. 127.

4. Quoted in O'Connor, *God and Inscrutable Evil*, p. 69.

takes to be such arguments. Indeed, nothing I have said shows that there cannot be a viable argument from evil against *some* variety of theism or that Rowe's conditions (1) through (4) are not necessary constraints on God's permission of evil. I do mean to suggest that the atheologian's circumstances significantly diminish the dialectical force of the argument from evil, which cannot live up to its common billing as an argument against the rationality of *all* varieties of theism.

I said early on in this paper that I seriously doubt that any remotely plausible theodicy, defense, or argument from evil can be constructed without presupposing, over and above generic theism, controversial philosophical or theological propositions. This may be so, even if those controversial claims are unrelated to moral claims. Thus I intend this paper to provide partial support for the following general principle:

(AE) Any argument from evil will implicitly or explicitly depend on at least one normative, metaphysical, or epistemological claim which is either (a) controversial among theists or (b) as controversial among philosophers as theism itself.

The general argument I endorse is therefore the following:

(1) All (remotely plausible) arguments from evil explicitly or implicitly depend on at least one normative, metaphysical, or epistemological claim that is both controversial and unnecessary for reasonable theistic belief.

(2) All claims that are both controversial and unnecessary for reasonable theistic belief can be rejected by some theists.

So, (3) No argument from evil succeeds as an argument against the rationality of all theists.

As Paul Draper has pointed out to me, (3) is ambiguous. It could mean:

(3a) There is no argument from evil that succeeds in making theism less rational for anyone, whatever their epistemic circumstances.

But this is not how I read (3), which should rather be taken to mean:

(3b) For any argument from evil A, there is a version of theism and a set of normative, metaphysical, and epistemological claims held

by some theist S such that argument A does not succeed in showing that S's believing that version of theism is not rational for S.

(3b), unlike (3a), follows from (1) and (2).

It may be objected that my position merely results from applying
the following general feature of all philosophical arguments to the problem of evil: Arguments about the truth (or falsity) of an interesting philosophical claim always deploy assumptions of a controversial sort not
(noncontroversially) entailed by that claim. So, runs the objection, my
conclusion about arguments from evil is both unsurprising and does little
to diminish the dialectical force of such arguments.

I admit the general point about philosophical arguments, but reject
the suggestion that no special insight has been gained into contemporary
presentations of arguments from evil. In defense of my position, consider
the following story. Suppose a man goes to his physician with a complaint about bad headaches. Following x-rays and a CAT scan, she sits
him down in her office and tells him that he has what appears to be an in-
operable tumor which typically kills most persons who have it within six
months. With a look of horror on his face, he says, "So this means I've
only got six months to live?" "Well, no," she replies. "It's true that the tumor is terminal in most people who have it, but only because 95 percent
of them are female. There's not a known case of a man dying from such a
tumor."

The point: What she initially said was true but misleading. It
seemed to imply something of mortal significance that it didn't in fact
imply. Her pronouncement did not mean what she justifiably said. Now
Rowe and other atheologians purport to have good arguments against
the reasonableness of theism per se — generic theism. They don't tend to
qualify the target of the argument — for good dialectical reasons, for the
aim is to show that generic theism is probably false. Therefore, the argument from evil is billed as (and is almost universally taken by
nontheistic philosophers who are not philosophers of religion to be) an
argument for the nonexistence of *God* — not as an argument for the non-
existence of a God *with middle knowledge* or *with perfect foreknowledge* or
who intends every event in history. As with the physician's comment to the
headache sufferer, the conclusions of Rowe's and other atheologians' arguments diminish drastically in dialectical force and relevance to belief
in God per se (i.e. to generic theism) as soon as the hidden assumptions
about divine nature are made explicit. For as soon as those assumptions
are made explicit, the theist (and nontheist) may simply take *them* to be

the problem. As I've already suggested, the only way for an atheologian to recover the dialectical force that his argument is supposed to have is to supplement the argument with an additional philosophical case that the following is necessarily or probably true: God can only exist if he has the nature presupposed by my argument. I don't know of any atheologian offering such an argument.

In concluding, let me suggest two ways that a theist may respond, in light of this discussion, when confronted with an argument from evil. First, consider the case of a theist who already rejects the key philosophical claim presupposed by the argument. For example, Rowe typically assumes middle knowledge in constructing his arguments from evil. One rational option for theists who reject middle knowledge is to grant Rowe that his argument is valid, but suggest that Rowe has merely constructed an excellent reductio of the view that God has middle knowledge. Grant me middle knowledge, says Rowe, and I have an argument to show that the probability of theism is very low. Hardly surprising, responds the theist who rejects middle knowledge: I already have an argument to show that the probability of the conjunction of *any* view with the claim that God has middle knowledge is zilch.

Second, this discussion suggests a general strategy for constructing defenses in response to arguments from evil. Suppose we say that a *good philosophical argument* must involve no premise p with the follow feature: It is as rational for a person to suspend judgment on the truth of p as it is for that person to believe that p. Then, when confronted with any putative argument from evil against the rationality of generic theism, the theist should look for those philosophical assumptions (metaphysical, epistemological, moral or meta-ethical) widely disputed either inside or outside the theistic (or nontheistic) philosophical community. She can then call attention to the fact that, since philosophers disagree about the truth of this key assumption, there must be some legitimate sense of rationality that renders it as rational to suspend judgment on the truth of this assumption as it is to believe the assumption. (Otherwise, it is hard to see how serious, honest philosophical inquiry ever generates rational beliefs.) So, in whatever sense it is rational for Eleonore Stump to disagree with Nick Wolterstorff, or for Bill Alston to disagree with Fred Dretske, or for Thomas Nagel to disagree with Daniel Dennett, in spite of the fact that they all understand each other's arguments, it must also be rational for a theist to reject the key assumption in the argument from evil. Hence, the theist may note that, due to this assumption, the argument cannot be a *good philosophical argument* for its conclusion.

So do all arguments from evil fail? Well, yes, precisely in the same way — and *only* in the same way — that all arguments for controversial philosophical claims fail. It all depends on what you mean by "failure." At any rate, if appeal to controversial claims or assumptions renders a philosophical argument unsuccessful, then there just are no successful philosophical arguments for controversial claims. Except, of course, the indubitably sound arguments in this paper.

The Problem of Pomegranates

Stephen Griffith

Foreword

The tone of this paper is likely to be offensive to atheists and to many theists as well. It may seem that the problem of evil is not being taken seriously, and that this displays an insensitivity to human and animal suffering. In response, it should be noted that no human being aware of the basic facts of life can reach adulthood without being painfully aware of the distribution and intensity of suffering that prevails in this world. Atheists should not be allowed the conceit that only they are sufficiently aware of these realities, and theists should not feel obligated to demonstrate their awareness and sensitivity by reciting a catalog of existing or hypothetical but realistic horrors whenever they discuss this problem, as if there were some of their readers who needed to be informed of such things. Having said this, it must nevertheless be once again acknowledged that the world does contain horrendous evils, and that the tone of this paper might make it inappropriate to be of much use in pastoral counseling of those who experience suffering. But in a purely abstract and intellectual discussion such as this, there would seem to be no point in being morbid or depressing.

Pomegranates are absolutely delicious, or at least some of us think so. Unfortunately, they are also notoriously difficult to eat. Other things being equal, the world would certainly be a better place if pomegranates were a more readily edible fruit. As it is, all lovers of pomegranates are faced with the practical problem of how best to indulge in their passion for this delectable delicacy. Pomegranatophilial theists, however, are faced with an even more difficult problem of a philosophical or theological nature known as the "Problem of Pomegranates." Here's the problem. God is said to be omniscient, omnipotent, and omnibenevolent. An omniscient deity, however, would know that, other things being equal, the world would be a better place if pomegranates were easier to eat. If this deity were also omnipotent, he would be able to create such a world, and if he were omnibenevolent, then he would want to do so, since, by hypothesis, such a world would be a better place than this one. But this has not happened. Therefore, there is no omniscient, omnipotent, and omnibenevolent deity, and thus no God.

Both philosophers and non-philosophers alike are likely to find this argument against the existence of God somewhat less than compelling. Most philosophers, however, will also notice that the "problem of pomegranates" (POP) as stated above bears a striking resemblance to what is often referred to as the "logical" form of the notorious "problem of evil" (LPOE) suggested by Hume in the eighteenth century and defended more recently by the firm of Mackie, McCloskey, and Flew, Atheists at Large,[1] as an argument against the existence of God. In particular, they will notice that although neither POP nor LPOE are presented as deductively valid arguments, they nevertheless have (or can readily be given) the same "formal structure" or "broadly logical" form. Thus, for example, both POP and LPOE could be described as consisting of propositions of the following form:

Schema

(1) God is said to be omniscient, omnipotent, and omnibenevolent.

(2) If God is omniscient, he knows that, other things being equal, the world would be a better place if the proposition (α) were true instead of the proposition (β).

(3) If God is omnipotent, he is able to create a world in which other things are equal, but in which the proposition (α) is true instead of the proposition (β).

(4) If God is omnibenevolent, he prefers a world in which other things are equal but in which the proposition (α) is true instead of the proposition (β).

---

1. See J. L. Mackie, "Evil and Omnipotence," *Mind* 64 (1955): 200-212; H. J. McCloskey, "God and Evil," *Philosophical Quarterly* 10, no. 39 (1960); Antony Flew, "Divine Omnipotence and Human Freedom," in *New Essays in Philosophical Theology*, ed. Antony Flew and Alasdair MacIntyre (New York: Macmillan, 1955), pp. 144-69.

(5) The proposition (β) is true, and the proposition (α) is false.

Roughly speaking, the POP could be generated from this schema by substituting a proposition like "pomegranates are delicious but difficult to eat" for (β) and a proposition like "pomegranates are a delicious, readily edible fruit" for (α), thereby obtaining

(1) God is said to be omniscient, omnipotent, and omnibenevolent.
(2) If God is omniscient, he knows that, other things being equal, the world would be a better place if the proposition "pomegranates are a delicious, readily edible fruit" were true instead of the proposition "pomegranates are delicious but difficult to eat."
(3) If God is omnipotent, he is able to create a world in which other things are equal, but in which the proposition "pomegranates are a delicious, readily edible fruit" is true instead of the proposition "pomegranates are delicious but difficult to eat."
(4) If God is omnibenevolent, he prefers a world in which other things are equal, but in which the proposition "pomegranates are a delicious, readily edible fruit" is true instead of the proposition "pomegranates are delicious but difficult to eat."
(5) The proposition "pomegranates are delicious but difficult to eat" is true, and the proposition "pomegranates are a delicious, readily edible fruit" is false.

Similarly, and with a corresponding roughness (and it is significant that this can be done only roughly), the LPOE can be generated from this schema by substituting propositions dealing with such things as the Holocaust, bubonic plague, or simply evil in general for (β) and the corresponding negations of such propositions for (α). In other words, an atheist who wished to use the LPOE to disprove the existence of God might say something like this:

(1) God is said to be omniscient, omnipotent, and omnibenevolent.
(2) If God is omniscient, he knows that, other things being equal, the world would be a better place if the proposition "it is not the case that evil exists" were true instead of the proposition "evil exists."
(3) If God is omnipotent, he is able to create a world in which other things are equal, but in which the proposition "it is not the case that evil exists" is true instead of the proposition "evil exists."
(4) If God is omnibenevolent, he prefers a world in which other things

are equal, but in which "it is not the case that evil exists" is true instead of the proposition "evil exists."

(5) The proposition "evil exists" is true, and the proposition "it is not the case that evil exists" is false.

So the POP and the LPOE have the same logical form. Indeed, if we regard the fact that pomegranates are delicious but difficult to eat as an "evil," the POP can be regarded as an instance or special case of the LPOE. Any logically competent atheist can use the schema employed in the generation of both the POP and the LPOE to generate a veritable plethora of similar "problems" for the theist. All he needs to do is to select contingent facts about the world that he finds displeasing (and that he suspects the theist will find displeasing both to herself and to God), and then substitute propositions asserting and negating those facts for α and β appropriately.

As mentioned previously, however, no one would find an argument against the existence of God which was based on the POP compelling. Superficially, based on the "logic" of the argument, it is tempting to suppose either that they both work or that neither does. But the POP is uncompelling. Under this supposition, then, it would appear that if the atheist wants to use the LPOE to disprove the existence of God, he must show either that the POP, despite all appearances to the contrary, actually works, or that the POP and the LPOE, all appearances to the contrary, are actually significantly different, which he can do only by reformulating the argument in a more complex way.

Now even the LPOE is uncompelling for most philosophers, or at least for most of those philosophers who attend most closely to the problem of evil in all its forms. It might thus appear that we have little to gain by examining the atheist's options here, but actually such an examination is quite instructive and can tell us something about the evidential argument from evil[2] as well. Since the POP is uncompelling, let us begin our examination by asking why. What exactly is wrong with the POP? Most people, no doubt, would be quick to point out that the fact that pomegranates are both delicious and difficult to eat is not really such an evil thing, if it is "evil" at all. It certainly is not the first thing one thinks of when pondering the "evils" of this world. As philosophers, however, we should not be so quick to beg this question. On the contrary, we should at least ask ourselves what we mean when we say that something is "evil"

2. This problem will be defined later (p. 91).

in a context of this sort. What sort of thing are we thinking of when we say of something that it is "evil" in any sense which might give rise to the LPOE? The most obvious answer we could give would probably be that we are thinking primarily of suffering, or better yet, of anything of which we can say "would that it were not so." Within this context, this would seem to include both the frustration of desires and the involuntary imposition of things to which we are averse. But this does not suffice to distinguish the POP from the LPOE.

Both the POP and the LPOE can be regarded as complaints about the actual world, or about some aspect of that world. The POP is of concern to Frustrated Lovers of Pomegranates (FLOPs), who complain about their frustrations in satisfying their desire to consume their favorite fruit, whereas the LPOE is of concern to Frustrated Awful World Naysayers (FAWNs), who complain about things as diverse as the Holocaust, the bubonic plague, and even the existence of certain parts of New Jersey. Moreover, neither FLOPs nor FAWNs would be satisfied with just any way of eliminating the cause of their complaints.

With regard to the POP, it is important to note that there are many sorts of possible worlds in which the POP would not have arisen. If, for example, there had been no people, or at least no sentient creatures of the sort who could enjoy eating pomegranates, there would have been no POP, and the same would be true if there had been no pomegranates. We can also imagine a world in which either the underlying chemical structure of pomegranates or the neurobiological structure of the human gustatory system (or perhaps we should say of their counterparts in another possible world) differ from the corresponding structures in the actual world in such a way that human pomegranatophilia does not exist in that world. FLOPs, however, would not prefer any of these alternatives to the actual world. On the contrary, they would prefer a world containing both lovers of pomegranates and an abundance of readily edible fruit tasting exactly like pomegranates. Similarly, there are many possible worlds in which the LPOE would not have arisen. We can readily imagine a world in which there are no sentient organisms (and thus no suffering), or perhaps a world in which there are no organisms at all (assuming that the concept of a non-sentient organism makes sense). FAWNs, however, would generally not prefer either of these worlds to the actual world. A FAWN would presumably be satisfied only with a world in which sentient organisms exist but never suffer, or at least do not suffer nearly as much as they do in the actual world. But is such a world really possible?

The POP is uncompelling because we simply do not think that the ability to eat pomegranates easily is very important. Thus, even if God could have (and perhaps should have?) made them (or their counterparts in another possible world) easier to eat, the fact that he has not done so does not bother us very much. The LPOE, on the other hand, to the extent that it is taken seriously, is so taken because the evils typically referred to in its formulation are quite bothersome and thus far more difficult to overlook. But in the case of these sorts of evils, it is not at all obvious that God could have avoided them in any way that would be satisfactory to a FAWN. More precisely, it is not so obvious that God could have created a world containing human beings like us but no FAWNs. One cannot satisfy one who is complaining about the state of the world simply by shooting him. In order to satisfy a FAWN, God would need to have created a world remarkably similar to this one, but without any of the evils that are upsetting to the FAWN. But what this shows is the unavoidable subjectivity of the problem. The status of the LPOE as a "problem" depends essentially on the existence of rational and sentient organisms whose "expectations" concerning the world (which are in this case based on a particular, admittedly somewhat traditional, concept of the Creator) do not match reality. But here we have a difficulty. Assume that the "logic" of the LPOE (and thus the POP) were unproblematic. Now imagine that our ability to consume and enjoy pomegranates were the only thing that mattered to us. If this does too much violence to the concept of a person, imagine some other sort of rational and sentient creature that cares only for one earthly thing. I am under the impression that koalas eat only eucalyptus leaves and have no natural enemies, so perhaps they care only about these leaves. If they were also rational and theistic, and if there were a severe shortage of eucalyptus leaves, they would have a problem (POEL)[3] reconciling this shortage with the existence of God, and their problem would seem serious, like the LPOE, rather than trivial, like the POP. On a more personal note, I have a pet pig, Newton, whose physical and emotional needs are entirely satisfied by his master. Newton is unaware of the existence of either predators or ham sandwiches. The only thing that ever happens in his life that seems to upset him in any way is having his hooves trimmed. Newton does not share his theological musings with me, but if he did, hoof trimming would undoubtedly be sufficient to generate the LPOE (or the POHT) for him. (If you wish, you may fill in the schema given earlier to see how this would be done.) The point is that if

3. I.e., the Problem of Eucalyptus Leaves.

the logic of the LPOE were sound, the only way of avoiding the "problem" it presents would be for God to create a "perfect" world, or at least a world which was perfect from the point of view of whichever creature ponders the LPOE.

This, of course, seems completely unreasonable, and moves us to the so-called "evidential" problem of evil (EPOE), which is based not on the mere existence of evil, but rather on the nature and extent of such evil as does in fact exist. In other words, the EPOE is the problem of explaining how an omnipotent, omniscient, and omnibenevolent deity could allow so much evil in the world, and evil of such a horrendous nature. Here we can see that, in the context of the EPOE, the POP is not really a problem. The frustrations experienced by FLOPs are simply not sufficiently evil to generate the problem, and from our point of view, at least, neither are the problems that concern Newton and the rational koalas. But we can also see that we are now faced with a new problem. The question now before us is this: How much evil is enough (or too much)? For many people, the Holocaust is certainly enough, or the plague, and for some the existence of certain parts of New Jersey does the trick. But how do we measure or compare different sorts of evil?

Suppose we could all agree as to exactly what features of our world are to be counted as evil, and suppose we could also agree on how to measure it, so we could agree as to the specific total amount of evil which exists in the actual world, say, E. Would this be too much? Would it be so much that we would be justified in saying that an omnipotent, omniscient, and omnibenevolent God simply could not permit it? The answer to this question obviously depends on our expectations. But what should our expectations be? This again depends on our exact understanding of what God is like. But simply listing the three traditional attributes mentioned above, unqualified, is inadequate. Paul Draper[4] suggests that $P(E/{\sim}G) \gg P(E/G)$, where G = God exists. In other words, he suggests that the probability of the world containing the exact amount of evil that it does on the hypothesis that God does not exist is much, much greater than the probability of the world containing that same amount of evil on the hypothesis that God does exist. He further insists that we not define the existence of God in such a way as to suggest that God might have an excuse

4. See, for example, Paul Draper, "Pain and Pleasure: An Evidential Problem for Theists," *Noûs* 23 (1989): 331-50; and "The Skeptical Theist," in *The Evidential Argument from Evil*, ed. Daniel Howard-Snyder (Bloomington, Ind.: Indiana University Press, 1996), pp. 175-92.

or justification for the evils in this world. But why should we agree to this? Does this not simply beg the question? We might just as well insist that the statement that there is such-and-such evil in the world not imply that there is any evil that cannot be reconciled with the existence of God. More appropriately, why not insist that God's goodness be defined in terms of the fact that he never permits the existence of evil without justification? Again, why not insist that the idea that God would prefer not to allow evil be an additional hypothesis that Draper needs for his inequality (instead of the theist needing an extra hypothesis about God's reasons)? The bottom line here is that $P(E/G)$ is either indefinable or defined unfairly, at least from a theistic point of view.

Still, what about FAWNs? Let's get our FAWNs in a Rowe.[5] Take any specific complaint (e.g., Rowe's complaint about the innocent fawn — Bambi, perhaps? — who is burned horribly in a forest fire and suffers a slow and agonizing death afterwards). How can or could we justify the existence of such an evil thing on theistic grounds? It seems that the request for a justification of this sort is inherently unreasonable. No matter what justification were given, the FAWN could always come up with an additional complaint, either real or hypothetical, and we would never be able to satisfy him, since, as mentioned previously, nothing less than a perfect world (from his point of view, of course) would do.

For the theist, the best course of action to follow at this point is to take the same sort of position that various philosophers have used so effectively against the LPOE. It would be beyond the scope of this paper to describe any such position in detail, but as I have argued elsewhere,[6] we might begin by sketching out a modified version of the free will defense so capably pursued by Alvin Plantinga. According to this line of argument, the omnibenevolence of God requires that his rational creatures be endowed with meaningful freedom. Meaningful freedom in turn requires that it be possible for those creatures who possess it not only to intend evil, but also to bring these intentions to fruition much if not most of the time. It also requires that the physical universe exhibit regularities of a sort that will inevitably produce a certain amount of suffering in the natural course of events. The theist is thus free to claim that all of the evil in the actual world can be explained in terms of one of these requirements, neither of which God can logically avoid without rendering our

---

5. William L. Rowe, "The Problem of Evil and Some Varieties of Atheism," *American Philosophical Quarterly* 16 (1979): 335-41.
6. In "Plantinga's Punt," unpublished.

lives inexcusably meaningless. The atheist, of course, will insist that the theist offer some proof of this claim, but this immediately raises the question as to where the burden of proof lies in this instance. After all, the atheist cannot prove that this claim is false either. So how should we decide whether to accept or to reject this claim?

At this point, the so-called "parent analogy"[7] seems to be appropriate. Imagine that during a visit to the home of some acquaintance, a toddler who has been playing in the backyard runs into the house with pink stains on her mouth and hands. The toddler is too young to indicate where the stains came from, but the host suggests that they might have come from berries on his yew bushes, which happen to be poisonous. This immediately raises the concern that the toddler might have ingested some of the berries. But again, the toddler is unable to answer any questions as to whether she has consumed any berries. Since there is no antidote, it seems that the best course of action is to rush the child to the hospital and have her stomach pumped, a rather unpleasant experience, especially for someone who has no idea what is going on. From the child's point of view, this experience is "evil" in a sense perfectly appropriate in the context of this paper. It is especially unpleasant, and yet it is clearly not only permitted but in this case brought about by the child's own parents, parents who supposedly love the child, would not want the child to suffer, and, as far as the child can see, have no reason to inflict this suffering on her. Why, she thinks, would her parents do this to her, or allow this to happen to her? After all, they must surely know that it is extremely unpleasant for her, since she is clearly expressing that fact through her tears. And they surely could have refrained from bringing her to the hospital and allowing this procedure to be performed. No one, in other words, forced them to do this. Finally, they surely would not want her to suffer. So why must this happen? This child is clearly in a position relative to her parents that is analogous to that of a FAWN with regard to God. She has a complaint about her parents that she does not know how to resolve. One important disanalogy here, of course, is that in

---

7. Cf. Stephen Wykstra, "The Humean Obstacle to Evidential Arguments from Suffering: On Avoiding the Evils of 'Appearance,'" *International Journal for Philosophy of Religion* 16 (1984): 73-93; and "Rowe's Noseeum Arguments from Evil," in *The Evidential Argument from Evil*, ed. Daniel Howard-Snyder (Bloomington, Ind.: Indiana University Press, 1996), pp. 126-50. The illustration as used in this paper differs slightly from Wykstra's in that the toddler is sufficiently developed mentally to not only suffer but also to feel a sort of frustration similar to that felt by a believer who "expects more of God."

this case there is no doubt as to the existence of her parents. Another disanalogy is that her parents, unlike God, are neither omnipotent nor omniscient, but this turns out to be irrelevant for present purposes because the parents need not be omniscient to know, as they do, that the child is suffering, and they need not be omnipotent to be able to, as they do not, refrain from inflicting that suffering. The point of this analogy, after all, has to do with the child's knowledge, not with any limitations the parents might or might not have. We, of course, are in a position to understand why the parents do what they do, and would presumably do the same thing. The child, however, does not understand why she is being made to suffer. More importantly, she is not, by hypothesis, even capable of understanding this. There is nothing her parents could say to her that would enable her to understand, and this is a limitation on her part, not on theirs. But our position with respect to God is quite similar. Not even the wisest among us is capable of understanding things in the manner that our Creator understands them. Our knowledge, and thus our ability to understand things, is even more deficient in comparison to that of God than the child's knowledge is in comparison to that of her parents. We are thus free to believe that there is some reason for all of the evil in the world, even if we do not always know what that reason might be. To claim that there is not, much less that there cannot be, such a reason, is to claim to know more than any human being could possibly know. The atheist, of course, would claim that the burden of proof is on the theist, but why should we accept this? If we know how to reconcile much of the evil in the world with the existence of God, and we do, and we know that we do not (cannot) know everything, we are certainly justified in at least entertaining the possibility that the remaining evil can be reconciled as well. After all, the toddler in the example given above not only knows that her parents exist, but also has good reason to believe that her parents love her, even though she does not (and, by hypothesis, cannot) comprehend their behavior in this instance. She has, in other words, a rational faith in their goodness and love. Should we not have the same with respect to God, and for similar reasons?

Suffering as Religious Experience

Laura Waddell Ekstrom

Introduction

Works of literature, accounts of human history, and the events of everyday life confront us directly with the reality of pain and suffering. Some of us of a melancholy (some might say morbid) disposition are overcome with worry over this reality. Lighthearted neighbors and friends perplex us. How do they carry on so, trimming their yards and enjoying the weather, all the while maintaining faith in a perfect and provident Lord of the universe? Is it out of callousness, shallowness, blessedness, or wisdom? Have they any dark nights of the soul or anguish over the cries and shed blood of their fellow creatures? The worry leads some of us to academic study of the problem of evil. But our answers are incomplete and fail fully to satisfy. O God, where are you through the violent violation of a woman? Why tarry when a child falls feverish and is ripped from life too soon? Why still your hand through war, betrayal, and pain?

Yet through our own suffering, confusion and bitterness may take a startling turn. Job's heartrending cries of injustice against the Almighty become the breathtaking utterance, "My ears had heard of you but now my eyes have seen you."[1] In his suffering, Job reports, he has met God. God has shown himself, made himself known to the sufferer. The philosopher Nicholas Wolterstorff gives something of a similar account in his report of a vision of God. As we strain to discern an explanation for divine permission of suffering, "instead of hearing an answer," Wolterstorff

1. Job 42:5.

writes, "we catch sight of God himself scraped and torn." He attests: "Through the prism of my tears I have seen a suffering God."[2] God is seen, God is known, in suffering.

The aim of this paper is to explore the idea of suffering as a kind of religious experience. It is argued by David Hume, William Rowe, and Paul Draper, among others, that pain and suffering constitute evidence against the existence of God.[3] But perhaps at least some such instances of pain and suffering are, rather, avenues to knowledge of God. Many individuals, Wolterstorff and Job among them, report that the times during which they have suffered the most deeply are the occasions of the most vivid of whatever glimpses they have been given into the character of God. The experiences are marked, that is, by intimacy with the divine. Is not precisely this the mark of (at least one important type of) religious experience? And is not suffering as a means to intimacy with God exactly what one would expect of a God who, on Christian scripture and tradition, took on human form and suffered along with and for the world?[4]

Understanding some instances of human suffering as means to intimacy with the divine makes available a line of partial theodicy distinct from the traditional soul-making, punishment, and free will theodicies. I call it the *divine intimacy theodicy*. The theodicy is suggested to an extent in the work of such contemporary philosophers as Marilyn Adams, Nicholas Wolterstorff, and Eleonore Stump, as well as in the writings of many Christian mystics of the medieval and later periods, including, for instance, Therese of Lisieux (1873-1897).[5] Why would the divine agent per-

2. Nicholas Wolterstorff, *Lament for a Son* (Grand Rapids: Eerdmans Publishing Co., 1987), pp. 80-81.

3. David Hume, *Dialogues Concerning Natural Religion*, ed. Richard Popkin (Indianapolis: Hackett, 1980); William Rowe, "The Problem of Evil and Some Varieties of Atheism," *American Philosophical Quarterly* 16 (1979): 335-41; Paul Draper, "Pain and Pleasure: An Evidential Problem for Theists," *Noûs* 23 (1989).

4. According to orthodox Christian tradition, the person of Jesus Christ suffered for us, yet God the Father is not capable of suffering.

5. Marilyn McCord Adams, "Redemptive Suffering: A Christian Solution to the Problem of Evil," in *Rationality, Religious Belief, and Moral Commitment*, ed. Robert Audi and William J. Wainwright (Ithaca, N.Y.: Cornell University Press, 1986), and "Horrendous Evils and the Goodness of God," *Proceedings of the Aristotelian Society*, supplementary vol. 63 (1989), pp. 297-310; Wolterstorff, *Lament for a Son*, and "Suffering Love," in *Philosophy and the Christian Faith*, ed. Thomas V. Morris (Notre Dame, Ind.: University of Notre Dame Press, 1988); Eleonore Stump, *Faith and the Problem of Evil: The Stob Lectures, 1998-99* (Grand Rapids: The Stob Lectures Endowment, 1999), and "The Mirror of Evil," in *God and the Philosophers*, ed. Thomas V. Morris (New York: Oxford University Press, 1994), pp. 235-47, and "The Problem of Evil," *Faith and Philosophy* 2:4 (1985): 392-418.

mit instances of evil? Perhaps a reply applicable to some instances of personal suffering is this: in order to provide occasions in which we can perceive God, understand him to some degree, know him, even meet him directly. In this essay I explore the plausibility of this line of thought.[6]

The Nature of Religious Experience

Religious experience is variously characterized. Rudolf Otto (1869-1937) describes it as experience in which the soul is "held speechless, trembles inwardly to the farthest fiber of its being," as it faces something so forceful and overwhelming that one feels oneself to be "dust and ashes as against majesty." The experience is one of "fear and trembling" but also of "wonderfulness and rapture."[7] The Christian mystic Teresa of Avila (1515-1582) reports an experience in which the mystic is

> conscious of having been most delectably wounded. . . . [The soul] complains to its Spouse with words of love, and even cries aloud, being unable to help itself, for it realizes that he is present but will not manifest himself in such a way as to allow it to enjoy him, and this is a great grief, though a sweet and delectable one. . . . So powerful is the effect of this upon the soul that it becomes consumed with desire, yet cannot think what to ask, so clearly conscious is it of the presence of God.[8]

John of the Cross (1542-1591) describes experience in which the understanding of the soul "is now moved and informed by . . . the supernatural light of God, and has been changed into the divine, for its understanding and that of God are now both one."[9]

One way of understanding religious experience is on analogy with sensory experience of the physical world. One might say that religious

6. The divine intimacy theodicy most likely has some measure of plausibility only when applied to human suffering and not to the suffering of non-human animals. Nonetheless, the matter is open in the absence of conclusive information concerning the capacities of members of other species.

7. Rudolf Otto, *The Idea of the Holy* (London: Oxford University Press, 1936), pp. 17-26, 31-33.

8. *The Interior Castle*, trans. and ed. E. Allison Peers (Garden City, N.Y.: Doubleday Image, 1961), pp. 135-36.

9. *The Living Flame of Love*, trans. and ed. E. Allison Peers (Garden City, N.Y.: Doubleday Image, 1962), p. 78.

experience is experience of the divine by way of some perceptual faculties, perhaps including a special spiritual faculty or a *sensus divinitatus*. So as not to beg any questions concerning the veridicality of the experience, religious experience might be defined more cautiously as experience that the agent *takes to be* of the divine: experience perceived by the perceiver as acquaintance or intimacy with God. William Alston, for instance, understands religious experience as "(putative) direct awareness of God."[10]

I propose to understand the category of religious experience rather broadly. I consider the term 'religious experience' to apply appropriately to at least the following three types of experience. First, a religious experience may be an experience in which it seems to one that one perceives God. Examples include a vision of divinity, a sense of God's presence during prayer or worship, and a feeling of God's nearness and comfort. Such experiences are regularly had by some theists. But an atheist may have them as well, as in Paul's experience on the road to Damascus.

Second, the category of religious experience includes experiences *like* those of God — experiences of the same sort as God's own experiences. In the Christian tradition, we could describe religious experience of the second sort as experience like that of one of the three persons comprising God. Or perhaps, so as not to beg any questions, we should describe the second type of religious experience as experience like what God would experience were God to exist with a nature as depicted by Christian scripture and tradition.

Third, an experience counts as a religious experience if it brings to consciousness the issue of God's nature and existence and makes vivid one's own attitude regarding this issue. Religious experiences of the third sort may include, for example, experience showing us ugly, horrifying or frightening aspects of the world; experience of our own capacity for evil; and experience of our frailty. Such experiences tend to bring to mind questions concerning the existence of God, as well as questions concerning the goodness, power, and knowledge of God. Religious experiences of the third type also include experiences carrying a sense of awe or wonder, such as witnessing the birth of a child or feeling moved by the beauty of a natural scene: the vista from a mountaintop or a seashore, for example.

Each of these types of experience has a legitimate claim to being re-

---

10. William Alston, *Perceiving God: The Epistemology of Religious Experience* (Ithaca, N.Y.: Cornell University Press, 1991), p. 35.

ligious in character. Consider an atheist who was raised in a religious family. She might sensibly describe her observations of pervasive poverty and disease during a visit to India as a *religious experience:* the experience raised vividly for her the problem of evil and occasioned her realization that she had become an atheist. A theist's sense of the majestic presence of God during worship is religious experience of a different (the first) sort: it is experience in which one is putatively aware of God. Further, insofar as it makes sense to describe experience like an eagle's (say, soaring above the rooftops) as *avian experience,* and insofar as it makes sense to describe experiences of running, jumping, and playing with toys *childhood experience,* so too there seems room for counting experiences similar to those of the divine being — if there is any — *religious experience.*

Why Count Suffering as Religious Experience?

Is it plausible to suppose that some instances of suffering qualify as religious experiences as characterized above? Testimonial evidence supports the claim that instances of suffering are sometimes instances of religious experience of the first type: experience in which it seems to the perceiver that he or she is aware of the presence of God. Consider, as one example, the divine vision recounted by Julian of Norwich in the midst of suffering a severe illness for which she had received last rites: "At once I saw the red blood trickling down under the garland, hot, fresh, and plentiful, just as it did at the time of his passion when the crown of thorns was pressed on to the blessed head of God-and-Man. . . . And I had a strong, deep, conviction that it was he himself."[11] She reports of the divine being: "I saw that he is to us everything which is good and comforting for our help. He is our clothing, who wraps and enfolds us for love, embraces us and shelters us, surrounds us for his love."[12] Many individuals in sorrow and pain have reported a vision of the divine or a feeling of God's nearness and comfort in their distress.

It is likewise reasonable to consider some occasions of suffering as religious experiences of the third type: experiences that vividly raise fundamental religious questions and illuminate one's commitments re-

---

11. Julian of Norwich, *Revelations of Divine Love* (New York: Penguin Books, 1984), p. 66.

12. Julian of Norwich, Long Text 5, quoted in *Enduring Grace: Living Portraits of Seven Women Mystics* (New York: HarperCollins, 1993), p. 88.

LAURA WADDELL EKSTROM

garding them. One's becoming the victim of a crime, for instance, or suffering a debilitating physical injury, commonly brings to one's mind the question of God's existence and nature. The experience of hardship is often a sort of testing experience in which one "shows one's true colors," demonstrating one's deepest commitments. Suffering is a religious experience of the third sort in driving us to seek God or in causing doubt, reinforcing unbelief, or in generating questions concerning God's nature and existence.

I would like to focus more attention on the notion that some instances of suffering qualify as religious experience of the second type: experiences *like* those of God.

Suppose that, as on traditional Christian doctrine, God created persons in order for them to love and to be intimate with him and to glorify him forever. Suppose that persons were once in a state of intimacy with God, but that we rebelled by choice, with the consequence that we suffer physical and emotional pain, as well as the spiritual pain of being out of harmony with the Creator. Suppose that God enacted a plan for reestablishing our harmony with him involving his taking on human form and suffering rejection, torture, and execution.

From the perspective of one who adopts this account, some human suffering may be viewed, in fact, as a kind of privilege, in that it allows us to share in some of the experiences of God and thus gives us a window into understanding his nature. Some instances of suffering are avenues for intimacy, oneness, with God. One cannot love what one does not know, and one means of knowing someone is to have experience like hers. Naturally we feel affinity toward and grow to understand and to cherish other persons with experiences similar to our own. These include educational, career, and family experiences, but also experiences of illness and adversity. A person whose experiences are quite different from one's own is difficult for one to come deeply to understand and fully to appreciate. Shared experiences facilitate dialogue in providing something in common about which to converse, and they make possible understanding that is beyond words, communicated perhaps with understanding looks or gestures. The parent of an ill newborn knows something about the other parents in the emergency room without their exchanging any words. Lovers become intimate through sharing experiences. Victims of a similar sort of oppression or injustice understand each other in a way that outsiders to their experience cannot.

For the Christian, then, instances of suffering can be occasions for identification with the person of Jesus Christ. Intimacy with Christ gained through suffering provides deeper appreciation of his passion.[13] I understand the notion of *identification with Christ* in a sympathetic rather than a mystical sense: the claim is not that the sufferer bears Christ's *actual* sufferings, as, first, it is unclear what the point of that bearing would be and, second, the mystical view would seem to require quite peculiar views concerning pain. Rather, I mean to suggest that the sufferer may sympathetically identify with Christ in sharing similar experience, as any other two persons identify with each other in the loose sense that they connect with, appreciate, or understand each other better when they share experiences of the same type or similar types.

Several objections immediately arise. The first is that this aspect of the theodicy is so thoroughgoingly Christian. Since I accept the truth of orthodox Christian doctrine, this objection is from my perspective otiose. But to widen the appeal of the theodicy, we can set aside reference to the person of Christ and understand suffering as experience like that of God, like that of the divine being, if we join Wolterstorff and others in affirming, against tradition, that God is not impassible but is, rather, a God who suffers. Suppose, for instance, that God grieves over human sin. Then in feeling deep sorrow over the neglect and abuse of children, and in having regret and disapproval over the poverty and arrogance in our world, a person may have experience *like* God's and so may have a glimpse into the divine nature. An individual's own sorrow and suffering may, then, be a means to understanding and having intimacy with the divine being.

---

13. Marilyn McCord Adams similarly suggests that instances of suffering, even horrendous ones, might be made *meaningful* by being integrated into the sufferer's relationship with God through identification with Christ, understood either as sympathetic identification (in which each person suffers her own pain, enabling her to understand something of Christ's suffering) or as mystical identification (in which the human sufferer literally experiences a share of Christ's pain). Alternately, Adams suggests, meaningfulness may derive from suffering serving as a vision into the inner life of God, either because God is not impassible, or because the sheer intensity of the experience gives one a glimpse of what it is like to be beyond joy and sorrow. She proposes, as well, that sufferings might be made meaningful through defeat by divine gratitude which, when expressed by God in the afterlife, gives one full and unending joy. "Horrendous Evils and the Goodness of God," *Proceedings of the Aristotelian Society*, supplementary vol. 63 (1989), pp. 297-310; reprinted in *The Problem of Evil*, ed. Marilyn McCord Adams and Robert Merrihew Adams (New York: Oxford University Press, 1990), pp. 209-21.

Divine Passibility

On the traditional conception of the divine nature, God is not affected by anything and so cannot suffer.[14] The doctrine of impassibility is defended primarily by appeal to philosophical considerations, including reflection on the natures of perfection, immutability, and transcendence. But the doctrine of divine impassibility has been recently criticized by a number of philosophers, including Alvin Plantinga, Charles Hartshorne, Charles Taliaferro, Kelly James Clark, Nicholas Wolterstorff, and Richard Swinburne. Like Wolterstorff's avowal of a suffering God, Plantinga, for instance, affirms the existence of a God who "enters into and shares our suffering." Plantinga writes: "Some theologians claim that God cannot suffer. I believe they are wrong. God's capacity for suffering, I believe, is proportional to his greatness; it exceeds our capacity for suffering in the same measure as his capacity for knowledge exceeds ours."[15]

Of the considerations in favor of rejecting divine impassibility, the most salient from my perspective are the scriptural evidence and the natures of goodness and love. Many biblical passages depict God as experiencing emotions that entail suffering. Consider the following: "The LORD was grieved that he had made man on the earth, and his heart was filled with pain" (Gen. 6:6). "I have seen these people, the LORD said to Moses, and they are a stiff-necked people. Now leave me alone so that my anger may burn against them and that I may destroy them" (Exod. 32:9-10). The writer of Psalm 78 describes how the Israelites "grieved [God] . . . they vexed the Holy One of Israel" (41-42) and speaks of God's "wrath, indignation and hostility" (49). Consider, as well: "Praise be to the Lord, to God our Savior, who daily bears our burdens" (Ps. 68:19).

Impassibilists dismiss such passages as mere anthropomorphism. Commenting on Genesis 6:6, for example, John Calvin writes:

> Since we cannot comprehend [God] as he is, it is necessary that, for our sake, he should, in a certain sense, transform himself. . . . Certainly God is not sorrowful or sad; but remains forever like himself in his celestial and happy repose; yet because it could not otherwise be

---

14. The Westminster Confession of Faith (II.1) states: "There is but one . . . true God, who is infinite in being and perfection, a most pure spirit, invisible, without body, parts, or passions. . . ."

15. "Self-Profile," in *Alvin Plantinga,* ed. James E. Tomberlin and Peter van Inwagen (Dordrecht: D. Reidel, 1985), p. 36.

known how great is God's hatred and detestation of sin, therefore the spirit accommodates himself to our capacity. . . . God was so offended by the atrocious wickedness of men, [he speaks] as if they had wounded his heart with mortal grief.[16]

According to Calvin, God permits biblical writers to use figures of speech about himself in accommodation to humanity's limited capacities of understanding. Given interpretive differences, the impassibility issue cannot be settled, of course, simply by citing biblical material. Nonetheless, a passibilist conception of God, it must be admitted, fits most naturally with the scriptural account of God's activities and involvement with human beings. The impassibilist must explain away or reinterpret numerous passages that, on their face, suggest that God is affected by and suffers over his creation.

On the traditional conception of the divine agent, God is not only omnipotent and omniscient, but also wholly good and perfectly loving. A number of philosophers, including Wolterstorff and Taliaferro, have registered their rejection of the Greek-influenced medieval conception of divine love as non-suffering benevolence. The argument is that apathy, unperturbed emotional indifference to the plight of humanity, is incompatible with God's love of humanity.

Here is why the incompatibility claim seems right. Suppose that we understand love, rather uncontroversially, as consisting in or at least essentially involving concern for the well-being or flourishing of a beloved object. This understanding of love applies equally to love of a cause or of an ideal or of a person, but I am concerned particularly with love of persons. In his recent work on love, Harry Frankfurt adds that the lover's concern for the beloved is disinterested, in the sense that the good of the beloved is desired by the lover for its own sake rather than for the sake of promoting any other interests.[17] Frankfurt emphasizes that lovers are not merely concerned for the interests of their beloveds; further, they *identify* the interests of the beloveds as their own.[18] And he argues that if the lover "comes to believe that his beloved is not flourishing, then it is unavoidable that this causes him harm."[19] Lack of

16. *Calvin's Commentaries,* vol. 1, trans. and ed. John Owen (Grand Rapids: Baker Book House, 1979), p. 249.

17. Harry Frankfurt, "On Caring," in *Necessity, Volition, and Love* (Cambridge: Cambridge University Press, 1999), p. 165.

18. Frankfurt, "On Caring," p. 168.

19. Frankfurt, "On Caring," p. 170.

flourishing in the beloved, by the nature of love, causes harm in the lover.

Of course, it could be claimed that this account applies only to instances of human love and not to divine love. But the move appears *ad hoc*. If love of someone consists in or essentially involves concern for her well-being, then it involves valuing, or having concerned approval for, her flourishing and disvaluing, or having concerned disapproval for, her harm. To say that I love my daughter, yet that I experience no sorrow, grief, or passion of any kind at her pain or disgrace, stretches the concept of love beyond comprehensibility. Furthermore, since one can love something only insofar as one is acquainted with it, it would seem that God cannot love us fully without knowing us fully. But our being fully known requires acquaintance on the part of the knower with our suffering and with the evil in our world.[20] Thus, reflection on the nature of love supports the conception of a God who suffers.

Further support for the possibility of God comes from the consideration of the nature of goodness. A morally good being grieves over evil. In a recent book offering an extended defense of the traditional doctrine of divine impassibility,[21] Richard Creel argues in part that it serves no *purpose* to attribute suffering to God, as God may act out of love and justice without being sorrowful. But to the contrary, we question the goodness of an agent who acts correctly towards victims of crime or disease, yet wholly without sorrow or empathy for the persons served. Passibilism, Creel argues, makes God worthy of our pity rather than our worship. But a great moral character, one worthy of worship, shows itself great in part by its sorrow, what it sorrows over and to what degree. Noble sorrow at witnessing a tragic occurrence is a good. Hence it would seem that God's goodness and love include sorrow, as well as joy, over the world. This sorrow is arguably not a defect, but a strength or an asset, a part of being supremely good.

Taliaferro understands divine sorrow as "concerned disapproval." "God disapproves of our cruelty and malice," he writes, "God cares about our failures, and this concerned disapproval may rightly be counted as an instance of sorrow."[22] Consider, for instance, Miriam's

---

20. Cf. Nicholas Wolterstorff, "Suffering Love," in *Philosophy and the Christian Faith*, ed. Thomas V. Morris (Notre Dame, Ind.: University of Notre Dame Press, 1988), p. 223.

21. Richard E. Creel, *Divine Impassibility* (Cambridge: Cambridge University Press, 1986).

22. Charles Taliaferro, "The Possibility of God," *Religious Studies*, vol. 25: 220.

rape. Taliaferro writes: "Part of what it means to be sorrowful here is that you do disapprove of it, the harming of someone who matters to you, and you disapprove of this profoundly. Any tenable notion of the goodness of the God of Christian theism must include the supposition that God exercises profound, concerned disapproval of creaturely ills."[23] It does seem reasonable to suppose that the God who is love, the God who is perfectly good, is deeply concerned for persons and suffers profound sorrow over their sins and afflictions. It is facile to presume oneself too sophisticated to go in for such supposed "sentimentalism." Proponents of the divine impassibility doctrine must defend it further against substantive religious and moral reasons for concluding that God suffers.

Objections: Pathology, Cruelty, and Inefficacy

In this section, I consider four central objections to a divine intimacy theodicy. The first, which I will address only briefly, comes from the direction of one unconvinced of the passibility of God. I have suggested that there is reason to think that God does suffer, provided by scripture and by reflection on the natures of goodness and love. But should the considerations in favor of the attribute of impassibility prove in the end more powerful, the divine intimacy theodicy is not thereby defeated. If suffering cannot be religious experience in the sense of being experience like that of God himself, it can qualify still as religious experience of the first and third sorts, and thus it can be justified as a means to intimacy with the divine. Furthermore, should traditional impassibilism survive recent attacks, Christian theism can yet make sense of suffering as experience shared with the person of Jesus Christ and so can count some occasions of suffering as avenues to intimacy with God through sympathetic identification with Christ.

A second and potentially more damaging objection is this: To view suffering as religious experience is evidence of a personality disturbance or psychological disorder. That is, it seems to indicate not right thinking but pathology that a person would glory in suffering or see spiritual dimensions to pain. The objection gains force from considering the physical conditions of the lives of some Christian mystics of the medieval and later periods who viewed suffering in such a manner. For instance, the Cistercian nun Beatrice of Nazareth (1200-1268), the author of *The Seven Manners of Love*, is reported to have deprived herself of food, worn un-

---

23. Taliaferro, "Passibility," p. 220.

comfortable garments, scourged herself, and slept on thorns.[24] Other religious figures may strike us as melodramatic and distressingly passive in their welcoming attitudes toward suffering. Consider the remarks of Therese of Lisieux concerning the onset of symptoms of the tuberculosis that took her life at the age of twenty-four:

> Oh! how sweet this memory really is! After remaining at the Tomb until midnight, I returned to our cell, but I had scarcely laid my head upon the pillow when I felt something like a bubbling stream mounting to my lips. I didn't know what it was, but I thought that perhaps I was going to die and my soul was flooded with joy. However, as our lamp was extinguished, I told myself I would have to wait until the morning to be certain of my good fortune, for it seemed to me that it was blood I had coughed up. The morning was not long in coming; upon awakening, I thought immediately of the joyful thing that I had to learn, and so I went over to the window. I was able to see that I was not mistaken. Ah! my soul was filled with a great consolation; I was interiorly persuaded that Jesus, on the anniversary of his own death, wanted to have me hear his first call. It was like a sweet and distant murmur that announced the Bridegroom's arrival.[25]

Therese welcomes the blood in her cough as the answer to her prayer that God consume her with his love, that God carry her to him quickly, and that she be allowed to share in the suffering of Christ. She declares in her "Act of Oblation to Merciful Love":

> I thank you, O my God! for all the graces you have granted me, especially the grace of making me pass through the crucible of suffering. It is with joy I shall contemplate you on the last day carrying the scepter of your cross. Since you deigned to give me a share in this very precious cross, I hope in heaven to resemble you and to see shining in my glorified body the sacred stigmata of your passion.[26]

In light of such passages, it may strike one as at best wishful thinking and, worse, indicative of a psychiatric condition, to believe that God is with one or is providing one intimacy with himself through suffering.

24. *Women Mystics in Medieval Europe*, ed. Emilie Zum Brunn and Georgette Epiney-Burgard, trans. Sheila Hughes (New York: Paragon House, 1989), p. 72.

25. *Story of a Soul: The Autobiography of St. Therese of Lisieux*, trans. John Clarke O.C.D. (Washington, D.C.: ICS Publications, 1996), pp. 210-11.

26. *Story of a Soul*, p. 277.

But of course those who report experience of supernatural phenomena are notoriously subject to the charge of being delusional. And certainly adopting the proposed partial theodicy need not lead one to self-mutilation or to other eccentric or damaging behaviors. The view under consideration is perfectly consistent with a mandate to *alleviate* suffering so far as possible and with a mandate not to self-impose pain. Furthermore, which views indicate spiritual insight and which indicate a condition in need of medical or psychological treatment is a matter of opinion. As it stands, the objection from pathology amounts to no more than the claim that it seems to the objector that the proposed view is crazy or, in other words, false. Without any further positive reasons to doubt the sanity of the proponent of the divine intimacy theodicy, other than that she believes the view, the objection is dismissible.

The objector might respond by pointing to such factors as social isolation, inadequate sleep, poor nutrition, and lack of medical care in the lives of some religious mystics. These circumstances, it may be argued, indicate that the view of suffering as religious experience is pathological and not reasonable. Yet surely these considerations are inconclusive. Recall C. D. Broad's remark that a person "might need to be slightly 'cracked' in order to have some peep-holes into the super-sensible world."[27] Difficult living conditions might in fact facilitate spiritual insight. Furthermore, a charge of insanity against every adherent to a divine intimacy theodicy is grandiose.

A third objection is an objection from cruelty. Why would a loving God create such a cruel way of our getting to know him? Why would suffering as a *means* to knowing God be preferable to direct divine self-revelation? Since permitting suffering is a cruel way of fostering intimacy, the objection goes, the perfect being would not be justified in this permission and so the account of suffering as religious experience fails as a partial theodicy.

It is surely troubling to conceive of God as declaring to created beings in a tone of sinister delight, "Suffer, and then I will let you know me," as if enduring a crucible of suffering were a passkey. But this image inaccurately reflects the divine intimacy theodicy. A perfect being does not, of course, delight over suffering, but rather causes or allows it when it is necessary to bringing about a greater good or preventing a worse evil. And the suggestion I am exploring is that, perhaps, some occasions

---

27. C. D. Broad, "Arguments for the Existence of God. II," *Journal of Theological Studies* 40 (1939): 164.

of suffering are necessary for certain individuals' coming to love of and intimacy with God. The objector may counter that some persons experience God in moments of great joy and beauty. Yet this may be true while it is also true that other persons' paths to God are paths through suffering. And it may be that the good thereby achieved could not be achieved in any other way: namely, the profound good of appreciation for and intimacy with a loving and suffering God.

The objector might be troubled with the question of why God would not simply show himself at all times, to everyone. Here the right line of response may be that for God to directly, constantly, and obviously manifest his presence would be coercive.[28] Perhaps God's remaining somewhat hidden protects our freedom, preserving our independence of thought and action. The rationale behind divine hiddenness may be something like this: I (the divine agent) will not intervene in the natural course of events to prevent your difficulties and your suffering, in part because perhaps then you will appreciate the ways in which I have loved and provided for you all along; perhaps you will freely come to recognize that acting wholly by your own lights is unsuccessful and that you need my help; perhaps you will be rid of some of your arrogance and will recognize your limitations. Suffering, that is, may be for some persons the most effective non-coercive means to achieving the end of love of and intimacy with God. Additionally, it may be that it is impossible fully to know God without personally experiencing suffering, because God himself suffers. If God is passible in emotion, then there is something that a person could not know about God if she did not suffer, one aspect of God's being that would remain entirely mysterious.

The fourth and final objection I will consider is this: a common reaction to suffering is not a sense of intimacy with the divine but rather confusion and rejection of God's existence. Suffering is easily interpreted as evidence that God does not exist or does not care about the sufferer. Hence, many cases of suffering, particularly those of non-theists, cannot plausibly be construed as religious experience.

In response, first, the divine intimacy theodicy is not designed to apply to all cases of suffering. Second, from the fact that some persons reject the existence of God on the basis of suffering, it does not follow that some occasions of suffering do not provide an *opportunity* for intimacy with God. We can choose, it seems, the manner in which we respond to

---

28. Michael J. Murray, "Coercion and the Hiddenness of God," *American Philosophical Quarterly* 30 (1993): 27-38.

suffering, including which types of attitudes we adopt in the midst of it. The thesis at issue is not that meaning *is* always found in suffering by everyone who suffers, but rather that a certain kind of meaning *can* be found in suffering, through divine intimacy.

Suffering might be religious experience without the sufferer recognizing it as such. This claim seems unproblematic, since a person can have an experience of a certain type without ever recognizing it as an experience of that type. Consider the following examples. First, suppose that Keith thinks that he is devising a novel line of reasoning. But in fact he is remembering a conversation in which someone else recounted a certain line of thought. Keith is having a memory experience, but he does not, and need not ever, recognize it as such. Second, suppose that Sandra begins thinking about chance and providence. Although she need not ever recognize the experience as such, she may be having a telepathic experience of the thoughts of Peter, who is across the room. Third, imagine a husband who begins to have indigestion, headaches, and back pain during the pregnancy of his wife. He consults his doctor, who finds his symptoms mysterious. He is, perhaps, having an empathic experience without realizing it. The concept of a religious experience, unrecognized as such, appears cogent.

Conclusion

A full justificatory account of suffering may be unattainable for us. I have simply sketched here and begun to explore the suggestion that one justifying reason for certain instances of suffering is that those occasions constitute religious experiences. Some cases of suffering may be viewed as kinds of experience that can bring a person closer to God, such that the good either in or resulting from them is intimacy with the divine agent.

The account of suffering as religious experience may have use not only as a partial theodicy, but also as a method for the theist for dealing with the existential problem of evil. That is, one way of enduring unchangeable occasions of pain and suffering may be to adopt an attitude of acceptance and, oddly, enjoyment in identifying with God. Consider how this might work, in particular, for a Christian theist. One in the midst of dealing with a deep betrayal of loyalty, for instance, might call to mind the thought, "As I have been rejected, Christ was rejected even by his close friend, Peter," and take comfort in the sympathetic identification. Likewise, although perhaps Christ never experienced precisely the particular physical pain from which one suffers, the sufferer is in part able to appreciate something about the person of Christ that perhaps not all others fully can: the sacrifice of his passion.[29]

29. I am grateful to Michael Murray and Kelly James Clark for comments on an earlier version of this essay.

The Gospel of Redemptive Suffering:
Reflections on John Paul II's *Salvifici Doloris*

Eduardo J. Echeverria

> *Through Christ and in Christ, light is shed on the riddle of sorrow and death. Apart from His Gospel, it overwhelms us.*[1]

> *The scandal of the Cross remains the key to the interpretation of the great mystery of suffering, which is so much a part of the history of mankind.*[2]

> *All who suffer in this world, the sick and incurable and dying, those in prison and tortured, the oppressed and those who are hopelessly poor, must know that, in their situation, they are not condemned to total powerlessness; if they unite their hopelessness with that of the crucified Son of God, they will do more to build the real kingdom of God than many an architect of earthly happiness.*[3]

> *The believing philosopher should not hesitate to include the redemptive vision of his faith in his speculation.*[4]

1. Vatican II Council, *Gaudium et Spes*, par. 22.
2. John Paul II, *Crossing the Threshold of Hope* (New York: Knopf, 1994), p. 63.
3. Hans Urs von Balthasar, "Hosanna — for Which Liberation Theology?" in *You Crown the Year with Your Goodness: Sermons through the Liturgical Year* (San Francisco: Ignatius Press, 1982), p. 74.
4. Louis Dupre, "Philosophy and the Mystery of Evil," in *Religious Mystery and Rational Reflection* (Grand Rapids: Eerdmans, 1998), p. 60.

111

> *Reason has its own domain, and faith hers. But reason can enter the*
> *domain of faith by bringing there its need to ask questions, its desire*
> *to discover the internal order of the true, and its aspiration to wis-*
> *dom — that's what happens with theology. And faith can enter the*
> *domain of reason, bringing along the help of a light and a truth*
> *which are superior, and which elevate reason in its own order — that*
> *is what happens with Christian philosophy.*[5]

Advice to Christian Philosophers

Pope John Paul II's reflections on the meaning of human suffering in his apostolic letter *Salvifici Doloris*[6] do not start from a religiously neutral position. This philosopher-Pope undoubtedly thinks it perfectly appropriate, in philosophical enquiry, to appeal to what he knows by way of faith. It isn't that John Paul leaves questions about God, evil, and suffering entirely in the hands of faith. He sketches some traditional arguments suggesting that the idea of a God infinite in knowledge, goodness, and power is compatible with the actual existence of evil. The philosopher-Pope accepts philosophical reason's modest yet legitimate demand, in Louis Dupre's words, "to perceive how an open conflict between a good God and an evil world is *not inevitable*."[7] And yet John Paul agrees, I think, with Dupre, who writes: "The very standards by which we mea-

5. Jacques Maritain, *The Peasant of the Garonne* (New York: Holt, Rinehart and Winston, 1968), p. 142.

6. John Paul II, *Salvifici Doloris*, apostolic letter, February 11, 1984. Subsequent references to this apostolic letter will be cited parenthetically in the text; hereafter the following abbreviations apply: *Salvifici Doloris* = SD, par. = paragraph number. Calvinist philosopher Alvin Plantinga praises this papal document highly: "*Salvifici Doloris* [is] surely one of the finest documents (outside the Bible) ever written on this topic, and surely required reading for anyone interested in the so-called problem of evil, or the problems that suffering can pose for the Christian spiritual life or, more generally, the place of suffering in the life of the Christian." Nicholas Wolterstorff, Richard J. Bernstein, and Alvin Plantinga, review of *Fides et Ratio, Books and Culture*, July/August 1999: 32. In the third volume of his trilogy on the notion of warrant entitled *Warranted Christian Belief* (New York: Oxford University Press, 2000), Plantinga repeats his judgment that *Salvifici Doloris* is "a profound meditation on suffering and a powerful effort to discern its meaning from a Christian perspective"; indeed, he calls it a "seminal work" in the "larger project of Christian scholarship, of discerning the ways in which Christian belief illuminates many of the important areas of human concern" (n. 38 and n. 46, at p. 488 and p. 493, respectively).

7. Dupre, "Philosophy and the Mystery of Evil," p. 54.

sure what does and what does not count as 'good' depend upon the acceptance or rejection of an intrinsically religious hierarchization of values. Any attempt to erect a system of values upon a religiously neutral basis, common to believers and unbelievers, fails precisely in the area where theodicy matters most, namely in deciding what must count as *definitive* evil." "Varying ontological commitments," adds Dupre, "'widen or narrow the range of options for defeating evil with good'."[8] Such value-theory pluralism justifies Christians to let revealed truth enter the domain of reason, says Maritain, "bringing along the help of a light and a truth which are superior, and which elevate reason in its own order — that is what happens with Christian philosophy."

Indeed, John Paul affirms that "revealed truth offers the fullness of light and will therefore illumine the path of philosophical inquiry."[9] Accordingly, engaging the data of revelation has enriched philosophical inquiry (*FR*, par. 74). Philosophical reason "is offered guidance and is warned against paths which would lead it to stray from revealed Truth and to stray in the end from the truth pure and simple." But the influence of faith is not exercised purely as a negative norm, as though Christian philosophers strive in their theorizing merely not to contradict the faith (*FR*, par. 63). "Instead," the Pope adds, "reason is stirred to explore paths which of itself it would not even have suspected it could take. This relationship with the word of God leaves philosophy enriched, because reason discovers new and unsuspected horizons" (*FR*, par. 73). Indeed, faith should have a positive influence on philosophical reflection.

Most important, the Pope not only accepts the concept of Christian philosophy as legitimate, but also boldly urges us to develop what he explicitly calls "Christian philosophy," which is not "an official philosophy of the Church, since the faith as such is not a philosophy"; rather it is "a Christian way of philosophizing, a philosophical speculation conceived [and practiced] in dynamic union with faith" (*FR*, par. 76). Philosophizing in faith, from an intrinsically Christian point of view, is not theology. Philosophy does respond to faith's own need for reflection, which is faith in search of understanding — *fides quaerens intellectum;* but that is theology. In a Christian way of philosophizing, faith enters the domain of

8. Dupre, "Philosophy and the Mystery of Evil," p. 59. The quote within quotes is from Marilyn McCord Adams, "Problems of Evil: More Advice to Christian Philosophers," *Faith and Philosophy* 5 (April 1988): 129.

9. John Paul II, *Fides et Ratio*, encyclical letter, September 14, 1998, par. 79. Subsequent references to this encyclical will be cited parenthetically in the text; hereafter the following abbreviations apply: *Fides et Ratio* = *FR*; par. = paragraph number.

reason "without ever demeaning the venture proper to reason" (*FR*, par. 78). And this is, the philosopher-Pope adds, "an undoubted boon for philosophy, which has thus glimpsed new vistas of further meanings which reason is summoned to penetrate" (*FR*, par. 101). In sum, he advises Christian philosophers "to illumine the range of human activity by the exercise of a reason which grows more penetrating and assured because of the support it receives from faith" (*FR*, par. 106).

One aspect of Christian philosophy is the subjective dimension in which "faith purifies reason" (*FR*, par. 76). "Faith liberates reason from [the] presumption [of self-sufficiency]," adds John Paul, "the typical temptation of the philosopher." This is intellectual pride, which is an expression of "gnoseological concupiscence," or a "carnal mind," as St. Paul puts it (Col. 2:18), the sinful inclination that sets us against God (cf. *FR*, par. 18-23). As a consequence, according to the Pope,

> The philosopher who learns humility [in faith] will also find courage to tackle questions which are difficult to resolve if the data of revelation are ignored — for example, the problem of evil and suffering, the personal nature of God and the question of the meaning of life or, more directly, the radical metaphysical question, 'Why is there something rather than nothing.' (*FR*, par. 76)

This paper is about all three of the problems John Paul alludes to in this last citation — the problem of evil and suffering raises the fundamental question of human life's meaning, particularly the question of the meaning of suffering, and, in brief, of a suffering person's relationship with the blessed Trinity, Father, Son, and Holy Spirit.

The Limits of Theodicy and the Idea of Salvation

"Human suffering evokes *compassion;* it also evokes *respect,* and in its own way *it intimidates.* For in suffering is contained the greatness of a specific mystery" (*SD*, par. 4). The mystery is adumbrated in the experiences of personally suffering or of sharing in the sufferings of those one loves. Suffering, in other words, "in its subjective dimension, as a personal fact contained within man's concrete and unrepeatable interior," says the Pope, "seems almost inexpressible and not transferable." Suffering is both subjective and passive, in the sense that it involves a submission such that I become the subject of suffering. But suffering is also marked by a "specific 'activity'," that is, marked by the "multiple and subjectively differentiated 'activity' of pain, sadness, disappointment, discouragement or even despair, according to the intensity of the suffering subject" (*SD*, par. 7). This suffering degrades and alienates my very being because it appears to me to make no sense, to have no purpose, no justification, and to be of no use (*SD*, par. 27).[10] Yet "nothing else requires as much as does suffering," he adds, "*in its 'objective reality'*, to be dealt with, meditated upon, and conceived as an explicit problem; and that therefore basic questions be asked about it and the answers sought" (*SD*, par. 5). In particular, in human suffering there is always the experience of some particular evil, whether in oneself or in others, as repugnant and this experience raises two questions: (1) Is suffering intrinsically evil? and (2) What is evil?

Consider the many forms that suffering may take: chest pains from a heart attack, grief, loss or emptiness when a loved one dies, sorrow, sickness, righteous anger in the face of unjust oppression, deep repentance and guilt for one's sins, and so forth. Can any of these kinds of suffering be shown to be good in some way? Pain has a biological function in serving as an alarm signal when something is going wrong with our body, warning us that we had better take appropriate action. As one author puts it, "It is known that approximately one out of every 400,000 babies born is fated to live a short life, due to a genetic disease called familial dysautonomia, a disease of feeling no pain. Such a child will cut himself, burn himself, fall down and break bones, without feeling any pain. Pain prevents us from doing any further damage. As Harold B. Kushner says, pain seems to be the price we pay for being alive."[11] "Suffering also tempers the individual's character," says Emmanuel Levinas. As Nicholas Wolterstorff observes, "In the valley of suffering despair and bitterness are brewed. But there also character is made. The valley of suffering is the vale of soul-making."[12] The pain and suffering that accompany punishment, discipline and education also have a social function, because this contributes to the social order of society. Lastly, "no pain, no gain," is the common adage,

10. On this aspect of suffering, see Y. A. Kang, "Levinas on Suffering and Solidarity," *Tijdschrift voor filosofie* 59, no. 3 (1997): 482-504; Stan van Hooft, "The Meaning of Suffering," *Hastings Center Report* 28, no. 5 (1998): 13-19; and Emmanuel Levinas, "Useless Suffering," in *The Provocation of Levinas: Rethinking Other,* ed. Robert Bernasconi and David Wood (New York: Routledge, 1998), pp. 156-67.

11. Kang, "Levinas on Suffering and Solidarity," p. 487.

12. Nicholas Wolterstorff, *Lament for a Son* (Grand Rapids: Eerdmans, 1987), p. 97.

and this seems right since there is no achievement in science, art, and architecture without paying the price of pain and suffering.

These and other instances of suffering involve accurate knowledge of human nature, our physical and moral makeup, which means that some suffering is, then, an appropriate reaction to some real state of affairs. Insofar as this is the case, then, despite the fact that human beings suffer whenever they encounter any kind of evil (*SD*, par. 7), the evil may be absorbed by an outweighing good and thus the suffering is not in itself evil; it is a positive reality, good in itself. As Germain Grisez has said: "Suffering generally also serves the important function of motivating people, as pain motivates animals to escape evil and/or struggle to overcome it. . . . The evil of a heart attack is the destruction of part of the heart's tissue, not the pain in the chest which a conscious victim of heart attack experiences. (The pain causes heart attack victims to rest and seek help; if they felt no pain, death would be more likely.) Just as some people are blind or deaf, some lack the sense of pain, and that lack is a serious handicap. . . . Similarly, the evil of being a sinner is not guilt feelings but the sin of which one is guilty, whether or not one suffers feelings of guilt. (Guilt feelings cause sinners to repent; if they feel no guilt, damnation is more likely.)"[13] One may thus say that the evil is logically necessary for producing an outweighing good, which has absorbed the evil.[14] Some suffering can be meaningful as a means with an end in view, and thus in itself it is not evil.

What, then, is evil? "Christianity proclaims the essential *good of existence* and the good of that which exists, acknowledges the goodness of the Creator and proclaims the good of creatures," according to John Paul II. So evil is not a positive reality in its own ontological right. The Pope embraces the Augustinian account of evil as a deprivation or distortion of a good that should have been but is not; in short, evil is an absence of the good. "We could say that man suffers *because of a good* in which he does not share," he adds, "from which in a certain sense he is cut off, or of

---

13. Germain Grisez, *The Way of the Lord Jesus*, vol. 2, *Living a Christian Life* (Quincy, Ill.: Franciscan Press, 1993), p. 32. See also John Saward, *Christ Is the Answer: The Christ-Centered Teaching of John Paul II* (New York: Alba House, 1995), especially pp. 85-89. I owe much both to Grisez's and Saward's short reflections on human suffering. Also helpful in this regard is Avery Dulles, S.J., *The Splendor of Faith: The Theological Vision of Pope John Paul II* (New York: Crossroad Publishing Co., 1999), pp. 89-93.

14. On the notion of absorbed evils, see J. L. Mackie, *The Miracle of Theism* (Oxford: Clarendon Press, 1982), p. 154.

which he has deprived himself. He particularly suffers when he 'ought' — in the normal order of things — to have a share in this good, and does not have it" (*SD*, par. 7).

Whence, then, comes evil? Here, too, John Paul assumes the Augustinian free will defense: the moral evil conceived and executed by human beings is a result of the misuse of their freedom; they introduced evil into God's good creation. According to the Pope,

> Sin was not only possible in the world in which man was created as a rational and free being, but it has been shown as an actual fact 'from the very beginning'. Sin is radical opposition to God. It is decidedly and absolutely not willed by God. However, he has permitted it by creating free beings, by creating the human race. He has permitted sin that is the consequence of the abuse of created freedom. This fact is known from revelation and experienced in its consequences. From it we can deduce that from the viewpoint of God's transcendent Wisdom, in the perspective of the finality of the entire creation [of human beings], it was more important that there should be freedom in the created world, even with the risk of its abuse, rather than to deprive the world of freedom by the radical exclusion of the possibility of sin.

So the risk of evil is logically implied by the good of significantly free and rational creatures.[15] But it isn't the generic good of human free-

---

15. John Paul II, *A Catechesis on the Creed*, vol. I, *God, Father, and Creator* (Boston: Pauline Books & Media, 1996), p. 260. He places great value on significant freedom: "Full of paternal solicitude, God's authority implies full respect for freedom in regard to rational and free beings. In the created world, this freedom is an expression of the image and likeness to the divine Being itself, to divine freedom itself. Respect for created freedom is so essential that God in his Providence even permits human sin (and that of the angels). Pre-eminent among all but always limited and imperfect, the rational creature can make evil use of freedom, and can use it against God, the Creator. . . . In the case of moral evil, however, that is, of sin and guilt in their different forms and consequences also in the physical order, this evil decisively and absolutely is not willed by God. Moral evil is radically contrary to God's will. If in human history this evil is present and at times overwhelming, if in a certain sense it has its own history, it is only permitted by divine Providence because God wills that there should be freedom in the created world. The existence of created freedom (and therefore the existence of man, and the existence of pure spirits such as the angels . . .), is indispensable for that fullness of creation which corresponds to God's eternal plan. . . . By reason of that fullness of good which God wills to be realized in creation, the existence of free beings is for Him a more important and fundamental value than the fact that those beings may abuse their freedom against the Creator, and that freedom can therefore lead to moral evil" (pp. 259, 271).

dom that is the finality of their creation. If I understand John Paul II correctly, the outweighing good that significant freedom produces is the friendship of God. He says, "At the root, there is no mistaken or wicked decision by God, but rather his choice — and in a certain manner the risk he has undertaken — of creating us free, in order to have us as friends. Evil too has been born of liberty. But God does not give up, and he predestines us with his transcendent wisdom to be his children in Christ, directing all with strength and sweetness, so that the good may not be overcome by evil."[16]

The claim that sin results from the misuse of our free wills has often been used as a way of justifying the connection between suffering, punishment, and justice. According to Aidan Nichols, "From such sin there flows certain other aspects of human suffering, such as the physical pain inflicted by evil people, or the fear and anxiety which good people undergo when faced with the prospect of evil people. From moral evil there may also follow kinds of suffering which could be seen as divine punishment for sin."[17] In this view, we find a common response to suffering, which is to think of it as just punishment. Suffering is a punishment inflicted by God for humanity's moral evil. John Paul defends this suffering as a positive reality, or good in itself; it seems to be meaningful as a means with an end in view. As he says,

> The God of Revelation is the *Lawgiver and Judge* to a degree that no temporal authority can be. For the God of Revelation is first of all the Creator, from whom comes, together with existence, the essential good of creation. Therefore, the conscious and free violation of this good by man is not only a transgression of the law but at the same time an offense against the Creator, who is the first Lawgiver. Such a transgression has the character of sin. . . . *Corresponding to the moral evil of sin is punishment,* which guarantees the moral order in the same transcendent sense in which this order is laid down by the will of the Creator and Supreme Lawgiver. (*SD,* par. 10)

16. John Paul II, *Catechesis on the Creed,* vol. I, pp. 316-17. On the same point, the Holy Father writes earlier in the same work: "By God's Providence, however, if on the one hand he has permitted sin, on the other, with the loving solicitude of a father, he has foreseen from eternity the way of reparation, of redemption, of justification and of salvation through love. Freedom is ordained to love. Without freedom there cannot be love. In the conflict between good and evil, between sin and redemption, love has the last word" (p. 260).

17. Aidan Nichols, O.P., *The Shape of Catholic Theology* (Collegeville, Minn.: Liturgical Press, 1991), p. 68.

So God sometimes causes suffering as a just punishment for the moral evil of sin. But even more, suffering in this sense has meaning not only because the one who suffers does so justly as a punishment for sin, says the Pope, "but first and foremost because it creates the possibility of rebuilding goodness in the subject who suffers." "This is an extremely important aspect of suffering," he adds, because "suffering must serve *for conversion,* that is, *for the rebuilding of goodness* in the subject, who can recognize the divine mercy in this call to repentance" (*SD,* par. 12). In brief, suffering in this life is an educative punishment that should be regarded as good and justified because its purpose is to cultivate or strengthen goodness both in oneself and one's relationship with others and especially with God (*SD,* par. 12).[18] Such suffering may produce moral virtues, and hence character building is the outweighing good that absorbs some evil.

Significantly, John Paul II does not estimate the value of all suffering in terms of teleology. For instance, pain is meaningful and valuable because as an alarm signal it alerts us when something is wrong in our body; but the gratuitous pain that strikes the cancer patient and isolates her in her suffering already suggests the breakdown of this teleology as a complete explanation as to the meaning or purpose of the pain of suffering. In general, as John Paul says, "It is true that universal experience teaches . . . the beneficial effects that pain has for so many as the source of maturity, wisdom, goodness, understanding, solidarity, so that one can speak of the fruitfulness of pain. But this observation leaves the basic problem unresolved."[19] Furthermore, though it is undoubtedly true that the suffering allied with punishment is meaningful as a means with an end in view, all suffering cannot be justified in this way, says John Paul, because *"it is not true* that *all suffering is a consequence of a fault and has the nature of a punishment"* (*SD,* par. 11). In other words, there is suffering without guilt, innocent suffering, because not all that suffer are being punished for moral evil. "Suffice it to mention," the Pope says, "natural disasters or calamities, and also all the forms of physical disability or of bodily or psychological diseases for which people are not blameworthy."[20] The Old Testament just man Job is decisive proof of this

---

18. Grisez correctly qualifies this point that suffering is an educative punishment. He says, "In the next life, of course, those who persisted in evil will experience their own wretchedness, and their punishment no longer will be educative" (*Living a Christian Life,* p. 32).

19. John Paul II, general audience (March 30, 1983), published in *L'Osservatore Romano,* 5 April 1983: 4.

20. John Paul II, *Catechesis on the Creed,* vol. I, p. 269.

claim. As John Paul says, "Already in itself it is *sufficient argument* why the answer to the question about the meaning of suffering is not to be unreservedly linked to the moral order, based on justice alone." "While such an answer," he adds, "has a fundamental and transcendent reason and validity, at the same time it is seen to be not only unsatisfactory in cases similar to the suffering of the just man Job, but it even seems to trivialize and impoverish *the concept of justice* which we encounter in Revelation" (*SD,* par. 11). In short, there is more to suffering than guilt.

While it is true to say that the innocent also suffer and hence they are not being punished for sin, it is also true and more important to understand that biblically there is only one class of persons, namely, sinners — all have sinned and come short of the glory of God (Rom. 3:23). Saint Thomas Aquinas makes this important point in his commentary on Job.[21] He reminds us of the sinful character of human beings, even of those who innocently suffer and that suffering and tribulation of all sorts may help the sinner forward to the ultimate good of union with God. We read in the Epistle to the Hebrews: "For whom the Lord loves he chastens. . . . Now no chastening seems to be joyful for the present, but painful; nevertheless, afterward it yields the peaceable fruit of righteousness to who have been trained by it" (12:6, 11).

Nevertheless, John Paul acknowledges that there are limits to estimating the value of all suffering as a just punishment for human sin. And so he wrestles with the traditional problem of evil that is usually presented as a dilemma for standard theism.[22] In his own words, the problem is thus: "How can evil and suffering be reconciled with that paternal solicitude, full of love, which Jesus Christ attributes to God in the Gospel? How are they to be reconciled with the transcendent wisdom and

21. On this, see Eleonore Stump, "Aquinas on the Sufferings of Job," in *The Evidential Argument from Evil,* ed. Daniel Howard-Snyder (Bloomington, Ind.: Indiana University Press, 1996), pp. 49-68. See also Paul Helm, *The Last Things: Death, Judgment, Heaven, and Hell* (Edinburgh: Banner of Truth Trust, 1989), p. 72.

22. By standard theism I am referring to what William L. Rowe has called "any view which holds that there exists an omnipotent, omniscient, omnigood being who created the world." Rowe also distinguishes within standard theism two views: restricted theism and expanded theism. "Expanded theism is the view that [God] exists, conjoined with certain other significant religious claims, claims about sin, redemption, a future life, a last judgment, and the like. (Orthodox Christian theism is a version of expanded theism.) Restricted theism is the view that God exists, unaccompanied by other, independent religious claims" ("Evil and the Theistic Hypothesis: A Response to Wykstra," in *The Problem of Evil,* ed. Marilyn McCord Adams and Robert Merrihew Adams [New York: Oxford University Press, 1990], p. 160).

omnipotence of the Creator? And in a still more dialectical form — in the presence of all the experience of evil in the world, especially when confronted with the suffering of the innocent, can we say that God does not will evil? And if he wills it, how can we believe that 'God is love'? — all the more so since this love is omnipotent?"[23] In other words, this problem is whether the propositions (1) "There is an omnipotent, omniscient, and perfectly good God" and (2) "There is evil in the world," are logically consistent in view of the claim that (3) "A perfectly good God would want to eliminate all of the evil that exists."

Besides the free will defense adumbrated above, John Paul sketches some other well-known theistic responses to the problem of evil and suffering. He accepts the validity of these arguments and thus he thinks that there are arguments available to show that evil's existence is not an insuperable intellectual obstacle to believing in a personal, infinite, and all-good God.[24] For instance, he accepts a version of the natural law theodicy in which evil is the result of the operation of a uniform natural order. God created a system of nature governed by natural laws for the sake of the goods that it alone can realize. Water is necessary for life but human lungs cannot absorb water without drowning. God foresees, but does not directly intend, that this and many other sorts of evil arise from the system of nature he has created. In other words, he permits but does not intend and approve such evils. This divine permission, of course, is not to will evil directly and for its own sake. The evil in question is an unintended but necessary consequence of a uniform natural order that produces certain kinds of good, for the victims of evil as well as for others. Something like this view is implied in the Pope's claim that God permits evil "in view of the overall good of the material cosmos."[25] This "indi-

23. John Paul II, *A Catechesis on the Creed,* vol. I, p. 269. The Pope raises a somewhat different but related question in *Crossing the Threshold of Hope,* pp. 60-61: "We cannot forget that in every century, at the hour of truth, even Christians have asked themselves a tormenting question: How to continue to trust in a God who is supposed to be a merciful Father, in a God who — as the New Testament reveals — is meant to be Love itself, when suffering, injustice, sickness, and death seem to dominate the larger history of the world as well as our smaller daily lives?"

24. John Paul II, *A Catechesis on the Creed,* vol. I, pp. 271-72: "Undoubtedly it is a great light we receive from reason and revelation in regard to the mystery of divine Providence which, while not willing the evil, tolerates it in view of a greater good." Yet, the Pope adds clearly, "However, the definitive light can come to us only from the victorious cross of Christ."

25. John Paul II, *A Catechesis on the Creed,* vol. I, pp. 270-71: "Sacred Scripture assures us that: 'against wisdom evil does not prevail' (Wisdom 7:30). This strengthens

cates," he adds, "that God permits evil in the world for higher ends, but does not will it."[26] So God is not the direct cause of evil, and he for a time tolerates evil only to bring about a greater good.

Nonetheless, there are definite limits to the rational-abstract approach to the problem of evil and suffering, according to John Paul. Unlike many critics of theoretical theodicy, however, John Paul does not consider philosophical reflections on evil as irrelevant and immoral, but he does recognize their limitations. As he says:

> Why evil, why pain, why this human cross which seems co-essential to our nature, and yet, in so many cases, is absurd? They are questions which have always tormented the heart and mind of man and to which perhaps there can be given partial answers of a theoretical order, but which continue to crop up again in the reality of life, sometimes in a dramatic way, especially when it is a case of the suffering of the innocent, of children, and also of groups and entire peoples subjected to overbearing forces which seem to indicate in the world the triumph of evil. Which of us does not feel pierced to the heart in the presence of so many painful facts, so many crosses?[27]

Two reasons, chiefly, stand out for the limitation of theoretical theodicy, as I understand John Paul's views. (1) Let us suppose that there are valid defenses against the problem of evil showing that (a) the evils are logically necessary to the best of all possible worlds, or (b) that each evil is logically connected with some great enough good like a perfect balance of retributive justice, or (c) that the risk of evil is logically implied by the good of free creatures. These logically possible reasons are part of

---

our conviction that in the Creator's providential plan in regard to the world, in the last analysis evil is subordinated to good. Moreover, in the context of the integral truth about divine Providence, one is helped to better understand the two statements: 'God does not will evil as such' and 'God permits evil'. In regard to the first it is opportune to recall the words of the Book of Wisdom: 'God did not make death, and He does not delight in the death of the living. For He created all things that they may exist' (Wisdom 1:13-14). As regards the permission of evil in the physical order, e.g., the fact that material beings (among them also the human body) are corruptible and undergo death, it must be said that this belongs to the very structure of the being of these creatures. In the present state of the material world, it would be difficult to think of the unlimited existence of every individual corporeal being. We can therefore understand that, if 'God did not make death', as the Book of Wisdom states, He nonetheless permitted it in view of the overall good of the material cosmos."

26. John Paul II, *A Catechesis on the Creed*, vol. I, p. 273.
27. *L'Osservatore Romano*, April 5, 1983: 4.

a general strategy for explaining why an omnipotent, omniscient, and perfectly good God would permit or allow evil to occur. This strategy expresses generic and global reasons, according to Marilyn McCord Adams. She explains, "generic in so far as some *general* reason is sought to cover all sorts of evils; global in so far as they seize upon some feature of the world as a whole." Following Adams, I will also distinguish between two dimensions of God's goodness in relation to creation: God as "producer of global goods" and God's "goodness to or love of individual created persons."[28]

Now I think that the Pope's concern with the meaning of human life and, with it, human suffering in the context of an individual person's life, leads him to think that fixing on generic and global goods as well as defending God's goodness *qua* producer of such goods is a mere abstract answer to the meaning of the individual person's suffering. Abstract insofar as, firstly, a theoretical global good theodicy discusses the evil of suffering at a general level rather than in terms of specificity and personal meaning, engaging the individual person who is suffering. As he sees it, an abstract general good theodicy does not clearly show God's providential care and love for human beings, leaving out of the picture how God, the transcendent good, relates himself to the evil of human suffering of individual persons. Secondly, this theodicy is abstract insofar as these generic and global goods offer only a set of immanent, created goods rather than the infinite and uncreated goodness of God. And though John Paul II insists that God values human freedom even to the point of permitting evil to occur, his permission is not for the sake of some global good like freedom; instead such permission is justified only if it brings that person into union with God, which is humanity's highest good.

(2) Let us suppose that a theoretical theodicy could show that the existence of God is compatible with the existence of evils of the amounts and kinds we find in the actual world, because they could be shown to be either not evils at all or evils necessarily built into the very idea of having a world in the first place. But even this approach has its limits. Father Nichols has made a decisive objection to it as a total response to the problem of evil, or so at least it seems to me. Were this argument and others like it, he says,

28. Marilyn McCord Adams, "Horrendous Evils and the Goodness of God," in *The Problem of Evil,* ed. Marilyn McCord Adams and Robert Merrihew Adams (New York: Oxford University Press, 1990), p. 213. See also her book-length treatment, *Horrendous Evils and the Goodness of God* (Ithaca, N.Y.: Cornell University Press, 1999), pp. 16-31, particularly pp. 29-30.

an adequate and total vindication of the 'justice of God', it would be exceedingly hard to find room for the theological concept of redemption, a concept which, however, lies at the heart of Christian faith. Thus Christian theodicists, aiming for total victory, swing their sabers and cut off their own heads. . . . [In other words,] if in theodicy we *could* clear up the problem of evil to our complete satisfaction, then there would be no need for salvation as presented in Christian revelation. God comes in His incarnate Son as the world's Redeemer, and by His Spirit as its Renewer, so as to repair the world's defects. But there would be no point in redemption if these defects could be shown to be either not defects at all or things built into the very idea of having a world in the first place.[29]

John Paul agrees, and he puts the point in his own words as follows,

In God's eternal plan, and in His providential action in human history, every evil, and in particular moral evil — sin — is subjected to the good of the redemption and salvation precisely through the cross and resurrection of Christ. It can be said that in Him God draws forth good from evil. He does it in a certain sense from the very evil of sin, which was the cause of the suffering of the Immaculate Lamb and of His terrible death on the cross as a victim for the sins of the world. The Church's liturgy does not hesitate even to speak, in this regard, of the 'happy fault' (*felix culpa;* cf. *Exsultet* of the Easter Vigil Liturgy). Thus a definitive answer cannot be given to the question about the reconciliation of evil and suffering with the truth of divine providence, without reference to Christ.[30]

The question arises here as to whether the Pope thinks that the unthinkably great good of the incarnation and redemption outweighs and justifies all the evil in the world. This passage clearly suggests that all evil in the world is absorbed by the single good of redemption and salvation. But what remains unclear is whether in his account of redemptive suffering John Paul II thinks that this good ultimately overcomes or defeats rather than justifies evil, in the sense that there is a logically necessary connection between the evils that occur and the good justifying God's permitting them.

Yet what is abundantly clear is John Paul's insistence that the cross of

29. Nichols, *The Shape of Catholic Theology,* pp. 70, 72.
30. John Paul II, *A Catechesis on the Creed,* vol. I, pp. 273-74.

Christ redeems both sin and suffering. "In the cross of Christ not only is the Redemption accomplished through suffering, but *also human suffering itself has been redeemed. . . .* In bringing about the Redemption through suffering, Christ *has* also *raised human suffering to the level of Redemption.*"[31] "Thus each man," the Pope adds, "in his suffering can also become a sharer in the redemptive suffering of Christ" (*SD*, par. 19). The cross does not only alter our perspective about suffering. Most important, by Christ's passion, John Paul says, all suffering is objectively and in principle changed, assumed in "a completely new dimension and a new order" (*SD*, par. 18). This means, as I understand it, that "suffering loses its prima facie negative character for the victim by being given a transcendent, positive meaning."[32] Says John Paul, "One can say that with the passion of Christ all human suffering has found itself in a new situation" (*SD*, par. 19). And as the Pope also says, "Christ's cross — the passion — throws a completely new light on this problem [of evil] by conferring another meaning on human suffering in general."[33] In other words, the right kind of connection is apparently made here between an individual's suffering and the single good of incarnation and redemption: not only is God's providential care and love for human beings definitively and unsurpassably manifested in his conquering or overcoming evil through the saving work of Christ crucified, but also suffering now possesses a redemptive and salvific value and power, and thus my suffering can be redemptive for myself and for others, provided I unite it with the sufferings of Christ. In short, I must take up my cross and follow the Lord (Mark 8:34).

31. I return later in the paper to the all-important question, in what sense is suffering redeemed? It seems clear to say, in the light of Christian soteriology, that our sins have been redeemed by the passion and death of Christ, but John Paul's frequent assertion in *SD* that "human suffering itself has been redeemed" (par. 19) is not easily understood.

32. Stan van Hooft, "The Meanings of Suffering," p. 15.

33. John Paul II, *A Catechesis on the Creed*, vol. II, *Jesus, Son and Savior* (Boston: Pauline Books & Media, 1996), pp. 453-54: "The redemption carried out by Christ at the price of his passion and death on the cross is a decisive event in human history, not only because it fulfills the supreme divine plan of justice and mercy, but also because it gave new meaning to the problem of suffering. No problem has weighed more heavily on the human family, especially in its relationship with God. We know that the value of human existence is conditioned by the solution of the problem of suffering. To a certain extent it coincides with the problem of evil, whose presence in the world is so difficult to accept. . . . Thanks to Christ, the meaning of suffering changes radically. It no longer suffices to see in it a punishment for sin. One must discern in it the redemptive, salvific power of love. The evil of suffering, in the mystery of Christ's redemption, is overcome and in every case transformed."

Furthermore, God is not an impersonal absolute that remains outside of human history, cold and distant from human suffering, according to John Paul II. "He is Emmanuel, God-with-us, a God who shares man's lot and participates in his destiny." "God is not someone who remains only outside of the world," the Pope adds, "content to be in Himself all-knowing and omnipotent. *His wisdom and omnipotence are placed, by free choice, at the service of creation.* If suffering is present in the history of humanity, one understands why His omnipotence was manifested *in the omnipotence of humiliation on the Cross.* The scandal of the Cross remains the key to the interpretation of the great mystery of suffering, which is so much a part of the history of mankind. . . . Christ is *proof of God's solidarity with man in his suffering.*"[34] Thus, in the mystery of redemptive suffering God himself participates in human distress.

As a personalist, John Paul understands God's response to human suffering to be a personal response of love. Indeed, the true answer to the question of why we suffer must be found in the revelation of divine love, which is the ultimate meaning-giving source of everything that exists, including suffering. "This answer has been given by God to man in the cross of Jesus Christ," according to John Paul (*SD,* par. 13). As the supreme mystery of divine love, Christ is the greatest possible answer to the question about suffering and the meaning of suffering. He is the answer, says the Pope, "not only by His teaching, that is, by the Good News, but most of all by His own suffering, which is integrated with this teaching of the Good News in an organic and indissoluble way." "And this is," adds John Paul II, "*the final,* definitive word of this *teaching:* 'the word of the cross', as St. Paul one day will say" (*SD,* par. 18). The cross is, then, the answer to the problem of evil, but this answer is not a theoretical one that refutes all objections. "Love is," according to the Pope, "the richest source of the meaning of suffering, which always remains a mystery: we are conscious of the insufficiency and inadequacy of our explanations. Christ causes us to enter into the mystery and to discover the 'why' of suffering, as far as we are capable of grasping the sublimity of divine love" (*SD,* par. 13).

So I now intend to look first at the whole matter of Christ's cross as God's response to suffering; then at how God in Christ is present in human suffering, and finally at the meaning of suffering in the light of Christ's passion, death and resurrection.

---

34. John Paul II, *Crossing the Threshold of Hope,* pp. 62-63.

Jesus Christ: Sufferings Defeated by Love

The very heart of Christian soteriology, the theology of salvation dealing with God's saving work in Christ, is the divine victory over the evils of human suffering. This suffering pertains not only to temporal suffering, however. Rather, the definitive evil and so the definitive suffering that humanity can know is eternal separation from God, who is the supreme good. As the *Catechism of the Catholic Church* states: "God put us in the world to know, to love, and to serve him, and so to come to paradise. Beatitude makes us 'partakers of the divine nature' and of eternal life. With beatitude, man enters into the glory of Christ and into the joy of Trinitarian life." Beatitude is, the *Catechism* adds, "not found . . . in any creature, but in God alone, the source of every good and of all love" (par. 1721, 1723). The loss of beatitude, rejection by God, damnation and the loss of eternal life is the fundamental and definitive meaning of suffering. According to the Pope, the love of the Father is manifested in the gift of his only-begotten Son, whose salvific work is communicated through the Holy Spirit. In his salvific mission, Christ strikes at the very roots of evil, which are sin and death, freeing humanity from the loss of eternal life and, with it, our suffering in its fundamental and definitive meaning. "The mission of the only-begotten Son consists in *conquering sin and death.* He conquers sin by His obedience unto death," says the Pope, "and He overcomes death by His resurrection" (*SD,* par. 14).

Because of the redemptive efficacy of Christ's salvific work in striking evil right at its roots, evil and definitive eschatological suffering is totally vanquished. "For God so loved the world that He gave His only-begotten Son, that whoever believes in Him should not perish but have eternal life" (John 3:16). Yet there is still more: *"evil and suffering* in their *temporal and historical dimension"* (*SD,* par. 15), says John Paul, are also struck at their roots. What this means is that in the death and resurrection of Jesus Christ there is also victory over sin and death in this earthly life. Nonetheless, though the dominion of sin and death are defeated in Jesus Christ, says John Paul II, "His cross and resurrection does not abolish temporal suffering from human life, nor free from suffering the whole historical dimension of human existence" (*SD,* par. 15).

So much is this the case, one might add, that there still remains about as much reason as ever to wonder whether perhaps Christ was victorious over the dominion of sin and death in his cross and resurrection. There's an obvious question: Why, if the dominion of sin and death has been defeated, isn't evil and suffering in their temporal and historical dimension abolished? In other words, why the divine permission for evil and suffering? Fr. Benedict Ashley makes the same point even clearer: "Even if the promise [of Romans 8:18-24] that God in his justice will more than compensate in our future life for every suffering in the present and will see to it that our efforts to help others will not have been in vain, the subjective problem remains. Why has an all-powerful God permitted us to suffer so much *here and now?* Why has he not eliminated the suffering and simply given us happiness that after all is ultimately his gift to give?"[35] The Pope faces this vexing question head-on, as we shall see below.

For now, it suffices to understand that Christ's saving work defeats the dominion of sin and, with it, its presence and power in human life that took root in human nature with original sin. We need to consider the doctrine of original sin, even if only briefly, in order to answer the question, in what sense is our suffering redeemed? What, then, is original sin?

Following the teaching of the Catholic Church, the orthodox Christian doctrine of original sin has the following four points, which the Pope develops in Volume II of his *Catechesis on the Creed: Jesus, Son and Savior.* First, original sin is *universal sinfulness,* consisting of attitudes, tendencies, and an inclination to sin, to evil, that the Council of Trent called "concupiscence," and which are contrary to God's will, at odds with his holiness, and present in all persons, in all areas of their lives. Second, original sin is *natural sinfulness:* it belongs to human nature in a real sense, and is present from birth; we are born with a fallen human nature. Third, original sin is *inherited sinfulness:* this fallen human nature is inherited which results in human beings that are born in a state or condition of hereditary moral weakness and alienation or estrangement from God, now having lost the grace of original holiness and righteousness. And fourth, original sin is *Adamic sinfulness:* it stems from Adam, who committed the first sin and whose disobedience toward God gave original sin a historical beginning, and which has left its consequence in every descendant of Adam, so that the sinful situation of humanity is connected with the fault of Adam, the first man and progenitor of the race.[36]

---

35. Benedict Ashley, O.P., *Choosing a World-View and Value-System: An Ecumenical Apologetics* (New York: Alba House, 2000), p. 316.

36. John Paul II, *A Catechesis on the Creed,* vol. II, pp. 17-77. On original sin as universal sinfulness, see pp. 31, 33-34, 36-37, 39, 41, and 46; on natural sinfulness, see pp. 28, 30; on inherited sinfulness, see pp. 28, 36-37, 39-43, 45-46, 48, and 55; on Adamic sinfulness, see pp. 23-27, 41, 43, 44-46, 48, and 60. I have profited much from Henri Blocher, *Original Sin: Illuminating the Riddle* (Grand Rapids: Eerdmans, 1997), espe-

We do not yet have original sin fully in view, however. Original sin underscores, firstly, the Church's insistence on the *contingency* of evil. As Father Nichols rightly states: "Sin must have entered human life at some historical moment. . . . For unless evil marred the creation of humanity contingently (i.e., historically), it could only have done so essentially (i.e., by God's own creative act), which is unthinkable. In claiming Adam (with Eve) as historical figures [*sic*], the Church is confirmed by the New Testament, especially by Paul's appeal to Adam's fall as the act which Christ's redemptive act inverted. Revelation presents both as historical events with metahistorical meaning."[37]

---

cially pp. 15-35. See also Peter Geach, *Providence and Evil* (Cambridge: Cambridge University Press, 1977), especially Chapter 5, pp. 84-101.

37. Aidan Nichols, O.P., *Epiphany: A Theological Introduction to Catholicism* (Collegeville, Minn.: Liturgical Press, 1996), pp. 175-76. One problem that arises from flattening out the difference between humanity as God created it and humanity as it exists in a fallen state is clearly identified by James Orr early in the twentieth century. He wrote, "If sin lies in the constitution of things by creation — if it is a necessary outcome of the condition in which God made man, and of the nature He has given him — how can the creature be asked to assume responsibility — at least serious responsibility for it" (*God's Image in Man and Its Defacement in the Light of Modern Denials,* 1903-1904 Stone Lectures at Princeton Theological Seminary [Grand Rapids: Eerdmans, 1948], pp. 206-7). The Pope upholds the essential historicity of the Fall in Vol. II of *A Catechesis on the Creed:* "The description of the first sin, which we find in the third chapter of Genesis, acquires a greater clarity in the context of creation and of the bestowal of gifts. By these gifts, God constituted man in the state of holiness and of original justice. This description hinges on the transgression of the divine command not to eat 'of the fruit of the tree of the knowledge of good and evil'. This is to be interpreted by taking into account the character of the ancient text and especially its literary form. However, while bearing in mind this scientific requirement in the study of the first book of Sacred Scripture, it cannot be denied that one sure element emerges from the detailed account of the sin. It describes a primordial event, that is, a fact, which according to revelation took place at the beginning of human history" (p. 27). If I'm not mistaken, what the Pope is saying in this citation is similar to the point made by Henri Blocher, "The real issue when we try to interpret Genesis 2–3 is not whether we have a historical account of the fall, but whether or not we may read it as the account of a historical fall. The problem is not historiography as a genre narrowly defined — in annals, chronicles, or even saga — but correspondence with discrete realities in our ordinary space and sequential time" (*Original Sin,* p. 50). See also, T. C. O'Brien, O.P., who writes, "Original sin is taken on the level of a *history* of salvation, and the state and the sin of Adam are treated as real events and parts of a divine plan, *economy,* for man. To regard the first sin and the fall as a mere symbol or mythological representation of men's collectivity in their sinful condition is incompatible with Catholic teaching, which envisages a real situation of a real person, namely a 'sin' actually committed by an individual together with its consequences for him." Again: "All the literary forms

Secondly, the consequence of original sin is death, so that "we die not because we commit individual sins of our own volition; rather we sin, and *inevitably*, we die, and *inevitably*, as a result of Adam's sin."[38] The upshot of the doctrine of original sin, says the Pope, is that it helps us to "understand the mysterious and distressing aspects of evil which [we] daily experience." Otherwise we "end up by wavering between a hasty and unjustified optimism and a radical pessimism bereft of hope."[39] John Henry Cardinal Newman was also persuaded that the doctrine of original sin was necessary to explain evil in our world in light of faith in God's goodness and omnipotence: "either there is no Creator, or this living society of men is in a true sense discarded from His presence. . . . And so I argue about the world; — if there be a God, *since* there is a God, the human race is implicated in some terrible aboriginal calamity. It is out of joint with the purposes of its Creator. This is a fact, a fact as true as the fact of its existence; and thus the doctrine of what is theologically called original sin becomes to me almost as certain as that the world exists, and as the existence of God."[40]

So temporal or historical evil and suffering entered the world with the Fall and original sin. In fact, the Holy Father says that "suffering cannot be divorced from the sin of the beginnings, from what St. John calls the 'sin of the world', *from the sinful background* of the personal actions and so-

---

are shaped and directed to bring out as history God's plan of man's creation, fall and redemption. There is a real link between past events, under whatever literary form they appear, and the conditions present to the author and explained in the light of these origins. Unlike the ancient myths these Biblical accounts are not a symbolic expression of some universal truth; they are an account of an actual situation in terms of its causes: the present is seen in the past, the past in the present" (Appendix 3 and 4, respectively, in Volume 26, *Original Sin,* of St. Thomas Aquinas, *Summa Theologiae* 1a2ae. 81-85, at pp. 115, 121).

38. Father Edward T. Oakes, S.J., "Original Sin: A Disputation," *First Things* 87 (November 1998): 23. See also John Paul II, *A Catechesis on the Creed,* vol. II: "Finally the whole of human existence on earth is subject to the fear of death, which according to revelation is clearly connected with original sin. Sin itself is synonymous with spiritual death, because through sin man has lost sanctifying grace, the source of supernatural life. The sign and consequence of original sin is bodily death, such as it has been experienced since that time by all humanity. Man was created by God for immortality. Death appears as a tragic leap in the dark, and is the consequence of sin, as if by an immanent logic, but especially as the punishment of God. Such is the teaching of revelation and such is the faith of the Church" (pp. 50-51).

39. John Paul II, *A Catechesis on the Creed,* vol. II, p. 42.

40. John Henry Cardinal Newman, *Apologia Pro Vita Sua* (London: J. M. Dent & Sons Ltd., 1864), part VII, p. 218.

cial processes in human history." "[O]ne cannot reject the criterion that, at the basis of human suffering, there is a complex involvement with sin," the Pope adds, "the sin that took root in this history both as an original inheritance and as the 'sin of the world' and as the sum of personal sins" (*SD*, par. 15). We live in a fallen world as a consequence of the original sin that amounts to the loss of our share in the divine life, or divine friendship, enjoyed by Adam and Eve, and thus of the integrity and immortality that stemmed from such sanctifying grace. Though the Pope urges us to exercise "great caution in judging man's suffering as a consequence of concrete sins" (par. 15), because there is no necessary connection between suffering and punishment, he nonetheless insists that humanity suffers as a result of the radical nature of our fall from sanctifying grace, which began with original sin and is extended through personal sins.

Thus, in defeating the dominion of sin and death brought about by the Fall and original sin through the saving work of Christ, God gives human beings a new supernatural principle, which makes them a new creation, to replace that given them by original sin and this makes it possible for humanity to live anew in sanctifying grace. In short, human suffering itself has been redeemed from the dominion of sin and death and raised to the level of redemption.

For our purposes here, then, the most important aspect of Christ's victory over sin and death is not only that he has taken upon himself the sins of all persons but *also their suffering*. If I understand the Pope correctly, Christ in his suffering and death on the cross not only takes upon himself suffering in its fundamental and definitive sense, accomplishing our redemption through it; but also, insists the Pope, Christ himself "in His redemptive suffering has become, in a certain sense, a sharer in all human sufferings" (*SD*, par. 20). Again: "Christ through His own salvific suffering is very much present in every human suffering, and can act from within that suffering by the powers of His Spirit of Truth, His consoling Spirit" (*SD*, par. 26). Still again: "Christ, the Incarnate Word, confirmed through his own life — in poverty, humiliation and toil — and especially through his passion and death, that God is with every person in his suffering. Indeed God takes upon himself the multiform suffering of man's earthly existence. At the same time Jesus Christ reveals that this suffering possesses a redemptive and salvific value and power."[41]

41. John Paul II, *A Catechesis on the Creed*, vol. I, p. 274. Elsewhere the Holy Father says, "The Gospel of suffering signifies not only the presence of suffering in the Gospel, as one of the themes of the Good News, but also the revelation *of the salvific*

The doctrine of God's suffering love goes beyond the hope of Romans 8 and touches present suffering itself. As Fr. Ashley explains this most important point:

> God the Father will wipe away our tears and give us ultimate and superabundant compensation in the future Kingdom. Yet he wishes us to achieve this not merely as a pure gift, but also as the just reward of our own achievements that because they are human necessarily involve pain and struggle. Human growth in knowledge, human growth in virtue, human transformation of the world must be in the human mode that works dialectically through contrasts, struggle, courage, and patience. Yet God understands that subjectively it is very hard for us to accept and endure this fact of actual, even if necessary, suffering. The only way to make our suffering easier and ultimately to compensate it superabundantly is by sympathy not merely in the sense of appreciating our pain, *but of experiencing it himself with us. Immanuel, 'God with us', Jesus Christ, has chosen to suffer and die with us and thus to enter into infinite delight through suffering with us.*[42]

Yet there is more: the Achilles heel of the doctrine of God's suffering love, at least on some interpretations, is found in this question: "if God is to suffer with us, how can we be assured that in the end we will be victorious with him?"[43] This question is particularly troublesome for those who imply that God must undergo change given that he suffers with us. This conclusion limits God, taking away his omnipotence and our assurance that he can surely save us. Ashley's response to this question is satisfying:

> The doctrine of the Incarnation avoids this, since God the Father does not become incarnate, but only God the Son, and God the Son suffers with us not through his divine nature but through his assumed human nature that unlike his divinity is capable of suffering. But does not this mean that he does not really suffer, but only that his human nature suffers? No, because it is one and the same divine Person who is both God and human. The suffering of his human nature is his suffering, no one else's, just as my bodily suffering is my suffering although I am not just a body. Moreover, this incarnate Son is anointed with the Holy Spirit whom he sends upon the Church and the world

---

power and salvific significance of suffering in Christ's messianic mission and, subsequently, in the mission and vocation of the Church" (*SD*, par. 25).

42. Ashley, *Choosing a World-View*, p. 317.

43. Ashley, *Choosing a World-View*, p. 317.

as his infinite strengthening and consoling power, so that the God who truly suffers remains infinite in his power to save us.[44]

So, on the one hand, Christ suffers in our place humanity's godforsakenness, our abandonment by God, this suffering which is the separation, the rejection by the Father, the estrangement from him, which is the ultimate evil of, and thus the price paid for, the turning away from God that is contained in sin (*SD*, par. 18). In this suffering we have the depth of Christ's sacrifice for us. As John Paul says, "Jesus knew that by this ultimate phase of His sacrifice, reaching the intimate core of His being, He completed the work of reparation which was the purpose of His sacrifice for the expiation of sins. If sin is separation from God, Jesus had to experience in the crisis of His union with the Father a suffering proportionate to that separation."[45] In an eloquent passage that bears quoting in full, John Paul II writes:

> Behold, He, though innocent, takes upon Himself the sufferings of all people, because He takes upon Himself the sins of all. "The Lord has laid on him the iniquity of us all": *all* human sin in its breadth and depth becomes the true cause of the Redeemer's suffering. If the suffering 'is measured' by the evil suffered, then the words of the prophet [Isaiah] enable us to understand *the extent of this evil* and suffering with which Christ burdened Himself. It can be said that this is "substitutive" suffering; but above all it is "redemptive." The Man of Sorrows of that prophecy [of Isaiah] is truly that "Lamb of God who takes away the sin of the world." In His suffering, sins are cancelled out precisely because He alone as the only-begotten Son could take them upon Himself, accept them *with that love for the Father which overcomes* the evil of every sin [i.e., estrangement from God]; in a certain sense He annihilates this evil in the spiritual space of the relationship between God and humanity, and fills this space with good. . . . This work, in the plan of eternal love, has a redemptive character. (*SD*, pars. 17, 16)[46]

---

44. Ashley, *Choosing a World-View*, pp. 317-18.

45. John Paul II, *A Catechesis on the Creed*, vol. II, p. 473.

46. In the background of John Paul II's account of Jesus Christ's suffering is a Chalcedonian Christology: "Here we touch upon the duality of nature of a single personal subject of redemptive suffering. He who by His passion and death on the cross brings about the Redemption is the only-begotten Son whom God 'gave'. And at the same time this *Son who is consubstantial with the Father suffers as a man.* His suffering has human dimensions; it also has — unique in the history of humanity — a depth and intensity which, while being human, can also be an incomparable depth and intensity of suffering, insofar as the man who suffers is in person the only-begotten Son Himself:

Yet, on the other hand, as Jacques Maritain has said, "It is indeed true that everything has been expiated by the suffering of Jesus alone, but as Head of Humanity, in communion with all other men, and [hence] recapitulating in Him all the sorrows of all other men." "There is but one single Cross," adds Maritain, "that of Jesus, in which all are called to participate. Jesus has taken on Him all the *sufferings* at the same time as all the *sins,* all the sufferings of the past, of the present, and of the future, gathered together, concentrated in Him as in a convergent mirror, in the instant that by His sacrifice He became, — in a manner *fully consummated* and through the sovereign exercise of His liberty and of His love of man achieving in supreme obedience and supreme union the work which was entrusted to Him, — the Head of humanity in the victory over sin."[47] John Paul is getting at the same dimension of Christian soteriology in claiming that "Christ's passion and death pervade, redeem, and ennoble all human suffering, because through the Incarnation he desired to express his solidarity with humanity, which gradually opens to communion with him in faith and love."[48]

As I see it, both Maritain and John Paul II are suggesting here a distinctly Catholic interpretation of the meaning of human suffering in light of Christian soteriology. John Paul II develops this interpretation, as I will show below. This interpretation is not merely about our identifying with Christ, who through his passion and death, says the Pope, "is a divine model for all who suffer, especially for Christians who know and accept in faith the meaning and value of the cross." Of course we should follow the way of the cross, John Paul adds, because "The incarnate Word suffered according to the Father's plan so that we too 'should follow in his steps' (1 Pet. 2:21). He suffered and taught us to suffer."[49] But this is not the heart of his interpretation.

'God from God'. Therefore, only He — the only-begotten Son — is capable of embracing the measure of evil contained in the sin of man: in every sin and in 'total' sin, according to the dimensions of the historical existence of humanity on earth" (*SD,* par. 17). On the relevance of Chalcedonian Christology for the problem of evil, see Marilyn McCord Adams, "Chalcedonian Christology: A Christian Solution to the Problem of Evil," in *Philosophy and Theology Discourse,* ed. Stephen T. Davis (New York: St. Martin's Press, 1997), pp. 173-198.

47. Jacques Maritain, *On the Grace and Humanity of Jesus,* trans. Joseph W. Evans (New York: Herder and Herder, 1969), pp. 41-42.

48. John Paul II, *A Catechesis on the Creed,* vol. II, p. 439.

49. John Paul II, *A Catechesis on the Creed,* vol. II, pp. 439-40. In *SD,* John Paul says, "Christ's sufferings" have "the power of a supreme example" (par. 22). In this light, we can understand the claim that "Suffering is also an invitation to manifest the moral greatness of man, his *spiritual maturity.*" That is, the *"spiritual tempering* of man

It is also not merely about the future resurrection and heavenly glorification that finds its beginning in Christ's cross (Gal. 6:14; Phil. 3:10-11; Rom. 8:17-18; 2 Cor. 4:17-18; 1 Pet. 4:13). "Christ's resurrection has revealed 'the glory of the future age' and, at the same time, has confirmed 'the boast of the cross': the *glory that is hidden in the very suffering of Christ*" (*SD*, par. 22). Nor is it merely about the triumphant love of God in Christ Jesus from which the very worst of human sufferings cannot separate us (Rom. 8:31-39). Of course the Pope understands well the evangelical motif of suffering and glory, especially with reference to the cross and resurrection. As he says, "The resurrection became, first of all, the manifestation of glory, which corresponds to Christ's being lifted up through the cross. If, in fact, the cross was to human eyes Christ's *emptying of Himself*, at the same time it was in the eyes of God *His being lifted up*. On the cross, Christ attained and fully accomplished His mission: by fulfilling the will of the Father, He at the same time fully realized Himself. In weakness He manifested His *power*, and in humiliation He manifested all *His messianic greatness*" (*SD*, par. 22). This interpretation is also not merely about what the Pope calls the "Gospel *paradox of weakness and strength*" (*SD*, par. 23; 2 Cor. 12:9; 2 Tim. 1:12; Phil. 4:13). Christ experiences the core and summit of human weakness and powerlessness in being nailed to the cross and, nevertheless, in his weakness he is lifted up, confirmed by the power of the resurrection. Similarly, "the weaknesses of all human suffering are capable of being infused with the same power of God manifested in Christ's cross." "In such a concept," the Pope adds, "*to suffer* means to become particularly *susceptible*, particularly *open to the working of the salvific powers of God*, offered to humanity in Christ" (*SD*, par. 23).[50] Only one who is open to the saving powers of God can hear and act on the Word of God: "My grace is sufficient for you, for my power is made perfect in weakness" (2 Cor. 12:9-11).

---

in the midst of trials and tribulations, which is the particular vocation of those who share in Christ's suffering. . . . Suffering, as it were, contains a special *call to the virtue* which man must exercise on his own part. And this is the virtue of perseverance in bearing whatever disturbs and causes harm. In doing this, the individual unleashes hope which maintains in him the conviction that suffering will not get the better of him, that it will not deprive him of his dignity as a human being, a dignity linked to awareness of the meaning of life" (par. 23).

50. The Pope is not suggesting that in our suffering we literally experience a share of Christ's pain, or mystically identify with the "inner life of God," because Christ "Himself in His redemptive suffering has become, in a certain sense, a sharer in all human suffering" (*SD*, par. 20). Marilyn McCord Adams sketches these and other possible interpretations of suffering in light of Christian soteriology in "Horrendous Evils," pp. 218-19; see also pp. 161-73.

Sharers in the Suffering of Christ

What, then, does John Paul II have particularly in mind when insisting that "the victory over sin and death achieved by Christ in His cross and resurrection . . . *throws a new light* upon every suffering: the light of salvation. This is the light of the Gospel, that is, of the Good News." Christ strikes, he says, "at the very roots of human evil and thus draw[s] close in a salvific way to the whole world of suffering in which man shares" (*SD,* par. 15). God the Father's love for us is most perfectly revealed on the Cross of Jesus Christ, where God the Son suffers all that we can suffer. Says Ashley, "Looking at him and believing that he is now at the Father's right hand sending the Holy Spirit upon us, our own present suffering is united with his. While it remains human pain, it is transformed by the hope of glory, a hope that is not merely future but present in the infinite power of God in Christ. And as Christ by his suffering saved the world, so by our suffering with him we save each other."[51]

Two obvious questions arise here. First, what sense can be given to the notion that Christ takes the whole world of human suffering upon his very self? Second, what sound theological sense can be given to the notion that by uniting our suffering with Christ's Passion we fulfill a role that God has given us, namely, to participate in the historical outworking of God's plan of salvation for the whole human race, which was accomplished in and through the finished work of Christ on the cross?

As to the first question, does the Pope mean to say that Christ actually experienced in his suffering and death on the cross, as humanity's head, the past, present, and future sufferings of all human beings? Yes, that is precisely what he is saying: the Son of God, Jesus, the Crucified, has taken upon himself the sufferings of all people and offered them up, in loving obedience, to his Father for the supreme good of the redemption of the world (*SD,* par. 18). In short, the vicarious suffering of Jesus on the Cross has redeemed human suffering itself. So not only is redemption accomplished through the suffering of Christ, but suffering itself, says the Pope, "has entered into a completely new dimension and a new order: *it has been linked to love,* to that love which Christ spoke to Nicodemus [John 3:16], to that love which cre-

---

51. Ashley, *Choosing a World-View,* p. 318. The phrase "we save each other" is potentially misleading. It suggests the heresy of Pelagianism, meaning thereby the teaching "that human beings can achieve salvation through their own sustained efforts." (*A Concise Dictionary of Theology,* edited by Gerald O'Collins, S.J., and Edward G. Farrugia, S.J. [New York: Paulist Press, 1991], p. 176). Of course I am not suggesting that Fr. Benedict Ashley had this meaning in mind.

ates good, drawing it out by means of suffering, just as the supreme good of the Redemption of the world was drawn from the cross of Christ, and from that cross constantly takes its beginning" (*SD*, par. 18). Having made his own the sufferings of all people, this suffering has a redemptive power. As Jacques Maritain says, "we are no longer alone in bearing our sufferings (we had never been, but we have known this only when He came). He has borne our sufferings before us, and He put into them together with grace and charity, a salvific power and the seed of transfiguration."

There is an obvious question: If human suffering has been redeemed, why has God not abolished the mass of sufferings engendered by original sin and our own personal sins? As I asked earlier, "why has an all-powerful God permitted us to suffer so much *here and now?* Why has he not eliminated the suffering and simply given us happiness that after all is ultimately his gift to give?" Maritain's reply, and the answer of John Paul as well, is that "human suffering is not abolished, because men, by the blood of Christ and the merits of Christ *in which they participate,* are with Him the co-authors of their salvation." This brings us to the second question I raised above, namely, the theological sense that can be given to the notion that by our suffering being united with Christ's sufferings we participate in the historical outworking of God's plan of salvation. Maritain's answer to this question is as follows: because Christ suffered our sufferings "He has rendered all these sufferings meritorious of eternal life, holy and redemptive *in themselves,* and co-redemptive *in the Church,* which is both His Spouse and His Mystical Body." That is, we share in Christ's suffering in such a way that our suffering, too, is redemptive, and even essential to furthering the plan of salvation, not in the sense of course that we can add anything to Christ's merits and to his blood, says Maritain, but rather in the sense that through our suffering and our love we apply the inexhaustible and infinite merits that Christ won for us on the cross.[52]

John Paul II develops this very same line of interpretation. All people, says the Pope, are *"called to share in that suffering* through which the Redemption was accomplished." They are called, he adds, "to share in that suffering through which all human suffering has also been redeemed. In bringing about the Redemption through suffering, Christ *has* also *raised human suffering to the level of Redemption.* Thus each man, in his suffering, can also become a sharer in the redemptive suffering of Christ" (*SD*, par. 19). In other words, "insofar as man becomes a sharer in the

52. The quotes in this paragraph are taken from Maritain, *On the Grace and Humanity of Jesus,* p. 42.

Christ's sufferings — in any part of the world and at any time in history — to that extent *he in his own way completes* the suffering through which Christ accomplished the Redemption of the world" (*SD,* par. 24).

This passage raises several questions. First, what does it mean to share in Christ's sufferings? It means, first, that through mystical union in faith with Christ we are indwelt by the third person of the Holy Trinity, the Holy Spirit. "God's love has been poured into our hearts through the Holy Spirit which has been given to us" (Rom. 5:5). Christ is in us and we are in him as sharers of God's life in Christ through the agency of the Holy Spirit. In this union, I discover that my sufferings are already Christ's and therefore are "enriched with a new content and meaning" (*SD,* par. 20). I have already mentioned some of this enrichment in the concluding paragraph of the last section. Let me single out just one of the points I made. The incomparable good of union with God in heaven compensates all the finite evils we suffer here (Rom. 8:18). The ultimate meaning of suffering and death is revealed in the resurrection of Jesus Christ. Says St. Paul, "For if we have been united with him in a death like his, we shall certainly be united with him in a resurrection like his. . . . But if we have died with Christ, we believe that we shall also live with him" (Rom. 6:5, 8). Germain Grisez makes this point well. "Just as Jesus willingly suffered, because he looked forward to the joy of resurrection (see Heb. 12:2), so Christians who are faithful can anticipate glory even amidst sufferings, and so can honestly say: 'When we cry, "Abba, Father" it is that very Spirit bearing witness with our spirit that we are children of God, and if children, then heirs, heirs of God and joint heirs with Christ — if, in fact, we suffer with Him so that we may also be glorified with him' (Rom. 8:15-17)."[53]

Yet there is still more: we walk in newness of life here and now. "We were buried therefore with him by baptism into death, so that as Christ was raised from the dead by the glory of the Father, we too might walk in newness of life" (Rom. 6:4). In other words, we are united with a resurrected, living Christ, and from this mystical union with this living Christ we have the high calling of bringing forth fruit to God. As one author puts it, "Christ is the vine, and we are the branches, abiding in him, bringing forth fruit."[54] This brings us to a second point. Most important, as a sharer in the sufferings of Christ, I discover through faith that in uniting my sufferings, in loving obedience, to Christ's sacrifice I am furthering the glory

53. Grisez, *Living a Christian Life,* p. 33.

54. Francis A. Schaeffer, *The Finished Work of Christ: The Truth of Romans 1–8* (Wheaton, Ill.: Crossway Books, 1998), p. 176.

of God and his plan of salvation. Says John Paul, "For, *whoever suffers in union with Christ* — just as the Apostle Paul bears his 'tribulations' in union with Christ — not only receives from Christ that strength already referred to but also 'completes' by his suffering 'what is lacking in Christ's afflictions [for the sake of his body, that is, the Church]' (Col. 1:24)."

Here, too, we meet the troublesome word "complete," and the question arises as to whether the Pope is suggesting that I am adding to Christ's sufferings, as if it takes my suffering and Christ's sufferings — the two together — to make up the full sum.[55] Let us look briefly at the entire verse in St. Paul's letter to the Colossians that plays a key role here in John Paul's interpretation of God's suffering love. "Now I rejoice in my sufferings for your sake, and in my flesh I complete what is lacking in Christ's afflictions for the sake of his body, that is the church." Again, is the Pope suggesting that the atoning work of Christ is still incomplete? Of course not: John Paul never wavers from insisting that nothing is lacking in the *finished* work of Christ on the cross. Nothing can be added and nothing need be added to his merits and to his atoning blood. He died saying, "It is finished" (John 19:30). Christ's actual death is efficacious, complete and once-for-all. Christ's sufferings are inexhaustible and infinite in their merit and saving power. But then what could St. Paul mean?

As New Testament scholar Eduard Schweizer says, "The decisive question in this case is that of the meaning of 'Christ's afflictions'." "This expression," he adds, "is never used in the New Testament for the Passion, nor for Jesus' experience of suffering in general." Rather, Christ's afflictions in this verse refer to the "sufferings endured in the community for the sake of Christ, or 'in Christ.' . . . If one understands the sentence thus, then the point is that the 'afflictions of Christ' are only endured in a way that still lacks something, that is, that they are not yet complete; but that 'Christ's afflictions' are . . . still outstanding."[56] Thus, if Schweizer is right in his exegesis of this verse then Christ's afflictions refer to "what is yet to come of the afflictions of the (corporate) Christ."[57] And since the body of Christ, the Church, is incorporated with Christ as its head, and is one with him, their sufferings are his, and his are theirs. Says Fr. Ashley, "The doctrine of the

55. On this, see Hans Urs von Balthasar, "Bought at a Great Price," in *You Crown the Year with Your Goodness,* pp. 76-81, and for this point, p. 81.

56. Eduard Schweizer, *The Letter to the Colossians: A Commentary* (Minneapolis, Minn.: Augsburg, 1982), pp. 101, 104-5.

57. C. F. D. Moule, *The Cambridge Greek Testament Commentary: The Epistles to the Colossians and to Philemon* (Cambridge: Cambridge University Press, 1958), pp. 76-77.

Incarnation includes the Church as the Body of Christ in that Jesus continues to be present really, though sacramentally. . . . Our consolation, therefore, is in the companionship of the suffering Christ present in our fellow Christians, the Church. We bear a common witness and carry on a common struggle that we believe and experience to be a share in Christ's sufferings, endowed with the power of transforming ourselves and the world."[58] As the Pope elaborates in a passage that repays meditation:

> The suffering of Christ created the good of the world's Redemption. This good in itself is inexhaustible and infinite. No man can add anything to it. But at the same time, in the mystery of the Church as His Body, Christ has in a sense opened His own redemptive suffering to all human suffering. Insofar as man becomes a sharer in Christ's sufferings to that extent he in his own way completes the suffering through which Christ accomplished the Redemption of the world. Does this mean that the Redemption achieved by Christ is not complete? No. It only means that the Redemption, accomplished through satisfactory love, *remains always open to all love* expressed *in human suffering*. In this dimension — the dimension of love — the Redemption that has already been completely accomplished is, in a certain sense, constantly being accomplished. Christ achieved the Redemption completely and to the very limit; but at the same time He did not bring it to a close. In this redemptive suffering, through which the Redemption of the world was accomplished, Christ opened Himself from the beginning to every human suffering and constantly does so. Yes, it seems to be part *of the very essence of Christ's redemptive suffering* that this suffering requires to be unceasingly completed. . . . [This Redemption] lives and develops as the Body of Christ, the Church, and in this dimension every human suffering, by reason of the loving union with Christ, completes the suffering of Christ. It completes that suffering *just as the Church completes the redemptive work of Christ.* The mystery of the Church — that body which completes in itself also Christ's crucified and risen body — indicates at the same time the space or context in which human sufferings complete the sufferings of Christ. (*SD*, par. 24)[59]

---

58. Ashley, *Choosing a World-View,* p. 319.

59. The Holy Father continues explaining: "Only within this radius and dimension of the Church as the Body of Christ, which continually develops in space and time, can one think and speak of 'what is lacking' in the sufferings of Christ. The Apostle, in fact, makes this clear when he writes of 'completing what is lacking in

It should be clear that the Pope is not claiming that individuals earn their salvation by the works of suffering. Salvation is through the finished work of Christ only. Yet suffering is an indispensable element in the redemption that was initiated and merited by Christ. Christ wants us to collaborate in his plan of salvation, and hence our sufferings, when offered up in love, uniting our sufferings to his all-sufficient suffering, can be of benefit to ourselves and others. This emphasis is not incompatible with the gratuity of grace. As Hans Urs von Balthasar says, "Even suffering, *particularly* suffering, is a precious gift that the one suffering can hand on to others; it helps, it purifies, it atones, it communicates divine graces. The sufferings of a mother can bring a wayward son back to the right path; the sufferings of someone with cancer or leprosy, if offered to God, can be a capital for God to use, bearing fruit in the most unexpected places. Suffering, accepted with thankfulness and handed on, participates in the great fruitfulness of everything that streams from God's joy and returns to him by circuitous paths."[60] It is through the overflowing, superabundant fullness of grace won by the cross of Christ, not because of any flaw, imperfection, or incompleteness, that a calling is given to us in the work of redemption.[61] "Suffering is," says the Pope, "a vocation; it

---

Christ's afflictions for the sake of his body, that is the Church'. It is precisely *the Church,* which ceaselessly draws on the infinite resources of the Redemption, introducing it into the life of humanity, *which is the dimension* in which the redemptive suffering of Christ can be constantly completed by the suffering of man" (*SD,* par. 24). That Christ's sufferings are inexhaustible and infinite in their merit and saving power is also expressed in the following passage: "And so the Church sees in all Christ's suffering brothers and sisters as it were a *multiple subject of His supernatural power. . . .* The Gospel of suffering is being written unceasingly, and it speaks unceasingly with the words of this strange paradox: the springs of divine power gush forth precisely in the midst of human weakness. Those who share in the sufferings of Christ preserve in their own sufferings a very special *particle of the infinite treasure* of the world's Redemption, and can share this treasure with others" (*SD,* par. 27).

60. Hans Urs von Balthasar, *You Crown the Year with Your Goodness,* p. 30.

61. John Paul II, *A Catechesis on the Creed,* vol. II: "[The] truth of our faith does not exclude but demands the participation of each and every human being in Christ's sacrifice in collaboration with the Redeemer. As we said above, no human being could carry out the work of redemption by offering a substitutive sacrifice 'for the sins of the whole world' (cf. 1 John 2:2). But it is also true that each one is called upon to participate in Christ's sacrifice and to collaborate with him in the work of redemption carried out by him. The Apostle Paul says so explicitly when he writes to the Colossians: 'Now I rejoice in my sufferings for your sake, and in my flesh I complete what is lacking in Christ's afflictions for the sake of his body, that is, the Church' (Col. 1:24). . . . Here we have one of the cornerstones of the specific Christian spirituality that we are called upon to reacti-

is a calling to accept the burden of pain in order to transform it into a sacrifice of purification and of reconciliation offered to the Father in Christ and with Christ, for one's own salvation and that of others."[62] Fellowship in Christ's sufferings (Phil. 3:10) is the only way to hear his answer to the question of the meaning of suffering.

Conversion to the Gospel of Suffering

We continue to write new chapters of the gospel of suffering in our Christian lives whenever we suffer together with Christ, in loving union with his salvific sufferings. Conversion is required to discover not only the salvific meaning of suffering, but above all to discover the calling that Christ gives us to collaborate in his work of redemption by suffering together with him, uniting our sufferings to his redemptive sufferings. This conversion does not lead us to think that in itself suffering is a good thing. No, says John Paul, "Suffering is, in itself, an experience of evil. But Christ has made suffering the firmest basis of the definitive good, namely the good of eternal salvation" (SD, par. 26). Rather, we discover the positive value of suffering only when it is united to the sufferings of the crucified Christ. As John Paul says, "Ever since Christ chose the cross and died on Golgotha, all who suffer, especially those who suffer without fault, can come face to face with the 'holy one who suffers'. They can find in his passion the complete truth about suffering, its full meaning and its importance. In the light of this truth, all those who suffer can feel called to share in the work of redemption accomplished by means of the cross."[63]

This kind of suffering bears witness to an interior maturity and spiritual greatness. As the Holy Father says, "This interior maturity and spiritual greatness in suffering are certainly the *result* of a particular *conversion*

---

vate in our life by virtue of Baptism itself which, as St. Paul says (cf. Rom. 6:3-4) brings about sacramentally our death and burial by immersing us in Christ's salvific sacrifice. If Christ has redeemed humanity by accepting the cross and death 'for all', the solidarity of Christ with every human being contains in itself the call to cooperate in solidarity with him in the work of redemption. This is the eloquence of the Gospel. This is especially the eloquence of the cross. This is the importance of Baptism, which, as we shall see in due course, already effects in itself the participation of every person in the salvific work, in which he is associated with Christ by the same divine vocation" (pp. 447-49).

62. Cited in Saward, *Christ Is the Answer*, p. 88. Saward states the Holy Father's view precisely: "To suffer in loving union with Christ is to be an apostle, a missionary, an active labourer in the vineyard of the Lord."

63. John Paul II, *A Catechesis on the Creed*, vol. II, p. 456.

and cooperation with the grace of the crucified Redeemer. It is He Himself who acts at the heart of human sufferings through His Spirit of Truth, through the consoling Spirit. It is He who transforms, in a certain sense, the very substance of the spiritual life, indicating for the person who suffers a place close to Himself. *It is He* — as the interior Master and Guide — *who reveals* to the suffering brother and sister this *wonderful interchange,* situated at the very heart of the mystery of Redemption. . . . For suffering cannot be *transformed* and changed by the grace from outside, but *from within*" (*SD,* par. 26). This process of sanctification may be lengthy, helping one to overcome the sense of the uselessness of suffering and thereby progressively bring oneself closer to hearing Christ's answer to the meaning of suffering and, with it, to the ultimate goal of union with God.

This interior process of conversion is often set in motion by a typically human protest and, with it, the question why. This protest is impelled by the perception that there doesn't seem to be a morally sufficient reason why God would permit these evils to actually occur. We are looking for some meaning to our suffering, and usually we are searching for that meaning on the human level. In particular, we have a sense that suffering is useless; this sense not only tends to engulf us, but it makes us a burden to others. Says the Pope, "The person feels condemned to receive help and assistance from others, and at the same time seems useless to himself" (*SD,* par. 27). We can overcome this feeling by sharing in the redemptive suffering of Christ.

An obvious question is this: how does discovering the redemptive meaning of suffering in union with Christ transform this feeling of uselessness? In this article, I have tried to show John Paul II's answer to this question. Perhaps even more basic is the question why God uses suffering to lead us to recognize, in some way, the sacrifice of Christ on the cross and, ultimately, to acknowledge and follow him. This question arises because the Pope suggests that "it is suffering, more than anything else, which clears the way for the grace which transforms human souls" (*SD,* par. 27). We know that individuals' souls need transformation because of their sinful character. But why choose suffering, more than anything else, as the instrument that makes us receptive or inclines a person to sanctifying grace? The Holy Father doesn't say exactly, but I think we can surmise that his answer would be no different than the answer C. S. Lewis gives in *The Problem of Pain:* pain and suffering of all sorts are God's instrument for getting the rebellious self to lay down its arms. God allows the evil of suffering, then, only because it may produce a benefit for the sufferer. Now, God either could not provide this benefit without the suffering, or at least suffering, more than anything else, seems the best means for attaining that benefit. As Fr. Benedict Ashley explains in a passage well worth quoting in full:

> If the end of the universe and its greatest good is for intelligent and free creatures to come to share knowingly and freely in God's life of self-giving love, then it is understandable why a loving God may permit them to sin if they freely so choose. This will be true, if only in this way they can from their own experience come to know best what God's love means in their lives. Thus the whole of human history can be understood as a school of love in that the lessons are not taught abstractly but from the experience of life lived in freedom. Because human beings only learn perfectly from actual experience and experience means they learn best from the contrast of good and evil, it is clearer why God has chosen this pedagogy. Is it not a fact that for humans love in its fullest sense is never achieved without a struggle between the lovers, without offense and forgiveness?[64]

The Holy Father directs his attention to the question regarding the meaning of our suffering. We often put this question to God-in-Christ. Christ replies from the cross, says the Holy Father, which is the heart of his own suffering. "It often takes time, even a long time, for this answer to begin to be interiorly perceived" (*SD*, par. 26). The Pope is sensitive to the individualized dynamics involved in coming to the interior perception that sharing in the sufferings of Christ is the only way to hear Christ's saving answer to the question of my suffering. What is it that I hear? "Faith in sharing in the suffering of Christ brings with it the interior certainty that the suffering person 'completes what is lacking in Christ's afflictions'; the certainty that in the spiritual dimension of the work of Redemption *he is serving*, like Christ, *the salvation of his brothers and sisters*. Therefore, he is carrying out an irreplaceable service." In some way, and it is a mystery that we shall never grasp in this life, in the mystical body of Christ, the sufferings of one member, when offered up in love, can be of benefit to another. As Saint Paul wrote in 2 Corinthians: "If we are afflicted, it is for your comfort and salvation" (1:5).

This answer to the problem of my suffering does not refute all objections. Says John Paul II, "Christ does not answer directly and He does not answer in the abstract this human questioning about the meaning of suffering. . . . The answer which comes through this sharing [in the suffer-

64. Ashley, *Choosing a World-View,* p. 308.

ings of Christ], by way of interior encounter with the Master, is in itself *something more than the mere abstract answer* to the question about the meaning of suffering." If I understand the Holy Father correctly, that we don't receive an abstract answer to our question implies that Christ's answer does not cover all evils at once; and it certainly does not focus on generic and global goods in the face of many and great evils.

The Holy Father's approach is a more person-centered one. Christ replies by calling us to a vocation and those who follow it must take up their own crosses. He "does not explain in the abstract the reasons for suffering, but before all else He says: 'Follow me'! Come! Take part through your suffering in this work of saving the world, a salvation achieved through my suffering! Through my cross! Gradually, *as the individual takes up his cross,* spiritually uniting himself to the cross of Christ, the salvific meaning of suffering is revealed before him." In other words, the individual discovers Christ himself as the personal answer to the problem of suffering. "He does not discover this meaning at his own human level, but at the level of the suffering of Christ." "At the same time," the Pope adds, "from this level of Christ the salvific meaning of suffering *descends to man's level* and becomes, in a sense, the individual's personal response. It is then that man finds in his suffering interior peace and even spiritual joy" (*SD,* par. 26). For him, evil and suffering are not irreconcilable with God's goodness and power; rather they have become an indispensable element in God's providential plan. As Father Avery Dulles correctly states, "God's love is manifested in weakness and humiliation — in what John Paul II calls 'the omnipotence of humiliation on the Cross'. Christ triumphs over evil and enables us to share in his triumph, provided that we follow the path to which he calls us. The scandal of the cross thus becomes the key to the interpretation of the great mystery of suffering. The *mysterium pietatis,* which coincides with the mystery of redemption, is God's response to the *mysterium iniquitatis.*"[65]

This interior process of conversion leads to the certainty that my suffering is not useless; indeed, it provides an irreplaceable service when united to the sufferings of Christ because, like Christ, I am serving the salvation of others. "In the Body of Christ, which is ceaselessly born of the cross of the Redeemer, it is precisely suffering permeated by the spirit of Christ's sacrifice that is *the irreplaceable mediator and author of the good things* which are indispensable for the world's salvation. It is suffering, more than anything else, which clears the way for the grace which trans-

65. Dulles, *The Splendor of Faith,* p. 92.

forms souls. Suffering, more than anything else, makes present in the history of humanity the powers of the Redemption. In that 'cosmic' struggle between the spiritual powers of good and evil, . . . human sufferings, united to the redemptive suffering of Christ, *constitute a special support for the powers of good,* and open the way to the victory of these salvific powers" (*SD,* par. 27). In short, Christ wills to be united with those who suffer, and somehow he allows their sufferings to complete his own. Of course there is no insufficiency in Christ's redemptive suffering; indeed, our 'making up' of what is 'lacking' derives its redemptive efficacy from Christ's cross and resurrection.

The Good Samaritan

This evangelical theology of redemptive suffering gives rise to compassion for the suffering of others. "If God so loved us [in Christ], we also ought to love one another" (1 John 4:11). Indeed, having united our suffering with the sufferings of the crucified Christ, we are impelled to love of neighbor. "The parable of the Good Samaritan belongs to the Gospel of suffering. For it indicates what the relationship of each of us must be towards our suffering neighbor" (*SD,* par. 28). The Holy Father insists that Christ's revelation of the redemptive meaning of suffering should in no way be identified with passivity, docility, and resignation to human suffering. We have a basic obligation to stop human suffering that is a result of injustice. This obligation is fundamental to the morality of all cultures and civilizations. It bears witness to the fundamental moral values of Christian love of neighbor and human solidarity (*SD,* par. 29). Yet there is more to this relationship to my neighbor than an obligation; we must also be internally disposed to be sensitive to the suffering of others — that is, compassionate. Says John Paul, "If Christ, who knows the interior of man, emphasizes this compassion, this means that it is important for our whole attitude toward others' suffering. Therefore one must cultivate this sensitivity of heart, which bears witness to *compassion* towards a suffering person. Sometimes this compassion remains the only or principal expression of our love for and solidarity with the sufferer" (*SD,* par. 28). At the root of compassion is the Christian understanding that "man can fully discover his true self only in a sincere giving of himself." "A Good Samaritan is *the person capable of* exactly *such a gift of self*" (*SD,* par. 28).[66] God

66. As the Holy Father explains, "Following the parable of the Gospel, we could

sometimes permits suffering, then, as an opportunity "to release love, in order to give birth to works of love towards neighbor, in order to transform the whole of human civilization into a 'civilization of love'. In this love the salvific meaning of suffering is completely accomplished and reaches its definitive dimensions. Christ's words about the Final Judgment [Matt. 25:34-45] enable us to understand this in all the simplicity and clarity of the Gospel" (*SD*, par. 30). Every work of love toward one's neighbor, especially a suffering neighbor, is directed toward Christ himself. "These words about love, about actions of love, acts linked with human suffering, enable us once more to discover, at the basis of all *human sufferings, the same redemptive suffering of Christ*. Christ said: 'You did it to me'. He Himself is the one who in each individual experiences love; He Himself is the one who receives help, when this is given to every suffering person, since His salvific suffering has been opened once and for all to every human suffering" (*SD*, par. 30).

There remains to make the concluding point that in light of the Holy Father's theology of redemptive suffering the proper response to suffering is a double one. "At one and the same time Christ has taught man *to do good by his suffering* and *to do good to those who suffer*. In this double aspect He has completely revealed the meaning of suffering" (*SD*, par. 30). On the one hand, by suffering in loving union with the sufferings of the crucified Christ we apply through our suffering and our love the superabundant good, infinite in its merit and saving power, of the world's redemption accomplished through the suffering of Christ. It is in this way that one does good by one's suffering. On the other hand, every work of love towards one's suffering neighbor is directed to Christ himself. "Assuredly, I say to you, inasmuch as you did it to one of the least of these My brethren, you did it to Me" (Matt. 25:40). It is in this way that we do good to those who suffer.

---

say that suffering, which is present under so many different forms in our human world, is also present in order *to unleash love in the human person*, that unselfish gift of one's 'I' on behalf of other people, especially those who suffer. The world of human suffering unceasingly calls for, so to speak, another world: the world of human love; and in a certain sense man owes to suffering that unselfish love which stirs in his heart and actions" (*SD*, par. 29).

"In the Bible, It Can Be So Harsh!"
Battered Women, Suffering,
and the Problem of Evil

Carol Winkelmann

> *I don't want it to be too late before I start doing what I'm supposed to do. In the Bible, it can be so harsh!*
>
> Carmen, *shelter woman*

> *Waiting on God can be a hard thing.*
>
> Lisa, *shelter woman*

> *Friendship, and not pleasure, is the opposite of suffering.*
>
> Mary E. Hunt, *theologian*[1]

> *As Chung Hyun Kyung says, "making meaning out of suffering is dangerous business." I would add that it is a business that women do everyday, and the closer theologians stay to those complex, organic processes, the more modes of meaning we uncover for dealing with evil and suffering.*
>
> Kathleen M. Sands, *theologian*[2]

---

1. *Fierce Tenderness: A Feminist Theology of Friendship* (New York: Crossroad, 1991), p. 129.
2. *Escape from Paradise: Evil and Tragedy in Feminist Theology* (Minneapolis: Fortress, 1994), p. 65. Chung Hyun Kyung is a Buddhist Christian theologian.

Introduction

Domestic violence is the single greatest threat to the health of American women. Stunningly, however, we are only beginning to understand its causes, nature, and effects. As I use the term here, domestic violence will refer to a pattern of male behavior in private, familial, or intimate settings used to control women. It is, in fact, a constellation of harmful behaviors, including physical, sexual, psychological/emotional, economic, and even spiritual/religious abuses.

In this essay, I wish to examine the language practices of African American and white Appalachian women who pass through the Women's House, a shelter for battered women in an economically depressed neighborhood in a mid-sized city in America's upper South.[3] I am interested in the religious content of the women's language as they attempt to survive partner abuse and to heal themselves. The religious beliefs of shelter women can hinder the healing process if those beliefs reflect traditional patriarchal ideologies. Yet the religious faith, including explanations of suffering and evil (theodicies) mostly related to the fundamentalist/evangelical Christian and Holiness/Sanctified backgrounds of the shelter women and reinvented out of the lived experience of domestic violence, can also serve to sustain the women through periods of profound suffering. This study concerns these complex and contradictory aspects of the religious discourse of survivors of domestic violence. The paradox: traditional Christian discourse creates suffering for battered women while their lived faith experience can provide the means to survive it.

The methodology of my study is feminist, ethnographic, and linguistic. Ethnography is social research that seeks to describe the lived experience of a group or subculture. Its methods include participant observation in field sites, ethnographic note taking, in-depth interviewing, and the collection and analysis of language practices and other semiotic information about the culture of (in this case) a shelter for battered women. For nine years I have collected and analyzed language in the shelter to uncover themes of significance arising out of largely naturalistic situations and linguistic routines, particularly story-telling or creative writing

3. This is a pseudonym for the shelter. All the names used in this study are likewise pseudonymous to protect the confidentiality of women's personal stories and the privacy of their often endangered lives. The words of the women in this study are used with permission. In my book *The Language of Battered Women: A Rhetorical Analysis of Personal Theologies* (Albany: SUNY Press, 2004), I elaborate on ideas in this essay, sometimes using different pseudonyms.

sessions that I facilitate. A goal of feminist ethnography is to advance women's well-being. Indeed, through the use of these qualitative approaches to language in a specific setting, I seek to contribute to conversations on domestic violence as a global phenomenon in critical need of address. I organize my findings in the following manner:

First of all, I will mention some of the basic facts about domestic violence and briefly describe the situation at my field site out of which my findings have emerged. Clearly the fundamental situation is one of intense suffering.

Second, I will situate the suffering of battered women within, first, a very brief, general, and traditional introduction to the problem of evil. Then I will quickly move on to situate the suffering of battered women within an elaborated ten-category typology (developed by Kristine M. Rankka) of both traditional and alternative theodicies. I use this typology to determine a fuller range of explanations to which battered women ascribe when they speak of their situations. I subsequently identify the several theodicies to which most battered women in this particular cultural context subscribe. When they are used with discernment, these theodicies have more and less potential to assist women in the healing process.

Thus, the third section of my presentation will be a description of how battered women do appear to move through the healing process when they do. I use a conversation layered with religious language to illustrate the process. My basic contention is that the healing process is energized by the intermingling of the diverse languages of battered women (secular and religious) as they speak out of their own backgrounds, their own experiences, their own social locations. Meaning shifts occur as words are transferred from one context to the next, thus thrusting language into new forms and functions and the speakers into new linguistic territory. In effect, battered women can accompany one another into greater levels of self-consciousness and social awareness.

Here this process applies to the religious content of their language. As they relate to other culturally diverse clients, staff, and volunteers in the shelter, shelter women are often able to develop new forms of religious discourse or "local theologies" to describe the realities of their domestic situations and to imagine new futures. The fourth and last section of my presentation concerns these local theologies. I have, at this point in my study, a few observations to make about the problem of evil as seen from the faith perspective of women whose bodies bear witness to the brutality of their partners who (more than most Christians would like to acknowledge, I am sure) use religion, use Christian scripture, to justify their brutality and maintain personal and social control.

Let me add only this: My project is critical; ultimately, I intend it to remain respectful to the gospel as I understand it in a critical and feminist light.

Domestic Violence and the Women's House

In May of 1992 I began volunteering at the Women's House. Over the years, I have had multiple roles: dishwasher, donation-sorter, gardener; then hotline counselor, office worker, caring listener, literacy worker, and, always, ethnolinguist. In 1994, I began volunteering once a week as a literacy worker in an effort to engage women who otherwise have little to do in the evening. In exchange, I am able to learn systematically from shelter women by listening to their stories. On any evening, I may work with one to five women or so. We sit around a table, choose a topic by consensus — any topic, although the women mostly write about their shattered lives. Then we write, we read aloud what we've written, and we talk. Whether the topics chosen are abstract (e.g., justice, hope) or concrete (e.g., why I left my partner; the worst day of my life), the talk and text is usually narrative and exposition on narrative: women telling the stories of their lives.

The shelter women are nearly all desperately poor. Domestic violence cuts across race, ethnicity, and class lines, but resources to escape it often do not. The women are typically underclass or working class African American and white Appalachian women. Many are mothers with children and they have just left behind nearly everything they have: marriages or intimate relationships, homes and material possessions, often jobs, families, sometimes even children. From these women I have learned much. Certainly the prevalence of partner violence in America is simply staggering; the statistics are nearly incomprehensible.[4] To wit:

4. The following information can be found in Jana L. Jasinski and Glenda Kaufman Kantor, "Dynamics and Risk Factors in Partner Violence," in *Partner Violence: A Comprehensive Review of Twenty Years of Research*, ed. Jana L. Jasinski and Linda M. Williams (Thousand Oaks, Calif.: Sage Publications, 1998); R. Bachman and L. E. Saltzman, *Violence against Women: A National Crime Victimization Survey Report* (Washington, D.C.: U.S. Department of Justice, 1994) and *Violence against Women: Estimates from the Redesigned Survey* (Washington, D.C.: U.S. Department of Justice, 1995); A. L. Kellerman and J. A. Mercy, "Men, Women, and Murder: Gender-Specific Differences in

- In the United States, over six million women are seriously assaulted by their partners each year.
- One woman is physically assaulted every eight to fifteen seconds in the United States and injuries are twice as likely to occur if the attack is perpetrated by a partner rather than by a stranger.
- One-third to one-half of all American women will be physically assaulted in their lifetimes by their partners, many repeatedly and some to death. This is no exaggeration; indeed, it is a well-known fact that 58,000 American soldiers were killed in the Vietnam War, but it is a very little known fact that, during the same time period, 54,000 American women were killed by their intimate partners.
- Half of all female homicide victims are killed by husbands or boyfriends while only 3 percent of male homicide victims are killed by wives or girlfriends (who are often acting in self-defense).

Such numerical data is stunning; nonetheless, experts agree that the figures are low estimates. Most instances of violence against women are not reported, often because of shame, fear, and/or a lack of confidence in the willingness or ability of the police or judicial systems to help.

Many battered women who pass through the Women's House do believe, however, that God does or will help them. Although the literature on battered women neglects or heavily critiques the influence of patriarchal religious ideologies on women's well-being, religious faith is very significant in the recovery process at the Women's House. A battered woman's concept of God, religion, and suffering often helps her to make sense of her situation and gives her strength in her struggle, albeit in very complex and sometimes contradictory ways.

Battered Women and Suffering

The suffering of battered women is multidimensional: it is physical, psychological, emotional, economic, and — I suggest — spiritual or religious. It manifests as broken bones or broken hearts, as withdrawal, as anger, or as despair. Truly the Women's House is a place of intense suffer-

Rates of Fatal Violence and Victimization," *Journal of Trauma* 33:1 (1992): 1-5; and J. E. Stets and M. A. Straus, "Gender Differences in Reporting of Marital Violence and Its Medical and Psychological Consequences," in *Physical Violence in American Families: Risk Factors and Adaptations to Violence in 8,145 Families,* ed. M. A. Straus and R. J. Gelles (New Brunswick, N.J.: Transaction Publications, 1990), pp. 151-65.

ing. It is nearly always filled to capacity, with additional women waiting to enter. Consequently, a rhetoric of hope and action is necessary in order to remain the allotted six weeks. In secular terms this means that, after the women enter the shelter, they must display activity aimed at gaining personal independence: that is, they must seek employment and housing, or psychological, drug and alcohol, and/or parenting counseling. If they do not articulate in some fashion a rhetoric of hope, the women are asked to leave the shelter.

Most shelter women, because of factors related to region, race/ethnicity, and class, are from fundamentalist/evangelical or Holiness/Sanctified backgrounds. Often they interpret their suffering, and formulate a language of hope and action, in religious or spiritual terms rather than in secular terms. They talk to and about God to interpret the meaning of their crisis and to seek out signs regarding its resolution. Many shelter women have deep religious faith, a faith that helps them to cope with suffering. Indeed, they usually have little else: They are fleeing relationships and households with little to offer in the way of material resources or emotional support. So whatever their current religious practice, God-talk is a typical and frequent feature of the language of shelter women.[5] They return again and again to their faith to seek explanation for their experience of unjust violence, to soothe themselves and other suffering women, and to sustain hope for the future.

This faith is expressed plainly. "I believe in God," says Jasmine, "I sit in the Lord's way." Jasmine is a woman I met in the shelter who had her jaw broken by her partner as he drove furiously down the expressway towards their home in Nashville, Tennessee. They had been arguing because he would not let her visit her family. After he smashed her face, he kicked her out of the moving van onto the side of the road. She lay there until the police came by. Jasmine, a twenty-three-year-old African American woman, is not defeated. Like Job, she has deep faith and it is her solution to the problem of evil. As we sit around the dining room table, her new friend and shelter companion, Millie, listens intently. Millie is a forty-year-old woman who has worked in social work. Her husband habitually locked her and their child in their home when he went out at

---

5. The religious backgrounds of women in the shelter are predominately Christian. A few women have been Muslim and I once met a woman who had been a Buddhist nun. I will address the issue of church-affiliation shortly. It is important, however, to recognize the diversity of women's religious views and experiences, across and within denominations. The current religious practices of shelter women, i.e., regular church attendance, daily prayer rituals, and so forth, are also diverse.

night. On the night before she came to the shelter, he tied her and tortured her with lit cigarette ends when he came home. In the course of their conversation, Millie responds to Jasmine in measure, deliberately and calmly, "This is a man's world." But, with a sense of the possibility of liberation, she adds, "One day, men will come back to the Lord's way. In a spiritual way, God brings justice. Now or later in life."

This language is typical in the Women's House. God-talk may very well be a primary common idiom of the many diverse languages of the shelter, that is, the variety of languages deriving from differences of race, class, ethnicity, religion, employment, education, age, sexual orientation, physical ability, and geographical origins. Although its patriarchal features are problematic, God-talk is a language of resistance and revitalization for many battered women, an "identity group" whose very existence is defined by the experience of suffering originating in male privilege and authority.

Suffering and the Problem of Evil

Suffering, according to anthropologist Clifford Geertz, is "an experiential challenge in whose face the meaningfulness of a particular pattern of life threatens to dissolve into a chaos of thingless names and nameless things."[6] In countless philosophical, theological, and popular reflections on it, a key thematic of suffering is a profound sense of a loss of control of one's own life, leading to human degradation, and finally to a loss of human meaning. What evils — natural, moral, or social — cause suffering? Why do such evils exist?

Philosophers, theologians, and others have debated the "problem of evil" for centuries. In traditional Christian thought, an omniscient, omnipotent, and perfectly good God created the world. But why would such a God allow the evil that causes the vast amount of profound suffering among humankind? Augustine, Aquinas, Hume, Kant, and many others have contributed to the discussion of logical or epistemic expla-

---

6. Clifford Geertz, *The Interpretation of Cultures* (New York: Basic Books, 1973), p. 103. The essay in which this quotation appears is entitled "Religion as a Cultural System" (pp. 87-125). In it, Geertz makes the point so often referenced by contemporary theologians that: "As a religious problem, the problem of suffering is, paradoxically, not how to avoid suffering but how to suffer, how to make of physical pain, personal loss, worldly defeat, or the helpless contemplation of others' agony something bearable, supportable — something, as we say, sufferable" (p. 104).

nations.[7] The scriptural treatments of suffering — such as the Book of Job — and the literary treatments of suffering — such as in the writings of Fyodor Dostoevsky, Albert Camus, and Elie Wiesel — have also demanded our attention. Three traditional reasons are usually given to explain suffering. One is that suffering is a test by God of one's faith, a test meant to help people appreciate by contrast the good things in their lives or to bring them to trust that what appears evil is in fact part of God's plan for ultimate good. A second reason is that suffering is caused by human beings, but allowed by God because God will not intervene in human freedom. A third reason is that suffering is admonishment or punishment by God for the self-centeredness of human beings.[8]

Increasingly, many ordinary people do not find these three classical theistic explanations of suffering credible. Any one of them can seem to lead to a God who does not care about the suffering of the innocent. Much suffering, human and animal, seems to be innocent suffering: It does not seem to be merited or educative. It seems caused by an indifferent God. The suffering of women and children caused by domestic violence, for example, does not seem to be merited — at least in the eyes of compassionate others if not for traumatized women and their abusive partners. Why would a caring God allow so many women and girl children throughout history, and across the world, for example, to be beaten, raped, enslaved, and killed at the whim of lovers, spouses, and other family members? Although some theists argue that God must necessarily protect human free will, and that these are examples of free will gone terribly awry, surely male free will cannot be a satisfactory explanation for the brutality of female victimization. To even explore such an argument in logical or epistemic terms seems to some persons singularly unethical.

7. The logical arguments explore the logical relations between the idea of an all-perfect, all-knowing, all-powerful God and the fact of evil. The epistemic arguments explore the subjective probabilities that an all-perfect, all-knowing, all-powerful God exists in view of the fact of intense instances of suffering. That is, the first type of argument is logical, deductive, or a priori; the second type of argument is empirical, probabilistic, or a posteriori. See Michael L. Peterson, ed., *The Problem of Evil* (Notre Dame, Ind.: University of Notre Dame Press, 1992) and Daniel Howard-Snyder, ed., *The Evidential Argument from Evil* (Bloomington, Ind.: Indiana University Press, 1996), especially pp. xi-xx.

8. See Brennan R. Hill, Paul Knitter, and William Madges, *Faith, Religion, and Theology* (Mystic, Conn.: Twenty-Third Publications, 1990), pp. 326-28, for this helpful introduction. See also Kristine M. Rankka, *Women and the Value of Suffering: An Aw(e)ful Rowing toward God* (Collegeville, Minn.: Liturgical Press, 1998), pp. 37-50, for a more detailed typology of both traditional and alternative theodicies.

The problem of evil and suffering continues to challenge philosophers and theologians, not to mention, of course, those persons among us who suffer — all of us, eventually and to some extent. In the view of some theologians, salvation history itself is a narrative of the search and struggle for redemption in the face of suffering and theology is its metalanguage. Thus theological views about suffering continue to develop and change across time.[9] Shelter women, too, have their own ideas about suffering based on their life experiences. Their own experiences of brutality and violence — in religious language, their own encounters with evil — form the basis of their own dynamic concepts of God.

"Why Does God Let Me Suffer?" Theodicies and Battered Women

Although the battered women who pass through the Women's House come from predominately evangelical/fundamentalist or Holiness/Sanctified backgrounds, their religious language covers a wide theological or philosophical spectrum. Their religious explanations of their suffering are restricted neither to the three traditional views listed above, nor to those spelled out in the doctrines, creeds, or other faith statements of their own congregations. The explanation for such diversity has to do, certainly, with language heterogeneity, the interplay between gender socialization, the women's levels of religious or theological education, the degree to which they understand and/or believe they must adhere to official church doctrine, the significance they place on personal interpretation and lived experience, their current religious practices, and other relevant immediate and contextual features, such as external expectations for discursive behavior.

I find it helpful, then, to filter the words of battered women about God and suffering through an even finer, more discriminating mechanism than the three-item list of basic perspectives held by contemporary Christians and other monotheists. In attending to the words of battered women, I have found that their theodicies may be more finely elaborated through a ten-item typology of both traditional and alternative theodicies. These ten systems of belief are dualistic, Augustinian, punishment/retribution, redemptive/atonement, Irenian/evolutionary, reme-

---

9. For an introductory survey, see Lucien Richard, *What Are They Saying about the Theology of Suffering?* (New York: Paulist Press, 1992).

dial/instructive, faith (solution), process, suffering God, and liberation.[10] In what follows, I will briefly define these systems and provide illustrative quotations from the written and spoken words of shelter women:

Dualistic

The universe is an arena for the great cosmic struggle between the forces of good and the forces of evil. The devil schemes for control over human souls. With divine aid and intervention, humans must struggle to resist evil.

> Dana: Domestic violence is the battleground over the good versus evil. The manipulating and anger are the evil terms. The faith and strength are the good tools. The devil can't handle faith, hopes, and dreams [of women who resist domestic violence].
>
> Corinne: I learned that, being a battered woman, I had to depend on the Lord. Only through him have I gotten deliverance. The more I see where God has brought me from, I know he's always been there.

Augustinian

Humans are given free will by an all-powerful God, but they often make destructive choices. God could prevent evil and suffering from happening but, in the interest of human free will, he does not. The lack of goodness is itself evil. This system is marked by a mistrust of the human body as a source of temptation and destructive choices. The adherent often accepts privation as a way to avoid temptation and accepts a hierarchy of religious authority for moral guidance.

> Carolyn: My suffering stems from decisions that I have made that were incorrect. These decisions may not be important but the accumulation accounts for something. God will help you, however, with a wrong decision.
>
> Dela: I think that's why I'm having such a hard time now, because I haven't been going to church or listening to the Word. I think I

10. See Rankka, *Women and the Value of Suffering,* pp. 37-50.

know too much. They say nothing can be accomplished without God. Well, I haven't been putting him in my life so I'm having trouble.

Punishment/Retribution

This system is a variant of Augustinian-influenced theodicy in that human choices do lead to suffering. Suffering does not always extend from bad human choices, but human sin is still the cause. Thus natural disaster can be explained. Sin demands repentance.[11]

> Penny: My God I have done wrong and I want to know my God that I used to know. . . . My God I am asking for forgiveness please! Lead me to your peaceful home. My God take away the guilt that I have of myself and lead me to you My God. Bring my family together and take away our pain and hurt and bring a family that prays together [and] stays together.
>
> Wanda: I [wish I could] start my life over the way it started — with good firm loving biblical principles. But stay, and not stray from that teaching. Because I have learned that God's way is not only the best way, but if you're looking for peace, it's the only way!

Redemptive/Atonement

In this theodicy, suffering is undertaken for several reasons, including for the sake of others. Suffering is expiatory. Like Jesus, the good Christian accepts it out of obedience to God. There is a willingness to accept suffering as part of God's plan for human salvation.

> Valencia: I think that everything will fall into place as long as you pray to God, pull yourself together, and concentrate on the positive things that happened in my life, have a good time with my family.
>
> Samantha: I know that my Redeemer lives. I need thee every hour of the day Most Holy One.

11. Traditional Calvinism, argues Rankka, is supported by such a theology.

Lise: One week prior to my severe beating I told a friend if God does not take me out of this situation soon I'm not going to be able to keep going on. I prayed over and over every day, asking God to take the burden and the whole situation off my shoulders, that I gave it to him to bear. I felt like God was not listening to me because the abuse — instead of things changing — became worse. I really felt like giving up on prayers but, right when I couldn't take anymore, God took me out the situation. I was put on a plane, sent with people I didn't know. I left my home, children, job, etc. I finally had the strength from out of nowhere to leave the abuse. God answers our prayers in his own precious time not in our time. So now, I continue to give it all to him and wait for his answer or what will be sent to me next. I know my whole life has changed now I walk in faith. God is good. Yeah! Yeah!

Irenian/Evolutionary

Suffering derives from the misuse of free will. It is the natural by-product of sinfulness. Through suffering, God shapes souls by providing them with a moral contrast between what happens as a consequence of sin and what happens as a consequence of goodness. Evil and suffering occur so humans have the opportunity to develop their souls in the face of affliction. (To compassionate outsiders, this view may seem completely unsatisfactory.)

Vanessa: Our feelings, sometimes they overwhelm or depress us. Learning how to deal with them and not allowing them to conquer us. Learn how to overcome is the answer to knowing how to cope. To stifle them without proper processing we do ourselves much harm, physically, mentally, spiritually, and especially emotionally. So if God gave us feelings, it must be good even if the feelings make us feel bad at that particular time. Staying in touch with our Creator is the way to stay strong and accept and get in touch with our feelings he gave us. For me, this is God's way of making us in his image.

Joanna: I love the Lord and he has always been apart of my life. I never blamed the Lord in what I went through, but it was very hard for me to talk to someone at church. I never questioned the Lord about what I went through because it felt like it was my fault and I didn't deserve to ask him for help when I knew I was wrong. I have always wanted to live a Christian life and serve the Lord, but all the man I encounter was not religious so it take me away from what I believe in. I return to church and that where I believe I got my strength to leave out of the relationship. I'm going to stay in church and do what I want to do. I know the Lord has never left me, but I did leave him. He was there for when I decide to come back to him.

Remedial/Instructive

This is a variant of the Irenian view. Suffering is soul-making. It leads to righteousness, compassion, and concern for others. It can be imposed by God or it can be self-imposed.

> Allie: Each day that I am away from home I am getting stronger and as I get stronger I become more comfortable with the changes that I'm making. My vision of myself in five years is to be a strong confident woman in a career helping to make a difference in women's lives. My experiences are preparing me for helping others. God is preparing me for something good.
>
> Linda: I think religion screwed me up big time. I hate that guilt I always have about everything. I think it helps me to be a good person but cripples me all the same time. I have the mentality that if I love John (truly love him), then I will put up with everything that he is or does, that I should accept these things. You know . . . love till death do us part.

Faith Solution

Evil is a mystery. There is no adequate explanation for it. Like Job, the good Christian surrenders to God. She may engage, like Job, in lamentation and protest; however, the ultimate response to God is trust and faith.

> Hettie: When my pain and troubles seem to get me down, I stand all amazed at the love Jesus offers me. Oh it is wonderful that Jesus cared for me enough to die for me. With God all things

(problems-pain) ends. There is no end of God's great love for me and you. I write this in the name of Jesus Christ. Amen.

Lisa: My name is Lisa and I am in pain. I just want to scream. I know it's time for me to carry my burden to God. Whatever the problem, I'll put it in God's hands.

Process

God works by persuasion, not coercion. He depends on human action to effect goals he sets. He takes risks to bring humans into community with himself and others. God is a co-sufferer in unjust situations and cannot or will not punish evil for once and for all.

Deana: This time it's about my own mistakes. If I had been in the church, I wouldn't have such hardship. He would have guided me to make better decisions. But I'm not being punished. God gave me something to think about. You have to take that first step by yourself. If you take the first step, God takes the next ten. . . . God is supposed to guide you through the valley of darkness, but you're not supposed to do something foolish.

Beattie: Together we can accomplish all things! If we just believe in ourselves and trust in God! I am going back to school so that I can make things better for myself and my children.

Suffering God

When humans suffer, God suffers. The sufferer has hope because God makes available compassionate care. The sufferer will experience both divine solidarity and human solidarity to strengthen her in the experience of (unjust) suffering.

Heather: God is my best friend and he's always there when I need him. I talk to him and ask him for help. He has helped me through some tough times. He kept my son from dying after he was born and he's helping me right now. He has put me in a Christian atmosphere with people who are Christians and in their own way they are helping even if they don't know it. I love my religion and I hope someday I will get to heaven but until then I can just pray and read.

Jewell: I had to weep because I can't do anything by myself. I had to wait on the Lord because of what he had in store for me and I had to wait on him. I was crying and this man came up to me and I asked him if he was a Christian and he said, "Yes, praise God!" And I wept because I knew then that the Lord brought him across my path to pray and lift my spirit. I not only stopped crying but I was smiling. He had such a pleasant face and his voice was so at peace. I know the Lord blessed me at that time in need.

Rosemary: Jesus stuck up for women in the bible. Such as Mary the Whore — when she was being stoned, he said, "Who [is] without sin cast the first stone."

Liberation

Suffering is caused by the oppression of others. Some sin is social; that is, social institutions can be oppressive. God is revealed to the oppressed, the poor. God is a "power-with" God, not a "power-over" God. As such, this theology often works in conjunction with the "Suffering God" approach. The sufferer engages in complaint, protest, resistance. The words of the sufferer are prophetic. Faith leads to action.

Millie: Man equals egocentric. They need to fulfill their masculine image. . . . They get abusive if you try to make them feel less than a man. This is a man's world. One day they [men] will come back to the Lord's way. In a spiritual way, God brings justice. Now or later in life.

Diana: Everyone here is losing a little suffering. Little by little, we are losing our suffering. Praise God who leads us out of exile.

The Theodicies of Battered Women

The theodicies to which women like Diana subscribe are not exclusive to battered women, of course; nor are the categories into which they fall mutually exclusive. Persons who are not theologically trained — and perhaps even those who are — may evidence contradictions in their cosmologies. Although my findings are based on data gathered over a nine-year period, I do not believe that through these brief statements we can fully understand the dynamic theologies[12] of the shelter women. If asked to present a systematic account, the women might very well try to rework their positions to fit into the parameters of their traditional faith communities. At the same time, and in keeping with functional linguistic views of the intimate connection between word and concept, I believe these statements of shelter women, collected in largely naturalistic situations or open-ended conversations, do reflect some of their most authentic, unself-conscious thinking on the nature of God and suffering. These are the candid utterances of women who are not being asked to regularize or defend their statements.

This being said, I have discovered that many women in the Women's House initially function within a redemptive/atonement model or a suffering God model of religious explanation for their suffering. The redemptive/atonement model, again, is the view that suffering is endured in expiation for the sake of others or out of obedience to God. The women often (at least in the initial days of their shelter stay) accept their suffering as part of God's plan for human salvation. The suffering God approach is the approach that recognizes that when humans suffer, God suffers. The sufferer experiences compassionate care through divine and human solidarity, both of which strengthen her in the experience of (unjust) suffering.

Both of these models, it should also be pointed out, are typical cultural behavioral templates in the gender socialization of girls and women. Girls and women traditionally have been taught to endure suffering in silence as part of their feminine or maternal duty. A good mother suffers hardships for her children without complaint, for example, or she defers to the patriarchal lines of authority in the interest of family peace, harmony, and order.

In addition, these two models are also not at all unfamiliar to either white or black Holiness/Sanctified or fundamentalist/evangelical congregations, in which most of the shelter women have been raised and many still attend. In a familiar black experience of religion, Jesus the innocent sufferer is a central divine image. Black women, according to theologian Jacquelyn Grant, have developed fervent feeling for Jesus as

---

12. I will argue shortly that shelter women in conversation develop "local theologies" and thus assist one another to greater levels of awareness about the immediate and social causes of their suffering.

friend and co-sufferer.[13] Above all, he is a co-sufferer, that is, not a regal king. Lavonia, a well-paid African American construction worker battered by a jealous partner, gives evidence of this experience:

> We understand Jesus more because of his suffering. In the black church, we understand his pain and sorrow. I'm not saying white women can't understand. But we understand more because we are closer to the suffering. Some white women can, but it's stronger in black women. . . . Black people are closer to God because we are oppressed like Jesus. And black women are closer to God than white women because we have been oppressed more. It's all the people who have been through the suffering, the hardships. Jesus went there. When you have been suffering, the praises go higher.

Where women in traditional black churches identify with the suffering Jesus, white women (and black women) in Holiness churches are primarily motivated and moved by the metaphors and images of the Spirit. Heather Mae, for example, says: "Just remember to pray and wait on the Lord. He is already there; he just can be really really busy. You are blessed just breathing in the Spirit." Jesus is a central image in these churches as well, however: according to doctrine, Jesus feels and suffers as a human being. By his suffering, he made full atonement for human sin. The Atonement is the only source of salvation and is "efficacious for those who reach the age of responsibility, only when they repent and believe." Believing often extends from personal experience.

With somewhat a different emphasis, then, the suffering Jesus is an important image in the religious experience, the song and worship, of both white Sanctified/Holiness Churches and traditional black churches.[14] Thus it is not completely surprising that battered women with fundamentalist/evangelical and Holiness/Sanctified backgrounds evidence these two types of theological approaches to suffering.

What is worthy of note are these three points: First of all, given their

13. See Jacquelyn Grant, *White Women's Christ and Black Women's Jesus* (Atlanta: Scholars Press, 1989), especially Chapter VII; and Emilie Townes, ed., *A Troubling in My Soul: Womanist Perspectives on Evil and Suffering* (Maryknoll, N.Y.: Orbis Books, 1993).

14. In my view, a difference between African American and white conceptions of redemption is the centrality of the act of belief for white women in contrast to the centrality of the experience of suffering for African American women. That is, African American women believe they are close to Jesus by virtue of similar experiences of unjust suffering; white women believe they are close to Jesus by virtue of belief. In this matter, the critical point is emphasis, not doctrinal differences.

traditional religious upbringing, gender socialization, and domestic situations there are relatively fewer women in the Women's House who adhere strictly or primarily to potentially more woman-threatening theodicies such as dualistic or Augustinian ones. (This may not be true of other denominational groups, such as Roman Catholics or Christian Scientists.)

Second, as battered women review, rehearse, or reenact domestic scenes, their language suggests that their abusers lay claim to different theodicies. The abusers, it seems, often do subscribe to dualistic, Augustinian, punishment/retribution, or Irenian/evolutionary explanations of suffering and evil. For example, abusers commonly cite Scripture passages that reaffirm the patriarchal order and traditional lines of authority. They very often refer to Genesis 2, in which *Adam* is incorrectly translated to signify the male only — and a male created before the transgressive Eve.

Third, I would like to point out the emancipatory potential of both the suffering God and the redemptive/atonement theological models. Although these models can instill or induce passivity in the face of pervasive or traumatic violence against women, they may also facilitate much more easily the growing social awareness and autonomy of battered women than the dualistic, Augustinian, punishment/retribution, or Irenian/evolutionary models of suffering and evil. Shifts may and often do occur in the theological perspectives of battered women.

To this topic, I would now like to turn, for it is out of this emancipatory potential that actual shifts — the remaking of meaning in acts of "local theologizing" — arise.

Shifts in Theological Language: The Remaking of Meaning

It is my contention that, during their stay at the Women's House, and depending on a variety of factors (one of which is the safe space to reflect on their inner experience) battered women may evidence some theological reconceptualizations based on local knowledge and lived experience, reconceptualizations moving mainly in the direction of remedial/instructive or liberation theodicies. That is, the women are sometimes able to move out of more individual-oriented theodicies (such as the punishment/retribution model) or away from their church communities' or their abusive partners' perspectives and into more socially oriented models such as the remedial/instructive model (personal action to help individual others) or the liberation model (social action for social change). Variants of these two latter models often surface when women are talking together about sexism and violence against women. In effect, they are sometimes able to co-create a new or alternative theological language as they remake theological meaning within their local context and lived experience.

Indeed, I will push this formulation further to suggest that women in conversation begin to help one another to develop "local theologies," their own particular explanations of the nature, causes, and consequences of suffering that depart to greater and lesser degrees from traditional or former explanations and that help the women make particular, personal sense of their situations. One variation of this dynamic that I will investigate forthrightly is this: Battered women who are more aware of the social causes and consequences of violence against women are able on occasion to lead more conservatively minded religious women into new levels of awareness; at the same time, women with more liberatory religious views can lead women with more traditional social views into increased awareness of the need for change. In short, women help women to move dialectically through the healing process, through stages of suffering, into states of greater autonomy and towards recognition of the need for both personal and social change.[15] From a feminist healing perspective, certainly, this is an ideal. It is also sometimes the reality.[16]

Before I illustrate this dynamic, I offer some explanation about how battered women do move through the healing process towards greater autonomy — of either the secular or faith-based sort. Women in the shelter often show evidence of passing through three linguistic or interpretative frameworks as they move through the intense suffering and isolation of their domestic crisis to more integrated and relational modes of being.[17]

15. This is a positive, progressive formulation of a dynamic that is not guaranteed; a regressive movement may very well be possible. The role of the facilitator can be important and will be discussed later.

16. James W. Pennebaker, psychologist, has offered convincing empirical evidence that the simple act of giving testimony about traumatic events (even to an inanimate object like a tape-recorder) actuates the healing process. See *Opening Up: The Healing Power of Confiding in Others* (New York: William Morrow, 1990).

17. This healing trajectory is suggested by Dorothee Soelle in *Suffering*, trans. Everett R. Katlin (Philadelphia: Fortress Press, 1975). Soelle's is only one of a number of schemas suggested by scholars. I use Soelle's work for two reasons. First of all, she is a respected feminist theologian trying to make sense of suffering in terms of theodicy and not simply psychology and, secondly, her schema is very simple. It suits the purposes of this brief essay very well. Soelle's schema, however, does not contradict the more detailed work of psychologists and other trauma scholars. For example,

The first phase is one of silence and isolation; the second phase is one of analysis and lament; the third phase is one of agency and solidarity. A qualification: the phases are not engaged by all women in the shelter. Nor are they linear or one-dimensional; that is, the sufferer may re-experience earlier phases in response to new concepts, events, or material conditions. This being said, I offer some examples of each phase.

Phase One characteristics: silence and isolation; numbness; the pressure of suffering turning the individual in on herself.[18]

> Mary Jo: Man, it feel like a dream. When am I gonna wake up? [. . .] It feels like I'm sleeping and when am I gonna wake up from this bad dream?
>
> Sheila: One time my husband put a pillow on my face and didn't take it off until I played dead. . . . My husband isolated me. He knew I had no family in the area. I completely relied on him.

Phase Two characteristics: lament; awareness; analysis of suffering within existing frameworks.

> Lynn: You have every right to hate this person for what he did/I was afraid of killing somebody.
>
> Wanda: [Feeling hatred for the abuser] might be very disturbing but it's very normal.
>
> Rose: I coulda been on death row. I could have and it wasn't that far away because my daughter was bleeding out of her rectum. The only thing I could say was "Lord have mercy! You've been killing my child." Then I had to look at her when she asked me, "Mama." She's 21 years old now. "You were my mother. Why didn't you know?" Wake up ladies! Wake up! He bad.

---

see Judith Lewis Herman, *Trauma and Recovery* (New York: Basic Books, 1992); Ronnie Janoff-Bulman, *Shattered Assumptions: Towards a New Psychology of Trauma* (New York: Free Press, 1992); Anna C. Salter, *Transforming Trauma* (Thousand Oaks, Calif.: Sage Publications, 1995); and Dee L. R. Graham with Edna I. Rawlings and Roberta K. Rigsby, *Loving to Survive: Sexual Terror, Men's Violence, and Women's Lives* (New York: New York University Press, 1994).

18. Notice that these are recollections or reflections of the battered women's Phase One internal states (i.e., of mind or feeling) while they were being abused. Their capacity to share in conversation indicates that they have moved beyond Phase One.

Phase Three characteristics: agency; autonomy of action; solidarity through suffering; changed structures or frameworks.

> Raylene and Jebba: We laugh together, we cry together, we support each other, we strengthen each other every day.
> Pat: We should have a Million Lady Walk.

As women like Mary Jo, Rose, and Raylene move through these phases of suffering towards survival and recovery, they may evidence some theological reconceptualizations based on local knowledge and lived experience and the development of a shared language.

As I mentioned earlier, they move mainly in the direction of remedial/instructive or liberation theodicies. That is, the women are sometimes able to move out of more individual-oriented theodicies (such as the punishment/retribution model) and into more socially oriented models (such as the liberation model). This new language develops when women are talking together about sexism and violence against women. In effect, they are sometimes able to co-create a new or alternative theological language.

To illustrate, I will focus on one story-telling session and on one particular type of mix in the language of the battered women. I choose a conversation that illustrates a particular intersection: the interplay of religious with secular languages. By "religious" language, I simply mean language relating to the divine or the transcendent or to Christian beliefs and practices. Broadly speaking, "secular" language is non-religious language; however, in this discussion, I will limit my focus to distinguishable varieties such as the languages of self-help, folk wisdom, human rights, and courts/criminal justice. These types of secular languages may be conceptualized generally as languages of self-consciousness and liberation, that is, languages regarding moving out of the condition of domestic crisis and into one of well-being. They may be drawn from the women's own life experience or community or assimilated from the language of other resident women and/or staff who advise, advocate, or teach group sessions on domestic violence, drug and alcohol abuse, codependency, and so on. In dealing with religious language, I will try to make qualitative differentiations between simply religious language and "spiritual" language, that is, language that expresses a sense of self, authority, or agency above and beyond the dogma, traditionalism, or habit of religion and its institutions. Very roughly speaking, in the following exchanges, secular and religious language are linguistic evidence of Phase Two concepts; social and spiritual languages are evidence of Phase Three concepts. Notice the ways in which secular and religious mix in dynamic or dialogic ways in the exchanges:

1   Venita: I always had my faith. I say my prayers at night. I put more
2   faith in God and not in [my abuser]. Do you know how I know?
3   Because I was torn enough to get out before it got too bad. I was
4   torn about him and God helped me to get out.
5   Carmen: It's different for Venita than for me. Venita came up in a
6   loving family. I had a bad life. . . . I had to try to believe in God. I
7   had to try. . . .
8   Venita: I felt it in my heart. You have to feel it in your heart. You
9   can't do it with your head.
10   Carol: What do you feel in your heart when you feel God?
11   Venita: I feel happiness in my heart. When it comes to God, it seems
12   like when I'm walking down this dark road I can see this light at
13   the end. I know there's a light ahead.
14   Carmen: I don't want it to be too late before I start doing what I'm
15   supposed to do! In the Bible, it can be so harsh!
16   Carol: Do you find out about God from the Bible?
17   Carmen: The Bible is very complex and real scary and other people
18   look at it as being the truth but the Bible contradicts itself.

[A short discussion of how most people think God is a male and how this leads some men to think they are better than women. Both women disagree with the image of God as male.]

19   Venita: [Men] do think they are better. Do you know the saying,
20   "Behind every good man, there's a woman"? It's never the other
21   way around.
22   Carmen: They think they are better because of Adam and Eve. . . .
23   Women believe more in God. They have to. They have to take so
24   much stuff. They have to have something to hold onto. Men have
25   each other. Men stick together. They have one another.
26   Venita: But a woman doesn't have anybody. Suppose you are just
27   out there by yourself. God is the only person you can believe in.
28   Carmen: Me too. I don't have no girlfriends when I get into trou-
29   ble. . . . If God were a woman, it would be wonderful. I know a lot
30   of men would be going to hell!
31   Venita: Me too. I know I would be standing. I try to be a good per-
32   son.

33   Carol: Does that mean God [as a man] lets men get away with stuff?

34   Venita: God lets men get away with stuff! Women pay more on
35   earth, more than men. Guys don't think about it. They are not go-
36   ing to get their consequences 'til after they die. Women get it
37   now. But when they die, they are going to get it.

38   Carmen: A woman God is for women.

39   Venita: In my case, I called the police. I was the one being abused.
40   He snatched my sons. I called the police and they said he can do
41   it because he is their natural dad. That's not fair! Turn the tables. I
42   would go to jail for kidnapping them. The laws are so messed up.
43   If a woman kills a man, she gets fifteen to twenty-five years in
44   jail. If a man kills his wife, he gets six years. I don't understand
45   that! It's not fair. They don't get what they deserve. We get pun-
46   ished a lot harder than a man. [. . .]

47   Carmen: Anyway, there's biases because of who has control. The
48   country is run by rich white men. The church too.

[A discussion about the patriarchal nature of another woman's shelter church.]

49   Venita: That's why I don't belong to no church. I read the Bible.
50   Now and then I read the Bible. I feel in my heart what I have to
51   do. I ain't going by his rules or her rules. No, I can't get into that.

52   Carmen: I be having a problem with the Bible all the time. Most peo-
53   ple do, but they just believe anyway. They don't admit the story
54   is wrong. [. . .] The Bible starts out with Adam and Eve. The
55   world thinks women are evil. Eve got Adam to eat the apple. Ev-
56   eryone says women are evil. So the stories in the Bible are like
57   that — against women. It is not right.

58   Venita: [My abuser] thinks God is on his side.

59   Carol: It's like a blank card to do anything.

60   Venita: There's your freedom to do anything you want to do.

In this series of exchanges, Carmen and Venita are engaging in dialogic activity with both religious and secular content. The secular languages can be characterized as those of folk wisdom (lines 19-21), criminal justice (lines 39-41), legal/judicial (lines 41-46); popular politics (lines 47-48), popular psychology (lines 19, 34-35, and throughout), domestic violence (line 39), human rights (lines 39-57); sub-clausally, there are secular themes and metaphors regarding the journey or escape (line 4), the moral trial (lines 5-7), justice/punishments (lines 43-46). Regarding the hetero-glossic mix of language, however, Carmen and Venita both contribute from their own differing standpoints. As Carmen points out, "It's different for Venita than for me. Venita came up in a loving family. I had a bad life. [. . .] I had to try to believe in God" (lines 5-6). Indeed, of the two women, Venita is the one who (initially at least) articulates the most conventional or uncritical religious perspective. Initially, her language appears to be largely Phase Two language; Carmen uses the most Phase Three language. Still the tension of the secular-religious hybridity creates a spiraling or recursive effect that results in both women engaging, if momentarily, in Phase Three worldviews.

To illustrate, I will first briefly consider the language of each woman, then I will discuss the ways in which their contributions propel the conversation forward. Notice, however, that there are traces of Phase One circumstances in the language of both women. They both recall a prior world — the days before they arrived at the shelter — in which they were isolated and alienated (lines 26-29). As she relives her Phase One experience, Carmen chooses the present tense: "I don't have no girlfriends. . . ." In the actual present, of course, she counts Venita and other shelter women as her friends. In contrast, Venita's language is speculative: "Suppose you are just out there by yourself. . . ." The chosen frame for her presentation — an imaginative world — indicates she now considers herself beyond (what I am defining as) Phase One circumstances; additionally, she is inviting her interlocutors — through the act of story-telling — to imagine this circumstance, to enter empathically into it, as she rehearses a past life that no longer exists.

Venita's Language in Terms of the Phases and Meaning Shifts

When she is not reliving her suffering, Venita uses Phase Two language, initially, about religious and secular issues. Lines 1-4 reveal a somewhat uncritical religious perspective. Lines 19-21 make clear a somewhat limited though still Phase Two awareness of her social situation. In these lines her language reveals a clear anger towards her abuser and her view appears to be shaped solely from her own experience with him (for surely not all men think they are better than all women and behind some women there are supportive men). That is, she initially does not have a full social awareness of her personal situation. Her language does not give evidence of social analysis. Yet her argument is coherent and cohesive: emotions and rationality are communicated together though her anger sometimes overwhelms her objectivity, that is, her ability to see other perspectives or possibilities.

There are additional Phase Two modalities in her language. For example, there are traces of a sense of righteousness in Venita's anger. Her abuser has clearly violated moral, criminal, and legal codes; yet, the legal and criminal justice systems and (interestingly enough) God seem to protect men — the latter, at least, while men are on earth. While Venita is angry about this, her language is psalmic: it is a language of lamentation. Lamentation is composed of both complaint and praise. In Venita's language, in addition to the plaintive modality, there is a tone of praise and worship. When asked what she feels when she "feels God," she says, "I feel happiness in my heart. When it comes to God, it seems like when I'm walking down this dark road I can see this light at the end. I know there's a light ahead" (lines 11-13). God is praised for being or showing the light even though — she complains — the road is dark. Ultimately, she counts on God to render justice. Hence, overall, her objectives are utopian. (And why not? She cannot count on the criminal justice or the legal systems to help her.) Pragmatically, however, she accepts her situation and, despite the recalcitrance of the criminal justice or legal systems, she seeks to change her own situation through existing social structures — "In my case, I called the police" (line 39). More precisely: of her own accord, she does not imagine alternative or more effective social structures, but she does imagine retribution — if only in a religious sense and a better life for herself. "But when they die [men], they are going to get it" (line 37).

By the time Venita utters the last exchange of the conversation, however, she has substantially altered both her religious and secular language. In lines 34-37, she is applying in a modest way a socio-cultural critique of religion. By lines 39-46, she is forming a critique of social institutions. Further, by lines 49-51, she is performing a full Phase Three sense of her own authority in spiritual matters and, by line 60, she is performing a full critique of religion as an institution. In short, she is demonstrating some clear Phase Three sensibilities. Her secular language has assumed a fuller social analytic; her religious language has been elaborated as more critical and more maturely spiritual. She recognizes that, when her abuser uses the Bible to justify his actions, he is giving himself an undue freedom (lines 58, 60). In contrast to this, she asserts her own authority in spiritual matters rather than any reliance on her abuser's authority or a church's rules or dogma: "I feel in my heart what I have to do. I ain't going by his rules or her rules" (lines 50-51).

Carmen's Language in Terms of the Phases and Meaning Shifts

Carmen displays somewhat more Phase Three language overall in the session, particularly regarding secular matters. She evidences less anger towards men than Venita. Carmen more evenly balances rationality and emotionality in the conversation: it would seem Carmen has slightly more willingness to think with equanimity about gender and gender relations. (She does believe women are more "spiritual" than men and she thinks women are closer to God, but this is because men have a different temporal frame of reference: "Men think for the day; women think for the future and God is their reward.") Though she has had "a bad life," she appears more willing to forgive. Carmen is not paralyzed by anger; she is not simply reactive. She is able to shape a perspective based on a wider view than solely her personal experience.

Ultimately, Carmen's perspective on both secular and religious matters is more fully socially analytical. She repeatedly offers a social analysis of religious matters. In line 22, she is offering a critique of dogmatic or fundamental religious views that surface in biblical interpretation. She understands (line 25) that men have an advantage because they "stick together" with the implication being that women suffer because they do not; she understands the consequence of the lack of solidarity in women's lives. In lines 29-30, she is again rendering a social/cultural critique by implying that justice is a gendered concept. Carmen clearly understands (lines 47-48) that the social system (including legal, criminal, and religious systems) is dominated by wealthy white males.

Although Carmen's view is more than simply religious or religiously doctrinaire, she is initially spiritually unsure of herself or she evidences contradictions in her thinking (lines 6-7 in contrast with lines 14-15). She does not share Venita's initial dogmatic religious point of view, but she accepts her basic perspective and so her sensibilities fluctuate. By line 38, however, her language is, in fact, imaginative, creative, prophetic. "A woman God is for women!" she declares, calling prophetically for a universe rectified or ordered by female justice. Surely these are signs of a Phase Three consciousness moving towards critical interdependence with other women. By lines 55-57, Carmen is performing a more fully mature spirituality, that is, she has assumed her own authority in matters spiritual: It is not right to use scripture to limit or control women socially. Her statements seem to broach issues related to the meaning of life and her place in it. She has clearly broken the habit of seeking the approval of others, including men, family, and the churches. Her mystical experience is a social or communal experience. Indicating traces of political conscious-ness, she says, "If God were a woman, it would be wonderful."

Neither Carmen's nor Venita's senses of the need for social connec-tion or solidarity with women are rendered, however, in explicitly politi-cal terms (i.e., in the sense of understanding the need to organize or en-gage in concrete actions). They do understand the problem of the lack of solidarity (lines 26-27). But they appear to seek to conquer this through changed personal or spiritual/cosmic structures rather than strictly so-cial structures. For example, Carmen implies that if God were female, jus-tice would be better served. Venita trusts only in divine efficiency: "God is the only person you can believe in" (line 27). The two women do not of-fer political ideas for social change, though clearly they understand the need for change. Indeed, as they told me more than once in our interac-tions, they viewed sharing their words in this study as a contribution to the battered women's movement.

Still, within this set of exchanges, the conversation moves on a gen-eral trajectory from worldly to religious matters and from legal to socio-political matters. The trajectory is not unilinear. Rather, it proceeds with spiraling (or recursive) "movements of mind" as Carmen and Venita re-turn again and again to basic issues of fairness, justice, and right living interspersed with moments of their own sexism, anger, and religious dogma. The ideas advance and recede. They are rearticulated and recast. The critical point, however, is this: in the end, Carmen and Venita have participated in a kind of dialectic activity that results in the co-production of a more liberatory worldview (temporary though it may prove to be). Perhaps neither could have arrived there alone.

Dialogism and the Spiral of Change

In relation to the curvilinear movement of the phases, there are contradic-tions in the worldviews of both women. For example, Venita does not question the discrepancy in the way God appears to divvy out justice to men as opposed to women. Elsewhere, in parts of the conversation not recorded above, both illustrate women's fundamental sexism against women though they decry the sexism of men. ("You can't trust a woman," Venita says; Carmen adds: "Women are conniving.")

Yet Carmen and Venita are learning from one another. They are clearly attending to relationality by listening carefully to one another, agreeing or accepting, modifying or yielding, challenging and meeting one another's challenges as they jointly construct (within the confines of this conversation at least) a mutually acceptable worldview composed of some clearly differing worldviews or languages. This creates the spiral activity and the "energy" or impetus to move their levels of perception or awareness.

Important moments in the conversation happen at specific junctures or locations. Carmen adds positively to the movement in lines 22, 28-30, and 38. Generally speaking, in these moments, she is applying social analysis or cultural critiques to religious matters. Venita engages and responds respectively beginning in lines 22 and 39. It is as if the exchanges are being meshed together and a spiral motion is being created.

Notice that, between lines 36-37, between lines 46-47, and certainly by the last utterance, Carmen and Venita are in positions of agreement and accordance: a kind of co-production made by acts of negotiations, respect, or reciprocity/mutuality. Conceived broadly, with Carmen's help, Venita moves from articulating a relatively uncritical religious and secular view to a more fully critical view. By the end of the conversation, she evidences more social and spiritual awareness. With Venita's help, Carmen moves from articulating an ambiguous or uncertain spiritual sense of self to a more fully authoritative spiritual stance. They are able to do this because the energy of each other's contributions — the dialogism — helps them to recast their initial articulations into language more self-consciously aware and mutually-accommodating. In short, together they create a new world.

Interestingly, Carmen and Venita are able to imagine this new world because they subvert traditional formulations about religion, an institution (they imply) that unduly influences gender roles and relations. In effect, two very religious women use resistance or subversion to reorder their worlds. Through the use of hybrid language forms and ensuing changes or shifts in meaning, they render God as female and her justice as sure. The effect of the converging and conflating of languages, fashioning a hybrid of sorts, creates a spiraling effect that results in both women (to different degrees) moving out of Phase Two concepts and into those of Phase Three by the end of the conversation.

As I have argued, some battered women move away from traditional explanations of the nature of their suffering and towards some alternative theodicies. Indeed, they may develop their own "local theologies" to make sense of their situations. The conversation between Carmen, Venita, and myself — in which the women begin to imagine a female deity — is an example of this movement. In terms of theodicies, I would characterize aspects of both of their utterances as moving away from aspects of an Irenian/evolutionary (misuse of free will; teaching by moral contrast) theodicy and moving into the direction of liberation theodicy. At the end of the conversation they've sealed the idea that suffering is caused by the oppression of others, of institutions. A girl-God, they seem to believe, would be a "power with" God instead of a "power over" God — and one who would bring justice to women.[19]

Other conversations with battered women suggest to me that the reverse gender designation is one trace of the development of what I am calling "local theologies." To this issue, we now turn.

Local Theology: Women Helping Women

The term "local theology" is a term most generally applied in missionary contexts in which it becomes recognized (by practitioners, prophets, insiders, and outsiders) that the theology inherited from traditional or mainline churches does not fit a particular set of cultural circumstances. New theological formulations are in order or perhaps have begun to develop. Women in the shelter are able to create local theology when they recognize as inadequate the theodicies and other theological arguments foisted on them by abusive partners who are trying to justify their dominance and by pastors and church communities that try — as so often they do — to effect reconciliation in the interest of family "stability" and/or a supposed scriptural mandate. In this essay, I do not have the space to show the preponderance of linguistic evidence I have gathered over the years that demonstrates how estranged battered women are from churches as patriarchal institutions and from scriptures and liturgies used as the tools of their batterer.[20] "They twist the scripture to get what they want! Twist it!" says Lisa. For many battered women, the problem of evil is a concrete problem, not an abstract one. It is men in a male-dominated society who often use religion to manipulate and ultimately harm women.

Instead of being grounded in male-oriented tradition or patriarchal authority, local theologizing is God-talk that defers to the role that partic-

19. I disagree personally with this strategy as a kind of reverse sexism or as a concept of God that retains "power-over" elements. I suggest, however, that when battered women imagine a female God, they are exploring new concepts of justice.

20. *The Language of Battered Women* (SUNY, 2004) treats in depth the issues in this brief essay.

ular circumstances play in shaping battered women's response to the gospel. As a community of faith (even if transiently and within the confines of the shelter), the women try to make sense of the Christian message within the context of local circumstances, that is, within the context of tremendous evil, cruelty, and harm perpetrated by men and their institutions. Battered women do local theology, I suggest, primarily when they try to figure out what their relationships with God and others would look like without the rules, orders, mandates, dogma, assignments of character, essence, or gender-based proclivities, and other authoritative explanations that are imposed upon them from an abuser, his or her church, or scripture.

According to theologian Robert Schreiter,[21] there are three recurring concerns for which to look in identifying local theology: Questions are raised about the broader culture, unsatisfactory theological explanations (theodicies, for example) are dismissed, and new ways of being Christian are explored. All three of these concerns can easily be evidenced in the talk of battered women.

To take these concerns briefly in order: First, local theology begins with an examination of the cultural context. Social, political, and economic questions engage energies that were once devoted to metaphysical questions. This is certainly true for battered women who agonize over the apparent ineffectiveness of the law enforcement, judicial, and penal systems. "There is no justice," Lisa says to Holly and me one day as she tries to figure out how her abusive partner had gotten released from jail just days after severely assaulting her. Later in the conversation she fantasizes that, if God were a woman, there would be childcare and more resources for domestic violence survivors. She also criticizes men for interpreting/constructing images and interpretations of God that work to their privilege. Still, when asked what gives her hope when secular and religious institutions have failed her, she immediately answers: "I think it's God."

To push this further: local theology derives from the dynamic interaction among the church, the gospel, and the culture. The dynamic is dialectic: one moves back and forth between these three aspects. This, I argue, is exactly what Carmen and Venita were engaged in as they talked about their situations within the context of shelter culture and influenced one another's religious/spiritual perceptions.

Secondly, unsatisfactory theological explanations (theodicies, for

---

21. I draw heavily on Robert Schreiter's *Constructing Local Theologies* (Maryknoll, N.Y.: Orbis Books, 1985) in this section.

example) are dismissed. Listen to other faithful shelter women — Christians all — dismiss scriptural explanation for women's particular suffering in childbearing:

> Lisa: Be subservient to your husband! That's what church is all about!
>
> Tina: Where does that leave us?
>
> Lisa: How can you remain faithful?
>
> Tina: I dropped out of church when I was twelve years old: I was a sinner! I tried to be a kid!
>
> Carol: Does it mean women aren't spiritual? Does it mean women can't have religion?
>
> Tina: Giving birth is a religious experience.
>
> Rita: It's the most beautiful thing! It brings tears to your eyes!

In this short dialogue, there has been an implied but definite repudiation of aspects of the myth of the Fall and the patriarchal identification of woman with evil, of woman as the scapegoat paying for her sins in the pain of childbirth. Then, in light of Schreiter's third concern, there is reinterpretation of childbirth as a positive, not negative, experience.

Surely new ways of being Christian are being explored. These women — Tina, Lisa, Rita — are faithful women, but they find religion and redemption (i.e., the Christ story) in the situation rather than bringing religion or redemption to the situation. They find redemption in their own stories. I will return to this issue directly.

Evidence of Dual Systems and Local Theology as Social Change

I would like at this point to take a minute to clear the theoretical air. You probably think I make much from tiny bits and pieces of linguistic evidence. I do. I claim that Lisa, Tina, Rita, and other battered women devise alternative theodicies or theologies by way of the interplay of diverse languages and lived experience. That's quite a change given that most women enter the shelter in late Phase One or early Phase Two stages of the healing process. But in linguistic/semiotic theory, change is not considered the total elimination of one system of signs. It's the incorporation of new signs, messages, or codes in an already existing system of signs. In fact, there may be operant dual systems of belief in which older theological systems continue alongside newer systems. Clearly this is what happens in the shelter. When Tina wonders that a female God might have "the PMS thing" in one breath and in the next says that a female God would make her life better, she's clearly operating out of two belief systems. But there is change, and from a feminist perspective, change for the better.

Most importantly, the development of local theology is itself evidence of social change. This is an essential point, given that many domestic violence activists believe that battered women are too traumatized to engage in street action or political work.

In Christian experience, salvation is change. Salvation means coming out of evil and experiencing deliverance into a new reality. Is it a stretch to suggest that this is what is happening for Venita and Carmen, or Tina, Lisa, and Rita? To escape from an abusive partner who so often uses the texts and traditions of patriarchal faith communities to justify his abuse is a deliverance — a deliverance (paradoxically) sustained by an abiding faith in God whoever she (or he) may be, however she manifests, and for whatever reason she must (or does) allow suffering to be the tragic reality of human life.

Rethinking the Problem of Evil

Before I move into my conclusion, I would like to visit very briefly a few themes that arise around particularly Phase Three battered women's notions of suffering and evil.[22] These are terms that arise in conjunction with some of the basic traditional language of theodicy: evil, sin, suffering, grace, salvation/redemption, and relations with God/other. These themes further suggest that local theologizing takes place by way of the dialogic language of shelter life.

In most religious traditions, evil is viewed as the opposite or absence of good. However, traditionally men have located evil in women or they have designated women as the cause or origin of evil (for example, the notion that women cause rape by their dress or behavior). For many battered women, particularly Phase Three women who are healing, evil is primarily located in systems that allow women to be harmed or to go

---

22. I use several theological handbooks in this section, including: Letty M. Russell and J. Shannon Clarkson's *Dictionary of Feminist Theologies* (Louisville: Westminster/John Knox Press, 1996); Gerald O'Collins, S.J., and Edward G. Farrugia, S.J., *A Concise Dictionary of Theology* (New York: Paulist Press, 1991); and Van A. Harvey's *A Handbook of Theological Terms* (New York: Macmillan, 1964).

without justice — for example, the legal, political, or religious systems. Evil is a violation of the well-being of women and their children that is a product of these systems. After the anger and protest against abusive partners subsides, women more easily see the constellation of factors that lead or allow abusive men to hurt women with so much impunity. The mixing of dialogue in the shelter — as in the mixing of secular social work language about domestic violence with battered women's religious language — facilitates this shift. For example, shelter women learn about the inefficacy of the law enforcement, judicial, and penal systems to protect them and their children from abusive partners. By extension, they learn to criticize religious institutions and the media for creating a climate in which it is possible to hurt women without censure.

Thus, for particularly Phase Three battered women, sin is epitomized by a violation of individual or communal well-being and it can be found to originate in systems whose activities lead to, for example, individual instances of domestic violence. Actions are interrelated and thus no one person or event is completely removed from others or another. One example of this is that battering partners come to be seen as men who make poor decisions about relationship, but who learned to make poor decisions from dysfunctional birth family relations, social institutions, and other culture-shapers, including churches. In the logic of many African American women, societal racism leads to individual frustration, which then leads to poor choices within domestic partnerships. No excuse is made for the batterers, but a shelter woman who has been in dialogue with staff members, for example, can see the interrelationship between such factors.

In traditional theology, grace is understood as God's mercy bestowed on humans in their sinfulness. Except for those in early Phase 1, most shelter women do not see themselves as fundamentally sinful and thus deserving of abuse. As they learn about the dynamics of domestic violence, they reject the name-calling and bodily harm doled out by abusers. While acknowledging some denominational differences, I believe many battered women see grace as arising in connection with other people; that is, grace is not simply God's divine power to forgive and transform, but their own relational openness in the context of family, particularly children, and community that redeems. This belief may come from the experience of being called out of shame and isolation by other women in the shelter in the process of healing. For example, as Tina's and Rita's words above suggest, there seems to be no, few, or permeable boundaries between the sacred and the ordinary. Battered women also find solace in one another — an opportunity they were denied before their escape from their partners. Their appreciation for one another as companions on the road to freedom is remarkable — a noticeable feature of community talk.

Suffering is a part of everyday life for battered women, poor women, violated women, to some degree and inevitably all women. In traditional theology, suffering derives from sin. In many battered women's view suffering is immediate, male-originating, and (for many Phase Three women) unrelated to the women's behavior. They learn that male violence is nearly always random. Women's broken bones and hearts, bruised flesh and feeling, carry the weight of evidence here. When battered women talk to other women who have experienced similar domestic situations or women who know about the dynamics of domestic violence, they learn that explanations based on individual sinfulness do not make much sense.

With respect to salvation or redemption, in traditional theology, the unique role of Jesus is emphasized and, for many black and white shelter women of the Holiness/Sanctified traditions, this holds. Jesus frees us from evil through his death and resurrection. However, in the throes of a dual system of belief — that is, a belief system composed of both traditional and alternative ideas — some (particularly Phase Three) women at the shelter seem to believe that salvation/redemption means righting relations so that women and their children might experience some freedom to live in safety and peace. To illustrate: most battered women are anxious to begin anew, to rethink the meaning and composition of family in order to be safe. Salvation is being realized as they enter the shelter and as their new life unfolds. There is generally a lot of language of praise and thanksgiving. There is a lot of hope for the future of their relationships with their children and other women, though admittedly there is usually little interest in relationships with men. If there is talk about relationships with men, it is not romanticized or idealized talk. As one battered woman said, "I haven't seen anyone pick up a romance novel here!"

In fact, and finally, relations with God and with others are desirable if they are characterized by mutuality. Many battered women who are healing see right relationship as being characterized by equality of power and responsibility and love that does not oppress or consume. Indeed, the model, the goal, of right relationship is friendship. For example, when a Phase 1 woman moves out of the isolation within which her abuser has imprisoned her, she rediscovers the strength that comes from networking with other women and the joy that comes from finding solace and support in a web of friends, allies, or companions. These are opportunities that are not available to many abused women, who feel that their needs are always subsumed to the cultural expectation of service to others. Perhaps Mary E. Hunt is right after all when she writes that the opposite of suffering is not pleasure; it's friendship.

The changes, I submit, are due to the mixing and merging of languages within the shelter — among them secular and religious languages. They are indicative of changes in theological thought. Given these subtle and not-so-subtle transformations, these manifestations of local theology, I — like theologian Kathleen M. Sands — believe it is time "to exorcise the patriarchal language of evil, sin, and suffering and to enlist ideals such as justice in the service of women." Or others, I add, who are held captive by unjust systems of domination. As Sands writes: "We might approach the topic of evil as a question for insight and judgment, not as a legitimating explanation" (67). The religious reflections of women can draw more wisdom from the living functions of community (69). In the Women's House, they undoubtedly and dialogically do.

Conclusion

In my experience at the Women's House, women survivors of domestic violence report all too often being held by their religious, social, and family communities, and particularly by their abusers, in theological belief systems — such as some of the theodicies I've explored — that are used to facilitate, justify, and sustain violence against them. Indeed, many women (especially Phase One and Phase Two women) adhere to theodicies that simply are unhealthy for them and for their girl children. Thus, in my view, contemporary religious feminists very correctly critique the patriarchal modes of religious belief; however, in the literature on domestic violence, little, no, or only negative attention is given to religious beliefs. Little or no attention is given to the deep faith and emerging women's spirituality that sustain many battered women as they try to survive and heal. The scholars and activists simply have not been able to make sense of the apparent paradox.

Many battered women have been able to make sense of the paradox of being violated as objects by men, the churches men have created, and the scriptures men have interpreted while at the same time being subjects and namers of their own faith journeys as Christian women. I do not mean to suggest that battered women have arrived at more mature, sophisticated, or better theologies or theodicies than the rest of us. To believe so would be to subscribe to a theodicy to which I do not wish to subscribe. But the lived experience of battered women, marked primarily by intense physical and emotional suffering, does give their thought, their feet-on-the-ground theology a legitimacy that perhaps — at this moment — few others of us (housed, clothed, fed, supported, loved, and employed) can claim.

In this ethnographic study, I try to explore this contradictory and complex religious language of battered women. I suggest that the particular language practices of battered women are worth attention. There is evidence that women, including those from fundamentalist/evangelical and Holiness/Sanctified traditions — can and do engage in some resistant, woman-favorable theological responses to their crises that do not fit neatly into their traditional male-defined systems — for, as Carmen said, "In the Bible, it can be so harsh!"

But then, as woman theologians point out: there are other ways to do theology than simply those ways with which we are now so familiar. In the Women's House, when they are not weeping about the trauma, the tragedy, the evil, the brutality in their lives caused by men and their institutions, including their religious institutions, battered women talk, laugh, play, and sing together with their children. They do rage and anger, but they also praise and lament. They teach and minister. They celebrate God's goodness and they hope for change. They form community and sometimes solidarity. These are language activities denied to many of them within patriarchal church and home. Some battered women in the shelter learn that it is even possible to laugh at the tragedy of their own suffering, suffering that is part of the fabric of a world lacking in justice for many. That laughter might be salvific, redemptive. At least, as they move toward healing, they are better able to put suffering in its place; that is, they see they have choices about how to respond to it. After all, as Lisa, a shelter woman, notes, "Waiting on God can be a hard thing." Given a safe space and a chance to talk honestly and openly about the life issues that matter, women can help women out of violent relationships, oppressive religious beliefs, and other harmful ideological systems. Salvation happens.

Additional Works Consulted

Comas-Diaz and Beverly Greene, eds. *Women of Color: Integrating Ethnic and Gender Identities in Psychotherapy.* New York: Guilford Press, 1994.

Desjarlais, Robert, Leon Eisenberg, Bryon Good, and Arthur Kleinman. *World Mental Heath.* New York: Oxford University Press, 1995.

Felman, Shoshana, and Dori Laub, eds. *Testimony: Crises of Witnessing in Literature, Psychoanalysis, and History.* New York: Routledge, 1992.

hooks, bell. *Sisters of the Yam: Black Women and Self-Recovery.* Boston: South End Press, 1993.

Laub, Dori. "Bearing Witness or Vicissitudes of Listening." In *Testimony: Crises of Witnessing in Literature, Psychoanalysis, and History,* edited by Shoshana Felman and Dori Laub. New York: Routledge, 1992. 57-74.

Mezirow, Jack, ed. *Fostering Critical Reflection in Adulthood.* San Francisco: Jossey-Bass, 1990.

Mouw, Richard J. *Consulting the Faithful: What Christian Intellectuals Can Learn from Popular Religion.* Grand Rapids, Mich.: Wm. B. Eerdmans Publishing Company, 1994.

Pennebaker, James W. *Opening Up: The Healing Power of Confiding in Others.* New York: William Morrow, 1990.

Salter, Anna C. *Transforming Trauma: A Guide to Understanding and Treating Adult Survivors of Child Sexual Abuse.* Thousand Oaks: Sage Publishers, 1995.

Sands, Kathleen M. *Escape from Paradise: Evil and Tragedy in Feminist Theology.* Minneapolis: Fortress Press, 1994.

Normal Narcissism and the Need for Theodicy

Richard T. McClelland

Introduction

In his great primer of moral psychology, Thomas Reid describes an "elation of mind" that is closely bound up with an agent's sense of his or her own self-worth. And in the same section, he goes on to describe a close connection between depression and self-worth.[1] One aim of the present essay is to sharpen the connection drawn by Reid and to place it in the context of contemporary psychoanalytic object relations theory and its treatment of normal narcissism. A further, and still secondary, aim of this essay is to support a new approach to the philosophy of the emotions. In a pair of recent essays, Bennett Helm has elaborated and defended an approach to the emotions that I find very attractive. In the following passage, Helm delineates two aspects of emotional states that will serve our analytic ends well:

> Emotions are commonly (and rightly) understood to be a certain kind of response to the significance of one's situation — that is, an evaluative response. Thus, fear is a response to (certain aspects of)

1. Thomas Reid, *Essays on the Active Powers of the Human Mind* (1788), ed. Baruch Brody (Cambridge, Mass.: MIT Press, 1969), pp. 187-92. Reid's emphasis on "regulation" of these emotions is particularly suggestive in the light of modern treatments of so-called "affect regulation" in developmental studies: see especially Allan Schore, *Affect Regulation and the Origins of the Self: The Neurobiology of Emotional Development* (Hillsdale, N.J.: Lawrence Erlbaum Associates, 1994). Schore's magisterial review has special value for the study of narcissistic functioning.

one's situation evaluated as threatening, a response which itself has certain effects on the subject and its behavior; and anger is a response to (certain aspects of) one's situation evaluated as offensive, a response having different characteristic effects on the subject. . . . That at which the emotion is directed (what I am afraid of or angry at) is the target of the emotion, and the characteristic kind of evaluation of the target at issue for a particular emotion (its threatfulness or its offensiveness, for example) is that emotion's formal object. The formal object of an emotion is thus what makes it intelligible that the subject has this emotion rather than some other emotion or no emotion at all.[2]

The theory of normal narcissism that appears below is, among other things, an attempt to specify the "space" within which the formal objects attaching to narcissistic emotions can usefully be found.[3] That is, I think that it is within this space that the formal objects of many of our most profoundly meaningful and most powerfully motivating emotions are to be found.

A further assumption underlying the present essay is the notion of multiple functions. It is my view that philosophical projects commonly serve more than one function, and that often some of the functions they serve are hidden from our overt view. The projects I have in mind here are what I will call *theodictic projects,* and these include positive theodicies (efforts to explain what might be the divine rationale for our experience of evil), propaedeutic theodicies (attempts, such as that carried forward recently by Marilyn Adams, to establish the general conceptual bound-

2. Bennett W. Helm, "The Significance of Emotions," *American Philosophical Quarterly* 31 (1994): 319-31, here p. 320; and "Emotional Reason: How to Deliberate about Value," *American Philosophical Quarterly* 37 (2000): 1-22. For an overview of the cognitive tradition see John Deigh, "Cognitivism in the Theory of Emotions," *Ethics* 104 (1994): 824-54. For recent studies in this tradition see especially Martha Nussbaum, *Upheavals of Thought: The Intelligence of Emotions* (Cambridge: Cambridge University Press, 2001); and Aaron Ben-Ze'ev, *The Subtlety of Emotions* (Cambridge, Mass.: MIT Press, 2000). For dissident views more in keeping with the approach taken by Helm, see also Stephen Leighton, "A New View of Emotion," *American Philosophical Quarterly* 22 (1985): 133-41; and Michael Stocker, "Emotional Thoughts," *American Philosophical Quarterly* 24 (1987): 59-69. I regret that Bennett Helm's superb full-length treatment of the issues came into my hands too late to be taken into account in this paper: *Emotional Reason: Deliberation, Motivation, and the Nature of Value* (Cambridge: Cambridge University Press, 2001).

3. For this use of "space," see further my paper "Autistic Space," *Psychoanalysis and Contemporary Thought* 16 (1993): 197-231. No reification is intended.

aries within which positive theodicies might be attempted), and defensive theodicies (efforts to overturn atheistic arguments from evil).[4] These projects have overt conceptual and logical functions that are well known to most philosophers. But they may also serve various social functions, as, for example, to present in a positive light, and to a particular audience, specific religious traditions and the communities that subscribe to them and are partially constituted by them. They may also serve political purposes within those communities, serving to advance the reputations and fortunes of their authors and others who may advocate for them. Academic careers can also be enhanced by the offering of effective theodictic responses to evil. It will be my central claim that theodictic projects also function on a psychological level, a function that belongs especially to that type of functioning that I will call normal narcissism.

Two disclaimers will complete my introduction. The first is to insist that the interpretation of theodictic activity that follows is not intended to be a reductive argument, nor is it intended to provide a premise in any such argument. That is, it is not my view that there is *nothing else* to theodictic activity than the narcissistic functioning that I go on here to describe. Nor do I assume that the psychological level of functioning is somehow more basic, more real (whatever that would mean), or more valuable than any other level of functioning that may apply to such projects. The levels on which philosophical projects function are really and irreducibly multiple. Fulfillment of one function does not automatically rule out fulfilling some other function or functions. The second disclaimer is that the present essay is not intended to be a "deconstruction" of theodictic activity. I believe that deconstructionism is a modern form of skepticism, and while I am skeptical about many things, I am not that kind of skeptic.[5] Associations commonly drawn today between psychoanalysis and deconstructionism should not mislead us into supposing that a psychoanalytic interpretation of some type of philosophical activity is *eo ipso* a deconstruction of that activity. I regard psychoanalysis as

4. Marilyn McCord Adams, *Horrendous Evils and the Goodness of God* (Ithaca, N.Y.: Cornell University Press, 1999). For more standard defensive or positive theodicies, see the papers collected in Marilyn McCord Adams and Robert Merrihew Adams, eds., *The Problem of Evil* (New York: Oxford University Press, 1990); and Daniel Howard-Snyder, ed., *The Evidential Problem of Evil* (Bloomington, Ind.: Indiana University Press, 1996).

5. An earlier draft of this essay was delivered to a conference at Calvin College in May 2000. Some listeners evidently understood the entire exercise as an effort to deconstruct theodictic projects.

part of the empirical branch of the philosophy of mind, and its theories are drawn upon here solely with the intention of illuminating the meaning of theodictic activity (i.e. as a heuristic device). That said, let us now turn to our central task.

Normal Narcissism and the Narcissistic Economy

I am not now thinking about narcissism as a form of psychopathology, and this study is not a contribution to the emerging field of philosophical psychopathology.[6] That is, I am not now concerned with the so-called narcissistic personality disorders, nor with those forms of self-involvement, self-absorption, and self-aggrandizement that we find commonly in social life and usually find so disagreeable. Rather, I here consider narcissism as a dimension of normal human psychosocial development, and as a normal functional structure to be found in all psychologically intact adult members of our species. I will treat narcissism under three broad headings: economic narcissism, and the two narcissistic emotions, elation and anxiety.[7]

6. The term is a little unfortunate for its *double entendre*. There is a useful introduction in George Graham and G. Lynn Stephens, eds., *Philosophical Psychopathology* (Cambridge, Mass.: MIT Press, 1994). One difficulty with Michael Stocker and Elizabeth Hegeman's otherwise splendid study, *Valuing Emotions* (Cambridge: Cambridge University Press, 1996), is that it treats narcissism from the outset as a form of pathology (pp. 268-86).

7. The psychoanalytic literature on narcissism is now immense. It began with Freud, "On Narcissism: An Introduction," *Standard Edition* 14 (1914): 67-102. The study of pathological narcissism owes a great deal to the work of Otto Kernberg, *Borderline Conditions and Pathological Narcissism* (New York: Jason Aronson, 1974), especially Chapter 10, "Normal and Pathological Narcissism," pp. 315-22; and Heinz Kohut, *The Analysis of the Self* (New York: International Universities Press, 1971), and *The Restoration of the Self* (New York: International University Press, 1977). There is a useful compendium of papers in: A. P. Morrison, ed., *Essential Papers on Narcissism* (New York: New York University Press, 1986). My own formulations owe much to Robert Stolorow, "Toward a Functional Definition of Narcissism," *International Journal of Psychoanalysis* 56 (1975): 179-86, and to the papers of Ronnie Solan: "'Jointness' as Integration of Merging and Separateness in Object Relations and Narcissism," *Psychoanalytic Study of the Child* 46 (1991): 337-52; "Narcissistic Fragility in the Process of Befriending the Unfamiliar," *American Journal of Psycho-Analysis* 58 (1998): 163-86; and "The Interaction between Self and Others: A Different Perspective on Narcissism," *Psychoanalytic Study of the Child* 54 (1999): 193-215.

Economic Narcissism

It seems that every psychologically intact human person past the age of three years has a self-representation which is comprised of images, memories, beliefs, values, internalized patterns of interrelatedness with emotionally significant persons, and patterns of affective regulation — all of these bound together in a more or less coherent narrative framework. Such a structure is at once a secure psychological "base" from which we extend, via our actions and relationships, our values and purposes into the world, and is also itself subject to challenges to its coherence resulting from our experiences in the world. Changing this structure is usually done at great cost to the person making the changes, including often a deep sense of confusion and considerable measures of anxiety (reflected in clinical depressions, psychosomatic disorders, and even outright, though usually temporary, psychosis). Such changes, nevertheless, are often felt by their subjects to be absolutely imperative, despite their costs, and they can also be the occasion of great exhilaration, momentous personal discovery, and increased creativity in living and working. We make them because the coherence of the inner narrative is vital to our sense of who we are, of what our most deeply held values are, and of what are our most cherished purposes in the world.[8]

According to this theory, we each of us have some method or pattern for maintaining the cohesion and the temporal stability of our self-representation, for maintaining its positive emotional coloring, and for maintaining its semantic coherence. Such maintenance patterns and techniques constitute a large part of the narcissistic economy. They constitute our capacity for self-soothing, for maintaining self-esteem, and for recovering from those blows, wounds, and insults that our self-representation undergoes in the normal vicissitudes of human life. The history of those vicissitudes, together with their sequelae in our emotional, imaginative, cognitive, and social lives, and the history of our success and failure in handling them, together with *their* sequelae, constitute a further significant element of the narcissistic economy. A third part of that economy is

---

8. For brief treatments of the role in personal identity of narrative structures, especially narratives of the self, see Jonathan Glover, *I: The Philosophy and Psychology of Personal Identity* (London: Penguin Books, 1988), pp. 139-53; and Oliver Sacks, "A Case of Identity," in *The Man Who Mistook His Wife for a Hat* (New York: Harper and Row, 1987), pp. 108-15. For the role of narrative in emotions generally, see Robert C. Roberts, *Emotions: An Essay in Aid of Moral Psychology* (Cambridge: Cambridge University Press, 2003), pp. 36-37, 50-52, et passim.

the particular pattern of sensitivities and vulnerabilities that we individ-
ually bring to the narcissistic dimensions of our experience, the specific
pattern of which vulnerabilities determines what it is that we find narcissistically wounding or rewarding, and the degree to which we find them
so. All this I shall call the narcissistic economy. I take it to be a functional
structure — indeed, a structure of functions or dispositions, and not an
independent agency within the human personality.[9] My interest here is in
its connections with the problem of evil and our responses to it. To establish that connection, we will need a closer look at the narcissistic economy itself and especially two of its attendant emotional states: namely,
narcissistic elation and narcissistic anxiety.

Narcissistic Equilibrium and Narcissistic Elation

The narcissistic economy is fundamentally a homeostatic system. That is,
it seeks to maintain the *status quo* regarding the coherence, stability,
meaningfulness, and positive affective tone of our self-representation. Its
function (or *telos*) is to keep us "on an even keel" in the face of the various
threats (perceived or actual) to our sense of narcissistic balance. Indeed, it
has as one of its functions immunizing us against at least relatively minor
threats to that balance. We can measure the narcissistic health of a person
by observing how well they maintain their sense of narcissistic balance in
the presence of such threats. It is not surprising, then, that various disturbances to the narcissistic system often present in association with various
kinds of vertigo, as a recent study by Danielle Quinodoz has shown.[10]
Such experiences of vertigo have a peculiar duality: they can be symptoms
of narcissistic disturbance or deficiency, and they are also sometimes

9. The dispositional character of such structures can be illuminated by Michael
Bratman's analysis of intentions, and especially what he calls "policies": see his *Intention, Plans, and Practical Reason* (Cambridge, Mass.: Harvard University Press, 1987),
pp. 87-91. Donald Davidson's notion of "sub-systems" is also pertinent: "Deception
and Division," in *The Multiple Self*, ed. John Elster (Cambridge: Cambridge University
Press, 1986), pp. 79-92; and cf. David Pears, "Self-Deceptive Belief-Formation,"
Synthese 89 (1991): 393-405. The whole issue should probably be placed in the framework of what some today call "scientific essentialism": see Brian Ellis, *Scientific
Essentialism* (Cambridge: Cambridge University Press, 2001) and the literature cited at
Richard McClelland and Robert Deltete, "Divine Causation," *Faith and Philosophy* 17
(2000): 13-14 and footnote 37.

10. See Danielle Quinodoz, *Emotional Vertigo: Between Anxiety and Pleasure* (London: Routledge, 1997).

sought for the particular pleasures they afford. Such pleasures seem to arise in the course of activities that court vertigo and also overcome it, or that stress our capacity to tolerate vertigo. We can think here especially of sporting activities, especially those that essentially involve our capacity to maintain somatic equilibrium: hang-gliding, mountain climbing, so-called "extreme sports," triathletic contests, and so on. Quinodoz has called the persons who pursue such activities "players with vertigo" and she is quick to note the addictive quality of the elation that attends their performances. One of the most insightful of them, the extreme climber Reinhold Messner, describes his own pursuit of such elation-pleasure this way: "I am seeking my limits. I need to exceed my limits much as some-one else needs drugs. Constantly. What I have reached so far interests me less. What I might (perhaps) reach now satisfies me, keeps me on my toes."[11] It is the capacity of a person to maintain that balance in the face of even extreme threats that brings the pleasure. The French tightrope walker Philippe Petit, who once essayed to walk a rope stretched between the towers of Notre-Dame, described it well: "Equilibrium is voluptuous. Notre-Dame belongs to me, Paris belongs to me, the vast sky belongs to me, it makes me forget to breathe." Elsewhere he says:

> No one must hear, no one must know that my heart is beating, that it is beating so slowly, that it has stopped beating, that my senses have multiplied tenfold, that my nose gathers in the scattered molecules of the air, that I become intoxicated with perfumes, that I invent colors. . . . No one must suspect that as I advance along the rope, my lips taste the sugary breeze, that I progress through sweetmeats.[12]

These are, of course, extreme cases. Mere mortals are more likely to derive a more modest degree of elation from our capacity to maintain or to restore narcissistic balance. It remains the case, I submit, that narcissistic equilibrium yields elation-pleasures similar to those described by these men, and also that the elation they report is narcissistic in character. Such elation is at once physiological and psychological; and is closely associated with the pleasures of mastery and triumphant victory.

We can get a vivid sense of what such pleasure is like from J. R. R. Tolkien's description of the young king of Rohan, Eomer, when he finds himself hard beset during the battle of the Pelennor Fields:

11. Quoted in Quinodoz, *Emotional Vertigo*, p. 161.
12. Quoted in Quinodoz, *Emotional Vertigo*, pp. 165-66.

> Stern now was Eomer's mood, and his mind clear again. He let blow the horns to rally all men to his banner that could come thither; for he thought to make a great shield-wall at the last, and stand, and fight there on foot till all fell, and do deeds of song on the fields of Pelennor, though no man should be left in the West to remember the last King of the Mark. So he rode to a green hillock and there set his banner, and the White Horse ran rippling in the wind.

> Out of doubt, out of dark to the day's rising
> I came singing in the sun, sword unsheathing,
> To hope's end I rode and to heart's breaking;
> Now for wrath, now for ruin, and a red nightfall!

> These staves he spoke, yet he laughed as he said them. For once more lust of battle was on him; and he was still unscathed, and he was young, and he was king: the lord of a fell people.[13]

That is narcissistic elation. It construes its bearer as full of power and able to project this power into the future, turning despair into hope, shame and humiliation into competence, grandiosity, expansiveness, and effective action. The presence of its *formal object*, the evaluative judgment of the young king, is signaled by the short phrase "and his mind clear again." His mind is clear because he knows and can present to himself the purpose of his actions, and because his purpose is undivided and undiluted by other considerations.[14] Such clarity of mind is a necessary, but not sufficient, condition for narcissistic balance and well-being (and, under some circumstances, for effective action). Given the archaic and fundamental importance of narcissistic equilibrium to our whole psychological health, it is not surprising that we might value such elation very highly. I will suggest later that some of the special features of theodictic projects attach to their role the maintenance or restoration of narcissistic equilibrium. But now let us turn to the darker side of narcissistic emotions: narcissistic anxiety.

---

13. J. R. R. Tolkien, *The Lord of the Rings*, Part III: *The Return of the King* (London: Allen and Unwin, 1966), Book V, chapter vi, pp. 122-23.

14. The matter of such clarity of mind merits a full treatment of its own, both with regard to its phenomenology and its aetiology. I hope to return to this subject in a future study.

Narcissistic Anxiety

Our sense of narcissistic balance, then, is more or less continually under threat. Narcissistic insults, blows, wounds, and catastrophes loom on every hand. Healthy persons evaluate these threats appropriately, deploying the emotional responses that constitute those evaluations. They are able to maintain their narcissistic balance in the face of these threats, and are able to recover, without undue strain, from the experience of those threats, wounds, blows, and insults, and to restore the homeostatic equilibrium of this motivational system. The emotion that appropriately accompanies narcissistic threats (perceived or actual) is narcissistic anxiety. We may revert to our image of the tightrope walker to characterize it. What the tightrope walker fears, of course, is falling into the void. The British object-relations theorist D. W. Winnicott once called fear of falling forever one of the "archaic anxieties."[15] Very severe narcissistic threats can call forth that degree of anxiety, for they may present to their bearer with such intensity as to be referred to as a "nameless dread," a fear that is so intense as to be formless, limitless, without bounds, a threat to the very coherence of our sense of self. Such fear can appear to be global, vast, and ineluctable. To some such patients, narcissistic coherence may seem like a psychological membrane holding them together. The threat is then like a small hole in that membrane, one that threatens to bring about its total, sudden and catastrophic collapse. Quinodoz, in her study of vertigo, refers to "narcissistic hemorrhage," the catastrophic nature of which often requires intense somatic feelings of vertiginous falling to symbolize it. And such symbolism is essential if the narcissistic economy is to come to grips with the threat and to metabolize its attendant fears. I once knew a narcissistically vulnerable patient who always had to wear several layers of tight-fitting clothing over as much of her body as possible, and also head coverings and dark glasses. Her coverings served as a second skin, holding her together, for she constantly felt that her own skin was too thin and was liable to collapse at any moment under the critical gaze of others.[16]

15. See D. W. Winnicott, *Psycho-Analytic Explorations* (Cambridge, Mass.: Harvard University Press, 1989), pp. 139, 196, and 260; and *The Maturational Processes and the Facilitating Environment: Studies in the Theory of Emotional Development* (Madison, Conn.: International University Press, 1965), p. 58. Related treatments can be found in J. L. Weiss, *Early Deprivation of Empathic Care* (Madison, Conn.: International University Press, 1992), pp. 185-87; and Ivri Kumin, *Pre-Object Relatedness: Early Attachment and the Psychoanalytic Situation* (New York: Guilford Press, 1996), pp. 10-18.

16. Closely related phenomena are treated in: D. Anzieu, *The Skin Ego* (New Ha-

Tolkien again gives a wonderful narrative image of such nameless dread at work in the climactic moment of his great epic:

> . . . as Frodo put on the Ring and claimed it for his own . . . the Dark Lord was suddenly aware of him, and his Eye piercing all shadows looked across the plain to the door that he had made; and the magnitude of his own folly was revealed to him in a blind flash, and all the devices of his enemies were at last laid bare. Then his wrath blazed in consuming flame, but his fear rose like a vast black smoke to choke him. *For he knew his deadly peril and the thread upon which his doom now hung.*[17]

Readiness to experience such dread usually belongs to pathological states or organizations of the personality, but a *capacity* for such dread belongs to everyone, given a sufficiently strong threat to their narcissistic balance. For, without that balance, and without the capacity to restore it, we cease to have a coherent and stable self-representation upon which to act in the world. The result may be a profound inner sense of being adrift in the world.

Such intense anxieties are likely to evoke equally intense defensive activity, and deep preoccupation with shoring up our narcissistic boundaries. Such preoccupation, in its turn, will almost invariably seem to others around us as a deep disregard for their vitality, and for their psychological depth. In Ovid's retelling of the myth of Narcissus, the nymph Echo has been deprived of her own speech by Hera and is only able to seduce Narcissus by using fragments of his own speech. He repulses her advances and she pines away with grief until only her voice (which is really his voice) remains (*Metamorphoses*, III. ll. 339-510). She has ceased to be a real character at all, so lacking in psychological depth and solidity as finally to be nothing but a disembodied and depersonalized voice. Even healthy persons who are deeply engaged in narcissistic repair often act in this self-sufficient fashion, as if they did not really need other people and as if other people had little or no independent reality. That is, they, too, can produce an "Echo effect." One commentator on problems of theodicy has complained of the German theologian Jürgen Moltmann that he "has listened to [Elie] Wiesel

---

ven: Yale University Press, 1989), and cf. Esther Bick, "The Experience of the Skin in Early Object Relations," *International Journal of Psychoanalysis* 49 (1968): 484-86; and D. Houzel, "The Concept of Psychic Envelope," in *Psychic Envelopes* (London: Karnac Books, 1990), pp. 11-16.

17. Tolkien, *Lord of the Rings*, Book VI, chapter iii, p. 223.

as a ventriloquist who listens to one of the voices he produces himself," which is similar to the sort of phenomenon I am trying here to describe.[18] But now we must turn away from these issues and consider theodictic projects more directly in the light of this theory of narcissistic functioning.

Normal Narcissism and the Need for Theodicy

My supposition is that theodictic projects can serve multiple purposes, and that among their many purposes are psychological functions, and in particular functions related to normal narcissism. It will help in making out this claim to revert to a closely associated notion, the *ego ideal*, which Freud treated first in his seminal 1914 paper on narcissism. A recent psychoanalytic lexicon gives this definition for the ego ideal:

> The images of the self to which the individual aspires consciously and unconsciously, and against which he measures himself. It is based on identification with the parents and other early environmental figures, as they actually are, were in the past, or as they have been idealized [to be].[19]

This concept can be useful to us in three ways:

1. The narcissistic economy makes use of some body of more or less coherently organized ideals. It uses these ideals in two basic ways: to set a standard against which the actions, performances and conditions of the agent can be evaluated; and to set a standard towards the achievement of which the agent can aspire. Such ideals have a curious push/pull quality, furnishing the narcissistic system with the values that it both seeks to realize in the world (in the agent and her performances) and over against which those performances are judged.[20]

2. These ideals, insofar as they represent an idealized object, person,

18. Marcel Sarot, "Auschwitz, Morality, and the Suffering of God," *Modern Theology* 7 (1991): 138. I make no claim about whether Sarot's complaint is warranted, and I note that it is not part of it to suggest that Moltmann's response to Wiesel is pathological.

19. B. E. Moore and B. D. Fine, *A Glossary of Psychoanalytic Terms and Concepts* (New York: American Psychoanalytic Association, 1967), p. 93.

20. Aquinas has noted something very similar to this push/pull duality: ". . . the will is directed to the end, both absent, when it desires it; and present, when it is delighted by resting therein" (*Summa Theologica* Ia2ae, Q. III, art. 4).

relationship or state of affairs, furnish the agent with a mental representation that stands over and against his self-representations. In that sense, they furnish us with our *ego ideal*. But they also represent performances, relationships and states of affairs that are understood to be *possible* for the agent. They are thus potential representations of the ego itself and thus furnish the agent with an *ideal ego*. Edith Jacobson called this "the double face of the ego ideal," and traced its motivational power to our archaic desire for oneness between ideal ego and ego ideal: "the desire to be one with the love object."[21]

3. For the religious believer, their representation of God is deeply related to both ego ideal and ideal ego. For here is the quintessential "love object," and here is also a representation that we both strive to emulate and long to be united with. The theme of divine-human union can be found in all of the traditions of classical theism. Its achievement — or near-achievement — in a person is described by the Jesuit psychoanalyst William Meissner this way:

> Such individuals reflect an inner life of lucidity, simplicity, and inner harmony that escapes the great majority of humans. The love of God in these souls seems wholly unselfconscious, stripped of the residues of [merely] infantile narcissism, and yet capable of integration into a life of activity, responsibility and generative fulfillment. They often seem capable of profoundly meaningful object relations that are characterized by selfless love and acceptance of others.[22]

21. Edith Jacobson, *The Self and the Object World* (Madison, Conn.: International University Press, 1964), p. 96. Cf. Peter Blos, "The Genealogy of the Ego Ideal," *Psychoanalytic Study of the Child* 29 (1974): 43-88. An especially nuanced treatment of the complexities of the ego ideal is in Roy Schafer, "Ideals, the Ego Ideal, and the Ideal Self," in R. R. Holt, ed., *Motives and Thought: Psychoanalytic Essays in Honor of David Rappaport* (New York: International University Press, 1967), pp. 131-74.

22. William Meissner, *Psychoanalysis and Religious Experience* (New Haven: Yale University Press, 1984), p. 157. And cf. Moshe Spero, *Religious Objects as Psychological Structure: A Critical Integration of Object Relations Theory, Psychotherapy, and Judaism* (Chicago: University of Chicago Press, 1992); and James W. Jones, *Contemporary Psychoanalysis and Religion: Transference and Transcendence* (New Haven: Yale University Press, 1991). For a much more reductive approach to the same issues, also within the framework of British psychoanalytic object relations theory, see M. D. Faber, *The Magic of Prayer: An Introduction to the Psychology of Faith* (Westport, Conn.: Praeger Publishers, 2002), especially chapters 1 and 2.

I think such conditions can be fairly described in terms of a non-infantile narcissistic equilibrium between a specifically religious ego ideal and ideal ego. The inner sense of peace and joy evident in such saints may represent, among much else of course, a species of narcissistic elation.[23]

But what has this to do with the problem of evil, or theodictic projects in general? Construing the problem of evil as a narcissistic threat will make the connection.

The logical and evidential problems of evil are not only challenges to our conceptual, epistemological, and metaphysical structures. They are also challenges to our narcissistic balance. We can invoke the twin concepts of the ego ideal and the ideal ego as heuristic devices to delineate two dimensions of that threat.

On the one hand, evil is a threat to the cohesiveness of our religious *ego ideal.* If our defenses against the arguments from evil should fail, then the threat may be perceived to be global, for the very existence of that ideal object is called into question. And if our defenses succeed, we may find ourselves forced by them to undertake a wholesale revision of our representations of the ego ideal. Hans Jonas, for example, in a famous essay, once argued that God cannot be understood in the traditional way as omnipotent, given the reality of evil.[24] Robert Audi imagines a person, Alice, who is

. . . a person of religious faith even if she has a kind of intellectual stance from which doxastic faith, as implying belief that God exists, is absent. While it is not consistent with her being a person of faith that she believe there is no God — since that would constitute too negative an intellectual commitment — she may be intellectually so affected by such things as the apparently negative force of the problem of evil and the power of naturalism as a worldview that she is forced

23. For consideration of the developmental issues involved in the transition from infantile narcissism to mature narcissism, see Meissner, *Psychoanalysis and Religious Experience,* pp. 137-84; also Esther Menaker, "The Ego Ideal: An Aspect of Narcissism," in *The Narcissistic Condition: A Fact of Our Lives and Times,* ed. M. C. Nelson (New York: Human Sciences Press, 1977); and Allan Schore, "Early Superego Development: The Emergence of Shame and Narcissistic Affect Regulation in the Practicing Period," *Psychoanalytic Psychology* 9 (1992): 187-250.

24. Hans Jonas, "The Concept of God after Auschwitz: A Jewish Voice," in *Mortality and Morality: A Search for the Good after Auschwitz* (Evanston, Ill.: Northwestern University Press, 1996).

to suspend judgment on the proposition that God exists, or less voluntaristically speaking, she simply does not form the belief that it is true. She is open to it, but she does not hold it.[25]

Alice, like Jonas, will have undertaken a considerable revision of any traditional representations of God that she may have entertained earlier in her life, to reach this condition. My contention is that insofar as the problem of evil has the power to even suggest to us such sweeping and deep-seated changes in our religious ego ideal (with which we perceive ourselves to be in union), it represents a deep threat to our narcissistic equilibrium. Our ensuing anxiety has as its formal object (to revert to Helm's terms) our evaluation of that threat, its seriousness and its scope. And it will mobilize our capacity for narcissistic defense, or, as the case may be, for narcissistic repair.

On the other hand, problematic evil is also a threat to the cohesion of the ideal ego — *of the theodicist.* Philosophers pride themselves on their conceptual, logical, and argumentative skills and powers. Moreover, such pride is an aspect of normal narcissism, part of that grandiosity that goes appropriately with a condition of healthy narcissistic equilibrium. But the problem of evil can represent a considerable threat to that pride and grandiosity. Suppose that our logical, argumentative, and dialectical powers should prove to be too weak to meet the challenge. We may then be precipitated into a condition of helplessness with respect to those very powers and skills. And helplessness, as we know, is the very essence of psychic trauma.[26] Among our most deep-seated fears, after all, is that of being found to be incompetent, impotent to deliver the solution to the

---

25. Robert Audi, "The Dimensions of Faith and the Demands of Reason," in *Reasoned Faith: Essays in Philosophical Theology in Honor of Norman Kretzmann,* ed. Eleonore Stump (Ithaca, N.Y.: Cornell University Press, 1993), pp. 70-89, here pp. 80ff. Comparison should also be made with Paul Draper, "Seeking but Not Believing: Confessions of a Practicing Agnostic," in *Divine Hiddenness: New Essays,* ed. Daniel Howard-Snyder and Paul K. Moser (Cambridge: Cambridge University Press, 2002), pp. 197-214.

26. For the connection of helplessness with psychological trauma, see S. Keiser, "Freud's Concept of Trauma and a Specific Ego Function," *Journal of the American Psychoanalytic Association* 15 (1967): 781-94; and H. Krystal, "Trauma and Affects," *Psychoanalytic Study of the Child* 33 (1978): 81-116, especially pp. 90-93. Freud drew the connection with special clarity in "Inhibitions, Symptoms and Anxiety," *S.E.* 20 (1926): 77-175. See also, now, Jonathan Cohen, "Structural Consequences of Psychic Trauma: A New Look at 'Beyond the Pleasure Principle,'" *International Journal of Psychoanalysis* 61 (1980): 421-31; Jonathan Cohen and Warren Kinston, "Repression Theory: A New Look at the Cornerstone," *International Journal of Psychoanalysis* 65 (1983): 411-22.

problems that we above all other mortals ought to be able to solve. We, after all, are supposed to be the conceptual tightrope walkers *par excellence;* we, after all, are supposed to be the ones who can climb the tallest logical peaks without benefit of oxygen. Such a threat of failure may invoke in some the archaic anxiety of falling forever into the void. As in the case of Sauron, Tolkien's Dark Lord, their fear may rise up to choke them.

In sum, both forms of threat are enough to elicit narcissistic anxiety, which, in its turn, will motivate defensive and/or reparative action. Such actions may take the form of redoubled efforts to meet the challenges of evil (thereby hoping to ward off the ultimate narcissistic catastrophe: the complete collapse of the ego ideal/ideal ego), or they may take the form of efforts to carry out the kind of interior revolution suggested by Jonas or by Audi (thereby hoping to mitigate the force and extent of the calamity). Now, if I am right to suggest that the problem of evil is also a narcissistic problem, are there any features of theodictic projects that betray their narcissistic significance? I believe that there are, and it is to them that I now turn.

Narcissistic Derivatives of Theodictic Projects

I repeat an earlier caveat: the argument here is not reductive. I do not think that there is *nothing to* theodictic projects other than their narcissistic components or functions. On the contrary, these projects are just what they present themselves to be: genuine efforts to meet real logical and conceptual challenges on the terms in which they are offered. My claim is that even so, they can be and often are the carriers of narcissistic work as well. It is a commonplace of psychoanalytic thinking that psychological truth is often hidden and is to be found in the mishaps that attend our activities, constituting what Lacan once called "meconnaisance," or misknowledge. One writer puts the point this way: "Our slips, lies, and unintended revelations come closer to unveiling fundamental psychological truths than our most finely tuned, most socially adapted, ego-syntonic attempts to be honest."[27] One thinks also of Freud's exploration of jokes and their capacity simultaneously to conceal and to reveal hostility.[28] In

27. Paul Hamburg, "The Lie: Anorexia and the Paternal Metaphor," *The Psychoanalytic Review* 86 (1999): 749.

28. "Jokes and Their Relation to the Unconscious," *Standard Edition* 8 (1905). For a contemporary discussion, see Christopher Bollas, *Cracking Up: The Work of Uncon-*

the same spirit, I shall attend especially to three features of theodictic projects that have aroused some of their sharpest criticisms. They constitute what I take to be unconscious derivatives of the narcissistic work that partially motivates these projects.

A generic feature of contemporary theodictic projects is their marked *defensive* quality. This is certainly due, of course, to the form in which the challenges to theism are cast. Given that the logical form of the problem of evil charges theism with logical incoherence, for example, it is not surprising that it should be met with arguments that are designed to fend it off; arguments, that is, that seek to show that the charge fails. It is a little more surprising that attempts to solve the evidential problem of evil should be similarly defensive in character. Here, too, the most successful attempts to meet the challenge generally try to show that the opponents' arguments fail. The secondary philosophical literature has begun to give rise to studies that seek to show that these theodictic arguments fail, that is, that arguments that arguments fail themselves also fail — defenses against defenses, as it were.[29] Of course, positive theodicies move beyond the defensive stance altogether. But that many responses to the problem of evil are primarily defensive in tone makes them perfect carriers of unconscious narcissistic work. Insofar as the challenges they seek to ward off are challenges to our narcissistic equilibrium, they are likely to mobilize all our energy and skills in repairing or otherwise defending the narcissistic balance upon which the mental health of the religious practitioner depends, and by which that health is partially constituted. Indeed, we can further account for the markedly *aggressive* quality of many theodictic arguments (a quality often conveyed by the almost painful technical virtuosity of many of these arguments, especially those invoking Bayesian inequalities) by considering how deep a threat evil poses to our narcissistic economy. To fail on this level is to fail absolutely, to fall into the void, to fall forever — or so it may appear to us. Narcissistically speaking, we are like the soldiers at Helm's Deep in Tolkien's story: they know "that to fail here is to yield the world of order, peace and light, to the chaotic forces of darkness and to yield it absolutely, world without end." As intense as are the

---

scious Experience (New York: Hill and Wang, 1995), pp. 221-56. There is a separate study to be made of the hostility that may be concealed within some theodictic projects. See further, below, on their aggressive quality.

29. E.g. Mark Bernstein, "Explaining Evil," *Religious Studies* 34 (1998): 151-63; and John Beaudoin, "Evil, the Human Cognitive Condition, and Natural Theology," *Religious Studies* 34 (1998): 403-18. My comments are not meant to derogate from the positive value of either essay.

anxieties associated with deep narcissistic threats, so intense are likely to be the defensive efforts they call forth, and so intense also is likely to be the aggression attending those defensive efforts. And in the psychological order, there are no more intense anxieties than the narcissistic anxieties.

My second derivative has to do with what I shall call the imperative of narcissistic defense. It can be reached by way of an observation James Wetzel makes, commenting on John Hick's theodicy:

> Evil, for Hick, may be real and threatening, but it is also inevitably defeated and 'made to serve God's good purposes'. And if evils even as grave as genocide can find their way into the scheme of human redemption, it is hard to see how theodicy manages to avoid trivializing human tragedy at the very moment it attempts to go beyond it. The vice of speculative theodicy is that it *cannot* accept the possibility of irredeemable evil . . . that in the balance of history, there are some losses which can never be recouped.[30]

I think Wetzel has not understood the psychological springs of this "cannot," a term which, like "can," is notoriously ambiguous and ambivalent. Given a certain ego ideal and a certain ideal ego, it is not possible, on the level of narcissistic functioning, to accept that "there are some losses which can never be recouped." The alternative is that we surrender our logical, conceptual, and dialectic weapons, and accept our inability to solve the problem. Such revisions of the ideal ego, as also of the ego ideal, may well be beyond us to bring about, and may even be beyond our capacity to contemplate. We cannot *face* the prospect. And this sometimes has the further effect that we cannot *see* it.

This further effect may have a bearing on Kenneth Surin's complaint that theodicy engenders moral blindness, and specifically blindness to the possibility of unconditional or irredeemable evil. He holds that:

> . . . theodicy, by its very nature, involves the application of the principles of reason to a cluster of problems which are essentially such that they cannot be resolved by the mere application of rational principles. Evil and suffering in their innermost depths are fundamentally mysterious; they confound the human mind. And yet the goal of theodicy is, somehow, to render them comprehensible, explicable . . . to slot oc-

30. James Wetzel, "Can Theodicy Be Avoided? The Claim of Unredeemed Evil," *Religious Studies* 25 (1989): 1-13, here p. 8.

currences of evil and suffering into a scheme of things consonant with the essentially rational workings of divine providence.[31]

D. Z. Phillips has said something very similar, commenting on Richard Swinburne's theodicy:

> There are screams and screams, and to ask of what use are the screams of the innocent, as Swinburne's defense would have us do, is to embark on a speculation we should not even contemplate. We have our reasons, final human reasons, for putting a moral full stop at many places. If God has other reasons, they are his reasons, not ours, and they do not overrule them. That is why, should he ask us to consider them, we, along with Ivan Karamazov, respectfully, or not so respectfully, return him the ticket.[32]

It is not my purpose here to judge whether anyone suffers from the kind of moral blindness that Surin and Phillips accuse theodicists of.[33] But I would once again like to suggest that if it is ever the case, then it may be because that person is deeply engaged in a narcissistic enterprise that makes it such that they cannot do otherwise. There are imperatives that belong entirely to the narcissistic economy, and are driven by its archaic needs. The possibility of such narcissistic absorption brings me to my third and final derivative.

Persons who are deeply engaged in defending their narcissistic equilibrium, or in reestablishing that equilibrium, or who are deeply engaged

---

31. Kenneth Surin, *Theology and the Problem of Evil* (Oxford: Blackwell Publishing, 1986), pp. 51-52. For similar views, see David Lewis, "Evil for Freedom's Sake?" *Philosophical Papers* 22 (1993): 149-72; Lawrence Langer, "Beyond Theodicy: Jewish Victims and the Holocaust," in *Admitting the Holocaust: Collected Essays* (New York: Oxford University Press, 1995), pp. 25-30; and Terence Tilley, *The Evils of Theodicy* (Washington, D.C.: Georgetown University Press, 1991).

32. D. Z. Phillips, "The Problem of Evil," in *Reason and Religion*, ed. Stuart C. Brown (Ithaca, N.Y.: Cornell University Press, 1977), p. 115; compare "On Not Understanding God," in *Wittgenstein and Religion* (London: St. Martin's Press, 1993), pp. 153-70. Similar concerns are at the heart of Stewart Sutherland's response to an earlier version of Marilyn Adam's theodicy: "Horrendous Evils and the Goodness of God, II," *Proceedings of the Aristotelian Society, Supplementary Volume* 63 (1989): 311-23, especially 313-19. For an insightful discussion of the issues, see Michael Scott, "The Morality of Theodicies," *Religious Studies* 32 (1996): 1-13.

33. Marilyn Adams, in *Horrendous Evils*, argues that divine reasons for evil and suffering are intrinsically beyond our comprehension. But this seems to me to amount to admitting the substance of Surin's and Phillips's charges, while denying their significance, and I do not think we can have it both ways.

in reconfiguring the fundamental set of ideals that inform their narcissistic economy, often relate to other people in their environment as if those others had no psychological depth. Narcissistically absorbed persons may very well need other people, even need them desperately. But their actions, moods, speech, emotional tonus, and other characteristics may be such as to ignore completely the needs of the other persons. The other person becomes a kind of mirror, reflecting only the needs of the absorbed one.

I have earlier spoken of this effect as the "Echo effect": just as Narcissus had no real vital human relationship with the disembodied Echo of his own voice, so the narcissistically absorbed person has no apparently real, vital, and emotionally deep relationships with the other persons around her.[34] Two further complaints often made about theodictic projects may be evidence of such absorption. The first such complaint is put well by Michael Scott:

> Despite claiming to have theories that account for the occurrence of evils in God's plan, the theodicist's explanations are plainly inadequate as a response to particular cases of evil. That is, theodicies have nothing to offer victims of evil. It is one thing to claim that moral evil is justified as the inevitable consequence of human beings being free and responsible; it is quite another to suggest to a person who has been raped that the suffering involved in that experience is in some way balanced out by God's gift of free will to human beings.[35]

The complaint is that theodicies, and especially so-called global theodicies, simply bypass the sufferings of particular persons. Nor is the situation relieved by replying that the proper purpose of a theodicy is to address such global concerns, rather than to provide practical relief of particular sufferings. For that merely reinforces the sense of having been bypassed. Now, whether this feature of theodicies is or is not a good reason to abandon the enterprise does not concern me. What does concern me is that we not overlook a possible psychological meaning of this phenomenon. It seems to me to be at least isomorphic to the kinds of object relations enjoyed by persons deeply absorbed in narcissistic repair or defense. That

34. Jorge Moldanado, "Narcissistic Resistances in the Analytic Experience," *International Journal of Psychoanalysis* 80 (1999): 131-45 discusses related phenomena in the treatment of narcissistically absorbed persons in psychotherapy. Compare also Christopher Bollas, *The Shadow of the Object: Psychoanalysis of the Unthought Known* (New York: Columbia University Press, 1987), pp. 154-55.

35. Michael Scott, "Morality of Theodicies," p. 2.

is, it is at least possible that theodicies bypass the full and individual reality of individual sufferings not only because of the logical and conceptual character of so-called theoretical theodicy, but also because such projects are a species of similarly deep absorption in narcissistic work. Theodicists may be unable to take in the full and unique reality of individual sufferings because they are utterly absorbed in *some other task.*

The second evidence is the staggering technical virtuosity of many theodictic projects, an element of them we have observed before. This has become particularly evident in contemporary responses to the evidential problem of evil, in so far as they have taken advantage of Bayesian confirmation theory to articulate their arguments. Such virtuosity belongs, of course, to the grandiosity that attaches to all narcissistic work. But it may also have a role to play in this bypassing of the individual, or what I am calling the Echo effect. For it tends to render the arguments opaque to ordinary persons grappling with the reality of evil in their lives and in the lives of those around them whom they see suffering and sometimes suffering abominably, and, often, at least apparently gratuitously. Even persons of good will, highly educated, deeply moral, profoundly spiritual in their outlook, may find such writing completely useless to them. Theodicists *themselves,* indeed, when in the grip of their own deepest sufferings, or when contemplating the very real and specific sufferings of others, may find them similarly useless and sterile. My contention is that theodictic projects are very likely to be bound up with the work of the narcissistic economy, and that one effect of this may be such degrees of narcissistic absorption and aggression that the Echo effect is *to be expected.* It may be this effect that the critics are responding to.

Conclusion

I would like to conclude this interpretation of philosophical responses to the problem of evil with three speculations.

1. Theodictic projects, like all philosophical enterprises, are very complex, working on many levels at once, and deriving many of their characteristics from more than one of the levels on which they function. My contention has been that among these functions are those of narcissistic defense and narcissistic repair. I further contend that some of the features of theodictic projects reflect these fundamental psychological dynamics. I have tried to stress throughout that such

narcissistic functions are entirely normal, and to be expected in every normally developed and psychologically intact adult human person. There is nothing pathological in any of this. It remains, however, a possibility that some theodictic projects might be carried out as part of a larger pattern of pathology (whether in an individual or in a group), and it remains a possibility that some traditions of theodictic inquiry might be pathological. That is, the newly coined term "philosophical psychopathology" may have to be applied in the sense of "pathological philosophy." There is a further study to be made of specifically pathological responses to the problem of evil. And that is my first speculation.

2. My second speculation has to do with the emotions that surround narcissistic disturbances and the work they give rise to. I do not think that emotions are essentially noetic or that they constitute, just *eo ipso*, a source of knowledge. That is, they have no essential epistemic value. But I think that they always contain information. This is especially obviously the case if we follow Helm and others in taking emotions to be evaluative states. Such information can be the basis for some kind of knowledge, and especially for self-knowledge. It seems to me to follow that the narcissistic emotions, elation and anxiety, as described in this essay, have similar value. I think we can learn from them with considerable accuracy what kind of threat (revealed by narcissistic anxiety) or payoff (revealed by narcissistic elation) has evoked them. That is, there may be a *metric* for narcissistic space, derivable from our experiences, when those experiences are understood in the light of the theory of normal narcissistic functioning. I certainly have no account to give of this metric, nor of the self-knowledge that belongs with it; and indeed I do not know for sure if such an account even can be given. But, if it can be given, then it is possible that we can turn the confrontation with the problems of evil into an occasion for self-knowledge, a self-knowledge that arises from some of the most archaic elements of that confrontation.[36] And that just might transform the terrain over which theodicists and anti-theodicists currently do battle.

36. This project will have to interdigitate with Ulric Neisser's classic essay "Five Kinds of Self-Knowledge," *Philosophical Psychology* 1 (1988): 35-59, and especially his concepts of the ecological self, the interpersonal self, and the conceptual self. Another very useful starting point is D. W. Hamlyn, "Self-Knowledge," in *Perception, Learning, and the Self* (New York: Routledge, 1983), pp. 239-66, a study redolent with connections to the topics treated in the present essay.

3. My third speculation has to do with Alice, the figure described by Audi, i.e. the agnostic person who is unable, in large part because of the impact of the problem of evil and the perceived failures of replies to it, to form a fully doxastic faith. The possibility of such persons seems to me one of the most interesting proposals to have been made in recent religious epistemology.[37] It is fair to ask, especially on behalf of such persons, what might be the alternative to traditional theodictic projects. One possible alternative is *silence*. This may seem paradoxical. After all, we customarily associate silence with the absence of vital human relationships, the absence of knowledge, the absence even of speech or thought. But there are forms of silence that can serve as forms of communication, as the medium for vital interpersonal exchanges, and even as forms of knowledge.[38] They have been known to the mystical traditions of classical theism for some time. They are reflected in such religious practices as sitting in silent solidarity with those who mourn the dead. The initial (and wisest) response of Job's friends was to sit in silence with him. I speculate that silence may be a viable alternative to theodicy, an alternative that succeeds in being the bearer of profound moral and spiritual values and attitudes. It is work for another occasion to suggest a conceptual framework within which to cast such an account of silence, and its associated spiritual disciplines.

37. From the point of view of developmental studies, if a capacity for basic trust in other persons depends on the vicissitudes of the earliest period, it is possible that there be persons who, as adults, simply have no psychological capacity to form the kinds of religious attachments required by most religious traditions. Such persons are likely candidates for the role assigned by Audi to his Alice. I hope to draw out these connections in more detail in a future study.

38. Most psychoanalytic literature treats silence as a form of defensive discharge or resistance, especially in the therapeutic setting. More positive views of silence are taken in, e.g.: M. M. R. Khan, "Silence as Communication," in *The Privacy of the Self* (New York: International University Press, 1974), pp. 168-80; Janet Hadda, "The Ontogeny of Silence in an Analytic Case," *International Journal of Psychoanalysis* 72 (1991): 117-30; and Stephen Kurz, "On Silence," *Psychoanalytic Review* 71 (1984): 227-45. There are models in this literature that should be of interest to the religious epistemologist. For a recent theological treatment, see Nicholas Wolterstorff, "The Silence of the God Who Speaks," in *Divine Hiddenness: New Essays,* ed. Daniel Howard-Snyder and Paul K. Moser (Cambridge: Cambridge University Press, 2002), pp. 215-28.

God, Evil, and the Thought
of Simone Weil

Robert Stanley

Simone Weil was, to put it mildly, a complex individual. She was born of parents who were ethnically Jewish but religiously agnostic. A brilliant woman, Simone Weil graduated in 1931 with her *agrégation* from the École Normale Supérieure, one of the pinnacles of the French intellectual establishment, where she studied under the philosopher Alain. After finishing her dissertation, she taught in a number of French *lycées*, where she rarely remained longer than a year or two. As a teacher, she was generally regarded as somewhat eccentric but deeply concerned for her students' academic well-being. Curiously, from one point of view, she then made a deliberate choice to work in an automobile factory, on an assembly line, where she observed and later commented upon the often harsh working conditions. Later she worked as an agricultural laborer in the vineyards of southern France, near Marseilles. In 1936, she went to Spain in order to lend her assistance to the Republican cause, but her natural awkwardness caused her to have a ludicrous accident (involving boiling cooking oil), thereby cutting short her "military" career.

In the last few years of her life — she was barely thirty-four and a half years old at the time of her death in 1943 — she was intensely interested in religious questions and matters of spirituality. She was deeply devoted to aspects of Christianity, especially the person of Christ, his sacrifice on the Cross, and the efficacy of the Eucharist. Yet in spite of this devotion to aspects of Catholicism and in spite of the fact that she frequently attended Mass, she steadfastly refused the sacrament of Baptism, insisting, instead, that by formally entering the Church, she would be cutting herself off from those outside the Church whom she admired: not only Jews, but also the Cathars, whose "Mediterranean" civilization she admired; and the Greeks, whose thought and literature she admired profoundly. Perhaps somewhat troubling for her Christian friends (and they were many) was her belief that the Greeks were better forerunners and harbingers of the coming of Christ than were the Jewish writers of the Old Testament. Indeed, she has been seen by some to be slightly anti-Semitic, in spite of the fact that both sides of her family were Jewish. In regard to her physical health, one has to say that it was not good: she suffered from migraine headaches for most of her adult life. Moreover, like many French intellectuals of her day, she smoked heavily. When she lived in wartime Britain (from December 1942 until her death on August 24, 1943), she had the somewhat fanciful notion (at least from a contemporary point of view) that she wanted to limit her food intake to the rations of a typical French person in Nazi-occupied France: in essence, it seems likely that she died in large part due to anorexia nervosa.

Many more things could be said about Simone Weil's life, interesting, complicated, paradoxical life that it was. But this is not primarily a biographical study. Rather, I would like to concentrate on her treatment of evil — its manifestations in the world, its impact on human beings, and its influence on us as concerns our relationship to God. But even here the task is anything but simple. Virtually all of Simone Weil's books were put together by others, from the voluminous writings she left behind, and were published posthumously. Her mind was brilliant but hers was not a systematic philosophy like that, say, of her friend Jacques Maritain. Nevertheless, a careful study of her œuvre to discover what she has to say about evil is quite rewarding.

Simone Weil's comments on evil are to be found in several books. But since one has to limit the consideration in some way, I have chosen to concentrate primarily on three of them: *Waiting for God* (1951), the translation of *Attente de Dieu* (1950); *The Need for Roots* (1952), the translation of *L'Enracinement* (1949); and *Gravity and Grace* (1952), the translation of *La Pesanteur et la grâce* (1947). Again, we must constantly keep in mind that virtually all of her publications were put together by other people and published after her death. *The Need for Roots* was essentially a report she wrote for the Free French Forces in London during World War II. At least it was conceived of and written as a whole; it, too, was published posthumously.

Because evil is such an important and recurring theme in *Waiting for God*, I have chosen to start with this book. We need to pause briefly to consider what Simone Weil's methods were. In the Introduction to *Waiting for God*, Leslie Fiedler writes,

Simone Weil's writing as a whole is marked by three characteristic devices: extreme statement or paradox; the equilibrium of contradictions; and exposition by myth. As the life of Simone Weil reflects a desire to insist on the absolute even at the risk of being absurd, so her writing tends always toward the extreme statement, the formulation that shocks by its willingness to push to its ultimate conclusion the kind of statement we ordinarily accept with the tacit understanding that no one will take it *too* seriously.[1]

It is very important to keep these facts in mind when reading Simone Weil or when considering the facts of her life. Many of her actions (such as going to Spain to fight for the Republican cause) and many of her written statements (such as repudiating much of the Old Testament and thereby downplaying Israel's contribution to Christianity) may seem either absurd or needlessly radical. Yet that was Weil's modus operandi. She wanted to make her readers reflect, to move out of old and perhaps inflexible ways of thinking, and for these reasons her statements tend to shock or at least surprise.

Waiting for God consists of six letters, five of which are addressed to Father J.-M. Perrin, O.P., on matters almost exclusively religious. The first two deal with Simone Weil's hesitancy to receive the sacrament of Baptism. In the very first letter to Father Perrin, she refers to evil as something that we must love as part of our submission to God's plan. She first speaks of our need to distinguish among what she calls "three domains," the first being that which is independent of us as human beings:

> In this [first] domain everything that comes about is in accordance with the will of God, without any exception. Here then we must love absolutely everything, as a whole and in each detail. Including evil in all its forms; notably our own past sins, in so far as they are past (for we must hate them in so far as their root is still present), our own sufferings, past, present, and to come, and [. . .] the sufferings of other men in so far as we are not called upon to relieve them.[2]

Weil seems to be arguing here that we must accept as God's will what occurs, has occurred, and will occur. This is most assuredly not to say that evil is not evil, or that we should not strive to avoid evil; rather, she advo-

---

1. Simone Weil, *Waiting for God*, trans. Emma Craufurd and intro. Leslie A. Fiedler (New York: Putnam, 1951), p. 29.

2. Weil, *Waiting for God*, pp. 43-44.

cates an acceptance of the fact that we are subject to evil and have to struggle against it, obviously with divine assistance. Much of the first letter is devoted to a detailing of reasons why she chooses to remain outside the Church: that also applies to her second letter.

The longest — and in some ways the most interesting — letter is the fourth, in which Weil gives a sort of spiritual autobiography. Several facets of this letter could be considered, but I will limit myself to three. (We need to remember that, although Simone Weil was never a member of the Catholic Church, she was deeply attracted to it for a variety of reasons.) The first two concern spiritual "events" associated in her life with two specific geographical locations: in 1937, while visiting the twelfth-century Romanesque church of Santa Maria degli Angeli in Assisi, Weil was obliged by someone or something to fall to her knees in prayer.[3] Even more astounding was what happened to her in the Benedictine abbey of Solesmes during Holy Week and the early part of Easter Week in 1938. She writes:

> I was suffering from splitting headaches; each sound hurt me like a blow; by an extreme effort of concentration I was able to rise above this wretched flesh, to leave it to suffer by itself heaped up in a corner, and to find a pure and perfect joy in the unimaginable beauty of the chanting and the words.[4]

Finally, while she was at Solesmes, Weil met a young English Catholic who introduced her to the poetry of George Herbert, one of the English metaphysical poets. Apparently his poem "Love bade me welcome" impressed her to such an extent that she committed it to memory. It must have been sometime thereafter that the following incident took place:

> Often, at the culminating point of a violent headache, I make myself say it [the poem] over, concentrating all my attention upon it and clinging with all my soul to the tenderness it enshrines. I used to think I was merely reciting it as a beautiful poem but without my knowing it the recitation had the virtue of a prayer. It was during one of these recitations that, as I told you, Christ himself came down and took possession of me.[5]

3. Weil, *Waiting for God*, pp. 67-68.
4. Weil, *Waiting for God*, p. 68.
5. Weil, *Waiting for God*, pp. 68-69.

She does not elaborate much on this encounter, except to say in the next paragraph "[. . .] I had never foreseen the possibility of that, of a real contact, person to person, here below, between a human being and God."[6] I would like to offer my own explanation of what is afoot here. Weil often expresses her belief in the loving kindness and the purity of God. Just as at Solesmes she had been able to "rise above this wretched flesh, to leave it to suffer by itself, heaped up in a corner," so with this deeply spiritual poem, whose efficacy was that of a prayer to the Almighty, she was able to overcome physical suffering, a form of evil, and to see it transformed into a mystical experience. Here the evil to be overcome was a violent migraine headache and it turned into what might be termed, without undue exaggeration, a life-changing experience. The beauty and the devotion of the poem, in some inexplicable manner, were able to cause her to have a mystical, otherworldly experience. Of this encounter, John Dunaway writes,

> From autumn 1938, however, her life was suffused with an awareness that she had encountered Christ and that she belonged to him. It was thenceforth an experiential truth converted to her by the person of Christ that was to guide her philosophy. In short, Simone Weil was converted to the Christian faith.[7]

One can argue with the literal veracity of that last statement. The word "converted" can be taken in various ways. Weil did not, as far as is known, ever formally become a member of the Roman Catholic Church or any other Christian group. Nevertheless, her devotion to the person of Christ and to his presence in the Eucharist were an undeniable part of her mind-set. It is doubtless in this broad sense that Dunaway considers her as having been "converted to the Christian faith." As we have seen, however, she very consciously elected to remain outside the confines of the Church, though she could never have distanced herself completely from it.

A lengthy essay entitled "Forms of the Implicit Love of God" is also a part of *Waiting for God,* and one of the essays under this broader title is called "The Love of Our Neighbor." About seven pages into this essay, Weil comments on the so-called "problem of evil," as it is usually known in philosophy. She does so in a way that is far from unambiguous.

6. Weil, *Waiting for God,* p. 69.
7. *Simone Weil* (Boston: Twayne Publishing, 1984), p. 16.

The spectacle of this world is another, more certain proof [i.e., of the fact that "[a]ll that man is capable of admiring is possible with God"]. Either God is not almighty or he is not absolutely good, or else he does not command everywhere where he has the power do so.

Thus the existence of evil here below [*ici-bas*], far from disproving the reality of God, is the very thing that reveals him in his truth.[8]

This is an extraordinary statement on Weil's part, all the more so as it is explained or justified in a way that some might object to vociferously. God's creation has room for those who accept and for those who reject him. Weil goes on to say:

On God's part creation is not an act of self-expansion but of restraint and renunciation. God and all his creatures are less than God alone. God accepted this diminution. He emptied a part of his being from himself. He had already emptied himself in this act of his divinity; that is why Saint John says that the Lamb had been slain from the beginning of the world. God permitted the existence of things distinct from himself and worth infinitely less than himself.[9]

This passage is not easy to parse. What Simone Weil seems to be saying is that evil exists, is a part of the world, not because God willed that evil should exist, but because God wanted to create the world and populate it with free creatures. The second sentence in the quotation mentioned above ("God and all his creatures are less than God alone") is a logical contradiction. But the next two sentences clarify, I believe, what Weil really had in mind: "God accepted this diminution. He emptied a part of his being from himself." In order to accommodate frail and finite human beings, she seems to be arguing, God accepted, as it were, a diminution of himself. This dovetails with her reference to St. John's allusion to "the Lamb [which] had been slain from the beginning of the world." It seems that in creating the world and its creatures God took a certain risk. As she says later in the paragraph of God's denying himself for our sakes: "This response, this echo, which it is in our power to refuse, is the only possible justification for the folly of love of the creative act."[10]

Simone Weil was very fond of the Lord's Prayer in Greek. She learned it, apparently, about the time she lived in the south of France,

8. Weil, *Waiting for God*, p. 145.
9. Weil, *Waiting for God*, p. 145.
10. Weil, *Waiting for God*, p. 145.

where she not only committed it to memory, but also recited it during the day, and even tried to teach it, in Greek, to some of her fellow farm workers near Marseilles. Because some of her commentary on the Our Father deals with her concept of evil, it is worthwhile to note a few pertinent passages. Under the rubric "Thy will be done," she has some interesting statements to make.

> We are only absolutely, infallibly certain of the will of God concerning the past. Everything that has happened, whatever it may be, is in accordance with the will of the almighty Father. That is implied by the notion of almighty power. The future also, whatever it may contain, once it has come about will have come about in conformity with the will of God.[11]

This is somewhat similar to what Weil expressed in the essay "Form of the Implicit Love of God," parts of which were quoted above. To say, as she does in the passage just cited, that "[e]verything that has happened, whatever it may be, is in accordance with the will of the almighty Father," is to make a statement that some thinkers would be loath to accept. But it dovetails with her belief that God is indeed almighty. Weil knows, however, that this position will cause difficulty for some of her readers. She concludes her commentary on "Thy will be done" by writing,

> We have to desire that everything that has happened should have happened, and nothing else. We have to do so, not because what has happened is good in our eyes, but because God has permitted it, and because the obedience of the course of events to God is in itself an absolute good.[12]

Again, some — indeed many — readers may disagree with her on this point, but Weil is, I think, being consistent with her earlier statements. Essentially, her position would seem to be that an omniscient, benevolent God not only knows what he is doing but also knows what is going on, for better or worse, in his own creation. She seems to have little difficulty with this belief.

Under the rubric of "Give us this day our daily bread," to which she appends her own words "the bread which is supernatural," Weil has several pertinent things to say. She believes that Christ is the bread that feeds

---

11. Weil, *Waiting for God*, p. 218.
12. Weil, *Waiting for God*, p. 219.

us and that we need to make daily intercession for his life-giving presence in our lives. We need to be aware of this need that we have. She writes,

> We should ask for this food. [. . .] We ought not to be able to bear to go without it for a single day, for when our actions only depend on earthly energies, subject to the necessity of this world, we are incapable of thinking and doing anything but evil. [. . .] The necessity that drives us toward evil governs everything in us except the energy from on high at the moment when it comes into us. We cannot store it.[13]

Again, we note Simone Weil's love of paradox. If one grants that the Christian believer depends on God for both physical food and spiritual sustenance, is it really true to say, as Weil does, that "when our actions only depend on earthly energies, subject to the necessity of this world, we are incapable of thinking and doing anything but evil"? In one sense, and a very real sense, this statement appears to be quite false: some persons who are complete nonbelievers carry out actions that a believer would be remiss not to praise and admire. But I think that Weil has nevertheless a real point to make: God's help is very real and very efficacious and can enable one to do more and better things than would perhaps be the case otherwise. Her use of paradox obliges us to look closely at the statement in order to determine if we agree or not.

Under the rubric "And lead us not into temptation, but deliver us from evil," Simone Weil stresses our need to remember that God's help — the supernatural bread, if you will — can benefit us, but it can be used only in the present. She writes:

> Although the soul has received supernatural bread at the moment when it asked for it, its joy is mixed with fear because it could only ask for it for the present. [. . .] The soul has not the right to ask for bread for the morrow, but it expresses its fear in the form of a supplication. It finishes with that. The prayer began with the word "Father," it ends with the word "evil." We must go from confidence to fear. Confidence alone can give us strength enough not to fall as a result of fear.[14]

---

13. Weil, *Waiting for God*, pp. 221-22.
14. Weil, *Waiting for God*, p. 225.

This is very much in line with what she had written earlier about the fact that divine sustenance, the supernatural bread, cannot be stored; it must be used at the moment it is requested by us and bestowed by God. The believer is assured that the Father, the heavenly creator, will provide him or her with whatever strength is needed. The confidence of which Weil speaks is not confidence in our own strengths and abilities, but rather confidence in our Father's help.

Weil's treatment of the Lord's Prayer is doubtless influenced by her deeply held belief that the true antecedents of the New Testament in general and of Christ's teaching in particular are to be found in the Greek philosophers much more than in the Hebrew scriptures. She especially disliked much of the Old Testament and almost everything to do with the Roman Empire, the latter because it epitomized and glorified the brutality and violence that she so deplored. Doubtless her antipathy to the harsh God of the Old Testament has to do with this same dislike. Of her attitudes and antipathies, John Hellman writes,

> This perception of Christ as the embodiment of Greek wisdom and sensitivity characterized her view of history and her bitter hatred of the Roman influence on the Western tradition. [. . .] With her strong feelings about the wisdom and virtue of the Greeks and the perverseness of the Romans, she could not wholly embrace the writings of the Fathers of the Church, or even of Paul, with the same rapture with which she encountered the word of Christ.[15]

It is interesting to see how fond Simone Weil was of the traditions of ancient Greece, India, and even Egypt, even as she displayed such hostility to ancient Israel and ancient Rome. Her love of compassion and mercy was equaled by her contempt for violence, brutality, and oppression. (Although even she admitted that the ancient Greeks could be brutal in their treatment of enemies.)

I would like to discuss briefly the book entitled *The Need for Roots* (the English translation of *L'Enracinement*), which Simone Weil wrote in London in 1943 and which was published in France in 1949. A. F. Wills, the translator, gives us this background information:

> Shortly after her arrival in England, the previous November [of 1942], Simone Weil had been asked by the Free French in London to write a

---

15. *Simone Weil: An Introduction to Her Thought* (Waterloo, Ont.: Wilfrid Laurier University Press, 1982), pp. 78-79.

report on the possibilities of bringing about the regeneration of France.

That report is this book, and in calling passionately upon her fellow-countrymen to set about recovering their spiritual roots before it is too late, and suggesting to them how this may be done, Simone Weil addresses herself to men of every nationality, but more particularly, of course, to those who share the spiritual heritage of the West.[16]

One can readily see the enthusiasm that the author brought to this task of prescribing what should be done for the moral and spiritual regeneration of France. She saw what she considered to be the great failing and the consequent great suffering of France. Her solutions are sometimes very practical, sometimes rather quixotic. Yet her keen intelligence was obviously fully engaged in her assigned task.

In Part Two of *The Need for Roots*, Weil discusses the problems of "uprootedness" both in urban and in rural areas. Although the specific problems are different between town and country, the resulting unhappiness, frustration, and misery — in other words, the evil — are remarkably the same. Rather early in this chapter on uprootedness she writes,

> Uprootedness is by far the most dangerous malady to which human societies are exposed, for it is a self-propagating one. For people who are really uprooted there remain only two possible sorts of behavior: either to fall into a spiritual lethargy resembling death, like the majority of the slaves in the days of the Roman Empire, or to hurl themselves into some form of activity necessarily designed to uproot, often by the most violent methods, those who are not yet uprooted, or only partly so.[17]

The two alternatives open to those who are uprooted, according to Weil, are equally unappealing, even dangerous. Uprootedness usually produces more of the same, and the condition spreads like a disease. Where people feel that they are uprooted and alienated, they are more vulnerable to demagoguery and to violent acts in general. In France, as she points out, the turbulence and dislocation of the First World War, soon followed by the economic and political upsets of the 1930s, were demoralizing for both urban and rural areas. She writes:

16. Simone Weil, *The Need for Roots*, trans. A. F. Wills (London: Routledge & Kegan Paul, 1952), p. xv.

17. Weil, *The Need for Roots*, p. 45.

In France, the uprootedness characterizing the proletariat had reduced vast numbers of workers to a state of pathetic stupor, and caused others to feel themselves at war with society. The same money which had brutally cut away the roots of the working-class, had at the same time gnawed at those of the middle-classes, for wealth is cosmopolitan; any feeble attachment to the country which these might still retain was very much outweighed, especially since 1936, by fear and hatred of the workers. Even the peasants had almost become uprooted since the 1914 war, demoralized by the rôle of cannon fodder they had played in it, by money which occupied an increasingly important place in their lives, and by far too frequent a contact with the corruption prevailing in the cities. As for intelligence, it was almost extinct.[18]

This is indeed a bleak portrait of her native France for the period between the two world wars. The images of grimness, of the breakdown of civility and community spirit, of the deep-seated antagonisms between workers and the middle classes, even, as mentioned elsewhere, between factory workers and farmers (or peasants, to use the translator's word) create a picture of a France almost in chaos. And, to be sure, many of these conditions described by Weil for France also obtained for other countries.

But Weil is not content merely to point out the social evils that were so glaring in France. Rather, she makes bold to suggest some solutions. For example, a system in which a young person is in school one day and virtually the next day goes to work in a dehumanizing factory is urgently in need of improvement. She suggests a more humane system, whereby new workers are made to feel that their contributions to the overall work process are valuable, that they are not merely cogs in a machine, that they realize "the value, social utility, and destination" of the products being produced. There should also be a reduction of "the complete divorce between working life and family life."[19]

As for agricultural workers, she suggests, perhaps not too practically, that they not be brought into contact with factory workers during military training. She writes:

The latter [factory workers] seek to impress the former [peasants], which is bad for both of them. Contacts of this sort don't really have the effect of bringing people together. Only a course of action pursued in common can do that; and, in the nature of things, there can be

18. Weil, *The Need for Roots*, p. 47.
19. Weil, *The Need for Roots*, p. 52.

no common action in barracks, since you are getting ready for war there in time of peace.[20]

She goes on to state her belief that young peasant recruits would be much better off in barracks far removed from the cities, because they would presumably not be with factory workers and because they would be less likely to have contact with prostitution. While some of these notions seem a bit fanciful, her prescriptions for improving conditions in the factories are quite pertinent. Let us remember that Weil herself worked several months in an automobile factory, so she had firsthand knowledge of the conditions she criticized.

The third book of Simone Weil I wish to discuss is *Gravity and Grace* (1952), the English translation of *La Pesanteur et la grâce* (1947). *Gravity and Grace* consists of some thirty-seven chapters, each one of which is placed under a certain heading or theme, e.g., "Void and Compensation," "Detachment," "The Self," "Decreation," and "Self-Effacement," to name a few. Gustave Thibon, to whom Simone Weil entrusted many of her writings when she left France, made these headings and grouped certain of her writings under them. In the introduction to a new edition of *Gravity and Grace*, Thomas R. Nevin speaks of the work of Gustave Thibon in preparing the volume for its initial publication. In his introduction, Gustave Thibon concedes the arbitrariness of his editing Weil's notes into topical, rather than chronological form. While the range of her interests is much greater than this volume suggests, *Gravity and Grace* is arguably the best introduction to her mind, and the best way to approach the entries is to read them not as final statements — Weil was too honest to be satisfied with conclusions — but as reflective experiments or arguments she made to herself, her first reader.[21]

I think it is important to keep in mind that, as Thomas Nevin says, Simone Weil was engaging in "reflective experiments or arguments she made to herself." These statements are revealing of her thinking, in this case on the subject of evil, at least at the time she wrote them. They may not, in any individual instance, be her "final word." In the interests of efficiency, I shall limit myself to a few of the comments on evil that occur in the chapter of the same name.

There are, in the chapter called "Evil," some thirty-nine entries that

20. Weil, *The Need for Roots*, p. 81.

21. Simone Weil, *Gravity and Grace*, trans. Arthur Wills (Lincoln, Neb.: University of Nebraska Press, 1997), p. xii.

range in length from two lines to twenty-one lines. Allow me to choose a few at random for analysis. Here is an entry from the second page of the chapter.

> *Literature and morality.* Imaginary evil is romantic and varied; real evil is gloomy, monotonous, barren, boring. Imaginary good is boring; real good is always new, marvelous, intoxicating. Therefore "imaginative literature" is either boring or immoral (or a mixture of both). It only escapes from this alternative if in some way it passes over to the side of reality through the power of art — and only genius can do that.[22]

One regrets that Weil gives here no specific examples of the literature of which she is thinking. She was obviously a woman of wide reading and high culture. When she wrote, "Imaginary evil is romantic and varied," she may well have had in mind a novel such as Mary Shelley's *Franken-stein* or some of Baudelaire's poems from *Les Fleurs du mal*. When she wrote, "[R]eal evil is gloomy, monotonous, barren, boring," she may have had in mind Flaubert's novel *Madame Bovary*, in which the heroine's adulterous escapades ultimately prove both boring and a bitter disappointment. She may, on the other hand, have had in mind the evil that is found in the everyday lives of real people — and it is that monotonous, barren evil which is portrayed in Flaubert's masterpiece and in other works of literature. While not presuming to know Weil's opinion on Flaubert and Baudelaire, I am willing to state that she would probably concede their genius in treating evil and the fallen nature of human beings.

I quote below a part of another statement on evil:

> The sin which we have in us emerges from us and spreads outside ourselves, setting up a contagion of sin. [. . .] But at the contact of a perfectly pure being there is a transmutation, and the sin becomes suffering. Such is the function of the just servant of Isaiah, of the Lamb of God. Such is redemptive suffering. All the criminal violence of the Roman Empire ran up against Christ, and in him it became pure suffering. Evil beings, on the other hand, transform simple suffering (sickness, for example) into sin.[23]

This statement has to be taken with some of Weil's statements elsewhere in her œuvre on purity. Basically, she seems to be saying that when ordi-

---

22. Weil, *Gravity and Grace*, p. 120.
23. Weil, *Gravity and Grace*, p. 122.

nary mortals come into contact with evil they often react by displaying negative traits: anger, hostility, the desire for revenge. But the contact between evil and "a perfectly pure being" is usually going to cause the sin to become suffering, according to Weil. Yet, let us remind ourselves, there are relatively few "perfectly pure beings," though there are innocent sufferers. The example she probably has in mind is Christ, against whom "[a]ll the criminal violence of the Roman Empire ran up," to use her words. His sacrifice on the cross, she implies, was so efficacious because of his — the sufferer's — perfect innocence and purity. It is equally evident that not all evil ultimately produces such a good result.

And here is a portion of yet another of the items in her chapter entitled "Evil." Here she discusses the problem of the transference of evil and the tendency it has to increase as a result.

> All crime is a transference of the evil in him who acts, to him who undergoes the result of the action. This is true of unlawful love as well as murder. [. . .]
>
> When there is a transference of evil, the evil is not diminished but increased in him from whom it proceeds. This is a phenomenon of multiplication. The same is true when the evil is transferred to things. Where, then, are we to put the evil?
>
> We have to transfer it from the impure part to the pure part of ourselves, thus changing it into pure suffering. The crime which is latent in us we must inflict on ourselves.[24]

Again, what do we make of this statement? It can be said that, in a certain sense, Weil is obsessed with evil and with purity. Evil was for her a dynamic principle, one that had all sorts of ramifications for humankind and for God. To the principle of evil she opposed goodness in general, but in particular she opposed purity. This idea comes up numerous times in her writings. Writing in *Simone Weil: Interpretations of a Life* (ed. George Abbot White), the critic Michele Murray has suggested that Simone Weil was influenced by Gnosticism, especially as exemplified in those practitioners of Gnosticism knows as the Cathars, who lived and flourished in the south of France until they were defeated and virtually exterminated by the forces of the king of France and Pope Innocent around A.D. 1209. Michele Murray writes,

> Simone Weil admired the Cathars. [. . .] During that time [in the early 1940s, prior to her departure for the U.S.A.], when personal survival

24. Weil, *Gravity and Grace*, p. 123.

was the chief, if not the only concern of those around her, she wrote two essays for a special issue of the *Cahiers de* [*sic*] *sud*, a journal published in Marseilles that specialized in the culture of Mediterranean France. In them she expressed her admiration for the Cathars even while admitting to insufficient knowledge of their closed and largely secret society.[25]

But what was there about the Cathars that drew Weil's attention and caused her intense, almost fanatical admiration? Murray suggests it was

> [. . .] their belief in absolute dualism. It is an attempt to reconcile God's existence with the problem of evil in the world, a problem that plagued Simone Weil throughout her life, as shown by her numerous journal entries on the subject.[26]

Weil's keen awareness of evil, her knowledge of the struggle between the forces of good and evil, her love of the Mediterranean culture of southern France: are these phenomena sufficient to justify one's belief that she was a Gnostic? That may be stating the case a little strongly, but it seems clear that she was very sympathetic to Gnosticism, at least to that form thereof exemplified by the Cathars. This may also at least give proof of why she was unwilling to become formally a member of the Roman Catholic Church, which, in her mind, to a certain extent paralleled or in a sense represented the continuation of the Roman Empire, an institution, as we have seen, that she cordially despised. In any event, her sympathies with Gnostic beliefs set her apart from standard, orthodox Christianity.

Even those who are very knowledgeable of and sympathetic to Weil cannot help but feel that aspects of her persona are a bit hard to take. Even so enthusiastic a Weilian as Eric O. Springsted has this to say:

> We are troubled by Weil's life, and by some of the ideas that have sprung from it, in a number of very particular ways. Religiously she often appears quite heterodox, even to the point of gnosticism in the popular sense of that term — at times her emphasis seems entirely on the spiritual at the expense of the physical.[27]

---

25. "Simone Weil: Last Things," in *Simone Weil: Interpretations of a Life*, ed. George Abbott White (Amherst, Mass.: University of Massachusetts Press, 1981), pp. 57-58.

26. Murray, "Simone Weil: Last Things," p. 58.

27. *Simone Weil and the Suffering of Love* (Cambridge, Mass.: Cowley Publications, 1986), pp. 5-6.

Weil's emphasis on the spiritual at the expense of the physical may perhaps be attributed to her extreme intellectualism. It may also be due, at least in part, to her tendency to overlook or perhaps underplay her own sexuality, and to her somewhat extreme asceticism. Again, to quote from Springsted:

> She had little interest in her own sexual identity and often attempted to be as man-like (or at least as unwomanly) as possible. As a joke, she would even occasionally sign letters to her parents as "your dutiful son." In the second place Weil was probably a victim of *anorexia nervosa*; this would partially explain the strict asceticism of her life and her almost blind lack of self-concern for her own person. Her attitude seems to indicate a spirit of self-immolation; her death, which occurred because of a refusal, and probably an inability, to eat while she was suffering from tuberculosis, seems to confirm this. All these facts taken together can easily lead to charges of self-hatred, suggesting an inhuman and fanatic quality about her that does not endear her to those to whom she is supposed to speak so eloquently.[28]

All of these aspects of Weil's life are basically evident, but that does not prevent her from being an original and insightful thinker. Springsted, for example, goes on to state that this skepticism on our part in regard to Weil is really misplaced and unjustified, especially when we read her own writings on suffering.[29] Her concern for suffering humanity and her empathy for suffering individuals are indisputable.

In doing research for this paper, I came across a collection of essays on aesthetics and language in the work of Simone Weil. One of the essays that particularly caught my attention was written by Diogenes Allen and entitled "The Character of Don Giovanni in Mozart's Opera."[30] Allen espouses the idea that Don Giovanni seeks sexual gratification from all women he comes across, thereby causing his partners degradation and wreaking havoc on the social fabric. Allen ties this in with the thought of Simone Weil by stating that the clue to Don Giovanni's defiance of social conventions and his refusal to repent is to be found in his (and other people's) wish to possess the whole universe, a wish that is not appropriate to any individual. In this regard, Allen quotes Weil as follows:

---

28. Springsted, *Simone Weil and the Suffering of Love*, p. 6.
29. Springsted, *Simone Weil and the Suffering of Love*, p. 6.
30. The essay appears in *The Beauty That Saves: Essays on Aesthetics and Language in Simone Weil*, ed. John M. Dunaway and Eric O. Springsted (Macon, Ga.: Mercer University Press, 1996), pp. 173-83.

There is in every man and in every group of men a feeling that they have a just and legitimate claim to be master of the universe — to possess it. But this possession is improperly understood, because they do not understand that each one has access to it (insofar as this is possible for a man on earth) through his own body; (through the *finite* part of himself).

Alexander [the Great] and a peasant proprietor, like Don Juan and a happily married husband.[31]

Allen goes on to say that, for Weil, this very human tendency to perceive everything from our own point of view gives us a very distorted picture of reality and therefore does not help us. As a solution, she suggests that we should allow ourselves to be convinced of the indifference of the natural world. Thus informed, as Allen puts it, of "the bitter truth of our vulnerability to nature, [. . .] we escape from our anthropocentricity and egocentricity. Freed of this false perspective we may now be content to possess the whole universe in a way that does not interfere with other people's possessions."[32] The evil that results or that can result from our egocentricity and self-centeredness is thus corrected by a proper view of our place in God's creation. Weil does not believe that an individual human being is unimportant to God — far from it — but neither is any human being the center of the universe.

Charles A. Riley II sees Simone Weil as part of a panoply of modern thinkers, writers, artists, and composers whose various and sundry works are characterized by asceticism, that is, by a turning away from sensual pleasure and a turning toward a denial of pleasure to embrace a greater good, though in the case of many of those to whom he refers it is not a religious good. It is in particular Weil's concept of "decreation" that places her in the context of asceticism and modern aesthetics. Riley states:

> Weil reveals the difference between what she calls decreation and what Modernism considers destruction. The distinction is vital: "Decreation: To make something created pass into the uncreated. Destruction: To make something created pass into nothingness. A blameworthy substitute for decreation."[33]

---

31. Allen, "Don Giovanni," p. 181. The quote is from *The Notebooks of Simone Weil*, 2 vols., trans. Arthur Wills (London: Routledge & Kegan Paul, 1976).

32. Allen, "Don Giovanni," p. 182.

33. *The Saints of Modern Art: The Ascetic Ideal in Contemporary Painting, Sculpture,*

This process of "decreation" places her in a position where she is better able to concentrate on what is significant in terms of meditation. She can free herself from the transitory points of irritation and grief and focus on that which really counts, namely, the love and the goodness of God.

How, then, can one summarize Weil's thought on evil? And is it even possible to do so? The task seems daunting but it must be undertaken. In attempting to summarize Weil's thought on evil, I have been greatly helped by Thomas R. Nevin's study entitled *Simone Weil: Portrait of a Self-Exiled Jew*.[34] Especially useful is Nevin's tenth chapter that is a masterful study of Weil's pivotal work *Attente de Dieu*, to which I have devoted some attention earlier in my paper. The tenth chapter Nevin entitles somewhat playfully, yet nonetheless seriously, "Waiting, with Vichy, for God." It is his contention that most — though not all — of Simone Weil's religious writings date from the Vichy years, that is, from June 1940, when France surrendered to Germany, until her death on August 24, 1943, approximately one year before the Vichy regime collapsed. She saw the moral and spiritual dreariness of the Vichy government of Pétain as symptomatic of the moral and spiritual dreariness of the world. It should also be pointed out, however, that her experiences with working conditions in France during the grim 1930s were not exactly conducive to a rosy optimism. Moreover, Weil would have been the first to admit that tyranny and cruelty did not begin with the 1930s and World War II.

The subject of evil occupied her in several works but that was especially true of *Attente de Dieu*. Because, as the four Gospels indicate, evil is such a powerful force, it can cause us to consider it even more overwhelming than it actually is. Nevin writes:

> [Weil] speaks of evil in Dantesque terms: it is monotonous, empty, trivial, vulgar, but it is also a false infinitude, a response of illimitable imagination to the void God's apparent absence from the world imposes on the mind. Imagination creates idols to fill the holes where grace might enter. [. . .] This evil contaminates even the relatively just, and it is inescapable: "It is for this reason that Christ did not come down from the cross, and did not even remember, in the moment of his greatest agony, that he would return to life."[35]

Architecture, Music, Dance, Literature, and Philosophy (Hanover: University Press of New England, 1998), p. 304.

34. *Simone Weil: Portrait of a Self-Exiled Jew* (Chapel Hill: University of North Carolina Press, 1991).

35. Nevin, *Simone Weil: Portrait of a Self-Exiled Jew*, p. 283.

Simone Weil, in other words, seems to be saying that evil is an element of almost overwhelming force in the world, but it is not something whose triumph is inevitable or permanent. God, through the Divine Person of Christ, had to contend with evil, and the struggle was of deadly import but, though it was not without terrible cost, ultimately successful. Such was the ferocity of this struggle that even God, as represented by Christ, almost forgot, indeed did forget, that evil would be overcome. To read a mind as brilliant as that of Simone Weil is to see oneself concerned with many phenomena, but the question of evil in God's creation is doubtless one of the most profound.

Seeing God Where the Wild Things Are:
An Essay on the Defeat of Horrendous Evil

John R. Schneider

"Horrendous" Evil: Where Philosophy and Theology Converge

In the last several decades, and especially since the appearance of J. L. Mackie's path-breaking essay "Evil and Omnipotence" in 1961, the classical problem of God and evil has evolved into a very complicated, technical debate among analytical philosophers of religion.[1] In this essay, I will not treat the problem in that technical manner. As I am a Christian theologian, I will treat it as a topic of Christian theology. The main body of the essay is therefore devoted more to the interpretation of biblical texts (mainly the book of Job) than to the analysis and construction of formal arguments. My main purpose is to offer a fresh interpretation of those texts and to forge from them the beginnings of a distinctly Christian theological view of God and evil.

However, in making this distinction between philosophical and theological techniques, I wish to make very clear that, unlike a good many theologians who weigh in on this problem, I do not mean to disparage the analytical methods of disputation, nor the intense focus of philosophers on theory as opposed to "interest-relative practice."[2] On the con-

---

1. J. L. Mackie, "Evil and Omnipotence," in *The Problem of Evil: Selected Readings*, ed. Michael L. Peterson (Notre Dame, Ind.: University of Notre Dame Press, 1992), p. 89.

2. So Kenneth Surin, "Taking Suffering Seriously," in *The Problem of Evil: Selected Readings*, ed. Michael L. Peterson (Notre Dame, Ind.: University of Notre Dame Press, 1992), pp. 339-49; on "interest-relativity," pp. 341-42. See my comments on Surin's approach to theodicy, below.

trary, I believe that the analytical disputation, as it has developed dialectically over time, has greatly clarified both the problem itself and the criteria for a satisfactory (rational) solution. I do not think that theologians can safely ignore these intuitions of reason in the name of practical faith. Furthermore (as this essay will show), I believe the course of the debate has produced grounds for seeing considerable convergence between the two disciplines, and that the arguments of certain philosophers have opened avenues for theologians (of a certain type, to be sure) to join the discussion and make contributions to it as they can. Before going forward to my main theological proposals, it will be useful as background and context briefly to explain my assumptions about the debate in philosophy.

First, on basic matters, I gladly accept the ontology, metaphysics, and view of language that engender the problem of God and evil in the first place. Among these commitments are that God exists in objective reality and is not mainly the construction of human minds; that concepts of personal agency really do apply to God; that God really is omnipotent and perfectly good; that God's goodness is not merely ontological but is moral; that we best understand God's moral goodness in the familiar human terms of love and justice; and that evil exists. A good share of this essay will make clear why I think Christianity is a species of theism, and why these philosophical commitments should be commitments of Christian theology, too. And because they should, Christian theologians cannot very well be indifferent to the analytical problem of God and evil, as some wish to be. As Job's friends learned the hard way, the problem grows directly from the logic of true faith. If someone like J. L. Mackie *proves* from our very own Christian concepts that theism is "positively irrational," as he claims to have done, then in my view he has proved theism *false,* and no amount of piety or "praxis" can make it otherwise.[3] To paraphrase Paul's argument to the Corinthians, if theism is proved false in that way, then we are still in our sins, and our faith is in vain. So as a theologian, I am very grateful to those Christian analytical philosophers, who have responded to Mackie and others in kind — by means of counterarguments. Whatever limitations their theories may have (and they do have them) these efforts have at very least kept the epistemic way open for theologians to engage the subject creditably.

But second, the analytical disputation has progressed toward sharper formulations of the problem that make it less the intellectual ab-

3. Mackie, "Evil and Omnipotence," p. 89.

straction it has too often been and more the sort of real-world topic that theologians can naturally engage. Most philosophers on both sides of the debate now acknowledge that Hume's original argument from evil has failed. Hume argued that if God exists then it is impossible for *any* evil to exist. But as Nelson Pike (among others) has shown, we routinely believe that morally good persons are justified in permitting certain *sorts* of evils, so long as they have a "morally sufficient reason" (MSR) for doing so.[4] Christian philosophers have forged ingenious theories to suggest what that MSR might possibly be — the creation of morally free beings (so Pike and Alvin Plantinga), or the desire to shape mature souls (so John Hick) — or proposed (more negatively) that we cannot know that God has no MSR (so Stephen Wykstra and William Alston).[5]

While opponents of theism are now divided over whether the argument should be formulated logically (so Mackie), or evidentially (so William Rowe, Paul Draper, and others), they now generally agree that not just any evil constitutes a first-order problem for belief in God.[6] They now generally agree that it is certain particular kinds of evils that do so. Some classify these evils as "pointless," some as "gratuitous," others as "dys-teleological." Marilyn McCord Adams simply calls them "horrendous," and I prefer this term to the others.[7]

Horrendous evils, according to Adams, are evils so devastating and dehumanizing to participants (both victims and perpetrators) that they engender "prima facie reason to doubt whether the participant's life can be worth living."[8] These evils are not just apparently gratuitous, pointless, or dys-teleological, although they fit these descriptions. What makes them

4. See Nelson Pike, *God and Evil* (Englewood Cliffs, N.J.: Prentice-Hall, 1964), p. 4, as discussed briefly in Marilyn McCord Adams, *Horrendous Evils and the Goodness of God* (Ithaca, N.Y.: Cornell University Press, 1999), pp. 9-11.

5. Alvin Plantinga, *God, Freedom, and Evil* (Grand Rapids: Eerdmans Publishing Company, 1977); John Hick, *Evil and the God of Love* (New York: Harper & Row, 1978); Stephen J. Wykstra, "The Humean Obstacle to Evidential Arguments from Suffering: On Avoiding the Evils of Appearance," *International Journal for Philosophy of Religion* 16 (1984): 73-93; William P. Alston, "The Inductive Argument from Evil and the Humean Cognitive Condition," *Philosophical Perspectives 5: Philosophy of Religion* (1991): 26-67.

6. William L. Rowe, "The Empirical Argument from Evil," in *Rationality, Religious Belief, and Moral Commitment,* ed. Robert Audi and William Wainwright (Ithaca, N.Y.: Cornell University Press, 1986), pp. 227-47; Paul Draper, "Pain and Pleasure: An Evidential Problem for Theists," in *The Evidential Argument from Evil,* ed. Daniel Howard-Snyder (Bloomington, Ind.: Indiana University Press, 1996), pp. 12-29.

7. McCord Adams, *Horrendous Evils,* pp. 26-28.

8. McCord Adams, *Horrendous Evils,* p. 26.

an acute problem for faith is not merely their apparent lack of purpose. It is that besides being without seeming purpose, these evils are *horrors.*

> Examples include the rape of a woman and axing off of her arms, psycho-physical torture whose ultimate goal is the disintegration of personality, betrayal of one's deepest loyalties, child abuse of the sort described by Ivan Karamazov, child pornography, parental incest, slow death by starvation, the explosion of nuclear bombs over populated areas.[9]

Adams's list should probably include other, less dramatic and more commonplace examples, such as the loss of a child in a freak accident or from disease. The testimonial of Nicholas Wolterstorff in his book *Lament for a Son,* or that of C. S. Lewis in *A Grief Observed,* relate experiences of death that are not uncommon, or sensational, but still horrifying to them.[10] The problem of defining what is horrendous is made more complicated still by differences in people's thresholds for suffering, but in my view none escapes. I believe that every human being participates, to some degree or other, in the experience of horrendous evil. Furthermore, we might add a distinction between horrendous evils that are deserved and ones that are undeserved. Hitler, for instance, was a participant in horrendous evil, but one might reasonably judge that any bad things that happened to him he had coming. On the other hand, when Nazi guards at Auschwitz tortured and hanged a little boy to death for their own amusement, the little boy did not have it coming, to say the least, and the horror is the worse for it.[11]

But the conditional definition that Adams gives is good enough for the purpose of this essay. Evils are horrendous in the event that they create prima facie reasons to doubt that someone's life has meaning and is worthwhile. Some evils do so "because it is so humanly difficult to conceive how such evils could be overcome."[12] They are thus grounds for doubting the goodness of God toward the victims. As a theologian I gladly accept the wisdom of this shift in the debate from evil in the abstract to horrendous evils in the actual world. As will become clear, my view is that the core traditions enshrined in sacred Scripture developed in the same way. Contrary to what some Christians think, there really are

---

9. McCord Adams, *Horrendous Evils,* p. 26.

10. Nicholas Wolterstorff, *Lament for a Son* (Grand Rapids: Eerdmans Publishing Company, 1987); C. S. Lewis, *A Grief Observed* (New York: Bantam Books, 1961).

11. Elie Wiesel, *Night* (New York: Bantam Books, 1982), pp. 60-62.

12. McCord Adams, *Horrendous Evils,* p. 26.

horrendous evils, evils so appalling, so devastating that we would not intuitively expect our God ever to permit them. Here the intuitions of philosophers converge with those of biblical tradition. In the next section we shall see that the book of Job is entirely focused, not on the general problem of evil, but on the problem of God permitting evils of this worst kind. And it remains to be seen what sort of distinctive biblical view emerges in response to the problem.

But to continue, a third point about the disputation in philosophy (and its convergence with theology) is that it has produced fairly widespread agreement about the limitations of theodicy. Philosophers on both sides agree that global theories about the existence of evil do not provide plausible explanations for the occurrence, amount, and distribution of particular horrendous evils. Most will concede that Mackie's judgment is on some level correct. Of the theodicies, he writes, "none has stood up to criticism."[13] While Alvin Plantinga will not concede that his famous Free Will Defense fails as an "epistemic defense" against Mackie's logical version of anti-theism, he freely admits that his theory offers no explanation for why God might allow certain particular evils. Some evils are so horrific, he admits, that we do not even have *candidates* for an explanation. He thus exhorts pastors and counselors to step in where philosophers must leave off.[14] John Hick has made similarly candid comments about his own influential approach, which is to argue that God permits evil to exist to further the making of "mature souls."[15] Some evils are empirically dys-teleological, and to such an extent that we cannot know how they might contribute to that end. In fact — and oddly — Hick judges that the Holocaust was so destructive to personal value and dignity that we must think the world would be better had it not happened.[16]

Hick's ambivalence is a little confusing, since elsewhere he treats his global theory as if it were an explanation for every particular horror.[17] But putting the matter of his consistency aside, it seems that Plantinga and Hick would agree that at most their global theories provide "partial

---

13. Mackie, "Evil and Omnipotence," p. 101.

14. See Alvin Plantinga, "Self-Profile," in *Alvin Plantinga*, ed. James E. Tomberlin and Peter van Inwagen (Dordrecht: D. Reidel Publishers, 1985), pp. 34-35.

15. See John Hick, *Evil and the God of Love* (New York: Harper & Row, 1966), p. 361; but also pp. 330-31 as discussed critically by Marilyn McCord Adams, *Horrendous Evils*, pp. 52-53.

16. Hick, *Evil and the God of Love*, p. 361.

17. Hick, *Evil and the God of Love*, pp. 330-31.

explanations," as Marilyn Adams calls them, and that horrendous evils create the need for fuller ones, if possible.[18] As will be clear, she contends that fuller explanation is possible, but that in order for that to happen our distinctively theological resources must come to the rescue.

In fact, there is growing support for the view that theology is better equipped to deal with the problem of horrendous evil than is philosophy. And theologians are indeed beginning to weigh in. Unfortunately, I am afraid to say, a huge rift has grown between Christian thinkers (typically philosophers) who see this fresh theological strategy as complementary to systematic theory, and those (typically theologians) whose stance toward theodicy is entirely adversarial.

Kenneth Surin is the most notable example of this common theologians' stance. Under the inspiration of Dorothy Soelle, Simone Weil, and others, Surin judges that theodicies do not only have limited powers of explanation when it comes to particular horrendous evils. In his judgment, they have no power of explanation at all. And worse, he contends, they are immoral, for (so he argues) to assert them to victims of evil is inherently to make those victims' suffering trivial. And still worse, because the suffering of such victims is sacred, something that ought not be touched, to assert theodicies in their presence is to commit blasphemy.[19] Instead of giving explanations, then, he argues, Christians should be still and listen to the narratives of victims themselves, and if we must speak at all, let it be about narrative of the suffering Christ.[20]

Now, there are undeniable truths embedded in this refusal of theory and speech. Few will disagree with the broad assertions that we should shut up and listen, that we must mourn with those who mourn, and that maybe — on right occasions, and with acute sensitivity — we should gently remind suffering believers (and perhaps receptive unbelievers) that they are not alone, that they stand in a long line of sorrows along with Jesus himself. In *Lament for a Son*, Nicholas Wolterstorff writes that the only thing that gave him any consolation at all during the worst of his grieving over his son's accidental death was the thought that he was not alone, and that in Christ we see that God identifies with us, and even suf-

---

18. See McCord Adams on the "partial" explanatory power of global solutions to the problem of finding a morally sufficient reason for permitting horrors, *Horrendous Evils*, pp. 53-54.

19. Kenneth Surin, "Taking Suffering Seriously," in *The Problem of Evil: Selected Readings*, ed. Michael L. Peterson (Notre Dame, Ind.: University of Notre Dame Press, 1992), pp. 341-45.

20. Surin, "Taking Suffering Seriously," pp. 345-46.

fers with us.[21] In my view, the trend to see God this way is a vast improvement over older classical notions of divine *apatheia* and impassibility, and we shall explore these fresh ideas just below. However, recognition of divine pathos in Christian narratives hardly entails anything like Surin's severe moral judgment against global theories, or his proposed divorce between theory and practice.

In a very incisive short piece, James Wetzel has observed that if speculative theodicies are disposed to an intolerable mood of triumph, the new practical theodicies of divine suffering are inclined to present the Christian story as a tragedy, and this, too, is unacceptable. Wetzel relates the judgments of Karl Jaspers and Paul Ricoeur, both of whom understood that the essence of tragedy is the fateful occurrence of irredeemable evil as a consequence of flaws in otherwise heroic figures.[22] On this understanding, they judged, whatever the Christian story is, it cannot be a tragedy — not so long as God is the main character and Jesus Christ the primary agent of God's action. Surely the judgment is correct. For these characters have no failings, and they do not become tragic victims, thwarted by forces that conspire against them. Of course forces do gather against them, but in Christ, to tell the story, God does not just enter into our suffering under the oppression of these powers, but rather God *defeats* them and seals *victory* over them forever. I believe this judgment applies broadly: Any Christian theodicy that stresses divine pathos instead of conjunctive goodness and sovereignty is prone to rewrite its story of victory into a tragedy. Wetzel seems absolutely right: "tragic theology would challenge the holiness and innocence of God and leave the religious consciousness in tatters."[23] And that of course would be of precious little help to victims of horrendous evil.

The dilemma between the triumphal and the tragic is made more difficult by the arguments of Roderick Chisholm. Chisholm argues that to be compossible with divine goodness, horrendous evil must not just be balanced off in an additive sense by the one who permitted it, but defeated.[24] We shall look at the sense of the term "defeat" in a moment, but

---

21. Wolterstorff, *Lament for a Son*, pp. 81-83.

22. James Wetzel, "Can Theodicy Be Avoided? The Claim of Unredeemed Evil," in *The Problem of Evil: Selected Readings*, ed. Michael L. Peterson (Notre Dame, Ind.: University of Notre Dame Press, 1992), pp. 351-65.

23. Wetzel, "Can Theodicy Be Avoided?" p. 359.

24. Roderick Chisholm, "The Defeat of Good and Evil," in *The Problem of Evil*, ed. Marilyn McCord Adams and Robert Merrihew Adams (New York: Oxford University Press, 1990), pp. 53-68.

its general sense makes clear that, if so, then the tragic vision and mood is of little help to the epistemology of theism. In other words, the view it generates leaves evil undefeated and so is irrational as a view of God and evil. Adams take Chisholm's requirement one step further by inferring from it and from the dignity of persons, together, that defeat must occur on behalf of the *individuals* who participate in horrors. Along this line assertions of divine pathos and suffering by themselves are precious little help to victims of ignorance and the irrational, either.

On that level, Adams correctly observes that religious narratives very often are themselves explanations. "*Reasons* why God permits suffering and *explanations* how God can make good on it are as much the stuff of narrative as of premises-conclusion arguments."[25] I would make the point even more strongly. We simply cannot recite the Christian narrative completely apart from certain "narrative theodicies" that it contains. These are in fact quite essential to the story as a whole.

The narrative of Christ's suffering and death, for instance, is inseparably connected in sacred tradition with the larger background narratives of creation, fall, and original sin; exodus, exile, and so forth — all partial explanations of the evils (sin and death) that Christ participated in by suffering, and only thereby conquered. The preferred reading (since Augustine) of Genesis 2–3 is that these root evils came into the world by means of free choices and actions made by angelic and human agents in circumstances created by God (support for some form of Plantinga's view). The established understanding of eschatology (since Irenaeus) is that God has acted ever since — in a great variety of ways, but centrally in Christ — to defeat these evils, that he will do so, and that the outcome of this defeat is the coming messianic kingdom of God. The account of Christ's incarnation, suffering, death, and resurrection is inseparable from this larger explanation. And furthermore, the account of divine providence and sanctification for both Judaism and Christianity is inseparable from explanations of the sort that emerge in the story of Joseph, in which God permits evil for good.

In the Olivet Discourse, Jesus encourages his followers to understand the travails of this world as analogous to the pains of labor — which are bad, to be sure, but necessary (alas) to the bringing forth of new life — and the outcome is well worth the pain (Matt. 24:8). In support of Hick and (as we shall see) Adams, the New Testament connects Christian sanctification in an essential way to suffering — suffering in

25. McCord Adams, *Horrendous Evils*, pp. 189-90.

identification with Christ. This is obviously the sense in which Paul meant the famous assertion that "all things work to the good for those who believe" (Rom. 8:28). My point is not that these are full explanations, or solutions to the problem of God and the occurrence of horrors (for they are not, as Job makes clear), but just that they *are* explanations of some evils, even perhaps some horrendous ones (such as Jesus' crucifixion), and that they are essential parts of the whole Christian story. We do not tell it completely without them. The challenge is how to do so properly. The proposed divorce between practical and theoretical Christian approaches to the problem is unacceptable.

But the philosophical disputation has produced still a fourth widely accepted intuition that helps bring clarity to theology. It is about the criteria for *rationality* in any purported teaching on the coexistence of God and horrendous evil. As noted, Marilyn Adams applies Chisholm's requirement of defeat to the lives of individuals who have been victims of horrendous evil. By the defeat of evil Chisholm means that the agent (in this case God) does not just balance off the evil by adding goods here and there to the whole. The defeat of evil happens if and only if the agent *integrates* the evil into the world in such a way that, as "value part," while still an evil, it now contributes positively to the "value whole."[26]

In that light, Adams contends that a horrendous evil is defeated in some individual's (*x*'s) life "by being relevantly integrated into *x*'s relation to a great enough good."[27] On the value that Christian tradition attaches to human personhood, she argues that God's goodness must extend to "each and every human person God created."[28] She concludes:

> At a minimum, God's *goodness* to individuals would require that God guarantee each a life that was a great good to him/her on the whole by balancing off serious evils. To value the individual qua person, God would have to go further to defeat any horrendous evil in which s/he participated by giving it positive meaning through organic unity with a great enough good *within the context of his/her life.*[29]

The challenge, then, is to show how God might just possibly accomplish the defeat of horrendous evil understood in this way. But where may we find plausible scenarios in which God achieves this outcome? Adams ar-

26. McCord Adams, *Horrendous Evils*, p. 29.
27. McCord Adams, *Horrendous Evils*, p. 29.
28. McCord Adams, *Horrendous Evils*, p. 31.
29. McCord Adams, *Horrendous Evils*, p. 31.

gues that our best place to find them is within our very own Christian tradition, and this leads to the heart of her proposals. Although her purpose is to engage the philosophical problem in its strictly logical formulation, her proposals constitute what is in essence an essay in systematic Christian theology on the problem of God and horrendous evil. This work merits attention in its own right, but I also wish to consider it in some detail for its importance to theology, and as a context (by both comparison and contrast) for proposals of my own.

First, Adams reviews the meditative writings of (in sequence) the process theologians Rolt and Hartshorne, the essayist Simone Weil, and the medieval mystic Julian of Norwich.[30] Adams finds insights in each of these approaches. But she also fairly detects serious limitations, especially as it comes to the crucial requirement that evil be defeated in the relevant sense. Process theology does not meet it, for instance. Our best hope for a plausible explanation — one that promises real defeat — lies elsewhere. She writes: "When it comes to defeating horrendous evils, the central doctrines of Christian theology — Christology and the Trinity — have considerable explanatory power."[31]

As for Christology, Adams judges that both doctrines of the Incarnation and the Atonement were best formulated by those theologians who stressed the notion of identification (as in God "identifies" with us) more than the idea of satisfaction (as in Christ "satisfies" a moral demand upon God).[32] In thinking about horrendous evil, let us be reminded that God himself became one with human beings — by becoming a human being, and then by suffering and dying for the sake of human beings. Particularly in the crucifixion, then, God has, in Jesus Christ, literally participated in our human experience of horror; and thereby God "integrates the experience into an incommensurately valuable relationship."[33] This integration takes place objectively, by the way, whether anyone knows it has happened or not. All that remains is recognition, the full therapeutic (my term) sense of which will come in a beatific post-mortem environment that God will bring about for everyone.[34]

Adams then takes on the controversial matter of God's suffering, which her proposals on the incarnation do not require, but is consistent with them. With considerable care not to commit anthropomorphic falla-

30. McCord Adams, *Horrendous Evils*, pp. 159-64.
31. McCord Adams, *Horrendous Evils*, p. 164.
32. McCord Adams, *Horrendous Evils*, p. 165.
33. McCord Adams, *Horrendous Evils*, p. 168.
34. McCord Adams, *Horrendous Evils*, p. 168.

cies, or to wax sentimental (or tragic) about the divine Being (which divine pathos approaches are prone to do), she at last commends a qualified version of the view. In Christ there is suffering in *both* natures, but she tries very hard to avoid the error of patripassionism (my descriptor) that too often emerges from theologies of this kind. Adams offers a helpful distinction between "God-sized" suffering and suffering of our common human sort.[35] So in Christ, God participates in horrors both from the inside, so to speak, as a human being, and from the outside, as the divine Son of God. And this proposal leads her naturally to consideration of Jürgen Moltmann's trinitarian work of dogmatics, *The Crucified God*.[36]

In this work, Moltmann places the ideal of divine suffering squarely in the context of the doctrine of the Trinity (which he understands in strongly social rather than psychological terms). He focuses (with Luther) upon the Christ's real experience of being abandoned by his very own Father, which he understands as deep alienation between the persons of the Father and the Son. This divine participation (somehow) absorbs and takes human suffering into itself and thereby toward a future, in which all will be well — for all human beings, but especially for innocent victims of horror.[37] We judge that Moltmann's trinitarian *theologia crucis* does not so much modify as intensify the proposals that Adams has just made about the extent of God's identification with the victims of horrendous evil. Thus Adams ends the theoretical part of her book, satisfied (as a self-styled "skeptical realist") that she has not resolved the problem perfectly but has at least shown that, compared with the global theories of Pike and Plantinga, "more expanded theisms are better able to explain how God can defeat horrors, precisely because of their richer assumptions."[38]

But as Adams constantly reminds readers, "nothing is free in philosophy!" It is also true in theology that we get nothing for free, either, and for all its many virtues, Adams's treatment invites critical questions.

One could launch criticisms on two separate grounds, which I will brush over lightly. First, the appeal to Nicene Christology is useless to anyone who is convinced that its assertions are themselves logically impossible. The use of this tradition-specific material makes it difficult to avoid shifting the entire ground of the debate, lest it become entirely pa-

---

35. McCord Adams, *Horrendous Evils*, pp. 168-74.

36. Jürgen Moltmann, *The Crucified God: The Cross of Christ as the Foundation and Criticism of Christian Theology* (Minneapolis: Fortress Press, 1993).

37. McCord Adams, *Horrendous Evils*, pp. 175-77.

38. McCord Adams, *Horrendous Evils*, pp. 179-80.

rochial and the purported solution acceptable only to Nicene Christians. Since Adams is engaging J. L. Mackie (who, I presume, would not accept without argument that the Incarnation is logically possible), I am not sure why she leaves this matter unattended as a premise in her argument. But secondly, a fiendishly complicated issue arises with the proposed sufficient condition for the defeat of horrendous evil. Is the integration of horrors into meaningful life-wholes for the victims by itself sufficient for its defeat? Or do we need the additional condition that no perfectly good agent would permit such evils unless it was morally necessary to do so?

This judgment of William Rowe, among others, seems right to me. The MSR exists if and only if it was necessary to permit the evil in order to bring about some indispensable great good.[39] Otherwise, evils such as the axing off of the woman's arms and the rape and ruin to follow were, for instance, no matter how meaningful to some now-flourishing whole, perforce unnecessary. Imagine that woman in her postmortem environment now at last able to approach God with the question she desperately wants to answer. Why, oh why, did God let this outrage happen to her? Why was it necessary (as she had always supposed it was)? Upon learning that in fact it was not necessary, but that God let it happen because it pleased him to build the whole of her life in a manner that included this horror, how will she rightly react? Not necessary? It did not *have* to happen in order to further some identifiable, indispensable good that God wished to bring about? What she endured was not in fact a "sacrifice" as she has supposed it was? It was more like an artist's intended blemish, a patch of the ugly in a beautiful work of art? God could have built a perfectly good life-whole for her without that experience? Imagine this same scenario as the ending to Wiesel's account of the little Jewish boy tortured at Auschwitz.

Would the woman or the boy embrace that answer? Should they? Or would they now have more questions than answers? Perhaps others (Simone Weil and Julian of Norwich, for instance) would try to console them and the debate over God and horrendous evil would erupt all over again in heaven! I assume in this essay that the criterion of necessity for permitting some horrendous evil is a necessary condition for it ever being defeated.

But it also seems that this therapeutically integrative and redemp-

39. William L. Rowe, "The Problem of Evil and Some Varieties of Atheism," in *The Evidential Argument from Evil,* ed. Daniel Howard-Snyder (Bloomington, Ind.: Indiana University Press, 1996), p. 3.

tive scenario of defeat for evil is not the only one in our store of specifically Christian traditions, and thus is not a *necessary* condition of defeat either, as Adams contends it is. By analogy, we often think of morally good persons or societies defeating evils in morally approvable (if controversial) non-redemptive ways. In instances where the agents and systems of evil are irreversibly resistant to the therapeutic advances of morality and reason, they may be left with no morally defensible alternative but to eliminate the evil by force. They may (so most Christians presume) justly wage war, they may imprison evildoers, or in extreme cases they may put them to death. Like it or not, biblical tradition about divine goodness is rich in narratives that mediate divine actions of this non-redemptive kind. We normally think of them as actions that execute retributive justice, and there is a strong analogy at times between them and retribution of the legal human kind.

But, in contrast to the therapeutic scenario, which is the ideal outcome, the ideal form of defeat for evil, perhaps we should think of this non-ideal scenario as a "surgical" one. For, so say our traditions, the agents of evil (angelic and human) have not just *done* evil, so that they are punished. They have *embraced* evil to such an extent that they have, in their moral habits, crossed a boundary of some sort. These creatures are no more just *fallen*. They have transgressed to an extent that makes them *evil*. Like it or not, narratives of the Flood, the Exodus, the Exile, and parts of the New Testament narratives of the Incarnation and Pentecost all have this sense embedded within them, and hence our historic teaching on divine judgment, damnation, and eternal separation from the love of God (hell).

In other writings and in this one, Adams protests that this human analogy for defeating evil cannot extend to an omnipotent, omniscient and eternal Being, whose therapeutic efforts would surely not return to him void.[40] But at minimum, this line of argument (pace Origen, Moltmann — and perhaps Barth!) is not just in keeping with universalism, but entails it. While this does not prove the argument unsound, it does make it extremely controversial for Christians, and perhaps even impossible for them to accept as counsel for their suffering. For in order to receive the argument as epistemic and existential consolation, in the throes of some great evil, the vast majority of Christians (and perhaps

---

40. Marilyn McCord Adams, "Hell and the Justice of God," *Religious Studies* 11 (1975): 433-47. See also her interaction with the defenses of belief in divine damnation by Jerry Walls, Eleonore Stump, and Richard Swinburne in *Horrendous Evils*, pp. 43-49.

also non-Christians) will have to be convinced first that orthodox tradition on divine judgment fails to represent true Christianity. They will instead have to adopt what is for them heresy, and many (especially if already bearing up under the burden of some great evil) will find this demand unfair, and maybe even cruel. Of course it is true that "nothing is free," and Adams will rightly reply that the evidence as she interprets it exacts just this price, and that none should be consoled by the thought that hell exists in any form. But now again the ground of debate shifts to the essence of true Christianity, and Mackie and others can sit back and wait to see if Christians can at least get their own story straight.

At very least, it seems good to explore a notion of divine defeat for horrendous evil that both satisfies the relevant criteria of rationality and is consistent with the teachings of orthodox Christian tradition. Still better, I suppose, if that notion could also be adapted to the unorthodox scenario of therapeutic universalism. With this background, then, I will now turn to the text of Job and propose that (properly interpreted) it contains the elements of just such a view.

Job, God, and the Wild Things

Recent Christian theologies of God and evil have focused almost exclusively on Christology, and particularly on God's identification with humanity in and through the suffering of Christ. I do not object to this application of New Testament narratives to the problem of horrendous evil. This stress on the pathos of God in Christ is a welcome improvement over classical assertions of God's impassibility. On the other hand, as just indicated, by itself this renovation of tradition is prone to rewrite the Christian story as a tragedy rather than relate it as the narrative of divine victory over evil that it is. As an exception, we have seen how Marilyn McCord Adams seeks to use classical Christology and its stress on identification and suffering to secure a plausible account of defeat for evil. I have argued that her account has many virtues, not least its rigorous attempt to satisfy Chisholm's criterion. On the other hand, as I have argued, it is very unlikely that most Christians will give up their orthodox belief in divine judgment in order to adopt Adams's account of divine victory over horrendous evil. In this section of the essay, my purpose is to relate the account of divine victory over evil that I believe emerges from biblical tradition. My main purpose is to show how that account emerges and what it teaches. In addition, I will give reasons (without attempting a complete demonstration) why I believe this account also satisfies the conditions for rational belief that God "defeats" evil.

The book of Job has been strangely missing from Christian theology on this problem. One reason may be the prevailing interpretation of Job, which is that the book gives no answer to the question, and that it in fact contains a strict prohibition against rational inquiry. In the Stob Lectures at Calvin College in 1998, Eleonore Stump issued a severe critique of this widespread interpretation, and her fresh reading of Job merits attention. While I will argue that her reading has serious flaws, parts of it will be helpful as a frame of reference for my own reading.[41]

The Anchor Bible Commentary enshrines the prevailing view that, in the two divine speeches at the end of the book, God throws Job's question back in his face. He thunders that he is omnipotent, and that Job is nothing by comparison. Properly chastened, Job cowers, admits that he has gotten in over his head, bows, apologizes, and departs in dust and ashes. On this reading, to pose the question as Job did is seriously wrong. It presumes that God is subject to merely human inquiry. It is the height of arrogance and impiety. That is more or less what the last speaker, Elihu, says to Job, and in the end Elihu's words stand uncorrected.

Stump finds this commonplace reading of Job to be on its face implausible. For it renders the character of Job pathetic. He turns out to be little more than a "pious windbag," someone who would challenge the boss behind his back, but not to his face.[42] Furthermore, this script of the ending renders the writer incompetent. Critics of the book, like George Bernard Shaw, would then be right. The climax of the book would then be nothing but a "noble irrelevance" (both to Job and to us).[43] Stump instinctively resists this condescending judgment of a text that has stood the tests of time. There has to be a better way to read it.

To prepare us for her alternative reading, Stump brings in the hermeneutical notions of "second-person" experiences and "second-person" accounts. In brief, a second-person experience (as distinct from first- and third-person ones) is just the encounter one has with a *person*. It is the direct experience of the person's presence, the apprehension of the person's true identity and character. I believe the notion is the same as Martin Buber's "I-Thou" relationship, which is an encounter between

---

41. Eleonore Stump, "First Lecture: Second-Person Accounts and the Problem of Evil," in *Faith and the Problem of Evil: The Stob Lectures of Calvin College and Seminary, 1998-99* (Grand Rapids: Stob Lectures Endowment, 1999), pp. 1-41.

42. Stump, *Faith and the Problem of Evil*, p. 21.

43. Stump, *Faith and the Problem of Evil*, p. 22.

persons that successfully brings about knowledge *between* them, as distinct from the knowledge that comes about between persons and things; this kind of relationship is an "I-it" relationship. In these second-person experiences we receive more than mere information from or about the person. In the demeanor, words, and other actions of the other, we encounter the person himself or herself.

Likewise, a second-person account (often a text, but not always) is one that mediates that sort of experience. Such an account mediates for us the essential identity and character of the person, portrays the person speaking and acting in characteristic ways, rather than simply giving predicative statements about the person, or factual reports of his or her doings. Stump contends that narratives just are texts (or oral accounts) that mediate second-person experiences. They are (usually) written stories that deliberately mediate the identities and characters of persons. If the accounts are successful, their readers actually *meet* the person in them, albeit in textually mediated form. In Stump's judgment, the speeches of God at the end of Job are dramatic narratives that mediate second-person experiences of God by Job.[44] And once we see this structure of the text, she argues, we begin to see that, contrary to the common reading, "Job does get an explanation of why he suffers."[45] And thus so do we.

Commentators typically read the first speech as divine chest pounding, as a thundering discourse on omnipotence, what "*I* can do, and *you* cannot." But Stump denies that divine power is the main feature of this speech. While she concedes that divine power is manifest, she maintains that the main feature is God's loving care for his creatures. When God speaks of his power over the sea, for instance, Stump argues that his point is not just that he can, and Job cannot, exert such control. His essential point is that he *takes care of* the sea. She appeals to the second-person character that is nested in the account. God does not speak *about* the sea and what he can do to rule it. God speaks *to* the sea, and the sea in turn responds to him. What emerges is a relationship of mutual love that exists between God, the sea, and all other creatures as well.[46]

The same pattern, or others consistent with it, she argues, runs through the entire speech. The first part is about God's relationship with inanimate forces of nature. God does not just *have* command over the morning — he *commands* the morning. God does not just *control* the light-

---

44. Stump, *Faith and the Problem of Evil*, pp. 5-17.
45. Stump, *Faith and the Problem of Evil*, p. 18.
46. Stump, *Faith and the Problem of Evil*, pp. 23-27.

ning — he *speaks* to it, and it to him. God does not just *order* darkness and light — he "shows them the way home."[47] He is not just *lord* of the rain and dewdrops, but is their *father*.

The second part of the speech is about God's relationship with living creatures. God reminds Job of his care for lions (provides their prey!), for wild donkeys (makes them a home in the wild), for hawks (gives them flight), and even ostriches (protects the offspring they foolishly forget).[48] Furthermore, the animals relate to God personally. The raven's young do not just depend on God, they cry for food, and the mighty wild buffalos "deign to serve" God.[49]

In the second speech, Stump notes that the focus shifts to two great beasts, Behemoth and Leviathan. She notes that scholars of Job are engaged in a most confusing debate over the identities of these creatures.[50] Are they mythological beasts? Are they ordinary creatures (Aquinas thought one was an elephant)? She decides to ignore the debate as irrelevant to core matters of interpretation, and to go ahead with her reading.[51] But going forward, she notes once again that the second-person accounts nested in this speech do not just mediate divine power, but depict God as caring intensely for his creatures, even for these monsters. To support this reading, she interprets God's question to Job about Leviathan to mean that God has a friendly relationship with it. "Will he [Leviathan] make long pleas to you, cajole you with tender words? Will he make a covenant with you, will you take him as an eternal slave? Will you play with him as with a bird, leash him for your girls?" (Job 41:3-5). What this passage indicates, according to her, is that "God has a close relationship with these great beasts that not only talk to him with tender words but cajole him, plead with him, play with him, and make covenants with him."[52] In conclusion, she judges: "It is a mistake, then, to characterize God's speeches as demonstrating nothing but God's power over creation. The speeches certainly do show God's power; but equally importantly, they show God having personal interactions with all his creatures."[53]

Stump thus thinks that Job does get an answer to his question. The answer he gets comes through this second-person experience of God

47. Stump, *Faith and the Problem of Evil*, p. 26.
48. Stump, *Faith and the Problem of Evil*, p. 26-27.
49. Stump, *Faith and the Problem of Evil*, p. 26.
50. Stump, *Faith and the Problem of Evil*, p. 27.
51. Stump, *Faith and the Problem of Evil*, p. 27.
52. Stump, *Faith and the Problem of Evil*, p. 28.
53. Stump, *Faith and the Problem of Evil*, p. 28.

speaking directly to him in terms that connote divine care — "a mother's care towards all his creatures, even the inanimate ones."[54] Stump compares Job's experience of God to that of a seriously ill child, whose mother's love comes through not only in what she says, but also, and more powerfully, in the demeanor of her person. The child will see the mother's love in her face, and will hear it in her voice.[55] Just so, when Job sees and hears for himself, he discerns that God loves him after all, and he withdraws his challenge. Job now knows firsthand that the God he has encountered and heard with his very own eyes and ears would never permit anything to happen to any creature of his that is not somehow good for it. "Job does have an explanation for his suffering; but it isn't the sort that philosophers have been interested in when they have considered theodicies."[56]

Stump's interpretation has important advantages over the common reading, as given in the Anchor Bible Commentary. I think it is correct to say that God validates Job's question. The three friends (and perhaps first readers) expected that God would destroy Job for his rebellious impudence. And in the prose ending, we hear that the friends have not "spoken truly" of God, as Job has done (Job 42:7). In a stunning reversal, God approves Job as "my servant," and puts him in the superior position now of praying for them. The ironic ending is that they — the very ones who thought they had God all figured out — are the ones who deserve punishment. And to add to their humiliation, God declares that he will nevertheless spare them — for Job's sake.[57] In this sense Job's social vindication could not be sweeter.

It is also good to stress that Job's understanding comes by means of a second-person experience of God. Until this encounter, Job says that he has heard of God, but now he has seen God with his own eyes. This seeing is not crudely literal, but rather a taking in of the whole divine performance — its form, demeanor, tone of voice, and the words themselves. It is all this together that absorbs Job's question and enables him to retreat and to withdraw his challenge.[58] Now that he has thus seen, he understands. But what exactly did Job see, and what did he understand?

---

54. Stump, *Faith and the Problem of Evil*, p. 28.

55. Stump, *Faith and the Problem of Evil*, p. 32.

56. Stump, *Faith and the Problem of Evil*, p. 34.

57. I am assuming the interpretation that this approval refers to Job's speeches and not only to what Job has just said to God. On this interpretive issue, see Norman Whybray, *Job* (Sheffield: Sheffield Academic Press, 1998), pp. 172-73.

58. The term *em' mas* means something like "I yield," and *niham*, "to change one's mind."

Despite the merits of Stump's explanation, recent studies of Job give grounds for judging that it oversimplifies the literary structure and substance of the text. There is little doubt that part of what Job sees in God, as Stump argues, is (for him) divine care for his creation. Scholars often note that the speeches convey both the omnipotence of God *over* creation and the goodness of God *toward* it.[59] But is this all that Job sees, or even the main thing that Job sees as God speaks to him from within the great turbulence? Does Job see in this presence what a little child facing chemotherapy would see in his mother doing her best to comfort him? The poetry makes this reading unnatural. Not just the windstorm itself, which is terrifying enough (as ancient Near Eastern readers understood), but the opening words of God to Job weigh against the analogy that Stump offers. "Who is this then that darkens counsel by words without knowledge? Gird up your loins like a man, I will question you, and you shall declare to me. Where were you when I laid the foundation of the earth?" (Job 38:1-4). The form, demeanor, tone of voice, and message would not make for a very good bedside manner.

As we shall see, the interpretation is prone to omit other similar parts of the speeches that evoke more dread than comfort. For instance, Stump omits the verses *preceding* the ones depicting God's covenantal relationship with Leviathan. In these verses, God declares his power to pull Leviathan out of the sea with a hook, like some small fish. God declares that he can lead him around at will, and these images are the context for the metaphor of the pet on a leash (Job 41:1). Stump also fails to notice that the raven ("vulture" is a better translation) is eyeing "the slain," dead human beings whose blood its young will suck for food (Job 39:29-30). Furthermore, the lion's prey might have some questions of its own about the means of divine care for the lion!

But a greater difficulty arises with the focus of the speeches. Job never expressed doubt that God governed nature properly. Job's vexation was over the apparent iniquity in God's governance of history. Perhaps the bitterest of his speeches is in Chapter 21, in which he matter-of-factly charges that (contrary to conventional wisdom) the wicked do not perish — they prosper. Meanwhile, the righteous often do not flourish — they suffer, they die, and meanwhile God does nothing (Job 21:1-34). Worse still, in Chapter 16, Job dares to charge that the horrors that have happened to him are not accidents (on divine omnipotence, they cannot be),

---

59. Gerhard von Rad, *Old Testament Theology,* vol. 1, trans. D. M. G. Stalker (New York: Harper & Row, 1962), pp. 416-17.

but are deliberate acts of God. The horrors have come directly from God, which (as his friends remind him) cannot be, but is nonetheless so. God, Job charges, has assaulted him, torn him to pieces, opened his kidneys, and poured his insides out on the ground (Job 16:1-13). God has become his enemy. Like a warrior, God has launched a relentless, brutal attack upon him. "He breaks me with breach upon breach, he runs upon me like a warrior" (Job 16:14). And God has done all this to a good man.

So when God goes on about his care for nature, what is it in the substance of the speech that Job finds directly relevant to his question? "Only in one passage (40:10-14)," writes Norman Whybray, "is there a reference to human affairs."[60] In Chisholm's terms, wherein does Job see the defeat of horrendous evil in what God says to him? Wherein exactly are we supposed to see it, too? Or was Shaw right after all, that the speech is a colossally disappointing letdown, as noble as it is irrelevant?

Recent historical-literary studies of Job can help us to better to see what Job saw. They also help to put the positive insights of Stump's reading into a context that makes them helpful. In a very recent book, Carol Newsom, who is a scholar of the Old Testament, offers a comprehensive treatment of Job in the dual contexts of ancient religious literature and modern narrative theory.[61] In her discussion of the divine speeches, she stresses their complexity as "rhetoric of the sublime."[62] "Especially where one is talking about the rhetorical sublime," she writes, "the aesthetic image mediates both experience and idea."[63] This description, I presume, is similar to Stump's notion of a second-person account. The book of Job contains prose (in the prologue and epilogue), poetry (the dialogues), and some of its parts make for a very awkward fit (especially the discourses of Elihu, Job 32–37). But as a whole, Newsom (with others) judges that Job is narrative, and that the divine speeches, far from being irrelevant, bring the book's dramatic dialogical plot to resolution and denouement.[64]

Newsom detects various connections of thought and image between the divine speeches and the earlier speeches of Job in chapters 29–

60. Whybray, *Job*, p. 157.

61. Carol A. Newsom, *The Book of Job: A Contest of Moral Imaginations* (New York: Oxford University Press, 2003).

62. Newsom, *The Book of Job*, pp. 236-37.

63. Newsom, *The Book of Job*, p. 237.

64. On the literary genre and structural problems of the composition, see Claus Westermann, *The Structure of the Book of Job: A Form-Critical Analysis*, trans. Charles A. Muenchow (Philadelphia: Fortress Press, 1981), especially pp. 1-15.

31. "What these details suggest is that the speech by Job and the speech by God stand over against each other somewhat like the facing panels in a diptych. Examined in this fashion, as contrasting but linked utterances, one can better see what they contribute to the complex conversation that is the book of Job."[65] She might have added that, at last, Job has a partner in conversation who is up to the job of handling his question. But how does God handle it, and why is Job convinced?

God does not handle it directly, in the conventional terms of deliberative rhetorical disputation, wherein one takes up the opponent's assertions one by one and dispatches them. Instead, the speeches constitute "an epideictic rhetoric that evokes more than it argues, a rhetoric in which the vivid presentation of images and tropes is foregrounded."[66] But what do these images and tropes convey? Here is where her treatment makes (in my view) its most incisive and valuable contribution, and is most helpful to this essay.

Newsom focuses on the dimension of the sublime and how the writer of Job has selected images and arranged them into a certain sequential *progression* in order to serve both the experiential and the cognitive power of the narrative. First, the most remarkable thing about the spatial imagery is not the vastness of the cosmos (as many commentators have thought), over which God reigns supreme. But nor is it the goodness of God in caring for the cosmos (so Stump), although both these ideas come along with the poetry. The most remarkable thing is the pattern and deliberately sequential progression of images that were, in the ancient Near East and in the Hebrew Bible, commonplace symbols of limits and boundaries between order and chaos. In the two divine speeches, the writer of Job has given this old poetic tradition dramatically new meaning.

In chapter 38, God begins with the cosmic edges: the bottoms of the earth's pillars, the boundary between darkness and light, and between the dry land and the seas. As Newsom observes (and as is well enough known in the field of Old Testament studies): "These mark the boundary between formlessness and structure, order and disorder, life and death."[67]

But familiar images now begin to mean something new — stunningly so. It is true, Newsom concedes, that the conventions of tradition

65. Newsom, *The Book of Job*, p. 239.
66. Newsom, *The Book of Job*, p. 239.
67. Newsom, *The Book of Job*, p. 242.

remain in place — God sets these boundaries against the forces of chaos. Thus the tradition narrates in mythic terms God's transcendence and sovereignty over basic disorder (of interest to Job). But as Newsom observes, striking differences come forth, particularly in the presentation of God and the sea in 38:11:

> In keeping with traditional imagery the sea is represented as violent and aggressive, 'bursting out,' and threatening to exceed its place until confined within the limits of 'doors and bars.' The description of the sea's waves as 'proud' anticipates a theme that becomes prominent in the second divine speech. This pericope radically departs from traditional imagery, however, in that it does not cast the sea as God's opponent in battle (cf. Ps. 74:13-14; 89:10-14; Isa. 51:9-10; *Enuma Elish* IV), but instead represents God as midwife who births the sea and wraps it in the swaddling bands of darkness and cloud. Whether this imagery represents an innovation of the Job poet or the use of an otherwise known tradition cannot be determined.[68]

To be sure, the imagery conveys a relationship of divine authority and restraint over this proud and violent creature. "Through this imagery both the traditional aggressiveness of the sea and the restraints placed upon it are taken up."[69] But the transformation of conventional wisdom (as Job's friends understood it) is unexpected.

> The metaphorical filter diminishes the sense of the sea as a hostile, alien power and associates it rather with the vigor of new life. Moreover, the restraints placed upon it are cast in terms of nurture and protection. The traditional resonance of the sea is not wholly overturned, of course, but reaccented. Here the chaotic waters of the sea are represented not only as the object of divine limitation but also of divine care.[70]

This of course resonates with Stump's reading of the passage, but puts it in a literary context that expands its meaning and importance for our theology, as we now begin to see.

The imagery of the speech now progresses from the limiting boundaries of creation to consideration of animals. However, as Newsom observes, these are not just any animals, making for a simple transition from

68. Newsom, *The Book of Job*, p. 244.
69. Newsom, *The Book of Job*, p. 244.
70. Newsom, *The Book of Job*, p. 244.

the inanimate to the animate creatures of God (so Stump). They are (almost) all *wild* animals, animals that make their home in the wilderness, which like the seas in Hebrew poetry is a commonplace image of danger, disorder, and chaos. And they seem to be carefully chosen wild animals, each also with a certain history of tradition in the ancient literature of religion. So it is a transition from one symbolic realm of chaos to another. And so Newsom: "Here, again, themes of nurture are presented through images of birth, food, and freedom. But the unsettling thing, still sometimes overlooked in interpretations of the divine speeches, is the fact that the animals selected for presentation almost all belong to the hostile and alien realm of the desert wilderness."[71] This transition from the chaos elements to chaos animals intensifies the sense of dislocation just described.[72]

In Babylonian theodicy, for instance, both the lion and the wild ass are, in different ways, harbingers of chaos, symbolic of wild forces, outside all human control. Wild deer and goats are a counterimage to the stock-in-trade, domesticated cattle that serve human purposes. The ostrich and the warhorse, both fearless in different ways, are anarchic in their elemental indifference to common wisdom. And finally, the typically noble image of the hawk in flight turns suddenly (as noted just before) to that of the vulture looking down upon a battlefield covered with human corpses — the food that God provides its nestlings.[73] This last imagery pretty clearly defies classification as material for a standard sermon on the providential care of God, or as an example a mother might give to calm a sick and terrified child (pace Stump).

Gathered as a collected whole, the poetry of the wilderness animals creates something greatly more distressing and elusive than a mere picture of God caring for his creatures. Convention shatters on the coincidence of beauty and horror, of cosmos and chaos in these images. God strangely celebrates basic disorder (such as the ostrich laughing witlessly at coming death). There is a vague reference it seems to Job's earlier cry that "I am a brother of jackals, and a companion of ostriches" (Job 30:29). The technique of the poet "seems unnervingly to place God in considerable sympathy with the emblems of the chaotic."[74] In some weird and troubling sense God seems to approve and even to nurture it as an integral part of the cosmos — and this is alien to common biblical tradition. It cer-

71. Newsom, *The Book of Job*, pp. 244-45.
72. Newsom, *The Book of Job*, pp. 244-45.
73. Newsom, *The Book of Job*, pp. 245-47.
74. Newsom, *The Book of Job*, p. 247.

tainly was alien to the theology of Job's friends. Nevertheless, somehow, within this collision of images, thoughts, and emotions, Job begins to see.

But perhaps nothing in the Old Testament is as unexpected in its defiance of convention as what comes next. That is the second speech, in which God speaks of his dealings with the great beasts Behemoth and Leviathan. In the last two centuries, as Stump noted, a vast body of literature has indeed grown up in disputation over the identity of these beasts, and over their place in the book of Job.[75] And the temptation (as Stump exemplifies it) is to write it off as yet another biblical scholars' muddle. But while understandable, this reaction is a serious mistake.

Literary common sense weighs against the typical judgment cited by David Wolfers — that the book builds us up for a resolution and then, inexplicably, "tails off into a description of two beasts."[76] Newsom's judgment once again is on target. This dismissive response is inexcusably dense.

> The perplexity of many nineteenth and twentieth century critics as to the function of the Behemoth and Leviathan speeches, a perplexity that often resulted in declaring them spurious, lay in their forgetfulness of what Burke and Lowth had analyzed so acutely. It lay in their failure to understand the divine speeches in the category of the sublime.[77]

This is her polite way of saying that too many scholars have not understood the poetics of Hebrew tradition. To Newsom and others the symbolic identity of the beasts is obvious.

> From the point of view of Job or any human, there is little question what Behemoth and Leviathan represent. Although they are unquestionably creatures of God (40:15; 41:25-26; cf. Ps. 104:26), they partake of the primordial (Behemoth, 40:15) and the mythical (Leviathan, 41:10-17). These are liminal beings who belong to the boundaries of the symbolic world. More emphatically than the wild animals of chapters 38 and 39, they manifest the alien Other, with the terror of the chaotic present in their very being.[78]

Norman Whybray observes that "certain features are those of the fire-breathing dragon of myth and legend (vv. 18-21); the Greek translation

---

75. David Wolfers, *Deep Things out of Darkness* (Grand Rapids: Eerdmans Publishing Company, 1995), especially pp. 161-94.

76. Wolfers, *Deep Things,* p. 161.

77. Newsom, *The Book of Job,* p. 243.

78. Newsom, *The Book of Job,* p. 248.

actually calls it a dragon — *drakon*. These verses probably reflect a current 'demonology' associated with the chaos monster."[79] Whether images of mere chaos or of demonic powers, Newsom's reading stands: "far from being alien to the divine speeches, [they] are simply the crescendo of the sublime terror developed throughout chapters 38–41."[80]

With the primordial image of Behemoth and the "fleeing dragon," Leviathan, then, the poetic progression has now reached the core of Job's lament and unmovable challenge to his friends. For according to the standard poetic traditions, the "chaos monster" is supposed to be dead, and doomed forever in the depths of the sea. Consider Psalm 74, which narrates poetically the triumph of God in conflated symbols of cosmic creation and the political exodus:

> You divided the sea by your might;
> You broke the heads of the dragons in the waters;
> You crushed the heads of Leviathan.
> You gave him as food for the creatures of the wilderness.
>
> (Ps. 74:13-14)

And consider Psalm 89, which has this same fusion of events and images (except Rahab appears instead of the parallel entity, Leviathan):

> Who in the skies can be compared to the Lord?
> You rule the raging of the sea,
> When its waves rise, you still them.
> You crushed Rahab like a carcass;
> You scattered your enemies with your mighty arm.
>
> (Ps. 89:6, 9-10)

The poetic tradition teaches and evokes trust that God's decisive actions in history — most notably the creation of the world and the securing of Israel and Torah (in which God reestablished divine cosmos) — were at bottom spiritual actions. They were final actions of warfare against spiritual entities, which (or who) would otherwise prevent divine order, or else destroy whatever they could of it. They were actions of divine *triumph* over these powers of chaos (and evil).[81] All that remained was for people of God to

---

79. Whybray, *Job*, p. 169.

80. Newsom, *The Book of Job*, p. 243.

81. To go further in this topic, see, e.g., Yehezkel Kaufmann, *The Religion of Israel*, abr. & trans. Moshe Greenberg (Chicago: University of Chicago Press, 1967), pp. 24-40.

connect with that triumph by means of righteousness, and they would triumph, too. They would prosper — just as Job had done.

As understood by Job's friends (and no doubt a good many Israelites), this poetic tradition (among others) ensured that no *intrinsic* disorder could exist in the world — no horrendous evil, so to speak. And much less could the worst disorder of all happen — the devastation and ruin of one deemed righteous by God. But Job's claim just is that the impossible has happened. Job's claim is that the chaos-monster is not dead, but is very much alive, and that it has somehow been unleashed to wreak ruin on the world. And — most offensive of all — this could only be the doing of God.

Interpreters seem almost completely to miss Job's use of the mythic tradition throughout the book to express his complaint. In his very first oration, Job uses the mythic tradition to curse the night he was conceived. The anti-cosmic symbolism is powerful: "Let those curse it who curse the day, who are skilled to rouse up Leviathan, let the stars of its dawn be dark" (Job 3:8-9). In his second oration he ironically equates himself with chaos. "Am I the sea, or a sea monster, that thou hast set guard over me?" (Job 7:12). His personal complaint is expanding swiftly to become global — better no world at all than one in which chaos lives. His distress over the injustice of history reaches its peak when Job considers God's power over chaos. "By his power he stilled the sea, by his understanding he smote Rahab, by his wind the heavens were made fair, *his hand pierced the fleeing serpent*" (Job 27:12-13, my italics). But this of course is no more the triumphant declaration of praise, as it functions in the tradition. In view of what has happened, and in the light of what Job now realizes about the world, it has become an ironic lament, the confession of a bitter, broken and thoroughly bewildered man.

So when we come to the ending, far from trailing off, the focus on Leviathan is riveting. Job understood perfectly (and so would the readers have understood). To use Stump's terms, Job gets a second-person experience of God amid the storm in which, among other things, God reasserts the way things really are between him and the chaos-dragon. This is exactly what Job wants to know.

This solves the problem raised earlier. If Job's question is about divine justice, how do God's speeches about nature constitute an answer? Leviathan just is the disorder that injustice represents, the challenge it poses to divine *mîspat* and *shalom*.[82] The response is entirely direct, Job

---

82. Newsom, *The Book of Job*, p. 248 on the reference to divine justice here.

takes it that way, and he concludes that, in spite of everything, God is not unjust after all.

But, again, exactly what does Job see that convinces him? To get at what the answer was, we must continue to build upon the work of Newsom (with whom at last we shall have to part ways, but not before considering her provocative solution). "At the end of the divine speeches three characters dominate the scene: Job, God, and Leviathan. The crucial hermeneutical task posed by the images is to discern the relationships among them."[83] But having chosen the right road, we could well take a wrong turn (and find ourselves in company with Job's friends in the arrogance of triumph). "The temptation," writes Newsom, "is to read these speeches according to the script of the divine warrior creation myth, that is, along the lines of Psalm 74 and 89 and Isaiah 51, in which God defeats the manifestations of chaos."[84] This would be mistaken, however, for "although this speech may draw on materials from those traditions, it does not 'say' the same thing."[85] She acknowledges that this straightforward reading of divine triumph would neatly support the traditional interpretation of Job, wherein God asserts his complete power over things that Job (and we) cannot begin to control. "That reading would deliver the comforting and deeply traditional view of the world as one organized and defended by a god who continually defeats the forces of chaos, even if he does not guarantee strict legal justice."[86] But as she observes, "things are not so simple."[87]

It is true, she judges, that these are proud and high-minded creatures, and that there is some evidence in the text of hostility between them and God. But it is also true, she argues, and a more conspicuous theme of the speech, "God describes them with evident admiration," and this spells grave trouble for the comforting divine warfare and triumph view.[88]

In the context of this difficulty, Newsom takes a closer look at the depiction of Leviathan. On the one hand, she discerns, "This depiction builds on the well known traditions of Leviathan the sea monster with which Yahweh in Israelite mythology and Baal and Anat in Ugaritic mythology do battle."[89] But in other texts, "the *tannînîm* are featured simply

---

83. Newsom, *The Book of Job*, p. 252.
84. Newsom, *The Book of Job*, p. 248.
85. Newsom, *The Book of Job*, p. 248.
86. Newsom, *The Book of Job*, pp. 248-49.
87. Newsom, *The Book of Job*, p. 249.
88. Newsom, *The Book of Job*, p. 249.
89. Newsom, *The Book of Job*, p. 250 and references.

as creatures of God (Gen. 1:21; Pss. 104:26; 148:7) without reference to any hostility."[90] She concludes that "both traditions appear to inform the description of Leviathan in Job 40–41."[91] This creates a devilish problem, to be sure. On one hand, "The significance of the Leviathan pericope can scarcely be overstated. It is both the climax and epitome of what God has to say to Job."[92] On the other hand, the conceptual and textual obscurities are profound, not least in 41:2-4, in which the speaker alternates between the first and third person in such a way as to "lead to very different translations and interpretations." However — and here we approach the end of our treatment of her work — Newsom finds this obscurity in the text strangely revealing.

Just as in the first speech, in which God identifies with chaotic, wild things, what we have in the second speech is "a curious level of identification between God and Leviathan. God represents himself as being in the image of Leviathan, only more so."[93] What Newsom takes from this curiosity of first-person expression, after extensive arguments to blunt the "hostility" that comes through in other verses, is that there in fact *is* identification between God and Leviathan, and that this fearsome, terrible, unexpected truth is what in the end Job accepts.

It seems that Newsom transposes the concept of the sublime, which she has attached to the experience of Job (and the world), into the very nature of God and final reality itself. The human rage for order is hubris, deception, and impossible to satisfy, even if it is, on its own side, inevitable and necessary in the human struggle. This "clash of two necessities," she judges, is "what makes for tragedy." And having heard and seen that the origins of the tragic are in God himself, Job is satisfied. "In response to what he has heard, Job briefly replies and then falls silent. Tragic knowledge gestures to the limits of dialogue, for there is nothing left to say."[94] What Job sees, then, she suggests, is akin to what William Desmond describes as experience of the tragic insight, which is like dying, drowning, suffocating.[95] With this negation, however, comes a countervailing elation, an ecstasy of release, resignation to reality, and so this is what Job received from his "Bakhtinian" encounter with divine discourse.[96] Job has at

90. Newsom, *The Book of Job,* p. 250.
91. Newsom, *The Book of Job,* p. 250.
92. Newsom, *The Book of Job,* p. 250.
93. Newsom, *The Book of Job,* p. 251.
94. Newsom, *The Book of Job,* p. 253.
95. Newsom, *The Book of Job,* p. 253.
96. Newsom, *The Book of Job,* p. 257.

least been closer to this truth than his friends, and can take some consolation in having been "right" about God's governance in the world all along. Little did he know!

But this solution does not seem right. For one thing (and Newsom grants the anomaly) it doesn't fit very well with the "happy ending" of the book, in which Job gets his good life back again. But for another (and mainly) it fails to capture the enigmatic relationships between God and the images of disorder in the speeches. I do think that Newsom is absolutely right about the standard reading — the imagery does not support a simple picture of God triumphant, with horrendous evil no longer a reality to contend with (pace Augustine). On the other hand, she concedes that the speeches are built conspicuously on just that tradition, and that the writer has used it with great imagination to create something new. But was that something a fairly complete deconstruction of the faith, as most people had come to understand it? The transition of consciousness from the triumphal to the tragic is a devastating and deeply sad experience, a loss of innocence and even, arguably, an exchange of faith for enlightened realism. On this reading, there is not much to satisfy Job in the ending, and (on Chisholm's criteria) it cannot be a plausible means of grace for us either. The word "checkmate" comes to mind.

In essence, Newsom's solution to what Job saw and heard in the windstorm was that the chaos is in *God*, that in spite of tradition the terrible yet ecstatic truth is that *God* is wild, that he is at home in the darkness, with the seas, in the wilderness. That he is in that aspect a brother to Leviathan, and we human beings cannot control him any more than we can change the winds. But I propose a different relationship. I believe the imagery of the speeches better serves the interpretation, not that the chaos is in God (pace Hegel and all other quasi-Manicheans), but that God is in the chaos. This is what Job needed to see and to hear in order to recover his faith.

Job's complaint was that chaos had not died, that it was alive and well, that it went "to and fro upon the earth," and he surmised this must imply the absence of God's goodness. The truth in Job's complaint just was in the empirical assertion (denied a priori by his comforters). His fallacy was in the inference, and the speeches are a kind of rebuke in the form of an evocative refutation. God appeared to him in the violent windstorm, and spoke to him in and through the thunder and lightning. In the first speech (as Stump rightly discerns, as does Newsom) the stunning feature is God's benevolent (albeit controlling) presence with the chaos-elements, most notably the raging sea, which he calms. In the progression, we see and hear God as present in the wilderness and with its inhabitants. God is at work unexpectedly not as the opponent of these creatures, but as their redeemer and friend, as one who brings life and good things even out of what we associate with death and evil — even horror. We are gradually unlearning one notion of divine victory (triumph) and replacing it with another more enigmatic teleological (surgical) one.

It is not control in the form of warfare and victory of the kind that naturally come to mind. It is control of the One who has already won the day, whose enemies are no real threat to him anymore, who can take his time, can do whatever he pleases with them, just as one leads a fish by a hook, a tamed beast by the nose, a pet on a leash. The images do not support Job's friends. Leviathan is not dead, is still powerful — so much so that nothing of human origin can resist him, for "upon earth is not his like," and unlike the ostrich he is justifiably "a creature without fear," which is the quintessence of chaos (Job 41:33). So far forth, God affirms Job's claim. But what Job has not yet seen, until now, is that God is completely at peace with what is happening — there is no trace of divine agony or pathos, no tragedy. He sees for himself that God is working *in and through* disorder to bring about his ordered cosmos.

God acknowledges the reality of the chaos, but he now reveals, and Job now sees, that he is in complete control of events. The relationship between God and Leviathan is not friendly, but rather one of grudging domestication. Not to press the point too far, but this understanding of the relationship between God and Leviathan is directly parallel to that between God and the Satan, with whose dubious activities the story began. If so, it may be that both are symbolic, in very different ways, of the same adversarial chaos that God has both tamed and (mysteriously) then unleashed upon the world. And if so, the common reading of the Satan as a benign creature would be false, too.[97]

So it is true that God has won the day, but the work is not yet finished, as it will be, and horrendous evil has a mysterious part left to play in the finishing. Here we are tempted to appeal to Chisholm's and Adams's notions of "value parts" and how their defeat must come by their integration into "value wholes," not by mere addition. There are suggestions of this sort of process in both my interpretation of the divine

97. On the tradition of Satan in Israel's religion, see Peggy Day, *An Adversary in Heaven: Satan in the Hebrew Bible* (Atlanta: Scholars Press, 1988).

speeches and in the ending. God is at work — omnisciently, omnipotently, caringly — in and with the darkness, the seas, the winds and the wilderness. On this view the poetry depicts God in creative and redemptive terms that mediate all his attributes — not just power or pathos.

On this view the poetry suggests that God is fully engaged in the work of bringing about a value-whole, the greatness and goodness of which is commensurate with those attributes. Furthermore, if we apply the criteria for defeat, as Adams does, to individuals who have suffered, so that the evil must be integrated constructively into the value-whole constituted by the victim's own life, the ending of Job seems to have applications, too. For in the end, Job is not left in resignation to the privilege of being a sacrificial victim for the good of the whole (pace Simone Weil). He receives caring attention as an individual, and he receives restitution for what he has lost. The restitution is imperfect, to be sure. The children of Job remain dead, for instance. But I attribute this imperfection to limitations that Israel's worldview imposed upon the writer. Israel had not yet developed a notion of the afterlife consistent with its intensely material anthropology — bodily resurrection would emerge as the solution in years hence. But without that concept, for the writer to bring the children back from the dead would have transgressed boundaries between the sublime and the ridiculous. The principle of personal restitution emerges clearly in Job, and believers in the resurrection of the body can use that belief to mediate the principle.

There is one last thing to ponder before transposing these thoughts into the distinctly Christian narratives of Christ in the New Testament. That is the criterion of necessity, which, as mentioned earlier, Rowe proposes is a condition for God to have a morally sufficient reason to permit any horrendous evil. It is very hard to see how what God permitted to happen to Job was necessary to bring about some indispensable great good. The only candidate I can see for this is the kind of wisdom that Job acquired — not in spite of his experiences, but directly because of them. Without them the speeches from the storm would have made no sense. Is it plausible to think that there is a kind of wisdom that God counts as indispensably good, but can only come about through some degree of participation in horrors? Perhaps it is the kind of wisdom that human beings must acquire and possess in order to have a mature relationship with God forever in heaven. I do not see why this scenario is implausible. Perhaps part of faith is to trust that it is so, and if so, there is real Christian truth both to Hick's pedagogical and Adams's moral-aesthetic solutions.

256

Mark's Christ: The Lord of the Sea

In this last section, I will carry the main themes of this essay over into a discussion of Christology and its applications to the problem of horrendous evil. In the light of preceding interpretations I will offer an approach that complements and allows for the expansion of recent theologies, which focus on the identification and suffering of Christ with us. My focus will rather be on important but neglected senses in which the New Testament teaches that, in Christ, God has achieved victory over evil in its worst forms. I will limit my discussion to selected parts of Mark's Gospel, which (as I will show) is uniquely suited to these purposes.

As is well known, Mark shows keen interest in relating his Christology to the experience of evil, and (so I will argue) he deliberately used the symbolic tradition that we have just explored, only he rewrites it in distinctly Christian theological terms. Furthermore, in doing so (as I will argue), contrary to majority opinion, Mark's stress is not one-sidedly upon the *suffering* of Jesus as a point of reference for persecuted and frightened believers. The old saying that his gospel is "a passion story with an introduction" does not do justice to the rhetorical and theological sophistication of the work. For the so-called "introduction," in the first several chapters, is on inspection a superbly crafted incarnational narrative (to use the term of C. Stephen Evans).[98] And in that narrative, recent studies show that Mark made creative use of the full range of poetic-religious symbols in Hebrew tradition in order to show and to persuade readers to believe that, in Christ's coming, God's victory over the sources and powers of every evil was secure.

Among the main narrative themes in early Mark is the pattern of confrontation between Jesus and the demonic. Modern Christians are often inclined to ignore or to the importance of this theme, to give it a naturalistic explanation, and to put it in terms of the demonic metaphor, rather than take it as literal warfare. I believe that this strategy is plausible, and that the theology I am proposing can stand upon either a literal or metaphorical view of the demonic. But Mark's narrative is as starkly literal as it could be, and the theme is at the core of his understanding of Christ.

In his book *Irony in Mark's Gospel*, Jerry Camery-Hoggatt comments extensively on how engagement of the demonic by Jesus became a major

---

98. C. Stephen Evans, *The Historical Christ and the Jesus of Faith: The Incarnational Narrative as History* (Oxford: Clarendon Press, 1996).

theme for Mark, and that he linked it with Jesus' deliberate choice to carry out his mission among the "multitudes."[99] Camery-Hoggatt shows persuasively that Mark depicts the crowds, in which Jesus immersed himself, as a kind of human sea, a place of constant danger and chaos. In this environment, the demons are aroused by his presence, which to them is an unexpected (and unwelcome) intrusion into their realm. Thus provoked, demonic entities invariably speak to him, and they loudly divulge to the crowds who he really is. This divulgence is not innocent, but is hostile and calculated to incite chaos, so that Jesus commands them to be silent, and he orders them to leave their wretched victims and to be gone. What is startling is that these entities obey him, and Mark relates that no one had ever seen anything like it, and that all were "amazed" (1:24-28).

In the third chapter, this theme rises and comes to its high point. The scribes who have been scrutinizing Jesus' actions begin to form their judgment. By elimination, they judge that Jesus must be animated by one of two beings: the only two beings with power to order demons about. Either it is the spirit of God that animates him, or it is the devil himself. They immediately rule out the first possibility and adopt the second one — Jesus is none other than the son of Beelzebub (Mark 3:22). Jesus responds by means of a scathing *reductio ad absurdum*. He asks, "How can Satan cast out Satan?" (3:23). The question implies that it is transparently ridiculous to think that, should Satan send a "son" into the world to embody his presence, this emissary would make it a primary part of his work to set people free from satanic oppression. What they should conclude, Jesus insinuates, is that God has sent someone to embody *his* presence, and that this "son" of God has invaded Satan's realm. Speaking cryptically he compares himself to someone who is about to "enter a strong man's house and plunder his property," and so he has first to tie the man up (3:27). It is on this momentous note, with Jesus about to make that invasive entry, that Mark makes more than a merely geographical transition. For the next several scenes, the location of all Jesus' extraordinary works will be the sea. Following this encounter with the scribes, Mark simply writes: "Again he began to teach beside the sea" (4:1).

To accept my approach to the rest of the narrative, one must accept that, while Mark narrates events, he does so with the imagination and purpose of a poet. Recent works by Camery-Hoggatt, already named,

---

99. Jerry Camery-Hoggatt, *Irony in Mark's Gospel: Text and Subtext* (Cambridge: Cambridge University Press, 1992), pp. 102-7; 134-38.

and also Rhoads, Dewie, and Michie strongly confirm this view of Mark.[100] As Rhoads comments comprehensively, "the Marcan settings connect for readers events in this story about Jesus with events of deliverance in Israel's history."[101] To our point, it is important to note his observation that Mark deliberately uses the sea this way, invariably to contribute to a desired mood of "chaos and destruction."[102]

At any rate, having now established his position by the sea, Mark relates that Jesus began telling his parables of the kingdom of God (Mark 4:2-33). It is as though, standing on the vestibule of evil's realm, Jesus is now ready to take it on right where it lives. Having finished, he tersely announces his intent to go out upon the sea and to go across to the other side (4:35).[103] But no sooner are they upon the sea, Mark writes, than a violent windstorm rises, arousing the sea, and terrifying the disciples to death. The weary Jesus is sleeping right through the tempest, and they cry to him for help in words that capture the essence of the problem: "'Teacher, do you not care that we are perishing?'"

At that very moment, Jesus awakens, and Mark writes that he "rebuked the wind, and said to the sea, 'Peace! Be still'" (4:39). At his command, Mark claims: "Then the wind ceased, and there was a dead calm" (4:39). Afterwards, Jesus rebukes the disciples for their lack of faith (and presumably goes back to sleep). Meanwhile, they pose the question that Mark wishes to put before readers — a question, which, if we are familiar with the poetic tradition, nearly answers itself. "Who then is this, that even the wind and the sea obey him?" (4:41).

The answer that follows from the second-person account, in the symbolic world in which it is said to have occurred, is strongly incarnational. As Ralph Martin has argued, in this event the disciples were in the presence of the same agent who is the subject of the Eighty-ninth Psalm, cited above. They were in the numinous presence of one who stood on a level no lower than that of Yahweh, the Lord.[104] But the point to be developed here is not the plausible use of Mark to support the Christology of the Nicene Creed. It is Mark's way of narrating the iden-

100. David Rhoads, Joanna Dewie, Donald Michie, *Mark as Story: An Introduction to the Narrative of a Gospel* (Minneapolis: Fortress Press, 1999).

101. Rhoads et al., *Mark as Story*, p. 69.

102. Rhoads et al., *Mark as Story*, p. 70.

103. Camery-Hoggatt's comments on the placing of these parables in just this setting does, I think, support the interpretation I am offering. See p. 132.

104. Ralph Martin, *Mark: Evangelist and Theologian* (Grand Rapids: Zondervan, 1973), p. 133.

tity of Christ as the Lord of the Sea, and what that means for a Christian theology of God and evil.

Paul Achtemeier has ably shown that Jesus' manner of speaking in the story continues the theme of his command over the demonic. His rebuke of the wind, Achtemeier demonstrates, is the same as that which he has been using against the demons. The story is a kind of cosmic exorcism.[105] And as with the imagery in Job, in which God calms and gives new life even to the sea, Jesus puts an end to the sea's violence and chaos, and he becomes its benevolent Lord. The symbolic link between this event and God's victory over evil becomes even stronger in the events that immediately follow.

As soon as the boat reaches the other side of the sea, Jesus and his disciples find themselves face to face with a man who has been completely taken over by the demonic. The man is a living chaos. He is naked, he runs like a wild animal amid the graves, crying out senselessly, no chains can bind him. He is uncontrolled and uncontrollable, and now he confronts, and is confronted by, Jesus.

The demons seem to have been ambushed, and are immediately put back on the defensive. They entreat Jesus not to torment them, to leave them alone, or at worst to let them go into the swine herding nearby. Jesus grants their request, they go into the swine, and Mark writes with typical irony, "they rushed down the steep bank and into the sea. And they were drowned in the sea" (5:13). The demons have returned to the realm from whence they came. The man, meantime, like the seas just before, is now completely sane, in his right mind, the violence and chaos gone, order and cosmos restored, and he views Jesus as his Lord. Jesus, however, instructs him to go back to his people and to tell everyone what *God* had done for him. Mark subtly changes what the man told everyone. He told them what *Jesus* had done for him (5:20).

Meanwhile, Jesus gets back in the boat, returns across the sea without incident to the other side, and resumes his position teaching "by the sea" (Mark 5:21), where he performs his most powerful miracles yet, even raising a little girl from the dead (5:35-43). His power over the demonic grows and spreads so that his disciples now, too, cast many of them out (6:12). In the Gospel, the demons never bother Jesus again. After performing the spectacular "messianic" miracle — feeding the multitudes in

105. P. Achtemeier, "Person and Deed: Jesus and the Storm-Tossed Sea," *Interpretation* 16 (1962): 169-76; cited and discussed in Camery-Hoggat, *Irony in Mark's Gospel*, p. 132.

the wilderness — Jesus sends his disciples alone out onto the sea, and winds arise again. In this account, Jesus comes to them striding effortlessly upon the waves, gets into the boat, and "the wind ceased" (6:45-52). On the other side they return to Gennesaret, where the chaotic man had been, only this time they are greeted by crowds of people in need, seeking but to touch the hem of his garment (6:53-56).

In these chapters we have something a good deal more profound than an introduction to the story of Christ's passion. Mark has related history in deliberately poetic form, finding in the events a symbolic connection with ancient biblical tradition. In that tradition God has achieved victory, if not yet triumph, over the powers of chaos and evil. In Mark's narrative we encounter God in the man Jesus, who enacts this victory in human form, and thus takes it further toward completion. In theology we are used to thinking of Christ's obedience, righteousness, suffering, death and resurrection as the means of divine victory over the evils of sin and death. To this thinking we should add the truths that emerge from the identity of (Mark's) Jesus in the symbolism of divine warfare with chaos and the demonic. In Jesus Christ, it seems, God himself has set human foot in our soil, and on behalf of humanity he has gone to the seas, engaged the chaos, and secured command over it as never before. It was in this position as Lord of the Sea that he suffered, went to his death, and rose again to the Father's right hand.

Sensitivity to the symbolism of God and evil in ancient biblical tradition, as applied in Job, and then reapplied in the Gospel of Mark, gives Christian theology powerful resources to add to discussion of the problem of evil and belief in God. The narrative of early Mark eloquently complements the more commonly exploited traditions of divine identification and suffering with human beings. It offers second-person experiences between Jesus, his disciples, the demonic, and the sea that expand our notion of his purported victory in terms of his identity and status as the sovereign, conquering Lord, whose name is above every name. It prevents the story of suffering from the distortions of tragedy, even as that story of his suffering prevents a distorted sense of triumph. And together, these features of the story as a whole make plausible the hope of our faith that some day the ambiguities of divine victory will dissipate, and the "defeat" of evil will be completed. As I have suggested, the story shows rich potential for meeting criteria for rational belief of that kind. Whether nonbelievers will find the account convincing as *truth* is a matter I will leave to them. Meanwhile, believers who know their tradition will find hope strengthened. If the narrative is true, then the victory of God over evil has advanced decisively toward final triumph, toward the day when, as promised, he will slay the dragon (Isa. 27:1), and he will cast the ancient serpent into the fire (Rev. 13:1-10; 20:10). But until he does, these stories can help believers to see and to hear God where the wild things are.

Innocent Sinfulness, Guilty Sin:
Original Sin and Divine Justice

Keith D. Wyma

As a college sophomore taking a course in Reformed theology, I was troubled by the doctrines having to do with original sin. Eventually I raised my questions in class. "How can it be just," I asked, "for God to create me in an already-sinful state? And if I *start* life with original sin, and so am sinful such that I *cannot help* but do evil, how can it be just on God's part to condemn and punish me for it?" In response, the professor stared at me, drew a long nasal breath, and in stern tones of righteous indignation proclaimed, "Well, I think that's the kind of question a good Christian just wouldn't ask!" After enduring the resultant witch-burning glares of my classmates, I shut my mouth and kept mum for the rest of the course.

But my questions remained, and they nag at me to this day. Apparently, I still just am not a good Christian (although good enough to have restrained my spiteful urge to identify the school and professor . . .). I see these questions as necessary for Christians to address, since they pose a serious challenge to Christian attempts to reconcile a just God with the evil humans do. For the doctrine of original sin seems to cripple the human freedom that crucially supports Christian theodicy. If we are born guilty of sin, then apparently at least some of our sin cannot be directly traced to any identifiable free choice on our own parts. Also, if original sin makes further sinful action inevitable, it's hard to see how those resultant sins can be attributed to our free and responsible action. In that case, though, it's not clear how God can escape responsibility for those sins; and it certainly seems that he cannot justly blame and punish us for sins we did not choose or could not help but commit.

In this paper, then, I shall examine original sin with two purposes:

first, to show that creating us in the state of original sin can be compatible with God's justice; and second, to show how the sins we perform from that state can still be our responsibility and thus justly be blameworthy.

Before analyzing aspects of the doctrine of original sin, however, we had better look at the doctrine itself. Christian thinking on this topic mostly reflects the view of Augustine of Hippo. Augustine set the tone for later Catholic theologians, including Thomas Aquinas. Moreover, the primary Reformers Luther and Calvin were both deeply influenced by Augustine. According to Augustine, then, since Adam's fall, every human being has been born already carrying the guilt and punishment of that first sin (not including those with miraculous births like Christ's, of course). Somehow Adam's sin has been transmitted and attributed to us (Augustine, *Confessions* VIII.x(22), X.xx(29)). Biblical texts appealed to in support of this view include Psalm 51:5, "Behold, I was brought forth in iniquity, and in sin my mother conceived me," and Romans 5:12, 18-19, ". . . through one man sin entered into the world, and death through sin, and so death spread to all men, because all sinned. . . . So then . . . through one transgression there resulted condemnation to all men . . . through the one man's disobedience the many were made sinners . . ." (NASB). Each of us thus begins life a guilty sinner condemned by God's righteous judgment (Augustine, *Confessions* I.viii(11-12)). Worse, the depravity of our faculties, which is part of the death-sentence punishment of that original sin, ensures that we cannot help but sin in our later actions (*On Free Choice of the Will* III, xix.180, 184, 185). Therefore, on our own we cannot please God by our actions (*Retractations* II, 4). This picture, or slight variations on it, has since dominated Christian doctrine on original sin.

In investigating this doctrine, the first difficult issue that I shall focus on concerns how we should understand God's justification in creating Adam's progeny in an already-sinful state. For it seems that God does us wrong by creating us in the punitive, morally-unable condition of original sin. Among its physical and mental effects, original sin damages our faculties for deciding upon and executing action, particularly as they relate to our abilities to know and to do the good. Does God not owe us a "clean slate" starting point? How can God justly extend the disordered faculties imposed on Adam as punishment for his transgression to us, who did not actually commit that sin?[1] In response to these questions, I

---

1. Of course, original sin was passd to us through both Adam and Eve, but because the Bible translation I use speaks of "through one man," I shall utilize that phraseology and refer to the Fall as *Adam's* sin.

shall propose two possible justifications. While they have distinct bases, they lend each other support, so that their combined justification will be stronger than either alone.

The first justification points to our complete inability to assert any moral obligation upon God with regard to the status of our creation. That is, in creating us, God graciously grants existence to us; it is as if God were giving us a gift. Since this existence is neither earned by us nor otherwise owed to us — after all, *before* we exist we cannot be the objects of any moral duty — it follows that we cannot make any claims on God as to *how* we shall exist. For example, that I exist at all is essentially a gift to me; with regard to moral obligation, God's act in creating me was *supererogatory* (at least in respect to any moral claims on *my* part). Given that, how could I possibly make any moral complaints about the qualities of that gift? May I accuse God of injustice because I'm not as insightful, not as good a writer, as I might have been? No. If God had chosen to create me in an earlier time period or in a nation racked by war, famine, or disease, could I claim that I was being wrongly treated, since I was being denied the easy, comfortable life I might have had? No. If God had chosen to create me with less ability or opportunity — or even let me be born with serious mental or physical disabilities or both — would that impugn God's justice? No. Why not? Because in a situation of non-obligatory giving, the amount of the gift is also a non-obligatory matter. God may give more or less ability or opportunity, as he pleases. In short, the initial circumstances of our lives and the innate extents of our capabilities — moral and otherwise — lie beyond the reach of moral obligations we can claim upon God.[2]

2. Please note that I am not claiming that God has, or can have, *no* moral obligations to us *at all*. Some thinkers have made this much stronger claim — cf. Marilyn Adams, "Duns Scotus on the Goodness of God," *Faith and Philosophy* 4:4 (October 1987): 486-505; and William Alston, "Some Suggestions for Divine Command Theorists," in *Divine Nature and Human Language: Essays in Philosophical Theology* (Ithaca, N.Y.: Cornell University Press, 1999); and a rebuttal of that position in Eleonore Stump's "God's Obligations," in *Philosophical Perspectives 6: Ethics*, ed. James E. Tomberlin (Atascadero, Ca.: Ridgeview Publishing Company, 1992) — but I do not. Moreover, my argument parses God's goodness and distinguishes between God's justice and his love and benevolence. So this point may commit me to maintaining that God could create us in *any* circumstances and with *any* capabilities (even, for instance, giving us lives of unending, unrelieved, unredeemed, mind-numbing suffering) and not violate justice; but it does *not* imply that God could do so and remain loving and benevolent. So while it might not be unjust for God to create in that way, God's character is necessarily such that he would/could never do so. It may seem that original sin makes for human lives

Moreover, this point is strengthened by the fact that the very nature of creaturely existence involves finitude. Any creature must fall short of the omnipotence of God; possession of that trait would imply divinity. However, to be less than omnipotent implies *some* limit to one's power to act. And if there must be limits to any creature's innate capacities to act, then where those limits fall is a matter for God's free discretion. For there is no point at which a capability-limit might be set such that no creaturely complaints might result.[3] Consider, for example, my ability to learn: it's good, but not great. I learn well enough to understand what I'm taught in most, but not all, areas. I never did gain a truly solid grasp of differential calculus. That failure bothers me; perhaps it even hindered my career choice — avoid engineering and physics, young man! Because of those sorts of hindrances, I have complained to God that I should have had more capability in these areas. But suppose God suddenly infused me with greater ability in all those areas. Differential calculus comes easily; I can jump higher, palm the ball, and dunk; and so on. But now I complain about difficulties with time-space theory, or my inability to "sky" and throw down jams off alley-oop passes. Shall God relent and increase my abilities again? And again when I complain that I can't leap tall buildings in a single bound? In truth, there is no discernible optimal ability-limit. Whatever the capacity and wherever the limit, ability-failures would remain possible, and creaturely complaints might be made. Thus God's creative choice is unconstrained by any set of capacities and limits that *should* or *ought* to be utilized; he may simply choose as he pleases.

To apply the general point to our question about original sin, our moral capacities to identify and to perform the good, or to identify and to avoid evil, must have some boundaries. As finite beings, we creatures necessarily have some circumstances possible in our lives such that under those conditions we could not know or could not do the good. Again, though, given that there must be some limit set, it is entirely up to God's free choice where to place that boundary. Therefore, even if we recognize our moral capacities, in the state of original sin, to be severely diminished in comparison to what they could be (or to what Adam's were before the Fall), that does not mean God has done us wrong. Were our moral capacities even lesser or greater, God would not thereby have done morally

that show that God has, in fact, acted in an unloving or malevolent manner, but that is another argument.

3. Several philosophers have made similar points, going back at least to Descartes in his *Meditation IV*, which deals with the explanation for the possibility of erroneous belief.

worse or better by us. For this reason, that we are created in a state of original sin, possessing moral capacities on a par with Adam's punitively weakened ones, does not impugn God's justice. Indeed, if Adam had never existed, God would still not wrong us by creating us with the moral capacities that we in fact have.[4] We simply receive what abilities God chooses to give us, with no question of justice involved at all.

But I think this justification faces some immediate objections. First, it has not explained how Adam's sin can be attributed to us; rather it treats our originally-sinful state as if God might have created us with it whether Adam fell or not. But a key aspect of original sin is that we receive it *from Adam* somehow, because of what he did. We're born in a punitive state through, and because of, him and our relation to him. Yet this justification conveys no sense of that, and so is incomplete.

Second, and more damagingly, this justification seems outright mistaken in that it ignores a crucial difference between our moral capacities and any other abilities we might possess: God does not demand a specified level of achievement in our use of those other abilities. Perhaps God may create me fast, slow, or even without legs; but he doesn't require me to run quickly. Perhaps he may create me with a low or high IQ; but he does not demand that I solve multivariable equations. Yet God does command me to do right. How then can he justifiably create me with an inability to do so? If God lays a demand, an 'ought', upon us, he must supply the 'can', the ability to carry out what's required. Yet in our condition of original sin, it appears impossible for us to meet the moral demands of God. Therefore, it seems that in the case of our moral capacities, God's choice of where to set our ability-limits is constrained by considerations of what he requires from us. But our originally-sinful condition seems to violate those constraints; God still appears unjust for creating us in such a state, while commanding us to do what that state renders impossible.

The former objection can be met, I believe, by appealing to the second potential justification, to which I shall turn next. Some help also will be offered for the latter, and more troubling, objection; but that will not have a complete defense until we see the second main argument of the

---

4. Augustine makes almost this same point: "If, therefore, a soul should start out — before it has sinned or even been alive — in the state that another soul was in after a blameworthy life, it still possesses no small amount of good. Therefore, it owes thanks to its Creator. . . ." (*On Free Choice of the Will*, trans. Anna S. Benjamin and L. H. Hackstaff [New York: Macmillan, 1964], III, xx.190). Here, I agree with Augustine, and the Medievals generally, that existence is itself a good thing — even when that existence is drastically limited or damaged.

paper. I think the interpretation of our moral obligations and moral inabilities included there will provide a plausible response. However, for complete consistency even that rebuttal will need to be accompanied by a minor revision to our understanding of original sin itself.

For now, though, let me lay out the second piece of the first main argument justifying God's creation of us in an already-sinful state. This justification utilizes counterfactuals of freedom and God's so-called middle knowledge. Counterfactuals of freedom are conditional (or "if-then") statements about free-willed agents, telling what they would have freely done, if circumstances had been different from what they were or are. For example, "If Bill Clinton were propositioned by one of his current interns, he would freely refuse," and, "If Judas had repented and asked for forgiveness instead of committing suicide, God would freely have forgiven him," are both counterfactuals of freedom. Moreover, many theologians and philosophers have thought that God's omniscience implies knowledge of which counterfactuals of freedom are true, including those concerning possible-but-uncreated free agent creatures. That is, in deciding whom to create, and in what conditions and circumstances to place them, God would have reference to truths about what any possible creature would freely do, in any circumstances possible for it. Those truths constitute what has been labeled God's "middle" knowledge (because it falls between God's knowledge of necessary truths prior to creation, and his knowledge of contingent truths about the world posterior to creation).

Unfortunately, the very possibility of true counterfactuals of freedom and very existence of God's middle knowledge are highly controversial. I cannot here present the argument in their favor; yet I do think they can be rationally defended.[5] For the purposes of this paper, then, I will operate under the assumption that such a defense is available, and that it is plausible that there are true counterfactuals of creaturely freedom, which God knows through his middle knowledge.

Now, all possible humans (presuming humans to be free agents) would then be the subjects of counterfactuals truly describing what they would freely do, in whatever states of affairs they might be found. God, in considering whom to create and where and when to place them, could make use of those truths. In creating Adam's progeny, God could restrict himself to the set of possible humans who would freely have done as

5. For a thorough and well-argued defense of the possibility of true counterfactuals of freedom, see Thomas P. Flint's *Divine Providence: The Molinist Account* (Ithaca, N.Y.: Cornell University Press, 1998).

Adam did in the circumstances of his temptation and fall. That is, I propose that the humans who exist, and who have existed and who will exist, constitute some subset of those possible humans who would freely have fallen, just as Adam did.[6] Thus, Adam's rebellion becomes a kind of paradigm for all of us, since his action represents what each of us would have done in his place. In him, we all sinned, *figuratively* speaking.

Because of that, God can justifiably create us in the same state to which Adam was punitively condemned. There's no point in replaying the Fall over and over to the same result. It's as if God said to himself, "The first scene will always be the same, so let us join the action *in media res;* begin with the second scene, where the lives follow their own unique paths." This justification then helps to make sense of why our state of original sin traces back to Adam. Because we are the ones-who-would-freely-have-acted-as-he-did, our relation to Adam allows the punishment his rebellion received to be applied to us as well. His action stands in for ours; on account of what he did, we too suffer the consequences and share in his condemned state.

Moreover, this justification also offers some vindication for God's creating us in a state from which we cannot fulfill his moral demands. God knows that even if we were created with more perfect moral capacities, like Adam's initially, so that we would be fully capable of carrying out his moral commands, we still would *not* do so, as Adam did not. Therefore, if we would not obey even if we could, God need not ensure that we could. It would be useless overdevelopment to give us increased moral capacities. For that reason, setting the limits to our moral capacities truly does resemble setting the boundaries of any of our other abilities; all such limiting falls to God's unconstrained, free choice, since it is not a question of moral obligation for God.

With both justifications in place, we can see each strengthening the

6. It might be asked, at this point, why God would choose to create from this set. That is, if God has middle knowledge, why wouldn't he simply create only those humans whom he knew would *not* fall? One answer might rely on Alvin Plantinga's notion of 'transworld depravity'. If every possible human is essentially such that in any world in which she exists, she freely does *some* evil, then God's choice would be constrained to the set of would-be-Adams ("God, Evil, and the Metaphysics of Freedom," in *The Problem of Evil,* ed. Marilyn McCord Adams and Robert Merrihew Adams [New York: Oxford University Press, 1990], pp. 83-109, esp. 101-5). Alternatively, one might appeal to supralapsarian notions that fallen-then-redeemed humanity makes for a better world than unfallen humanity (cf. Plantinga's "Supralapsarianism, or 'O Felix Culpa'" in this volume). In either case, it would involve argument beyond the scope of this paper.

case for original sin's being compatible with God's justice. In the first proposal, we saw how God's choices regarding the initial conditions and capacities of a creature's existence are completely free and unconstrained by moral obligations to the created being. That establishes the general point that even if our native abilities and capacities are not sufficient to succeed at all we might attempt with them, we do not thereby possess grounds to complain against God's justice to us. So although our moral abilities are recognizably impoverished, that does not necessarily imply God has wronged us. In spite of the fact that we ourselves committed no actual sin to bring on the punitive reduction of our moral abilities, God can still justifiably create us in such a reduced condition.

The second proposal showed how our originally-sinful state traces back to Adam's rebellion through our counterfactual concurrence with his action. If God creates only from among those possible humans who would freely have done as Adam did, then he can justifiably skip the replays of the Fall and simply start us out in post-Fall condition. Moreover, this justification provides a plausible interpretation for the biblical passages on original sin. Sin and death (i.e., the punishment for sin) "entered into the world" and "spread to all" because Adam's action was just what we would freely have done in his place; thus "through one transgression there resulted condemnation to all." Further, this proposal aids the first by supplying reason to think that God justifiably could create us with moral abilities insufficient to the moral directives he issues. If it is true that we would have rejected those commands anyway, even if we could have kept them perfectly, then it seems pointless for God to have to give us those higher abilities.

However, a significant obstacle remains in that even though we can now see how God might be justified in creating us in the disordered and limited condition of original sin, we still have not seen how God can justly *blame* us for being in that state. That is, one piece of the standard view on original sin is that it is a state not simply of disorder but of *guilt* (it's a *sin*, after all). We inherit more than Adam's post-Fall faculties; we also receive his guilt. Yet the proposed justifications don't seem to imply that. If it's true that we would have rebelled as Adam did, it's one thing to skip giving us his test; but it seems a much farther step to blame us for failing it. As an analogy, take one of the unfortunate subjects of Stanley Milgram's famous experiments involving authority and electric shock. Suppose a test subject has displayed willingness to inflict extreme pain on the word of an authority. Further suppose this confirms that the subject would also have been willing to follow orders in carrying out Hitler's genocidal plan in Nazi Germany. Let's say, then, that it's true of this subject that she would freely have helped to commit genocide if her governmental authorities had told her to. Do we then blame her for the Nazi atrocities? Does this counterfactual concurrence make her guilty of those crimes? No; because although she would have committed the acts, she in fact did not. Similarly, it seems unjust for us to share Adam's guilt, as only he actually committed the transgression in question.

On that account, even with the justifications in place, the predominant view on original sin needs alteration. I propose this: the state itself of original sin should be understood more as a *shortfall* than as a *transgression*. That is, rather than being a kind of wrongdoing, original sin resembles the Old Testament states of *uncleanness*. Having leprosy might have indicated imperfection that made an Israelite unfit to enter the wholly perfect presence of God, but it didn't count as a crime against the Almighty. Similarly, the disorder of original sin might in itself prevent one from being fit to see God; so original sin still needs fixing and baptism is not in vain (one of Aquinas' concerns should original sin not be a source of guilt [*On Evil*, q.4, a.1, resp.]). However, seen this way, original sin does not constitute a damning offense. Original sin is a sinful state in that its disorder disposes us to become actual sinners (and even inevitably so, as we shall see), but is not in itself grounds for guilt.[7] It is a state of *innocent sinfulness*.

I conclude this portion of the argument by appealing to authority for legitimization. In formulating my view, I was troubled by its implications in altering the traditional Christian doctrine; my position seemed on the fringes of orthodoxy and perhaps even slightly heretical. However, I have lately discovered that my explication closely matches statements by Zwingli and Wesley on original sin.[8] So it turns out Christian thinking on this point is not monolithic. And if my position prevents me from being a "good Christian," at least I'm in good company.

However, in beginning the second main argument, I seem to have undercut myself. If the first argument establishes the innocence of the initial sinful state of original sin, and if the disordered disposition of that

7. Surprisingly, even Augustine shows some support for this point. He writes, ". . . if ignorance of the truth and difficulty in behaving rightly are the natural points from which man begins . . . no one properly condemns the soul because of its natural origin" (*On Free Choice*, III, xxii, 220).

8. Zwingli, from his *Fidei Ratio*, and Wesley from *On Original Sin* and the *Confession of American Methodists*, quoted in William T. Bruner, *Children of the Devil* (New York: Philosophical Library, 1966), pp. 186-87, 193, 200.

state makes committing sins inevitable, then apparently these further sins will not be reason for guilt, either. As an analogy, consider a drunk person, who may be held responsible for things she did while inebriated and unable to control her actions *if* she freely and knowingly drank herself to that condition. Yet suppose she was the thirsty but unwitting victim of spiked punch at a Sunday school party — if she had no control over getting drunk, can she be blamed for her subsequent blacked-out drunken brawl with a deacon? Seemingly not. Similarly with the innocent sinfulness of original sin: we don't enter that state by any actual action or choice on our parts. This starting point is beyond our control. However, that initial disposition ensures that we will actually commit sins; such necessity seems to take those actions out of our control, too. Therefore, it appears that we cannot be considered guilty of those, either. If God holds us responsible for them, he seems to accuse us unjustly. Yet vindicating God's accusation is the second goal of this paper's argument. Has my earlier position made that impossible?

I think not, based on an important distinction between the inevitability of *sinning* and the inevitability of *committing a particular sin*. I believe a correct view of original sin includes the former but not the latter. The disordered faculties of post-Fall humanity make sinning unavoidable, but that doesn't mean they necessitate committing any particular sin. Because of the inescapability of sinning, it may not make sense to hold us accountable for entering the general state of being sinners. Yet we may still bear responsibility for the specific sins we commit. I thus propose that not only should the initial disposition of original sin be considered guiltless, but so also should the necessarily-subsequent *state* of being a sinner. However, that excuse does not extend to committed sinful *acts;* for those, responsibility, blame, and punishment can justly be assigned.

It works like this — suppose that my original sinfulness necessitates the following (vastly simplified) disjunction:

> (S1) Four-year-old Wyma covets his older brother's Christmas present, *or* (S2) seven-year-old Wyma falsely accuses his younger brother of breaking a lamp, *or* (S3) ten-year-old Wyma mocks a classmate's disability, . . . *or* (Sn) twenty-year-old Wyma presents a false I.D. to buy beer, . . . *or* (Sz) on his deathbed Wyma curses God.

I cannot, then, complete my life without making at least one disjunct true. However, that does *not* mean I must make true any *particular* disjunct. Suppose further that at ten, I mock my classmate and that, astonishingly, it is my first sin. The disjunction is now true; I'm a sinner. More precisely, though, (S3) is now true; I'm an uncharitable mocker. Given original sin, I could not help but become a sinner, but I needn't have been uncharitable to my classmate. Thus, I can bear no guilt for being a sinner, but I can be held responsible for my uncharitable act. In judgment God might ask, "Could you have avoided mocking that classmate?" My honest reply would have to be affirmative. "Then," God might justly respond, "We condemn you for your mockery; proceed to your punishment."

Or again, consider this analogy: a man is kidnapped by terrorists who rig him with a bomb controlled by a "deadman" switch in the form of a spring-compress-grip. If the man relaxes his grip, the spring decompresses and the bomb detonates. The terrorists then bind, gag and conceal the man on the side of a continuously busy roadway. Eventually he must tire and release his grip, and the bomb will destroy whatever vehicles are passing. He lets go at time $t(n)$. The resultant explosion takes eleven lives (including his). In judgment God asks if the man could not have released the grip earlier at $t(n-1)$ or even held it a bit longer to $t(n+1)$. The man responds affirmatively. Obviously, the man can't be held responsible for detonating the bomb; in no way could he have avoided that (or his own death). But can he be held responsible for the *particular other deaths* he caused? I think so — although admittedly to a diminished degree in these circumstances; for *those* deaths weren't necessary, but occurred through the man's chosen and avoidable release at $t(n)$. It can legitimately be asked: why did the man trigger the bomb when he did? Suppose he answers this question with, "I saw my hated business rival's car passing, and thought, 'that cheat really deserves to be blown up.'" Wouldn't the man then at least be responsible for the act of killing his rival (and perhaps so to a lesser degree, regarding killing the others caught in the blast)? Cases like this show that we are willing to assign responsibility and blame, even in circumstances similar to our condition due to original sin.

My thesis would have a problem accounting for guilt assigned to persons who refrained from sinning until their last possible action. If I were to live sinlessly my whole life, but then, because of original sin, were to curse God on my deathbed (Sz), it isn't clear that I could be held responsible for that act. That *specific* action would become unavoidable, and guilt for it appears to be excluded. Similarly, the kidnap victim might well remain entirely blameless, if he only released the trigger in dying of exhaustion. However, with regard to sinning, the simple truth is that no one who survives past (early) childhood waits till the end of his or her life to sin.[9] Indeed, God might — through his middle knowledge — choose to create only those possible humans who freely would sin in some action prior to their last opportunity. In that way, God could preserve the justice of his condemnation for our sins, by eliminating any instances in which someone's committed sin would be unavoidable due to original sin.

However, my view still faces the objection that our responsibility for our sins may be significantly diminished; therefore, punishment might be inappropriate. As admitted above, the kidnap-victim certainly bears less responsibility for the death of his business rival than if he had set up the bomb himself. But the key is, he is responsible to *some* extent and does incur *some* blame. Similarly, lessened responsibility for sin may still allow God justly to blame and punish us. Even hell might yet be jus-tifiable punishment. Aquinas points out that any unrepented sin against the infinite majesty of God constitutes an infinitely grave and eternal of-fense (*On Evil*, q.1, a.5, rep.15; q.2, a.10, resp; q.7, a.10, rep.1). And infinity reduced by any portion or percentage leaves infinity, so an eternity in hell might be appropriate punishment even for diminished-responsibility sins. Thus, while our responsibility for our committed sins might be less-ened by the necessitating impact of original sin, that guilt is not removed. On that account, God justly can punish us for those sinful acts.

Further, by placing the focus of responsibility and blame on specific committed sins, this argument can offer additional support for the pa-per's first main point. One problem for the first argument — that God could be justified in creating us in the state of original sin — was that God's moral demands seemed illegitimate, given his creating us in a con-dition from which we are unable to fulfill those demands. However, we now see that God's moral requirements can be understood from two per-spectives. First, we might think that God commands us not to be sinners. Second, we might view God's laws as forbidding us to commit any par-

9. Here it might be objected: But what about infants who die unbaptized? They clearly don't commit any actual sins. Are they condemned merely because of original sin? In fact, I think my view can answer this query better than the traditional, main-stream view of original sin. It seems quite possible that such infants would be *saved*, for if Christ's death-to-sin can be shared by the living through baptism, couldn't it also be shared by the dead through death itself? So perhaps infants lose their original sin-fulness in death, and thus approach judgment as true innocents. Note, too, that even if older, guilty sinners also share in Christ's death when they die — and so lose the de-fect of original sin — they would still be subject to judgment for their committed sins (unless they had accepted Christ, of course). Thus, while universal infant salvation is compatible with my view, universal salvation is certainly not entailed by it.

ticular sins. From the prior perspective, God requires more than we are capable of doing, given original sin — but not so, from the latter. Even while acting from original sin's disordered disposition, we still possess the freedom to perform or to avoid individual sins as their opportunities arise. Therefore, if God's moral law forbids specific commissions of sins, then it does *not* demand more than we're capable of doing.

Now perhaps this seems like a distinction without a real difference. After all, if I'm able to refrain from performing (S1), and from (S2), and from (S3), and so on through (Sz), doesn't that mean that I'm able to refrain from becoming an actual sinner? Shouldn't the conjunction of the possible refrainings imply that the disjunction of possible sins may be false? No. Even if it's possible for me to refrain at every opportunity to sin that I face, that does not mean it's possible for me to refrain from becoming a sinner. I think we frequently see analogous examples of this point. As I write this, my beloved Indiana Pacers have just lost to the boorish Miami Heat. The loss snapped a twenty-five home-game winning streak. Could the Pacers have won the game? Yes. For each of the particular home games remaining this season, can the Pacers win it? Yes. Could the team then have won a home-streak stretching from November of '99 (when the actual streak started) through the end of the '00 season? Regretfully, I think not. In general, it is within the team's power to win *in each* game they play, but it's beyond their ability to win *all* their games. Or again, consider an alcoholic who cannot make and successfully execute a decision to stay sober "for the rest of her life," but who can refrain from taking *this* drink and thereby can stay sober "one day at a time." I believe we occupy a similar position with respect to our original-sin-diminished ability to keep the moral law.

Moreover, I think this paper's interpretation of the moral law is plausible beyond the considerations of the immediate issue. After all, the divine commandments direct *specific* actions — to refrain from stealing, to honor one's parents, to love one's neighbor, etc. — so this perspective seems biblically grounded. Further, with this support added to the earlier argument, we can conclude that God's justice is not violated by creating us in an already-sinful state; for in spite of first appearances, our *original* moral abilities are not insufficient to meet his moral demands.[10] So this interpretation solves the problem that dogged the first argument.

---

10. Note that I do not claim that no one ever finds herself in the position of necessarily committing a particular sin, only that that never happens based *solely* on original sin. Such necessary sinning may still occur in other ways — perhaps through sinfully-entered dilemmas, or through the force of sinfully-gained habits — but that need not impugn the moral abilities we are originally given.

In summary, then, I propose that original sin necessitates our becoming sinners; it makes it unavoidable that we shall actually commit sins. Given its unavoidability, I do not think the *state* of being a sinner can count as blameworthy or as a source of guilt. However, original sin does not necessitate the commission of any *particular* sinful action. Hence God may justly blame and punish us for our committed sins, which confer guilt because of their avoidability.

Joining this argument to the first, I submit that God's moral uprightness and justice are compatible with creating us in the severely limited and disordered condition of original sin, but that we are guilty and blameworthy only for the individual sins we actually commit. We cannot claim any moral obligation on God with respect to the status of our creation — i.e., to the capacities and powers we possess by nature — no matter the limits imposed. Moreover, God might justifiably create us in the punitive state earned by our first parent, if God knows through his middle knowledge that we would freely have rebelled just as Adam did. However, while our creation in original sin is thus morally justified, that does not make original sin a morally guilty state. Further, if original sin necessitates that we actually sin, the state of being an actual sinner remains guiltless too. But by distinguishing the necessity of sinning from the necessity of committing a particular sin, we can see how our individual sins may not be necessary, but rather may be freely committed. Thus God can justly blame and punish us, because those sins can still be matters of responsibility and guilt.

I think this view of "innocent sinfulness and guilty sin" upholds the righteousness of God; preserves the essential inheritance and corruptive power of original sin; and leaves human freedom intact enough to provide grounds for moral responsibility, so that our committed sins may be our own and no fault of God's. On that account, in contrast to my professor's warnings, I think my questioning has brought me to a more convinced reverence for God's holiness, and to a more convicted realization of my own guilt.

Faith Confronts Evil

Barbara Omolade

In 1761, a young girl "snatched from Afric's distant happy seat" huddled in a corner of a Boston slave market. "Born in Africa, captured, enslaved, and transported via the notorious transatlantic crossing known as the Middle Passage," this girl "was sold in Boston . . . to John Wheatley as a personal servant to his wife Susannah." By allowing their young slave, called Phillis, to read and write, the Wheatleys recognized and encouraged her gift of poetic expression. John Wheatley helped to authenticate and later managed the publication of Phillis Wheatley's writings, and in 1773 she "became the first African and only the second woman in America to publish a book of poetry."[1]

In spite of the privileges of travel and learning she received as a slave who wrote poetry, Phillis Wheatley declared in a 1774 letter to Reverend Samson Occom, a Mohegan minister,

> . . . in every human Breast, God has implanted a Principle which we call Love of Freedom; it is impatient of Oppression, and pants for Deliverance; and by the Leave of our Modern Egyptians I will assert, that the same Principle lives in us.[2]

---

1. Katherine Clay Bassard, *Spiritual Interrogations: Culture, Gender, Community in Early African American Women's Writing* (Princeton, N.J.: Princeton University Press, 1999), p. 30.

2. John C. Shields, ed., *The Collected Works of Phillis Wheatley*, The Schomburg Library of Nineteenth-Century Black Women Writers (New York: Oxford University Press, 1988), p. 177.

In the eighteenth and nineteenth centuries, African American Christians, or Afro-Christians, such as Phillis Wheatley often compared white America to Pharaonic Egypt and their own enslavement to that of the enslaved children of Israel. Inspired by divine intervention on behalf of the Israelites, Afro-Christians prayed for deliverance from their own hard-hearted owners. They looked to God for a Moses to lead them out of bondage.

A delivering Moses did arise from among the suffering Africans. Named Harriet Tubman, she was an escaped slave who made several dangerous trips south to lead hundreds of the enslaved — young and elderly, men and women — out of slavery and to help them settle in New York and Canada. Tubman once declared, "When I think of all the groans and tears and prayers I've heard on the plantations, and remember that God is a prayer-hearing God, I feel that his time is drawing near. . . . God's time is always near. . . He gave me my strength, and He set the North star in the heavens, he meant that I should be free."[3]

Although they experienced different forms of slavery in different historical eras, both Harriet Tubman and Phillis Wheatley held on to faith in God's promises of deliverance and liberty for themselves and their people. In speech acts such as prayers, songs, speeches, diaries, sermons, poetry, letters, and interviews, other African American Christian women of the antebellum era, among them Sojourner Truth and Jarena Lee, expressed similar views. They often spoke in the tradition of a "black Jeremiah," constantly warning whites of the judgment coming from God for their support of the sin of slavery.[4] Undaunted by the consequences of her assaults against slavery, Maria Stewart, an Afro-Christian orator, declared that she was not afraid to "suffer for pleading the cause of oppressed Africa" because she was "firmly persuaded that the God in whom I trust is able to protect me from the rage and malice of mine enemies and from them that will rise up against me. . . ."[5]

In this study, the antebellum United States is considered an evil society because its racialized slave system and national polity oppressed and dehumanized both enslaved and free Africans causing them enormous suffering, deprivation, and social dislocation. However, in a twist that sug-

3. John Blassingame, ed., *Slave Testimony: Two Centuries of Letters, Speeches, Interviews, and Autobiographies* (Baton Rouge: Louisiana State University Press, 1977), pp. 463-64.

4. Marilyn Richardson, ed., *Maria W. Stewart: America's First Black Woman Political Reporter* (Bloomington, Ind.: Indiana University Press, 1987), p. 16.

5. Richardson, *Maria W. Stewart*, p. 30.

gests divine intervention, the racist and culturally restrictive Protestantism practiced by white British colonialists and their American descendents was transformed by African Americans, especially women, into a faith that "unleashed their silenced tongues" and unfettered their restricted bodies. Rather than addressing the theodicy question of how a good God could allow human suffering, this paper seeks to understand how African American Christian women sustained their faith while living in an evil society.

Their experiences demonstrate that faith provided the enslaved with a way to construct a symbolic universe with a moral and social order that could then frame their fight for freedom. Not all African American Christians had such faith or were consciously involved in these constructions. Many had instrumental or pragmatic religious beliefs that were mixed with African primal religious notions. Others were drawn to Christianity for the benefit of the social services and companionship that came from belonging to the church. Many turned to Christianity for a rationale for their resistance to slavery and a justification for their acts against slaveholders.

While many women who resisted slavery are known today as abolitionists and supporters of women's rights, they are less recognized as devoted Christians who considered their oppression in symbolic terms informed by their faith. They viewed Jesus as their personal redeemer and spiritual friend, and they called on his Holy Spirit for help in times of trouble. These women were also compelled to speak about the enslaving grip of sin on all human beings, and how faith could confront both individual and societal evil. Afro-Christian women understood that they were not wrestling by themselves against human enemies and their oppressive social system, but were rather engaged in spiritual warfare *with* God ". . . against principalities, against powers, against the rulers of the darkness of this world, against spiritual wickedness in high places" (Eph. 6:12). One enslaved woman explained,

> . . . I know nothing about what God said to the prophets of old, but I do know what he has said to me. And I know that I have a counselor in him that never fails. When danger comes, he works on my mind and conscience and causes me to walk around the snares set for me by my enemies.[6]

When the European rulers and owners began to use race and religion as the rationale for their political and economic expansion on race,

6. Clifton Johnson, ed., *God Struck Me Dead: Voices of Ex-Slaves* (Cleveland: Pilgrim Press, 1993), p. 157.

the struggle of African Americans became a moral and spiritual one as well as a political one. The treatment of Africans by Europeans was not merely exploitative but replete with gruesome and evil acts. Christianity posits that the source of these kinds of acts lies in the innate human capacity for sin. The sin nature is at the heart of the internal and eternal battle between evil and good. Yet the sacrifice of Jesus enables believers to overcome this capacity and, when imbued with his Holy Spirit, become "more than conquerors" against evil.

African American women of faith became pivotal in the spiritual and political battle against the evils of slavery and racism. As abolitionists and prayer warriors, these women of faith fought against the sin of slavery and the slavery of sin using the spiritual weapons of speaking and preaching, writing and talking in prophetic and political language against evil. Along with African American men, these women carved out spiritual spaces and built churches where they worshipped and fellowshipped according to their own cultural values and political views. From these sites, they envisioned and struggled for emancipation from both sin and societal evil.

Societal Evil

> When I looked for good, then evil came unto me: and when I waited
> for light, there came darkness.
>
> Job 30:26

We have come to view evil social orders as twentieth-century phenomena, as dictatorships and other totalitarian regimes that use technology and bureaucracy to commit mass murder and torture. We now measure such evil by the enormity of senseless suffering and oppression they inflict upon innocent victims. Yet in the slave coffles and coastal factories we see the models for the means of mass deportation used by more recent regimes. Slave ships and plantations were precursors of concentration camps and forced labor camps. The death of millions in the middle passage foretold the concentration camps of the Nazis, the gulags of Stalin, the killing fields of Cambodia, and the mass murders of Rwanda. While no evidence suggests a direct link between the Atlantic slave trade and American slave societies and twentieth-century regimes of malevolence and inhumanity, they certainly share similar themes, patterns, and practices. The racist ideology adhered to by slaveholders and by ordinary citizens in the antebellum United States could be understood as the primer for Nazi societal evil and ideas of racial superiority.

For the purposes of this essay, an evil society is one in which legitimate rulers use power or force to commit rational, deliberate, and conscious malicious acts against a group designated racially inferior or genetically unfit. These evil acts must not be equated with mere rage. A society attacked by an enemy frequently retaliates with brute force, but an evil social order commits acts that inflict great harm on internal, noncombatant populations: men, women, the elderly, and children. Indeed, all members of the victimized groups are viewed as criminals, whose presence, rather than their commission of any specific deed, is a crime.

In an evil society, the military, police, and civilian militia routinely use violence as well as public shaming and humiliation rites against individuals in the victim group while closely monitoring all aspects of their behavior. Regardless of whether the intention is genocide, in evil societies both laws and customs support torture and abuse as a precursor for and adjunct to extreme exploitation and ultimately extermination. While acts of torture, shame, and brutality afford political, economic, and ideological benefits to rulers and citizens, dehumanization and excessive sadism exposes the demonic or irrational amoral character of societal evil.

Rulers of evil societies depend on ordinary citizens to go along with their views and with their treatment of victims. Indeed, ordinary citizens are permitted and even encouraged to terrorize, rape, rob, and even murder members of the targeted group. Because of the human tendency to compartmentalize acts of evil, they can do this and still view themselves as morally decent, especially in their own communities whose "common-sense morality draws a sharp distinction between family members and friends, on the one hand, and those not close to us, on the other."[7] Sometimes ordinary citizens in evil societies will commit impulsive and limited acts of kindness toward the targeted group, but only a few would place themselves and their families at risk of ostracism or even punishment by doing so consistently or openly. Most often citizens go along with evil acts because they hold the same or similar views about the superiority of their race, culture, history, or religion in the social order. Most believe that members of the victimized group are inferior outsiders and pariahs who, at least on some level, deserve the maltreatment they are receiving.

---

7. Laurence Mordekhai Thomas, *Vessels of Evil: American Slavery and the Holocaust* (Philadelphia: Temple University Press, 1993), p. 46.

In evil social orders that last for several decades or generations, brute force and sadistic violence are necessary, but they are not sufficient for controlling the victimized population. Evil societies that are multigenerational must also control the reality of everyday life, the symbolic universes, and the minds of their victims. The racial social order in the British colonies and later in the United States lasted from the early 1600s until 1865. The maintenance of slavery and race in antebellum America, for example, required that free and enslaved Africans submit to or accept without question the whites' worldview, in particular whites' natural right to rule them. Crushing the minds of the Africans became as important to sustaining the evil social order as systematic violence and humiliation. Owners, rulers, and even ordinary citizens fostered their social death by attempting to destroy and at least contain the capacity of Africans to envision or remember themselves as social subjects with the ability to construct their own everyday reality.

Philosopher Charles Mills suggests that

> To be an African American was to be, in Aristotle's conceptualization, a living tool, property with a soul, whose moral status was tugged in different directions by the dehumanizing requirements of slavery on the one hand and the (grudging and sporadic) white recognition of the objective properties blacks possessed on the other, generating an insidious array of cognitive and moral splits in both black and white consciousness.[8]

The founding of the Atlantic world split human experience into whiteness and blackness, in which whites were considered human and blacks their antithesis. Moreover, Christianity and democracy were also divided by race. Social evil coexisted with Christianity, which purported to be the nation's code of moral goodness; and its democratic principles were conjoined to white nationalism and African American suffering and social death. To survive in the midst of these conflicts and splits meant that Africans had to construct and create an oppositional moral universe of their own while also resisting the evil social order in all ways possible.

---

8. Charles W. Mills, *Blackness Visible: Essays on Philosophy and Race* (Ithaca, N.Y.: Cornell University Press, 1998), p. 7.

Societal Evil, Slavery, and Social Death

We have as far as possible closed every avenue by which light may enter the slave's Mind. If we could extinguish his capacity to see the light our work would be done, Then they would be on the level of the beast of the field and we should be safe.

Senator Henry Berry, 1832

The emergence of the Atlantic world in the 1500s signaled an abrupt removal of Africans from societies of their own making to ones replete with violence, chaos, and racial hostility directed at them. For nearly four subsequent centuries, western Europeans, especially the English, French, Dutch, Spanish, and Portuguese, would engage in economic and political ventures of conquest and settlement in the Americas. The development of the Americas depended upon one of history's largest forced removals of a human population and involved the mass dislocation, forced labor, and enormous suffering of millions of enslaved Africans. From the early 1500s to the late 1800s, "upwards of 12 million Africans survived the middle passage and were distributed throughout the Americas — North, Central, and South America — and the Caribbean." Twelve million survived, but between fifty and one hundred million Africans lost their lives in all the facets of the slave trade, capture, transshipment, and sales.[9] The surviving captives entered the netherworld, a "hell without fire" where, although physically alive, they were considered subhuman and socially dead by their European captors and owners and worked like chattel.

Theologian William Jones describes the suffering endured by Africans in America as "mal-distributed, enormous, and non-catastrophic."[10] It occurred within a series of violent dislocations that began when individuals were bought from local slave markets or suddenly captured from their villages. They were then marched from thousands of villages located along winding rivers and roads that crisscrossed the coasts and interior of West and Central Africa. After being sold and even re-sold by several African owners, the enslaved arrived at the coast, to wait in forts and "factories" run by European traders before being transported across the ocean.

9. Howard Dobson, "The Slave Trade and the Making of the Modern World," *New York Amsterdam News* (September 30–October 6, 1999), pp. 10-11.

10. William R. Jones, "Theodicy: The Controlling Category for Black Theology," *Journal of Religious Thought* 30 (1973): 34.

The captive Africans were then plunged into the Middle Passage, an abyss of darkness, stench, and terror aboard ships that took up to two months to cross the Atlantic. As they boarded the ships, both men and women were stripped of their clothing and had their heads shaved. Historian Michael Gomez states that "the psychological implications of denuding are both clear and clearly intended — profound humiliation and disintegration of identity."[11]

While men were crowded and chained in the hold, women were allowed small quarters nearer to the deck, where they were frequently subjected to rape and sexual abuse by the sailors. African captives were often suicidal and depressed. But the Middle Passage was, of course, only a prelude to further violence, shame, and displacement. There would be more torturous journeys along the American coastal ports, from slave market to owner. Many enslaved Africans eventually went to work in the American wilderness, chopping down forests and preparing the land for growing the cash crops that would make their owners wealthy. Others worked feeding and caring for the personal needs of their owners' families.

In his comparative study of slavery worldwide, sociologist Orlando Patterson observed that much of the hard work, physical punishment, social stigma and alienation endured by enslaved African Americans were common to slaves in nearly all societies. He asserts that slaves are always considered "socially dead" because "slavery is the permanent, violent domination of natally alienated and generally dishonored persons."[12] Patterson also concludes that slavery in the United States was harsher than in other slave systems. In other slave societies, the enslaved performed a wide variety of administrative, military, and other functions, often in service of the state. Gifted slaves were rewarded with manumission or greater rights. Moreover, other societies provided more consistent and systematic forms of manumission and privileges for slave children, especially those fathered by their owners.

In the first century of British North American colonization, the slave system was not unlike these more flexible forms. Imported Africans entered a society where they usually worked and lived among the laboring classes of indentured and free white workers and often worked alongside their

11. Michael Gomez, *Exchanging Our Country Marks: The Transformation of African Identities in the Colonial and Antebellum South* (Chapel Hill, N.C.: University of North Carolina Press, 1998), p. 159.

12. Orlando Patterson, *Slavery and Social Death: A Comparative Study* (Cambridge, Mass.: Harvard University Press, 1982), p. 13.

owners. In his study of American slavery, Peter Kolchin noted that "their small size and dispersed nature facilitated rapid acculturation and individual autonomy" of enslaved Africans.[13] But during the late seventeenth century and the eighteenth century, as plantation economies grew, the need for enslaved African labor increased and slaves' condition worsened. The previous mixed labor arrangement gave way to "a true slave society, the transformation in which some people were slaves (relatively few, at first) into one in which slave labor formed the basis of the economy and social order."[14] As the thirteen British colonies moved toward independence,

> members of the aristocratic elite espoused in the political arena of the colonial society the virtues of republicanism, self-government, and freedom in . . . their relations with England. At the same time they stood as white masters atop a racially segmented colonial structure they had built on the backs of the enslaved blacks.[15]

The national leaders professed democracy but remained committed to a social and political ethos that promoted racial definitions of citizenship and personhood in its laws and founding documents. The new nation was divided into free and slave states within which a fully instituted racial slave society emerged that regarded enslavement as the perpetual state for all Africans for all times. In order to maximize blacks' perpetual and unfettered use as laborers, all efforts were made by white owners and the ruling elite to deny them any legal or social recourses or protections. Under the confluence of slavery and freedom, democracy and racial dictatorship that defined the new nation, both free and enslaved African Americans endured enormous suffering. One North Carolina minister, a slaveholder, admitted with resignation that "slavery and tyranny must go together — and there is no such thing as having an obedient and useful slave without the painful exercise of undue and tyrannical authority."[16]

According to historian Lerone Bennett, enslaved Africans were subject to their owners' "fascist regimentation." He adds that "military disci-

13. Peter Kolchin, *American Slavery, 1619-1877* (New York: Hill and Wang, 1993), p. 48.

14. Kolchin, *American Slavery*, p. 28.

15. Benjamin Ringer and Elinor Lawless, *Race-Ethnicity and Society* (New York: Routledge, 1989), p. 106.

16. James Oakes, *The Ruling Race: History of American Slaveholders* (New York: W. W. Norton & Co., 1998), p. 109.

pline prevailed on most plantations which had a chain of command rang-
ing downwards from the plantation owner to the white overseer and the
black driver."[17] In addition, "an immense police apparatus was created
by every Southern state to awe the slaves and to beat them into submission. Slave patrols, authorized by state laws, policed plantation areas and
made periodic searches of slave cabins."[18]

As this restrictive form of African bondage grew rather than de-
clined, African Americans found themselves living under a "racial dictatorship" that reinforced the tyranny of the slave system and extended to
Africans who were not slaves. Denied political and social rights, these
blacks usually lived in all-black enclaves and worked in menial jobs
while surrounded by a sea of hostile white citizens. Routine racial terror
and threats of violence reinforced a rigid color line that defined racial
identity and social place. Owners and other white people tended to regard Africans as subpersons. According to the philosopher Charles Mills,
"the peculiar status of a subperson is that it is an entity which, because of
phenotype, seems, (from . . . the perspective of the categorizer) human in
some respects but not in others. It is a human . . . who, though adult is not
fully a person."[19]

The suffering of African Americans was an ethnic suffering that did
not strike quickly and then leave after a short terrible siege.[20] It was
intergenerational, mundane, and ordinary — and therefore enormous. In
order to survive the multiple assaults of being considered subpersons
within a racial dictatorship, Africans had to develop multiple ways to resist both the physical manifestations and the social and spiritual dimensions of both slavery and racism. Africans throughout the Atlantic world
sought social space in order to sustain their families and build communities where they could be free of direct control of the racial dictators. Social
space offered Africans in the Americas a place where they could interpret
their condition, comfort each other, and plan ways to develop effective
means of resistance. For Africans in the Caribbean and Brazil, their large
numbers on vast plantations facilitated the creation of a social world that
resembled the African societies left behind. But in areas like the United
States, where they were scattered among and dominated by European
populations, Africans had to (re)construct other kinds of social worlds.

17. Lerone Bennett, *The Shaping of Black America* (Chicago: Johnson Publishing
Co., 1970), p. 147.
18. Bennett, *The Shaping of Black America*, p. 147.
19. Mills, *Blackness Visible*, p. 6.
20. William Jones, "Theodicy," pp. 34-35.

While it took several generations, eventually both enslaved and free Africans during the antebellum era created communities framed and facilitated by Christianity.

Gender made the entire enterprise of creating supporting community while living in the midst of the everyday reality of the racial dictatorship and evil social order more complicated. First of all, in all societies women's everyday social world differs dramatically from that of men, even when both are enslaved. Sociologist Dorothy Smith notes that

> Characteristically for women (as also for others in the society similarly excluded), the organization of daily experience, the work routines, and the structuring of our lives through time have been and to a very large extent still are determined and ordered by processes external to, and beyond, our everyday world.[21]

Secondly, in the United States, gender roles and gender-based divisions of labor constrained all women. White women in antebellum America often viewed themselves as enslaved to the patriarchy just as Africans were enslaved to white owners. Indeed, most white women shared household labor with their African American women slaves and servants. They worked together to prepare and serve meals, nurse the sick, and care for children and the elderly. Equality between black and white women who daily co-labored in the white household went only as far as the racial limits set by white women and their men, however. While enslaved and coerced into helping white women sustain their families and households, African American women were prevented from being solely tied to the domestic concerns of their own families. Moreover, household labor reinforced rather than detracted from racial abuse and domination.

While the abuse of enslaved women was endemic to all slave societies, sexual abuse of African American women often within the owner's household was among the most egregious moral evils in antebellum America. Slave women, historian Deborah White asserts,

> were the only women in America who were sexually exploited with impunity, stripped and whipped with a lash, and worked like oxen. In the nineteenth century, when the nation was preoccupied with keeping women in the home and protecting them, only slave women

21. Dorothy Smith, *The Everyday World as Problematic: A Feminist Sociology* (Boston: Northeastern University Press, 1987), p. 65.

were so totally unprotected by men or by law. Only black women had their womanhood so totally denied.[22]

While also forced to labor like men in both the homes and the fields of their owners, enslaved women were also expected to bear children without any sustained concern for their health, choice, or virtue. As one former slave remembers, owners factored pregnancy and childbirth into their profits: "My mother was young — just 15 or 16 years old. She had 14 children and you know that meant a lots of wealth."[23] Often literally worked to death by the double burden of childbearing and forced labor, the production and procreation extracted from African women made the system successful. The United States had become the only New World slave society to successfully reproduce its population by natural increase. As Raboteau notes, "By the time of emancipation in 1865, the number of slaves in the United States has grown to above four million, a figure ten times the number imported from abroad."[24]

Although the slave society in the United States was populated with large numbers of sexually abused and overworked women and children often enslaved by their own fathers, owners of these women and children suffered neither penalty nor censure for adultery, sexual abuse, or cruelty. The usual patriarchal standard of the father recognizing and caring for his children did not apply to the progeny of owners and enslaved women. These men continued to be regarded by their white families and communities as decent husbands and fathers and civic, business, and religious leaders. The moral implication of the sexual abuse of African American women was simply ignored.

But being tied to the daily rhythms, routines, and patterns of white households gave African American women access to "the inner and backstage world" of white men and their families. They saw contradiction and irony between their claims of racial purity and their actual sexual behavior. They knew intimate details about their owners' women and children, and silently they watched and waited for ways to use the knowledge they gleaned to sustain their own families. Enslaved women used their forced participation in the construction of the social world of

22. Deborah Gray White, *Aren't I a Woman? Female Slaves in the Plantation South* (New York: W. W. Norton & Co., 1985), p. 162.

23. *Unwritten History of Slavery* (Nashville: Fisk University Social Science Institute, 1945), p. 2.

24. Albert J. Raboteau, *Slave Religion: The Invisible Institution in the Antebellum South* (New York: Oxford, 1978), p. 91.

the white owners and their families to sustain a furtive social world for their loved ones and children (including the children fathered by their owners). According to historian Angela Davis,

> ... with the Black slave woman ... in the infinite anguish of ministering to the needs of the men and children around her through the daily routines of domestic household labor, she was performing the only labor of the slave community which could not be directly and immediately claimed by the oppressor. . . .[25]

It is "[p]recisely through performing the drudgery which has long been a central expression of the socially conditioned inferiority of women, the Black woman in chains could help lay the foundation for some degree of autonomy for herself and her men. . . . Even as she was suffering under her unique oppression as a female, Black women were thrust into the center of the slave community and became essential to its survival."[26]

Addressing the basic needs of both white and African American household members afforded African Americans a unique angle of vision on racial dictatorship and societal evil. Social theorist Patricia Hill Collins notes that

> Accounts of Black domestic workers stress the sense of self-affirmation the women experienced at seeing white power demystified. But on another level these Black women knew that they could never belong to their white 'families', that they were economically exploited workers and thus would remain outsiders. The result was curious outsider-within stance, a peculiar marginality that stimulated a special Black women's perspective.[27]

From their outsider-within stance as enslaved domestic workers African American women attempted to "make sense of" the evil interiority of slavery and racism. They created Christian speech acts reflecting their experiences of and resistance to the unholy mixture of sexual exploitation and white Christian religiosity, and the curious juxtaposition of democracy and racial terror. Faith and speech acts enabled African American women to endure daily exposure to the contradictions of evil and encour-

25. Angela Davis, "Reflections on the Black Woman's Role in the Community of Slaves," *The Black Scholar* (November-December 1981), p. 7.

26. Davis, "Reflections on the Black Woman's Role," p. 7.

27. Patricia Hill Collins, *Black Feminist Thought: Knowledge, Consciousness, and the Politics of Empowerment* (Boston: Unwin Hyman Press, 1990), p. 11.

aged their constant struggles to "shine as lights in the midst of a crooked and perverse nation" (Phil. 2:15).

African American Women Confront Evil

In her poem to the Rt. Hon. William, Earl of Dartmouth, Phillis Wheatley asks:

> Should you, my lord, while you peruse my song,
> Wonder from whence my love of Freedom sprung,
> Whence flow these wishes for the common good,
> By feelings hearts alone best understood,
> I, young in life, by seeming cruel fate
> Was snatched from Afric's fancy'd happy seat; . . .
> Steel'd was that soul and by no misery moved
> That from a father seiz'd his babe beloved:
> Such, such my case. And can I then but pray
> Others may never feel tyrannic sway?[28]

Wheatley learned English quickly and wrote poems, like this one to Lord Dartmouth, that reflected her thoughts about being captured and enslaved. Her work captures the excitement of both the Great Awakening and the American Revolution. She wrote at the "beginning of the African American community building, black collective consciousness, and African American cultural production."[29] During her lifetime, "African Americans became an identifiable collective in terms of language, religious practice, and literary and cultural production."[30] She was a precursor of both illiterate and literate African American Christian women who relied on their faith to help them interpret the promise and the sorrow of slavery and the promise of freedom in the "perverse nation" in which they lived.

In the seven existing letters of her correspondence to Obour Tanner, her confidante and fellow enslaved woman, Phillis Wheatley discusses the meaning of the "saving change" of conversion to Christianity for herself and her people. In her May 19, 1772, letter to Tanner, she says "it gives me very great pleasure to hear of so many of my nation, seeking

28. Shields, ed., *Collected Works of Phillis Wheatley*, p. 63.
29. Clay Bassard, *Spiritual Interrogations*, p. 13.
30. Clay Bassard, *Spiritual Interrogations*, p. 23.

with eagerness the way of true felicity" — that is, becoming Christians.[31] In another letter she tells Tanner of her "desire to dwell on and delight in him alone above every other object."[32] Katherine Clay Bassard concludes that "for the two women, both brought from Africa to serve in America as slaves, religious conversion provided a common experience and the language of Christianity provided a common language in America."[33]

In his study *Christianity in Africa*, Ghanaian theologian Kwame Bediako posits that, although transmitted by European colonial missionaries, Christianity was interpreted and appropriated by Africans for themselves. The deeper insight, Bediako argues, is

> that Christ already present in the situation, called in His messengers to that by proclamation and incarnation, might be made manifest. The cross-cultural transmission is thus a confirmation of the divine initiative in the local situation, extending its ramification beyond the range of former horizons, and demonstrating the ecumenical significance of local history.[34]

Therefore, rather than coercion to white religion, Africans and their descendents in the Americas saw in the biblical descriptions of Christ and the moves of God confirmation of their own humanity and their individual and collective search for the divine. In North America, African conversion to Christianity was intertwined with acquisition of the English language. By the late eighteenth century, most free and American-born Africans were fluent in English and had heard about Christianity from other Africans who learned to read and interpret the Bible. As slavery spread with the forced migration of the enslaved from the upper south to western and lower southern regions during the antebellum period, Christianity also spread among the enslaved. Where possible, oral or written literacy and knowledge about the Bible accompanied its spread.

Bediako observes that, because of Pentecost,

> language itself becomes, then, not merely a social or psychological phenomenon, but a theological one as well. . . . God speaks to men and women — always in the vernacular. . . . The ability to hear in

31. Shields, ed., *Collected Works of Phillis Wheatley*, p. 165.
32. Shields, ed., *Collected Works of Phillis Wheatley*, p. 181.
33. Clay Bassard, *Spiritual Interrogations*, p. 23.
34. Kwame Bediako, *Christianity in Africa: The Renewal of a Non-Western Religion* (Edinburgh: Edinburgh University Press, 1997), p. 226.

one's own language and to express in one's own language one's response to the message which one receives, must lie at the heart of all authentic religious encounter with the divine realm.[35]

Whether it was the languages spoken by African captives or the Africanized English of their progeny, hearing the Word in their own vernacular gave Africans an authentic and autonomous understanding of Christianity that went beyond the intentions or interpretations of European American transmitters. As purveyors of societal evil, these white Christians used religion to rationalize slavery and racism and demonize African primal religions. Most owners refused to allow enslaved Christians to read the Bible, observe the Sabbath, or participate in the church as equals.

Yet because it was heard and interpreted in their own vernacular, African American Christians were able to construct affirming African cultural and social liturgies and theologies. Christianity gave them access to God and a (re)constructed spiritual life that continued rather than disrupted their connections to Africa. As they went beyond the imposed limitations of their everyday reality to speak and pray in their own voice, Afro-Christians increased their faith in the God of the Bible. African American women and men believed that the biblical God was no respecter of persons (per Acts 10:34) and that in the church "there is neither bond nor free, there is neither male nor female: for ye are all one in Christ Jesus" (Gal. 3:27). Because of their experiences of humiliation and suffering, they identified with Christ and believed him to be in their midst (per Matt. 18:20).

While they shared the same basic tenets of faith, the location and legal status of African American believers did shape their religious practices. Free African American believers, especially in the North and Midwest, developed churches and denominations independent of white control. There they could freely worship God, develop their religion, and support their own leaders and causes. According to historian Elizabeth Higgenbotham, the African American church was more than a center for worship. It also functioned as a "discursive, critical arena — a public square in which values and issues were aired, debated and disseminated throughout the larger black community."[36] Although they were not citi-

35. Bediako, *Christianity in Africa*, p. 60.

36. Elizabeth Brooks Higgenbotham, *Righteous Discontent: The Women's Movement in the Black Baptist Church, 1880-1920* (Cambridge, Mass.: Harvard University Press), p. 7.

zens and had no legal protections, free African Americans vigorously protested the enslavement of their brethren and made their churches centers of anti-slavery activity and actual stops on the Underground Railroad.

In the meantime, enslaved African American Christians were severely restricted, punished, or even martyred by their owners for practicing their faith. While some owners required attendance at church services and family prayers, the enslaved had to read the Bible in secret and could only freely worship in invisible and underground churches. These secret services provided arenas for the enslaved to learn about God, help each other, and pray for an end to their bondage. Increasingly, enslaved African Americans shared powerful spiritual and political networks with their free brethren. Their simultaneous attacks on slavery were slowly eviscerating the institution.

Both free and enslaved African American women expanded the reach and meaning of Christianity to help them "wade through their sorrows, managing their suffering, rather than being managed by it."[37] Hardly docile believers, these women were emboldened "to go beyond biblical sanction in order to denounce contemporary injustices such as slavery, racism, sex discrimination, wherever these evils seemed to be hindering God's work."[38] Through preaching and praying, singing and testimony, as well as their writings, they used their voices to both profess faith and protest bondage. The literate, mainly free women wrote or dictated their personal testimonies or spiritual biographies for publication and distribution. Enslaved and illiterate women dictated their stories and testimonies to abolitionist activists and journalists. Both described their conversion, sanctification, and faith walk in terms of personal encounters and visions of Jesus and his Spirit and attributed their acts of courage and perseverance to God's intervening and ordering their steps.

For thirty years, Sojourner Truth was the public face and voice of these dual dimensions of antebellum African American Christian women. Truth was above all an itinerant preacher; she traveled throughout America between 1840 and 1870 condemning slavery and speaking

37. M. Shawn Copeland, "Wading through Many Sorrows: Toward a Theology of Suffering in Womanist Perspective," in *A Troubling in My Soul: Womanist Perspectives on Evil and Suffering*, ed. Emilie Townes (Maryknoll, N.Y.: Orbis Books, 1996), p. 118.

38. William Andrews, ed., *Sisters of the Spirit: Three Black Women's Autobiographies of the Nineteenth Century* (Bloomington, Ind.: Indiana University Press, 1986), p. 16.

out for freedom, women's rights, and temperance. Biographer Nell Painter declares that "No other woman who had been through the ordeal of slavery managed to survive with sufficient strength, poise and self-confidence to become a public presence over the long term. . . . Truth would have explained that the force that brought her from the soul murder of slavery into the authority of public advocacy was the power of the Holy Spirit."[39] By the time of her death, no other African American woman's life and thought had been as chronicled and publicized. Though illiterate, her self-published biography, *The Narrative of Sojourner Truth*, dictated to Olive Gilbert in 1850, "marks a turning point . . . her first step into deliberate representation of self."[40]

Painter explains that in 1875, Frances Titus "republished Olive Gilbert's *Narrative* together with Truth's Book of Life — her scrapbooks."[41] While editions of Gilbert's biography are extremely rare, Titus' 1875 edition most closely approximates an authorized biography of Sojourner Truth. Since Truth could not write, this study of her faith walk and life combines Titus' 1875 reprint of Olive Gilbert's *Narrative*, an oral history, with contemporary biographer Nell Painter's 1996 interpretive and analytical historical study *Sojourner Truth: A Life, a Symbol*.

Truth was born Isabella in the late 1700s to African-born parents, James and Elizabeth, also known as "Bomefree" and "Mau mau Bett," who were owned by Johannes Hardenbergh, a Dutch landowner in New York. Truth explained to Gilbert that "her mother talked to her of God" and that even as a young child, she was "ever mindful of her mother's injunctions, spreading out in detail all her troubles before God, imploring and firmly trusting him to send her deliverance from them."[42] Her prayers, or "talks with God," as she called them, were partially the Lord's Prayer spoken in Low Dutch as taught by her mother. Truth explained that she would implore and ask God to help her "out of all her difficulties" and "she talked to God as familiarly as if he had been a creature like herself."[43]

In 1807 or 1808 Isabella, then nine years old, was separated from her parents and became the only slave of a local farm family. She was subse-

---

39. Nell Irvin Painter, *Sojourner Truth: A Life, a Symbol* (New York: W. W. Norton & Co., 1996), p. 4.

40. Painter, *Sojourner Truth*, p. 110.

41. Painter, *Sojourner Truth*, p. 259.

42. Olive Gilbert, ed., *Narrative of Sojourner Truth: A Bondswoman of Olden Time, Edited by Frances Titus for the Author* (Battle Creek, Mich., 1875), p. 59.

43. Gilbert, *Narrative of Sojourner Truth*, p. 61.

quently sold twice more and stayed with the last family for sixteen years as she grew into adulthood, "married," and had five children. Like most slaves, Isabella was beaten and deprived while also suffering the physical abuse of overwork and deplorable working conditions. Painter also asserts that Truth's male and female owners also sexually and emotionally abused her.[44] Yet Truth, inspired and instructed by her mother, says she continued to pray to God.

Like most enslaved Africans, Isabella's prayers were pleas for help to survive and to be free from bondage. Emancipation of slaves in New York was a gradual and complex process that began in 1799 but would not be complete until July 4, 1827, due to a law requiring former slaves to "serve a further period of indentured servitude."[45] In 1826 Isabella's owner, John Dumont, reneged on his promise of freedom, and Isabella fully discharged her responsibilities and freed herself. That is, she "heard the voice of God instructing her when to set out on her own as a free woman."[46] Leaving an enslaved husband and four other children, Truth took her baby and went to work for the Van Wagenens, a family living nearby, where she awaited the legal end of her enslavement.

It was during this time, she told Gilbert, that "God revealed himself to her, with all the suddenness of the flash of lightning"[47] and she became aware of her sin and worthlessness. She continued "the travail of sanctification, as she wrestled with ambivalence and the experience of God's awesome, immediate presence."[48] She had a vision of Jesus as a divinity "who loved her, had always loved her, who would stand between her and God's fury."[49] Truth told Gilbert that she "felt Jesus . . . a friend, standing between me and God, through who, love flowed as from a fountain."[50]

After this powerful vision, Isabella became sanctified, born again, and baptized in the Holy Spirit, and in the years following the legal end of slavery, she lived and worked in religious communities, eventually moving to New York City. Truth had "an assurance of salvation that gave her the self-confidence to oppose the rich and powerful of this world. . . . This assurance of her sanctification and God's constant support released

44. Painter, *Sojourner Truth*, p. 15.
45. Painter, *Sojourner Truth*, p. 25.
46. Painter, *Sojourner Truth*, p. 23.
47. Gilbert, *Narrative of Sojourner Truth*, p. 65.
48. Painter, *Sojourner Truth*, p. 29.
49. Painter, *Sojourner Truth*, p. 30.
50. Gilbert, *Narrative of Sojourner Truth*, p. 69.

Isabella from the crippling conviction that she was nothing."[51] Gilbert also notes that

> The sense of her nothingness, in the eyes of those with whom she contended for her rights, sometimes fell on her like a heavy weight which nothing but her unwavering confidence in an arm which she believed to be stronger than all others combined could have raised her from her sinking spirit.[52]

Describing the legal battle she underwent to get her son out of slavery, Truth recalled that, "Oh God only could have made such people hear me; and he did it in answer to my prayers."[53]

On June 1, 1843, on Pentecost, at the leading of the Holy Spirit, Isabella Van Wagenen became Sojourner Truth, her name now defining her new spiritual calling as a traveling minister for truth. Gilbert asked whether Sojourner Truth was always her name.

> She replied "No, 'deed! My name was Isabella; but when I left the house of bondage, I left everything behind. I wa'n't goin' to keep nothin' of Egypt on me, and so I went to the Lord an' asked him to give me a new name. And the Lord gave me Sojourner, because I was to travel up and down the land, showing the people their sins, and being a sign unto them. Afterward I told the Lord I wanted another name, 'cause everybody else had two names; and the Lord gave me Truth, because I was to declare the truth to the people."[54]

She left New York "strong in the faith that her true work lay before her, and that the Lord was her director, and she doubted not that he would provide and protect her."[55] As she traveled west, "she saw her mission as lecturing to the people, testifying and exhorting them to embrace Jesus and refrain from sin."[56] While her ministry and mission led away from regular denominations and churches, Truth became nevertheless an imposing spiritual presence, ministering in various religious communities.

Gilbert gives an example of Truth's preaching and ministering by describing an encounter at a religious camp meeting in 1844. As was not un-

51. Painter, *Sojourner Truth*, p. 30.
52. Gilbert, *Narrative of Sojourner Truth*, p. 70.
53. Gilbert, *Narrative of Sojourner Truth*, p. 70.
54. Gilbert, *Narrative of Sojourner Truth*, p. 164.
55. Gilbert, *Narrative of Sojourner Truth*, p. 100.
56. Painter, *Sojourner Truth*, p. 74.

common at such meetings, a gang of violent young men interrupted the service and threatened the worshipers. Truth was preaching at the time, and at first she sought to hide, for she was the only African American present and feared being singled out for attack. But then she asked herself,

> "Shall I run away and hide from the Devil? Me, a servant of the living God? Have I not faith enough to go out and quell the mob. . . . I'll go to the rescue, and the Lord shall go with and protect me."[57]

So while the religious leaders hid and the congregation trembled, Truth continued to preach and sing until the roughnecks left.

As her reputation as an evangelist and a speaker against slavery grew, in 1851, she was invited to join the antislavery and women's rights circuit sponsored by William Lloyd Garrison. She became popular because her most political insights were peppered with biblical references, Christian songs, and wit and savvy insights. In her famous "Ain't I a Woman?" speech, delivered in 1851 at the Woman's Rights Convention in Akron, Ohio, Truth rhetorically questioned the authenticity of traditional notions of womanhood when she and hers sisters had to work like men and were oppressed as mothers. As Painter notes, she also affirmed the friendship of Jesus, "that made possible survival and autonomous action when all other means fail."[58]

Truth's remarks at the convention and in other settings became nationally known when in 1863 Harriet Beecher Stowe wrote an article entitled "Sojourner Truth, the Libyan Sibyl" for the *Atlantic Monthly*. In the article, Stowe describes an encounter that endeared Truth to white abolitionist audiences: in a Boston abolitionist meeting, after hearing Frederick Douglass despair of African Americans ever gaining justice from white people and his consideration that they might have to seize their freedom by armed struggle, Truth merely asked, "Frederick, is God dead?" The question, Painter observes, made Truth a "symbol of Christian faith and forbearance, a talisman of non-violent faith in God's ability to right the most heinous of wrongs."[59] Stowe and other abolitionists used her question to assert the myth of the Christian slave's love and forgiveness of white people in spite of abuse and bondage. But within the context of her political and religious thought as well as the conversations among their African American Christian contemporaries, her question seems less

57. Painter, *Sojourner Truth*, p. 105.
58. Painter, *Sojourner Truth*, p. 30.
59. Painter, *Sojourner Truth*, p. 161.

about forgiveness and more about exhorting Douglass to have faith, as she does, in the power of God to free African Americans. For Truth and many other African American Christians, faith in God, not simply human strategies and plans, would ensure victory over slavery and injustice. Truth's political assessments about forcibly combating the evils of slavery and gender oppression were, like her life, guided by her faith in God.

Sojourner Truth enjoyed a successful career as a public speaker and advocate for women and the freed long after the end of slavery. While she was uniquely vocal, courageous, and popular, she was part of a cohort of nineteenth-century African American Christian women, former slaves and servants who felt called by God to move through the country preaching and ministering to both white and black believers in and out of pulpits and public forums. These "sisters in the spirit" carved out a distinct Christian faith walk that challenged existing political boundaries and social roles. Their call to preach, according to Jarena Lee, was

> as if aided from above. My tongue was cut loose, the stammerer spoke freely; the love of God, and of his service, burned with a vehement flame within me — his name was glorified among the people.[60]

Unlike Truth, these sisters were literate and could therefore provide written descriptions of their life and thought without white mediation. *The Life and Religious Experience of Jarena Lee,* the first of several spiritual autobiographies written or dictated by African American women, was published in 1836. Ten years later, *The Memoirs of the Life, Religious Experience, Ministerial Travels and Labours of Mrs. Zilpha Elaw, An American Female of Colour; together with Some Account of the Great Religious Revivals in America (Written by Herself)* appeared in print.

The spiritual autobiographies of Jarena Lee, Zilpha Elaw, and Julia Foote, three nineteenth-century African American Christian women, were edited and introduced by William Andrews in *Sisters in the Spirit.* Andrews explains the "fate of the individual soul" is the central question of the genre of spiritual autobiography:

> Whether written by blacks or whites, American spiritual autobiography chronicles the soul's journey not only from damnation to salvation but also to a realization of one's true place and destiny in the divine scheme of things.[61]

---

60. Andrews, *Sisters of the Spirit,* p. 48.
61. Andrews, *Sisters of the Spirit,* p. 10.

These autobiographies were written by women who were among the first generation of free northern African Americans. Yet, at an early age, because of poverty, they were separated from their families and worked as live-in domestic servants for white households. Although denied formal schooling, most became literate and learned to read the Bible after they were converted to Christianity. Lee lamented that she "never had more than three months of schooling; and wishing to know much of the way and law of God have therefore watched the more closely the operations of the Spirit, and have in consequence been led thereby."[62] Being servants tested their faith, because in the midst of their daily household chores, their masters frequently questioned, ridiculed, and interrupted their attempts to be true followers of Christ. Nevertheless, their conversions were accompanied by spectacular spiritual encounters in which they heard from God, faced demons and satanic apparitions, and were finally released into the saving grace of Jesus' love.

After repenting and receiving salvation, the young women joined local congregations, and spent many years attending Bible schools and serving various ministries in the church. They married and had children, but continued to struggle for a deeper and more meaningful relationship with the Lord. Lee and Elaw learned about, and then sought, sanctification in which the believer "enjoys the inner peace that comes of being convinced that, having been liberated from sin, one is now completely identified with God in thought, word, and deed."[63] Lee described sanctification as lightning darting through her; after praying to be sanctified she found herself standing in the yard "with my hands spread out, and looking with my face toward heaven." As she ran to tell others of her experience, "a new rush of the same ecstasy came upon me, and caused me to feel as if I were in an ocean of light and bliss."[64]

This state of spiritual joy compels believers to seek righteousness with God and to respond "to a 'call' to a mission that command[s] their total allegiance and loyalty."[65] These "sisters" spent many years attempting to be obedient wives and dutiful mothers, and hesitated in answering God's call to preach and minister. Their guilt over disobeying God often

---

62. Andrews, *Sisters of the Spirit*, p. 48.

63. Andrews, *Sisters of the Spirit*, p. 15.

64. Andrews, *Sisters of the Spirit*, p. 34.

65. Sandy Dwayne Martin, "Providence and the Black Christian Consensus: A Historical Essay on the African American Religious Experience," in *The Courage to Hope: From Black Suffering to Human Redemption,* ed. Quinton Hosford Dixie and Cornel West (Boston: Beacon Press, 1999), p. 19.

drove them to illness and sorrow. Julia Foote advised women to "not let what man say or do, keep you from doing the will of the Lord or using the gifts you have for the good of others. How much easier to bear the reproach of men than to live at a distance from God."[66]

Eventually they rejected their socially defined roles as mothers and wives or widows and became totally committed to ministry. Their writings describe their faith walk from sin to salvation and sanctification and from personal hesitancy, doubt, and difficulties to triumph as evangelists and ministers. After her husband's death, Lee "clearly did not identify herself as a mother first and foremost, but as a worker whose first duty was to her calls, her preaching career."[67] After leaving her sick child for a week with friends, she wrote, "during the whole time, not a thought of my little son came into my mind; it was hid from me, lest I should have been diverted from the work I had to do, to look after my son."[68] In a similar way, rather than maternal anxiety, Zilpha Elaw thought that her "natural anxiety" about her daughter "did not comport with an absolute submission to the will of God."[69] Eventually, both Lee and Elaw broke up their households and placed their children into the care of relatives and friends, "forsaking all to preach the everlasting Gospel."[70]

But even after divesting themselves of their domestic responsibilities, the women found their call to preach limited and restricted by the prevailing notions of the proper place for women within both white and black church communities. Using scriptural authority and social custom male church leaders objected to any woman preaching or pastoring a church. After being told that "our Discipline . . . did not call for women preachers," Lee wrote,

O how careful ought we to be, lest through our by-laws of church government and discipline, we bring into disrepute even the word of life. For as unseemly as it may appear now-a-days for a woman to preach, it should be remembered that nothing is impossible with God. And why should it be thought impossible, heterodox, or improper for a woman to preach? Seeing the Saviour died for the woman as well as the man.[71]

66. Andrews, *Sisters of the Spirit*, p. 21.
67. Andrews, *Sisters of the Spirit*, p. 19.
68. Andrews, *Sisters of the Spirit*, p. 45.
69. Andrews, *Sisters of the Spirit*, p. 76.
70. Andrews, *Sisters of the Spirit*, p. 46.
71. Andrews, *Sisters of the Spirit*, p. 36.

Nevertheless, male clergy and custom confined most "sisters of the spirit" to preaching in homes, tent meetings, or special church services rather than in church pulpits. Eight years after being told that women could exhort and hold prayer meetings but not preach during a service at Bethel Church, Jarena Lee "sprang as by an altogether supernatural impulse, to her feet and was aided from above to give an exhortation on the same subject as the minister." Although she believed her lack of decorum would lead to expulsion from the church, Richard Allen, now bishop of the African Episcopal Methodists, said "that he now as much believed that I was called to that work, as any of the preachers present."[72]

Lee then proceeded to preach with more confidence and support, but at many of the same venues where she had preached before her outburst. She describes a rigorous itinerary that included a meeting at her uncle's house, a week later a meeting at the Court House, another at a schoolhouse, and from there to preaching engagements before large congregations. She often walked miles to fulfill her commitments to ministry and preaching. Lee noted that an elderly white man who was once a notoriously cruel slaveholder attended several meetings at which she preached. At first he expressed doubt whether African Americans even had souls, but then declared that Lee's preaching "might seem a small thing, yet he believed she had the worth of souls at heart" and accordingly "seemed to admit" that African Americans had souls.[73]

The ministries of Lee and others were direct challenges to white doubters, racists, and slaveholders. Zilpha Elaw's ministry called her to make several trips into slave states to preach to both slave and free, black and white. These efforts were dangerous because law required the arrest of any person of color entering the slave state without papers proving his or her freedom. However, Elaw attributed to God the fact that she was never detained or required to show her documents when preaching "on the soil of slavery." After preaching at a service to an enslaved congregation, Elaw grew fearful of being kidnapped and tried to hide from view, but her "faith rallied and her confidence in the Lord returned."[74] At one of her worship services, a cruel, alcoholic slave driver knelt in repentance, causing Elaw to travail for him in the spirit.[75] She reflected on the paradox of preaching to congregations of slaveholders "who were not de-

72. Andrews, *Sisters of the Spirit*, p. 45.
73. Andrews, *Sisters of the Spirit*, p. 47.
74. Andrews, *Sisters of the Spirit*, p. 91.
75. Andrews, *Sisters of the Spirit*, p. 100.

ficient of pastors and reverend divines, who possessed all the advantages of talents, learning, respectability and worldly influence."[76] Elaw's explanation of her popularity was that

> the power of truth and of God was never so manifest in any of their agencies as with the dark coloured female stranger who had come from afar to minister amongst them. But God hath chosen the weak things of the world to confound the mighty. Divine goodness raised me and honored me as an angel of God.[77]

When recalling the powerful words and courageous feats of these "angels" and messengers of the Lord, it is easy to forget their impoverished social backgrounds. Indeed, their lives were marked by the endless toil, dislocated family life, and poverty faced by nearly all free African American women. While ministering with courage and devotion, they had to eke out a living performing domestic work, often as live-in servants. They often relied on the charity of other believers for their food and shelter. These women suffered from poor health and injuries, probably resulting from hard work, poor nutrition, and lack of medical care. Elaw and Lee both wrote about illnesses that left them bedridden for months.

The lives of these "sisters of the spirit" combined vulnerability with endurance, toughened wills with physical and emotional weaknesses. Yet they tried to think through and make sense of themselves, their fate, and the issues of God and evil without the time and tools we associate with this kind of philosophical and theological endeavor. Indeed, their material conditions and personal backgrounds support their claims that their own strength and intelligence was not the source of their speech acts, ministry, or bold resistance. They declared that the Holy Spirit of God enabled them to change their names, unleash stammering and silenced tongues, freely move and preach, and most of all engage in "spiritual interrogations" of the religious and political social order.

These broken African American Christian women became earthen vessels that "the excellence of the power of God could be treasured" (2 Cor. 4:7). They were able to minister and write under the relative freedom of states that had ended slavery. However, the majority of African Americans were still enslaved and forced to express their faith while under far more restrictive and dangerous circumstances. In the

76. Andrews, *Sisters of the Spirit*, p. 92.
77. Andrews, *Sisters of the Spirit*, p. 92.

following narrative, a woman believer describes slavery as "hell without fire":

> I was born in Franklin, long before the Civil War. I belonged to the family of B. . . . I was born in a little log cabin in the cabin lot. This was a place fenced off and filled with cabins for the slaves. My mother was the mother of nineteen children. . . . My master gave me and us children to his son. . . . When I was little I used to work around the big house, cleaning floors, polishing silver, wiping floors, waiting on the table, and everything. My mother was the cook. My mistress was awful mean and exciting. . . . She used to beat me like I was a dog. . . . I worked like a dog. Everybody was mistress and master, even the little children. They were awfully fine and swell and did everything but say their prayers. . . . On Sunday they usually sat around and plotting some devilment and meanness for us. I actually saw old man F. walk through the field and seeing a baby crying, take his stick and knock its brain out and call for the foreman to come and haul off the nasty, black rat. Yes, in them days it was hell without fires. This is one reason I believe in a hell. I don't believe a just God is going to take no such man into his kingdom.[78]

Christian faith, as historian Albert Raboteau indicates, "was no easy faith for slaves exposed to constant toil and regular violence at the hands of professed fellow Christians."[79] Unfortunately, most slave owners professed Christianity and used scripture to support the existence of the fireless hell of human bondage. They often held church services on their farms and plantations, and even permitted white or even black preachers, as confirmed by Elaw's experiences, to minister to the enslaved. Sometimes the enslaved were allowed to travel to nearby religious services in town or on other plantations. But owners' attention to religious activities was not intended to incorporate the enslaved into their faith community, bur rather to transform the legitimate desires of the enslaved to worship and to learn about Christianity into opportunities for reinforcing obedience to white authority.

Owners used Ephesians 6:5-8 to instruct slaves to obey their masters, and have respect for them and please them, "with a single motive and their whole heart as if serving Christ himself." One former slave said

---

78. Johnson, *God Struck Me Dead*, pp. 153-61.

79. Albert J. Raboteau, *Slave Religion: The Invisible Institution in the Antebellum South* (New York: Oxford University Press, 1978), p. 31.

that "ministers used to preach — 'Obey your masters and mistresses and be good servants' I never heard anything else."[80] Susan Boggs, an escaped slave, noted that her owner said, "You must 'obey your masters and be good servants.' That is the greater part of the sermon when they preach to colored folks." She however, viewed the "obedience" message and the controlled church services with skepticism.

> I didn't see any difference between the slaveholders who had religion and those who had not. Why the man that baptized me had a colored woman tied up in his yard to whip when he got home, that very Sunday and her mother belonged to the same church. We had to sit and hear him preach and her mother was in church hearing him preach [about obedience].[81]

Another enslaved woman, Ms. Joseph Smith said, "Those who were Christians and held slaves were the hardest masters. A card-player and drunkard wouldn't flog you half to death . . . the Christians will oppress you more." She pointed to the irony that although Sunday was considered a day of rest, the enslaved were expected to continue with their chores. But "if you do the least thing in the world that they don't like, they will mark it down against you, and Monday you have got to take a whipping. . . . Now the card player and horse racer won't be there to trouble you . . . would rather be with a card-player or sportsman, by half, than a Christian."[82]

Harriet Tubman reported in her narrative that when she was quite young, she lived with a very pious mistress but the slaveholder's religion did not prevent her from whipping the young girl for every slight or fancied fault. In rebellion against such hypocrisy, when invited to participate in the family prayers, Tubman chose to stay on the landing and pray for herself, "and I prayed to God . . . to make me strong and able to fight and that's what I allers prayed for ever since."[83]

The brutality and hypocrisy experienced by Boggs, Smith, Tubman, and other enslaved African American women did not deter them from being Christians. As the hymn "Ole Satan's church is here below/Up to God's free church I hope to go" demonstrates, the enslaved distinguished between the legitimacy of their own church and the false faith of their

80. Blassingame, *Slave Testimony*, p. 411.
81. Blassingame, *Slave Testimony*, p. 420.
82. Blassingame, *Slave Testimony*, p. 411.
83. Blassingame, *Slave Testimony*, p. 458.

owners.[84] While owners persisted in controlling when, where, and how their slaves prayed and worshipped, enslaved believers were equally determined to build underground churches in "hush harbors" or obscure wooded areas. In one such service, a slave explains, "we had to take boards for seats and go to the graveyard, rain or shine, cold or wind. It was the only place we could meet, but there, on our humble seats, we met and praised God."[85]

The secret religious gatherings were where "they would steal off to the field and in the thickets and there . . . they called on God out of heavy hearts." African American enslaved Christians, Raboteau notes, "perceived in their own experiences the paradox of the gospel, the redemptive power of Christ's suffering repeated once again in the pattern of their own lives." Enslaved believers practiced "a joyful sorrow, sorrowful joy, or more accurately, sorrow merging into joy arose from the suffering of the slaves' lives, a suffering that was touched, however, and so transformed, by the living presence of God."[86]

Since owners prohibited the enslaved from Bible reading and study, they learned of their faith through "oral modes of African American preaching, singing, spirituals, hymnody, clapping, shouting, testifying, praying, speaking in tongues."[87] These expressions of theology, social commentary, and cultural resistance were not supplementary, but the very essence of the Afro-Christian experience. Congregational and collective singing became emblematic of Afro-Christian worshippers, for it solidified the ties among believers and described their enslaved condition while also expressing their relationship to God. W. E. B. Du Bois called them "sorrow songs" because "it was the music of an unhappy people, of the children of disappointment; they tell of death and suffering and unvoiced longing toward a truer world, of misty wanderings and hidden ways."[88] But much of the singing was also a joyous outpouring of the good news of the gospel and of God's faithfulness. They were also a code used to signal escape plans. Harriet Tubman, for example, explained that she sang,

84. Copeland, "Wading through Many Sorrows," p. 119.

85. Blassingame, *Slave Testimony,* p. 448.

86. Albert J. Raboteau, "The Blood of the Martyrs Is the Seed of Faith: Suffering in the Christianity of American Slaves," in *The Courage to Hope: From Black Suffering to Human Redemption,* ed. Quinton Hosford Dixie and Cornel West (Boston: Beacon Press, 1999), pp. 29-30.

87. Clay Bassard, *Spiritual Interrogations,* p. 98.

88. W. E. B. Du Bois, *The Souls of Black Folk,* ed. Henry Louis Gates Jr. and Terri Hume Oliver (New York: W. W. Norton & Co., 1999), p. 157.

"When that old chariot comes, I'm going to leave you, I'm bound for the promised land, Friends, I'm going to leave you," to alert her family members to when she was planning to escape.[89] She also recalled that

> Slaves must not be seen talking together, and so it came about that their communication was often made by singing, and the words of their familiar hymns, telling of the heavenly journey, and the land of Canaan, while they did not attract the attention of the masters, conveyed to their brethren and sisters in bondage something more than met the ear.[90]

According to musician and scholar Cheryl Kirk-Duggan there are some instances of terrible evil — Auschwitz, Rwanda, and so on — for which "no songs of liberation have been sung." However, the "praxis of slavery and racism was often met by the utterances of song, of the Spiritual. As instruments of praxis these 'chants of collective exorcism' were sung by those trapped in the bowels of slavery and racism as they voiced their existential pain. Those who sang knew a God who cared. Black folks had a lived theology and theodicy."[91]

African American Christian women, both free and enslaved, learned of a God who cared while living in an evil society, where most white people who also claimed to be Christians believed their faith endorsed bondage and subordination. Because they knew God and Jesus loved and recognized their humanity, African American believers rejected white faith claims as untrue and implausible and as a group of slaves succinctly told their mistress after their conversion: "We be holy; you not be holy."[92]

The speech acts of African American Christian women grew out of their need to walk a delicate balance between the command to love their enemies and the equally compelling need to confront evil. Their acts express the "new political option" posed by Jesus and the faith that was the heart of their theology. According to Kwame Bediako,

> Jesus' way was one of engagement and involvement through a new way of overcoming, which arose from a unique concept of power: the

---

89. Bradford, *Harriet Tubman: The Moses of Her People* (Secaucus, N.J.: Citadel, 1974), p. 28.

90. Bradford, *Harriet Tubman*, p. 27.

91. Cheryl Kirk-Duggan, *Exorcizing Evil: A Womanist Perspective on the Spirituals* (Maryknoll, N.Y.: Orbis Books, 1997), p. 47.

92. Raboteau, "The Blood of the Martyrs," p. 35.

power of forgiveness over retaliation, of suffering over violence, of love over hostility, of humble service over domination.[93]

The believing women dared to apply Jesus' "unique concept of power" to their own situation and condition. Paul's admonition to "[b]e not overcome of evil, but overcome evil with good" (Rom. 12:21) expressed Christ's demand that his followers love their enemies and not seek revenge upon them. Since they were already overcome by an evil social order and surrounded by enemies, "overcoming evil with good" posed a seemingly impossible challenge to African American believers.

For them, the apparently inconsistent question of why a good and omnipotent God allows evil was important, but not central to addressing their responses to evil. Many African American Christian women like Truth, Lee, and Elaw first recognized, as they approached God, their own sin and the difficulty of doing good. Although individuals' evil acts differ in scale, scope, and moral impact from societal evil, addressing the reality of one's own desperately wicked heart initiates the ability to overcome social forms of evil. By consciously addressing their own sin nature and working out their "salvation," these women were rejecting the notions that they were subhuman chattel and claiming their authority as human beings capable of reflection and moral reason.

They recognized that believers, especially those oppressed by evil, should not become so overwhelmed by evil that they fail to take responsibility for doing good to others including their enemies. As historian Albert Raboteau notes, "When slaves forgave and prayed for slaveholders, they not only proved their humanity, they also displayed to a heroic degree their obedience to Christ's command: 'Love your enemies. Do good to those who persecute and spitefully use you.'"[94] Moreover, they knew that revengeful responses to evil would make Christians no different in character from their enemies and, most importantly, leave no room for God to supernaturally intervene on their behalf. "Vengeance is mine, I will repay, saith the Lord" (Rom. 12:19).

Conclusion

The women in this study believed that, in addition to the material world with its physical and social dimensions, there existed a spiritual

---

93. Bediako, *Christianity in Africa*, p. 245.
94. Raboteau, "The Blood of the Martyrs," p. 36.

realm unseen by the human eye. Through the eyes of faith, they viewed God as actively intervening in human history, especially through the agency of believing human beings. For them, the boundary between the material and spiritual was so porous that believers could be in continuous relationship with Christ while carrying on the affairs of their daily lives. It is in this sense that faith and its paradox of "intangible substance" and "unseen evidence" are manifested as a social fact of the material world.

Social scientists can document the substance of the lives of social actors with evidence from primary and secondary sources. But what is difficult to document is how "broken vessels" — or human social actors who lacked material or social means — could produce powerful oppositional speech acts. What social facts can the scholar point to that explain the source of Wheatley's poetry, Truth's speeches, Lee's released tongue, or Tubman's moves?

Harriet Tubman's escape from slavery, her aid to escaping slaves, and her bravery as a spy have all been documented and accepted by historians. But Tubman, through her biographer, identified that her ability to act was not derived from her own mind, bravery, or material conditions. She proclaimed that her source was God. While describing many of her narrow escapes, Tubman would always reply,

> Don't I tell you, Missus, it wasn't me, it was the Lord! Just so long as he wanted to use me, he would take care of me, and when he didn't want me no longer, I was ready to go; I always told him, I'm going to hold steady on to you, and you've got to see me through.[95]

Bradford says that Tubman clung to God with an "all-abiding confidence." For "hers was not the religion of a morning and evening prayer at stated times, but when she felt a need, she simply told God of it, and trusted Him to set the matter right."[96] She "expected deliverance when she prayed, unless the Lord had ordered otherwise. . . ."[97] Her prayer "was the prayer of faith and she expected an answer."[98] Other "sisters of the spirit" also claimed their strength and insights came from God, who directed their steps and offered protection against both seen and unseen enemies or forces of evil. Since the spiritual and physical worlds were

95. Bradford, *Harriet Tubman*, p. 61.
96. Bradford, *Harriet Tubman*, p. 23.
97. Bradford, *Harriet Tubman*, p. 61.
98. Bradford, *Harriet Tubman*, p. 57.

connected, these women believed God would help them defy the limitations imposed by human beings and social structures.

While the manifestation of evil always causes physical suffering and material harm, Afro-Christian women believed that evil had to be opposed on both material and spiritual levels. They had to go beyond evil's representation in the social order of white supremacy and white power and were compelled to pray against the spirit of evil and its demonic origins. The crucifixion and resurrection of Christ assured them of evil's ultimate defeat.

Faith in the Christian God is counterintuitive because of Jesus Christ and his confrontation with evil on the cross, where he was publicly tortured, humiliated, and lynched. Jesus could have called on a host of angels for protection, yet was "broken for the transgressions and sins" of believers. His resurrection promises them his love and protection on earth and everlasting life in heaven. African American Christian women understood the counterintuitive power of resurrection from the dead after public crucifixion, for it mirrored their own daily lives of bondage and brutality and informed their new life in Christ as agents of faith and resistance. They were physically weak, economically destitute, poorly educated, and socially insignificant, but when moving with the spirit of God, these women were able to go beyond their normal human capabilities. Their faith made them unafraid to plot, plan, and pray for the end of slavery — or at least for the slaveholder's reach to be limited and proscribed. In other words, when related to issues of spiritual and political power, these women were able to "take on the mind of Jesus." "When related to the questions of politics and power," Kwame Bediako explains, "his mind, is not a dominating mind, not a self-pleasing or self-asserting mind, but rather a saving mind, a redemptive mind, a servant mind."[99]

The faith walk of African American Christian women connects the morality and agency of the Christian victim with their faith in God's interventions against evil. Many people assume that if there is a God, that God should supernaturally intervene to prevent evil and stop victims from suffering. In this view, the ability of the victims to resist is ignored while the perpetuators of evil seemed endowed with power that can only be contained by supernatural acts. But God's plan for addressing evil seems to focus at least in part on the agency and responsibility of the victim-believer to act. In the case of the evil social order of antebellum

99. Bediako, *Christianity in Africa*, p. 247.

slavery and white supremacy, God intervened by empowering African American Christian women to resist evil through speech acts. From the experiences of these women, God's spirit moved on and through the social and political narratives of other human agents.

The competing views of evil and faith that emerged in the lives of the enslaved and their owners and oppressors support the notion that God works through rather than simply over human beings. Human free will is fundamental to God's plan for human beings and God protects the agency of both the sinner who commits evil acts and their victims who are encouraged to respond and resist those acts.

While seemingly destined for perpetual enslavement and servitude to the white and the mighty, African American Christian women such as Maria Stewart believed

> that the oppression of injured Africa has come up before the majesty of Heaven; and when our cries shall have reached the ears of the Most High, it will be a tremendous day for the people of this land; for strong is the hand of the Lord God Almighty.[100]

African American Christian women who lived through the antebellum period would concur with those scholars and politicians who point to the political and economic factors that led to the Civil War and the end of slavery. However, they would add that these historical events were also evidence of the hand of God moving in response to their prayers and supplications for freedom for their people.

The New World was riddled with the enormity of the Christlike suffering of Africans, yet the goodness of God, always at war with evil, persisted victoriously in the lives of African American Christian women. Sojourner Truth contrasted the permanency of the goodness of God, with the transitory nature of evil. "Goodness," she said, "never had any beginning, it was from everlasting, and could never die. But evil had a beginning, and must have an end."[101] By becoming sanctified and holy "vessels of honor for Him," African American Christian women helped to bring about the demise of slavery by actively confronting both the spirit and the social forms of evil.

---

100. Richardson, *Maria W. Stewart*, p. 63.
101. Painter, *Sojourner Truth*, p. 115.

Works Consulted

Andrews, William, ed. *Sisters of the Spirit: Three Black Women's Autobiographies of the Nineteenth Century.* Bloomington, Ind.: Indiana University Press, 1986.

Bediako, Kwame. *Christianity in Africa: The Renewal of a Non-Western Religion.* Edinburgh: Edinburgh University Press, 1997.

Berger, Peter, and Thomas Luckmann. *The Social Construction of Reality: A Treatise in the Sociology of Knowledge.* New York: Anchor Books, 1966.

Blassingame, John, ed. *Slave Testimony: Two Centuries of Letters, Speeches, Interviews, and Autobiographies.* Baton Rouge: Louisiana State University Press, 1977.

Bradford, Sarah. *Harriet Tubman: The Moses of Her People.* Secaucus, N.J.: Citadel Press, 1974.

Clay Bassard, Katherine. *Spiritual Interrogations: Culture, Gender, Community in Early African American Women's Writing.* Princeton: Princeton University Press, 1999.

Collins, Patricia Hill. *Black Feminist Thought: Knowledge, Consciousness, and the Politics of Empowerment.* Boston: Unwin Hyman Press, 1990.

Copeland, M. Shawn. "Wading through Many Sorrows: Toward a Theology of Suffering in Womanist Perspective." In *A Troubling in My Soul: Womanist Perspectives on Evil and Suffering,* edited by Emilie Townes. Maryknoll, N.Y.: Orbis Books, 1996.

Davis, Angela. "Reflections on the Black Woman's Role in the Community of Slaves." *The Black Scholar* (November-December 1981): 4-15.

Degler, Carl. "Slavery and the Genesis of American Race Prejudice." In *The Making of Black America: Essays in Negro Life and History,* edited by August Meier and Elliott Rudwick. Vol. 1, *Origins of Black Americans.* New York: Atheneum Press, 1996.

Dobson, Howard. "The Slave Trade and the Making of the Modern World." *New York Amsterdam News* (September 30–October 6, 1999): 10-11.

Du Bois, W. E. B. *The Souls of Black Folk.* Edited by Henry Louis Gates Jr. and Terri Hume Oliver. New York: W. W. Norton & Co., 1999.

Ekstrom, Laura Waddell. "Suffering as Religious Experience." In *Christian Faith and the Problem of Evil,* edited by Peter van Inwagen. Grand Rapids: Eerdmans, 2004.

Fraser, David A., and Tony Campolo. *Sociology through the Eyes of Faith.* New York: HarperCollins, 1992.

Gilbert, Olive. *Narrative of Sojourner Truth: A Bondswoman of Olden Time, Edited by Frances Titus for the Author.* Battle Creek, Mich., 1875.

Gomez, Michael. *Exchanging Our Country Marks: The Transformation of African Identities in the Colonial and Antebellum South.* Chapel Hill: University of North Carolina Press, 1998.

Higgenbotham, Evelyn Brooks. *Righteous Discontent: The Women's Movement in the*

Black Baptist Church, 1880-1920. Cambridge, Mass.: Harvard University Press, 1993.

Johnson, Clifton, ed. *God Struck Me Dead: Voices of Ex-Slaves.* Cleveland: Pilgrim Press, 1993.

Jones, William R. "Theodicy: The Controlling Category for Black Theology." *Journal of Religious Thought* 30 (1973): 28-38.

Kirk-Duggan, Cheryl. *Exorcizing Evil: A Womanist Perspective on the Spirituals.* Maryknoll, N.Y.: Orbis Books, 1997.

Kolchin, Peter. *American Slavery, 1619-1877.* New York: Hill and Wang, 1993.

Martin, Sandy Dwayne. "Providence and the Black Christian Consensus: A Historical Essay on the African American Religious Experience." In *The Courage to Hope: From Black Suffering to Human Redemption,* edited by Quinton Hosford Dixie and Cornel West. Boston: Beacon Press, 1999.

Marty, Martin E. *Righteous Empire: The Protestant Experience in America.* New York: Dial Press, 1970.

McGary, Howard, and Bill Lawson. *Between Slavery and Freedom: Philosophy and American Slavery.* Bloomington, Ind.: Indiana University Press, 1992.

McKivigan, John, and Mitchell Snay. *Religion and the Antebellum Debate over Slavery.* Athens, Ga.: University of Georgia Press, 1998.

McNeil, Genna Rae. "Waymaking and Dimensions of Responsibility: An African American Perspective on Salvation." In *The Courage to Hope: From Black Suffering to Human Redemption,* edited by Quinton Hosford Dixie and Cornel West. Boston: Beacon Press, 1999.

Memoirs and Poems of Phyllis Wheatley A Native African and A Slave. Salem, Mass., 1838.

Mills, Charles W. *Blackness Visible: Essays on Philosophy and Race.* Ithaca, N.Y.: Cornell University Press, 1998.

Oakes, James. *The Ruling Race: History of American Slaveholders.* New York: W. W. Norton & Co., 1998.

Omi, Michael, and Howard Winant. *Racial Formation in the United States from the 1960s to the 1990s.* New York: Routledge, 1994.

Omolade, Barbara. "Hearts of Darkness." In *The Rising Song of African American Women.* New York: Routledge, 1995.

Painter, Nell Irvin. *Sojourner Truth: A Life, a Symbol.* New York: W. W. Norton & Co., 1996.

———. "Representing Truth: Sojourner Truth's Knowing and Becoming Known." In *This Far by Faith: Readings in African American Women's Religious Biography,* edited by Judith Weisenfeld and Richard Newman. New York: Routledge, 1996.

Patterson, Orlando. *Slavery and Social Death: A Comparative Study.* Cambridge, Mass.: Harvard University Press, 1982.

Plantinga, Alvin. "The Free Will Defense." In *The Problem of Evil: Selected Readings,* edited by Michael Peterson. Notre Dame: University of Notre Dame Press, 1992.

Raboteau, Albert J. *Slave Religion: The Invisible Institution in the Antebellum South.* New York: Oxford University Press, 1978.

————. "The Blood of the Martyrs Is the Seed of Faith: Suffering in the Christianity of American Slaves." In *The Courage to Hope: From Black Suffering to Human Redemption,* edited by Quinton Hosford Dixie and Cornel West. Boston: Beacon Press, 1999.

Richardson, Marilyn, ed. *Maria W. Stewart, America's First Black Woman Political Writer.* Bloomington, Ind.: Indiana University Press, 1987.

Riggs, Marcia, ed. *Can I Get a Witness? Prophetic Religious Voices of African American Women.* Maryknoll, N.Y.: Orbis Books, 1997.

Ringer, Benjamin, and Elinor Lawless. *Race-Ethnicity and Society.* New York: Routledge, 1999.

Shields, John C., ed. *The Collected Works of Phillis Wheatley.* The Schomburg Library of Nineteenth-Century Black Women Writers. New York: Oxford University Press, 1988.

Six Women's Slave Narratives. The Schomburg Library of Nineteenth-Century Black Women Writers. New York: Oxford University Press, 1988.

Smit, Laura A. "In Your Light, We See Light: The Continuing Viability of a Christocentric Epistemology." Paper presented at Calvin College Faculty Seminar and Conference on Christian Scholarship, May 2000.

Smith, Dorothy. *The Everyday World as Problematic: A Feminist Sociology.* Boston: Northeastern University Press, 1987.

Surin, Kenneth. "Taking Suffering Seriously." In *The Problem of Evil: Selected Readings,* edited by Michael Peterson. Notre Dame: University of Notre Dame Press, 1992.

Thomas, Laurence Mordekhai. *Vessels of Evil: American Slavery and the Holocaust.* Philadelphia: Temple University Press, 1993.

Townes, Emilie, ed. *Troubling in My Soul: Womanist Perspectives on Evil and Suffering.* Maryknoll, N.Y.: Orbis Books, 1996.

Unwritten History of Slavery. Nashville: Fisk University Social Science Institute, 1945.

White, Deborah Gray. *Aren't I a Woman? Female Slaves in the Plantation South.* New York: W. W. Norton & Co., 1985.

Contributors

Paul Draper is Professor of Philosophy at Florida International University in Miami, Florida.

Eduardo J. Echeverria is Associate Professor of Philosophy at Sacred Heart Major Seminary in Detroit, Michigan.

Laura Waddell Ekstrom is Robert F. and Sarah M. Boyd Associate Professor of Philosophy at The College of William and Mary in Williamsburg, Virginia.

Stephen Griffith is Professor of Philosophy at Lycoming College in Williamsport, Pennsylvania.

Del Kiernan-Lewis is Executive Director of the Rainbow Center for Women, Adolescents, Children, and Families at the University of Florida Health Sciences Center in Jacksonville, Florida.

Richard T. McClelland is Associate Professor of Philosophy at Gonzaga University in Spokane, Washington.

Barbara Omolade is Dean of Multicultural Affairs at Calvin College in Grand Rapids, Michigan.

Richard Otte is Professor of Philosophy at the University of California at Santa Cruz.

Alvin Plantinga is John A. O'Brien Professor of Philosophy at the University of Notre Dame in Notre Dame, Indiana.

John R. Schneider is Professor of Religion and Theology at Calvin College in Grand Rapids, Michigan.

Robert Stanley is Associate Professor of Foreign Languages and Literatures at the University of Tennessee at Chattanooga.

Peter van Inwagen is John Cardinal O'Hara Professor of Philosophy at the University of Notre Dame in Notre Dame, Indiana.

Carol Winkelmann is Associate Professor of English and Director of Graduate Studies in English at Xavier University in Cincinnati, Ohio.

Keith D. Wyma is Associate Professor of Religion and Philosophy at Whitworth College in Spokane, Washington.